D0897743

MODERN MUSLIM INTELLECTUALS AND THE QUR'AN

THIS volume examines the writings of ten Muslim intellectuals, working throughout the Muslim world and the West, who employ contemporary critical methods to understand the Qur'an. Their work points to the emergence of a new trend in Muslim interpretation, characterised by direct engagement with the Word of God while embracing intellectual modernity in an increasingly globalised context. The volume situates and evaluates their thought, and assesses responses to it among Muslim and non-Muslim audiences. The ten chapters highlight the diverse arenas in which such intellectuals draw on the Qur'anic text, through their fresh readings of its verses.

SUHA TAJI-FAROUKI is Lecturer in Modern Islam, Institute of Arab and Islamic Studies, University of Exeter, and Research Associate, Department of Academic Research and Publications, The Institute of Ismaili Studies. Her publications include *A Fundamental Quest: Hizb al-Tahrir and the Search for the Islamic Caliphate* (1996); *Muslim–Jewish Encounters: Intellectual Traditions and Modern Politics* (co-edited, 1998); and *Islamic Thought in the Twentieth Century* (co-edited, in press).

MODERN MUSLIM INTELLECTUALS AND THE QUR'AN

Edited by
Suha Taji-Farouki

OXFORD
UNIVERSITY PRESS

in association with

THE INSTITUTE OF ISMAILI STUDIES
LONDON

OXFORD
UNIVERSITY PRESS

Great Clarendon Street, Oxford OX2 6DP

Oxford University Press is a department of the University of Oxford.
It furthers the University's objective of excellence in research, scholarship,
and education by publishing worldwide in

Oxford New York

Auckland Bangkok Buenos Aires Cape Town Chennai
Dar es Salaam Delhi Hong Kong Istanbul Karachi Kolkata
Kuala Lumpur Madrid Melbourne Mexico City Mumbai Nairobi
São Paulo Shanghai Singapore Taipei Tokyo Toronto

with an associated company in Berlin

Oxford is a registered trade mark of Oxford University Press
in the UK and certain other countries

Published in the United States

by Oxford University Press Inc., New York

British Library Cataloguing in Publication Data
Data available
Library of Congress Cataloging in Publication Data
Data applied for
ISBN 0-19 720002-8

1 3 5 7 9 10 8 6 4 2

Printed in Great Britain
on acid-free paper by
MPG Books Ltd. Bodmin, Cornwall

The Institute of Ismaili Studies

THE INSTITUTE OF ISMAILI STUDIES was established in 1977 with the objectives of promoting scholarship and learning on Islam, in historical as well as contemporary contexts, and fostering a better understanding of Islam's relationship with other societies and faiths.

The Institute's programmes encourage a perspective which is not confined to the theological and religious heritage of Islam, but seeks to explore the relationship of religious ideas to broader dimensions of society and culture. The programmes thus *encourage* an interdisciplinary approach to Islamic history and thought. Particular attention is given to the issues of modernity that arise as Muslims seek to relate their heritage to the contemporary situation.

Within the Islamic tradition, the Institute promotes research on those areas which have, to date, received relatively little attention from scholars. These include the intellectual and literary expressions of Shi'ism in general and Ismailism in particular.

The Institute's objectives are realised through concrete programmes and activities organised by various departments of the Institute, at times in collaboration with other institutions of learning. These programmes and activities are informed by the full range of cultures in which Islam is practised today. From the Middle East, South and Central Asia, and Africa to the industrialised societies in the West, they consider the variety of contexts which shape the ideals, beliefs and practices of the faith.

In facilitating the *Qur'anic Studies Series* and other publications, the Institute's sole purpose is to encourage original research and analysis of relevant issues, which often leads to diverse views and interpretations. While every effort is made to ensure that the publications are of a high academic standard, the opinions expressed in these publications must be understood as belonging to their authors alone.

QUR'ANIC STUDIES SERIES

THE QUR'AN has been an inexhaustible source of intellectual and spiritual reflection in Islamic history, giving rise to ever-proliferating commentaries and interpretations. Many of these have remained a realm for specialists due to their scholarly demands. Others, more widely read, remain untranslated from the primary language of their composition. This series aims to make some of these materials from a broad chronological range —the formative centuries of Islam to the present day—available to a wider readership through translation and publication in English, accompanied where necessary by introductory or explanatory materials. The series will also include contextual-analytical and survey studies of these primary materials.

Throughout this series and others like it which may appear in the future, the aim is to allow the materials to speak for themselves. Not surprisingly, in the Muslim world where its scriptural sources continue to command passionate interest and commitment, the Qur'an has been subject to contending, often antithetical ideas and interpretations. This series takes no sides in these debates. The aim rather is to place on record the rich diversity and plurality of approaches and opinions which have appealed to the Qur'an throughout history (and even more so today). The breadth of this range, however partisan or controversial individual presentations within it may be, is instructive in itself. While there is always room in such matters for personal preferences, commitment to partic-ular traditions of belief, and scholarly evaluations, much is to be gained by a simple appreciation, not always evident today, of the enormous wealth of intellectual effort that has been devoted to the Qur'an from the earliest times. It is hoped that through this objective, this series will prove of use to scholars and students in Qur'anic Studies as well as other allied and relevant fields.

Contents

Contents

Notes on Contributors

Asma Barlas obtained a B.A. in English Literature and Philosophy and an M.A. in Journalism from Pakistan, and a Ph.D. in International Studies (from the USA). She has published as a journalist, poet, and short story writer. Her scholarly work includes papers on the Qur'an and Muslim women's rights (published in the *Journal of Qur'anic Studies*, for example). She has also published two books, most recently *"Believing Women" in Islam: Unreading Patriarchal Interpretations of the Qur'an* (2002). Born in Pakistan, she was one of the first women to be inducted into the Foreign Service, but was then removed by the military ruler General Zia ul-Haq for her criticism of him. She joined the *Muslim*, a leading opposition newspaper, as assistant editor. In the mid-1980s she left Pakistan for the USA, where she eventually received political asylum.

Andreas Christmann received his M.A. and Ph.D. from the University of Leipzig. For the last five years he has been Lecturer in Contemporary Islam in the Department of Middle Eastern Studies at the University of Manchester. His current research interests include Qur'anic hermeneutics as developed in nineteenth- and twentieth-century Islamic thought, and the life and work of the Damascene Kurdish scholar Muhammad Sa'id Ramadan al-Buti.

Ursula Günther studied Arabic, Islamic Studies and Romance languages and literature in Tübingen, Paris and Hamburg. She was awarded her Ph.D. on Mohammed Arkoun at the University of Hamburg. She is currently engaged in research on Islam and the transition process in South Africa, at the University of Hamburg. Her research interests include gender studies, North Africa, the history of ideas, and inter-religious/intercultural dialogue. Her publications include *Mohammed Arkoun: ein moderner Kritiker der islamischen Vernunft* (forthcoming), and chapters on aspects of Islam in South and sub-Saharan Africa, in Algeria, Muslim feminism, and Islamic modernism and fundamentalism.

Anthony H. Johns completed a degree in Arabic and Malay at the School of Oriental and African Studies, University of London; his Ph.D. thesis was on Sufism in the Malay world (1954). After four years in Indonesia he was appointed to the Australian National University in Canberra where he taught Arabic and Islamic Studies for many years. In the course of his distinguished career he has held visiting appointments in Jerusalem, Toronto, Tokyo and Oxford, and spent many research periods in Cairo. He has published numerous major papers in journals, and chapters in books, on various aspects of the Qur'an and Qur'anic exegesis, and on the vernacularisation of the foundation texts of Islam in Indonesia. Now Emeritus Professor, he is Visiting Fellow in the Division of Pacific and Asian History of the Research School of Asian and Pacific Studies at the Australian National University.

Navid Kermani has taught at the University of Bonn and is currently Long-Term Fellow at the Institute for Advanced Studies (Wissenschaftskolleg) in Berlin. Among his publications are: *Gott ist schön: Das ästhetische Leben des Koran* (1999); *Iran – Die Revolution der Kinder* (2001), *Dynamit des Geistes: Martyrium, Islam und Nihilismus* (2002); *Das Buch der von Neil Young Getöteten* (2002). In 2000, he was awarded the Ernst-Bloch-Förderpreis by the city of Ludwigshafen. Kermani has also worked as an artistic director at the theatres of Frankfurt and Mülheim an der Ruhr.

Ronald L. Nettler is University Research Lecturer in Oriental Studies, University of Oxford, Fellow of the Oxford Centre for Hebrew and Jewish Studies, and Fellow of Mansfield College. He has written widely on Islamic thought, medieval and modern, and on Muslim–Jewish relations.

Abdullah Saeed is Associate Professor and Head of the Arabic and Islamic Studies Program at the University of Melbourne, Australia. He holds a B.A. in Arabic and Islamic Studies, a Masters Degree in Applied Linguistics, and a Ph.D. in Islamic Studies. His research interests include modern Islamic thought, Qur'anic hermeneutics and Islam in Australia. His recent publications include *Islamic Banking and Interest* (1999); *Muslim Communities in Australia* (co-edited, 2001); *Islam and Political Legitimacy* (co-edited, 2003); and *Islam in Australia* (2003).

Suha Taji-Farouki is Lecturer in Modern Islam at the Institute of Arab and Islamic Studies, University of Exeter, and Research Associate at The Institute of Ismaili Studies, London. Her publications include *A Fundamental Quest: Hizb al-Tahrir and the Search for the Islamic Caliphate* (1996); *Muslim Identity and the Balkan State* (co-edited, 1997); *Muslim-Jewish Encounters: Intellectual Traditions and Modern Politics* (co-edited, 1998); and *Islamic Thought in the Twentieth Century* (co-edited, in press).

Osman Taştan is Associate Professor in the Department of Islamic Law at Ankara University's Faculty of Divinity. He obtained his Ph.D. from Exeter University, UK. He is a member of the editorial board of *İslamiyat,* an Ankara-based Turkish journal of Islamic studies. His work includes a chapter on "Religion and Religious Minorities" in Turkey and articles on the theory and history of Islamic law. His research also covers population policy in Islamic Law, and war and peace in Islamic Law.

Farzin Vahdat is a sociologist interested in critical theory and the development of modernity in the West and the Middle East. He teaches Social Studies at Harvard University, and is the author of *God and Juggernaut: Iran's Intellectual Encounter with Modernity* (2002). His articles have appeared in such journals as *Critique* and the *International Journal of Middle Eastern Studies.*

1

Introduction

SUHA TAJI-FAROUKI

THE FORCES of modernisation have brought unprecedented disruption and change to Muslim societies during the twentieth century. Indigenous to Western historical development, they largely have been perceived as alien elements in the Muslim experience, and the changes brought by them as enforced from without. Even when such changes were welcomed, Muslims' relation to the modern was rendered profoundly ambivalent by their experience of the imperialist project, with which it was inextricably linked. The old and the 'traditional' thus survived the introduction of the new and the 'modern', leading to a state of continuous tension in Muslim societies. As the relationship with the self-past became problematised and cultural dignity was compromised, Islamic thought in the twentieth century itself became a discourse of crisis.

The responses of Muslim thinkers to the challenges posed by modernity, and to its philosophical underpinnings and overwhelming effects,[1] provide one example of the ways in which adherents of the great religious traditions have dealt with modernity, and how they deal with change more generally.[2] At the heart of these responses is a struggle to define the place of the sacred and that of human reason, and the role and implications of a commitment to transcendence. In facing the inexorable forces of rationalism, liberalism and secularisation radiating from the West, Muslim thinkers have elaborated disparate responses, justified through the resort to Islamic tradition. Tradition is recruited either to legitimise change, or to defend against perceived innovation and to preserve threatened values. Consequently, tradition itself becomes the very substance of change.[3] Reflecting the absence of any level of consensus in Islamic thought in the twentieth century, Muslim thinkers have become polarised between two extreme types. There are those who argue from a defence of tradition for a comprehensive rejection of modern Western influences, and the 'return' to a 'pure' Islamic cultural mode: this is commonly accompanied by a utilitarian stance vis-à-vis the material and technological products of modernity. Others, in contrast, start from the embrace of Western modernity (or specific contemporary frameworks or worldviews generated by it), and radically remould tradition to justify this.[4]

Late twentieth-century thinkers of the latter tendency have caught the attention of Western academic and media observers in recent years, against a backdrop dominated by the successes, failures and radicalisation of Islamist forces in the Muslim arena. While rejecting traditional Islamic thought outright as inadequate to the demands of the modern context, these thinkers also repudiate the numerous shades of Islamist formulation. They advance their own projects as appeals – and potential contributions – towards a renaissance in Islamic cultural and intellectual life, and progress and reform in the material, social and political conditions of Muslim countries. Their political ideas are often close to the heart of the liberal tradition, based on reason and values of freedom, liberty and democracy. Calling for detachment of the entire public sphere from the purview of religion, they often project the Qur'an – Islam's foundational text – as a source of general ethical guidelines, rather than the answer to all human issues. Reflecting their exposure to Western culture and intellectual life, their own approach to this text and its meanings is often informed by contemporary intellectual trends and critical methods.

A selection of such thinkers from diverse national and cultural backgrounds, and their intellectual projects, form the subject of this volume. As Muslims constitute increasingly diverse reading communities around the foundational text, projects of the kind advanced by such thinkers might be expected to multiply in coming years. Muslims thus increasingly occupy a growing variety of cultural and intellectual settings, and participate in ever widening and diversified networks. They increasingly contribute to the global debate on the hermeneutical quest for meaning, and function as Western scholars, breaking down boundaries and assumed dichotomies.[5] This is one reason for studying these projects. At the same time, study of such projects highlights salient aspects of Islamic thought and Muslim experience in the twentieth century, especially as this moves into and is viewed from the vantage point of the early twenty-first century. Three major themes in particular are illustrated by these thinkers and their projects, and form the focus of this introductory chapter: (1) They demonstrate the continuing validity for contemporary Islamic thought of the problematic of 'Islam and the West' or 'Islam and modernity'. While these formulae may be somewhat jaded, and can be legitimately critiqued and deconstructed on many fronts,[6] they continue to capture a vital debate in Muslim thinking against the background of the long and complicated history that has bound Muslims to the West, and vice versa. While several of the thinkers studied offer responses, if only implicitly, to this problematic, their own projects at the same time illustrate a particular mode in the internalisation of Western or modern ideas and concepts in contemporary Muslim discourses. (2) These thinkers exemplify the fragmentation and diffusion of intellectual authority in contemporary Muslim societies. They reflect the expanding multiplicity of voices and unprecedented uncertainty concerning who speaks for Islam, engendered by the cumulative impact of modernisation on traditional concepts and modes of intellectual authority. (3) These projects highlight the absence of consensus concerning the purpose and methods of Islamic reform and its legitimate boundaries. Several of the thinkers studied offer responses, again at times implicitly, to this fundamental question, and it is in this context specifically that their views concerning the Qur'an come into play. In this respect, their projects also illustrate the continued centrality of the Qur'an (and discourses constructed on its basis) to contemporary Muslim debates and politics, as the ultimate legitimising text of the Islamic tradition.

Before considering these themes in turn, as with all collected works observations concerning the approach of this volume and associated questions are in order.

Reflections on approach and some key questions

Any discussion of Muslim intellectual life in the twentieth century must take into account the defining context of modernisation, with its dislocating effects on structural, economic, societal, political and cultural realities in Muslim countries. Without these profound transformations, the unparalleled change on every front, and the problems this has generated, the projects studied here would hardly have been possible, and there is much to be gained from viewing them as products of these changes. They form an intrinsic part of the evolving Muslim discursive arena, shaped by the nation-state and its associated discourses, colonial and post-colonial trends, the Islamic *sahwa* (revival) and its impacts, and processes of globalisation.

Reflecting this, the present volume eschews an exclusively textually based approach, aspiring to strike a balance between analysis of the main texts and ideas studied on the one hand and exploration of their multiple contexts on the other. Contributing authors were encouraged to take into consideration thinkers' personal and professional trajectories, and to examine thinkers and texts within the contexts of their origination and development, paying particular attention to national and ideological dimensions. The essays collected here ultimately reflect their authors' own preferences and interests, however, and the degree of attention to contextual matters hence varies widely from one to another. Nevertheless, it remains an essential dimension in the attempt to position the thinkers studied, to understand what drives them to produce their texts, and to illuminate reactions to these. For example, certain of these thinkers directly or implicitly critique Muslim regimes for their privileging of Islamists and their capitulation to Islamist demands in a bid to pre-empt their effectiveness as vehicles of dissent. They also criticise these regimes for their failure to foster democracy, nurture civil society, or respect

4

human rights. Official postures concerning their texts (and concerning attacks on these by other actors) must thus be understood in terms of the endeavour by states to manage both Islamist pressures and the force of a public opinion, especially among younger generations, considerably under the sway of Islamist ideas.

Out of further consideration for the multiplicity and complexity of the contexts of their production, the present volume also aspires to avoid as far as possible the imposition of a single preconstituted category or label on the projects studied. Thinkers studied here engage in widely scattered fields of activity. Were they to be asked many, if not all, might not wish to identify themselves with some or all of the others. Subsuming them under a single label would obscure their diversity and distort their individuality, each of which forms a significant dimension of this study.[7] Underlining this, they are approached as individual voices in specific contexts: as ways of articulating a human existence in a given society and culture under a particular political system, and in the context of collective struggles engaged therein.[8] Their provenance within Muslim societies unites them.[9] They also share a role as modern intellectuals,[10] who are products of a modern 'secular' education or combine elements of this with aspects of 'traditional' Islamic learning. The place of the Qur'an and its meanings for contemporary Muslim life forms a prominent theme in their texts. Situated within a general concern with reform and an interest in intellectual modernity, it can be described as a unifying focus of their projects. Nonetheless, the diverse contexts and specific concerns of these thinkers and their consumption patterns as readers exposed to disparate intellectual influences and spanning different generations are clearly reflected in their texts, and are highlighted here.

Contributing authors were encouraged to explore perceptions of thinkers and texts, and their reception within various contexts and specific audiences, especially the Muslim one (in the specific national-regional-linguistic context of the thinker concerned and beyond this), and the 'Western' one. The reactions of Muslim audiences illuminate struggles in Muslim societies reflected in the discursive arena, and point to their general intellectual and cultural milieux. The reception of these projects among Western audiences illustrates some contemporary Western attitudes towards Muslim societies, and expectations regarding their future in a globalising world. To establish a precise profile of patterns of consumption of these texts among these two audience types, to quantify them or to map their distribution is a tall order. However, impressionistic comments concerning their reception among Muslim and Western audiences are possible as a first step toward exploring the sociology of this literature. Many Muslims familiar with certain of these thinkers dismiss them outright, deeming them unqualified to contribute to the debates in which they engage. Some are condemned for failing to respect the historical Muslim consensus concerning issues fundamental to the Islamic religion, and the legacy of Islamic scholarship that expresses it. Others are accused of violating the sacred, and working to destroy 'Islam' from within. A common Muslim view emphasises how marginal certain of these projects are in contemporary Muslim contexts, pointing to their failure to resonate with Muslim concerns and needs. In this view, such projects have no intrinsic value, and any interest in them derives from the ideological contexts of their production exclusively. A perception of the small circulation of their texts is contrasted with the widespread circulation enjoyed by other twentieth-century works on Qur'anic meaning for the modern world.[11] Some Muslims might agree to disagree on specific aspects of these projects, nevertheless seeing in them a potentially valuable contribution to illuminating the future development of Muslim culture and society, whether internally or in relation to significant others. Yet others embrace certain of these projects unreservedly. Such positive Muslim evaluations can be confined to specific constituencies, such as women, the youth, and those who are Western-educated,[12] or educated to a high level in modern educational institutions in Muslim countries. In comparison with competing Islamic formulations, however, it is fair to say that the appeal of these projects among Muslim circles in general appears to be confined to a relatively small minority.

In contrast with a limited and perhaps overwhelmingly unreceptive Muslim response, there is evidence of great interest in some of these projects in European and American circles. University courses devoted to them are being introduced and some of the thinkers behind them have been enthusiastically hosted and adopted. This raises a number of questions. What role have Western academia and media played in promoting these thinkers? Who benefits from the sale of their texts and who controls the means of their production? How has a Western involvement impacted on Muslim perceptions of them? Has Western interest in them bestowed an arbitrary and artificial weight on projects with little inherent intellectual substance when measured against historical Islamic thought and its towering figures? What assumptions about these thinkers' self-identities lie behind their projects? How do they wish to be received, and by whom: for whom are they writing? What does a lack of receptivity to some of these texts reveal about many Muslims' orientations and concerns during the late twentieth and early twenty-first centuries? What is revealed by an exaggerated Western interest in projects that are unrepresentative of more influential discursive interpretations in contemporary Islamic thought? Specifically, what does this interest reveal about Western attitudes towards Muslim societies, or the ideological leanings of Western scholars of Muslim societies, Islamic civilisation and culture?[13] Does this interest manifest an innocent Western yearning for a Muslim 'other' whose values resonate closely with those of the self? It should not be forgotten in this regard that perceptions of a long-standing Western interest in dissident voices are common in Muslim societies. Conversely, what do Muslim attitudes towards these projects reveal concerning perceptions of the Western 'other' as internalised in the self-world and the formulation of its religious discourses?

While it is not possible to answer all of these questions here, it is important to draw attention to the fact that neutrality is ultimately unattainable in any analysis (including what follows), given that every context of analysis brings its own horizons, special concerns and biases. The deconstruction of underlying methodological expectations, presuppositions and assumptions in any attempt to assess their projects is further necessitated by the fact that several of the thinkers studied here represent marginal voices. Their simultaneous if implicit critique both of regimes and Islamists places them in a particularly vulnerable position, while they themselves are often rejected by Islamists, Islamic traditionalists and Islamic officialdom alike, and even sometimes by secularists. The intention here is neither to praise them nor to privilege negative perceptions of them. Nor is it to suggest their intrinsic or relative merit by drawing attention to them. It is rather to offer some elucidation of the bases of their reception among different audiences, while at the same time presenting their projects for further comparison and debate. The long-standing conventions and methodologies of the Islamic tradition clearly shape the expectations of many Muslim critics: from this perspective, these projects are unwholesome, hybridised, unconvincing and threatening. In contrast, Western enthusiasm for such thinkers – as an *avant-garde* of 'Islamic liberalism' or members of a new elite advocating an Islamic 'reformation' – expresses an underlying assumption that this is what Islam 'needs' to render it capable of existing cooperatively in the modern world.

In what follows, Muslim expectations reflecting more traditionally oriented positions are given particular attention. While this partly reflects this author's own interests, it is a legitimate analytical perspective for two reasons. Firstly, most of the thinkers studied here self-consciously frame their discourse in terms of the texts and culture of Islam. Secondly, their Western admirers adopt and fête them in their capacity as *Muslim* thinkers specifically, perhaps seeing in them a desirable model of Islamic spokespersons.

Islam and Western modernity

In the nineteenth century, responses to the growing Western presence in Muslim societies took three distinct courses. At one end of the spectrum ultra-conservatives called for a rejection of any interaction with the modern West, while at the other end secularists urged its wholesale embrace. The *via media* characterised what is often termed the 'Modernist' trend. This crystallised during the late nineteenth and early twentieth century in the form of a synthesis between modern values and systems on the one hand, and what were seen to be eternal Islamic values and systems on the other, creating an 'Islamic-Western' composite.[14] This paradigmatic response to Western modernity has been assumed by much recent scholarship to underpin projects such as those collected in the present volume, as evidenced by the positing of a line of continuity between the historical 'Modernists' and certain of these contemporary projects. All are subsumed under a distinct trend, described either as 'modernist Islam' or 'liberal Islam'.[15]

The assumption of common underpinnings can be usefully explored here. The late nineteenth- and early twentieth-century ulama, statesmen and intellectuals who advanced a synthesis between Islamic and modern Western values referred to themselves as *muslihun* (reformists),[16] or salafis,[17] terms which underscore the Islamic character of their self-perceptions.[18] While the impetus for their reform project was provided by the challenge of modern Europe, its impulse lay within the Islamic tradition,[19] and although modernity provided answers, the Islamic culture furnished the integrating framework for these. The Islamic parameters and commitment of the early reformists' endeavours reflected the reality that this culture represented the only frame of reference imaginable to them.[20] In the late twentieth-century Muslim experience, in contrast, multiple frames of reference have become imaginable, thanks to the relentless penetration of competing worldviews and cultural forms amidst the social, political and economic dysfunctions caused by modernisation. This is evidenced by some of the projects discussed here, for which Western modernity appears to be the starting-point and ultimate goal, whether consciously adopted or unconsciously assumed. This perspective might be projected through a discourse that resorts to Islamic tradition in a bid to lay claim to its culturally authenticating force, and by way of response to competing Islamic formulations.

Both Muslim imaginings of the 'West' and Western self-imag-
inings have undergone significant shifts since the era of the early
reformists. Their approach to the West and their understanding
of Western modernity was largely selective and apologetic. For
example, they failed to discern, or preferred to ignore, its imperialist dimensions. The success, force and internal stability of the
nineteenth-century Western experience had precluded the
emergence of any serious critique of the Enlightenment and its
consequences within Europe itself, let alone on the part of
Muslim reformists. Their enchantment with modernity and its
Enlightenment values can thus largely be explained in terms of
the fact that its intrinsic crises and shortcomings were yet to be
seen. Three important differences separate the experience of
Muslim thinkers of the late twentieth century from that of the
early reformists in this regard. First, the Western modernity they
encounter is significantly transformed from that encountered at
the century's turn. In the course of the twentieth century, its
pillars were shaken and its self-confident narrative of emancipation and progress was undermined. World wars, unjust effects and
destruction of the environment caused by science and industry,
social disintegration and the trivialisation of life reflected in much
of modern culture have all reduced confidence in the project of
modernity. While its inherent problems have been starkly
exposed, internal fragmentation, erosion and self-critiques have
grown.[21] Second, compared with the early reformists, Muslim
thinkers of the late twentieth century are generally more intimately familiar with Western modernity and its complexities.
While for the early reformists it was a new discovery, made from
the perspective of traditional Islam, contemporary Muslims have
long been exposed to its realities. The old enchantment has gone,
and they are better placed and equipped to critique it. Finally,
contemporary Muslims are widely convinced that an element of
cultural imperialism permeates Western attitudes and policies
where Muslim societies are concerned. This creates an inhos-
pitable climate for projects perceived to call for assimilation of the
worldview or the cultural–intellectual products of Western
modernity as a basis for the reform of Muslim societies and insti-

tutions, and for projects which are openly grounded in Western thought or enthusiastically supported by Western parties.

For their part, the reformists generally developed a critical facet to their overwhelmingly positive projection of the West only after the outbreak of World War One.[22] The fate of their imagining of the West and its implications for future efforts to create a cultur- ally synthetic formula can be traced with particular clarity in the Arab context. The dashing of Arab expectations and the ensuing colonial policies cast serious doubt on the view of the West held by the Arab-Islamic reformists, and led ultimately to the unravelling of their synthesis of 'Islam', the 'West', and a largely cultural Arabism. Its constituent elements took shape in the inter-war period in trends of Westernised, secular intellectuals, radical Arab nationalists, and those upholding an increasingly ideologised, 'post-reformist' Islam. Rejection of Western imperialism became the universal point of departure, while throughout the new discourses the West was increasingly imagined in terms of an irreconcilable animosity, projected as an unjust organisational model and a morally degenerate and culturally corrupt society. Arab fascination with the West had been dealt a fatal blow by the end of the 1930s. As Nafi puts it:

> [G]one was the clean, harmonious, charitable, prosperous west that was depicted in al-Tahtawi's *Takhlis al-Ibriz*; the west of the enlight- enment, of the French revolution ... under whose impacts and in whose image Khayr al-Din al-Tunisi ... Muhammad Abduh and the young Rida moulded their visions of modern Islam. In its place, a new version was being pieced together of a ruthless, exploitative, self-destructive and lethal west.[23]

In spite of their self-conscious rejection of the West, however, it soon became apparent that the self-same 'West' had reappeared, to occupy a significant place within these new discourses.[24] For example, Arabism was cast in an overwhelmingly Western conceptual mould, while Islamists gradually adopted Western political methods in their bid for state power, assuming the modern nation-state as the arena for their struggle. The West had in fact remained to haunt even those discourses that explicitly and vehemently rejected it.[25] The Arab experience in this respect was

11

not unique: throughout the Muslim world, major ideas, assumptions and methods of the modern West have become unconsciously internalised, where they have not been consciously adopted, in all types of ideological and discursive formulation.

Certain of the projects studied here demonstrate the extent of this unconscious internalisation, others the degree of conscious adoption, in the context of discourses that engage primarily with the Islamic texts and tradition. At the same time, these projects – and Muslim reactions to them – bear witness to the persistence in contemporary Muslim thinking of the problematic of 'Islam and Western modernity', with its attendant challenge of cultural authenticity or self-referentiality. Its continuing relevance is confirmed by Muslim perceptions of the threat to traditional cultural distinctions inherent in processes of globalisation, and the perceived failure of the West to establish relations with the Muslim world based on cultural equality and exchange. For Muslims exercised by such concerns, some of the projects explored here appear to actively discourage confidence in the cultural resources of Muslim societies, and do the West's work of cultural imperialism for it.[26] In this view, it is no accident that these thinkers, projected as agents of Westernisation, have spent lengthy spells in the West and its academe. The Muslim experience of the twentieth century has been one of enduring crisis, precipitated by the onslaught of Western modernity with its thirst for domination, and perpetuated by continuing Western injustice towards the Muslim world. In light of this, those who appear to advocate Western solutions to the problems of Muslim societies are naturally denounced as spokespersons for the 'West', rather than for Muslim concerns or for 'Islam', even when they relate their ideas directly to the Islamic textual tradition.[27]

Who speaks for Islam?

In traditional Muslim societies, a single social group spoke authoritatively for Islam: this was the class of the ulama. It had held the societal nexus throughout Islamic history, while safeguarding the tenets of the faith from a position of semi-independence from the political system. From the late nineteenth century, the comprehensive changes produced by the impact of European colonialism and modernisation gradually eroded its position. The control of the ulama over the educational process and legal systems was broken, and the bases of their economic power and independence were lost. The ulama class would discover that its languages and methods were not those of the emerging order,[28] while its traditional Islamic learning was perceived to be less relevant to the new concerns and preoccupations of Muslim societies. New social classes created by modernisation rose to prominence, while modern education produced a new educated elite, professionals and modern intellectuals. As the social position of the ulama class shrank, a rising intelligentsia with a self-professed commitment to Islam occupied a significant part of the resulting vacuum. Various social actors entered the cultural arena with claims to speak for Islam: alongside intellectuals and professionals such as engineers and medical doctors, these included government officials and military personnel, for example. In the course of the twentieth century, the traditional impulse to solicit and defer to the opinion of the ulama has been considerably weakened, not least by their cooperation with the modern state, and their failure to respond effectively to the overwhelming discursive challenges of the modern era.[29]

The intellectual authority of the ulama class in pre-modern Muslim societies derived from societal recognition of its members' piety, and their specialist training in elite institutions of Islamic learning. In *madrasa*s and 'mosque-universities' such as al-Azhar, formal Islamic knowledge and the authoritative interpretation of tradition were transmitted directly from generation to generation, in a system where customs of *ijaza*-granting signalled mastery of a more-or-less fixed canon of traditional texts and the principles of interpretation established therein. The monopoly of the ulama both on the transmission and the interpretation of formal Islamic knowledge was first broken by the introduction of print culture in Muslim societies. This produced a revolution in access, through the mass production of books:

> Books, which they [the ulama] literally possessed … could now be
> consulted by any Ahmad, Mahmud or Muhammad, who could make
> what they will of them. Increasingly from now on any Ahmad,
> Mahmud or Muhammad could claim to speak for Islam. No longer
> was a sheaf of impeccable *ijazas* the buttress of authority.[30]

The 'democratisation' of direct access to the traditional texts of
Islam made possible by print has been complemented by the
'massification' of modern education in Muslim countries since
the mid twentieth century, creating unprecedented levels of
popular literacy. The practical necessity to consult those with
'ulamatic' training has thus been greatly reduced.[31] The traditional, hierarchical concepts of Islamic intellectual authority were
dealt a further blow by the contribution of the reformists to the
revival of the salafi notion of returning to a direct understanding
of the primary texts of Islam. Their argument effectively liberated
Muslims from the need for specialist expertise, theoretically
removing all barriers of learning between the texts and their
readers. This greatly weakened the assumption of 'ulamatic'
training as the necessary credentials for speaking on behalf of
Islam, throwing open the doors of interpretation to those without
the skills and qualifications that might ensure a degree of continuity in this. Increasingly today those without formal training in
the Islamic disciplines claim direct interpretive rights over the
Islamic texts as equals with the ulama, and in direct competition
with them.[32] Any possibility of uniformity or continuity of interpretation, or of a controlled diversity of readings, has been lost.

New claims to Islamic intellectual authority are tied to the
norms and expectations created by modern education.
Compared with the exclusive, erudite and at times inaccessible
repertoire of the ulama, new spokespersons for Islam frame their
discourses in forms accessible and relevant to modern-educated
readerships, and adopt innovative techniques of interpretation.[33]
Marked by diffusion, diversification, and above all fragmentation,
new modes of authority are linked to the rise of the professions, to
political and social activism, and to the introduction of new information and media technologies in Muslim countries. As claims to
Islamic intellectual authority multiply, new spokespersons for

Islam are able to disseminate their interpretations to ever wider, anonymous audiences, while the control of information and opinion has become increasingly difficult, thanks to communicational changes reflecting an increasingly information-rich global context.[34] Increasingly, it is a matter of circumstance, indeed accident, which of the myriad 'authoritative' voices, texts and discourses are encountered and embraced, as Muslims access information across all boundaries. A 'spectacularly wild growth of interpretations'[35] in recent decades reflects the absence of any guiding or uniting concept of intellectual authority, and of the credentials that might underwrite it.

Several of the intellectuals explored in the present volume provide clear illustration of this trend. For the most part, they neither graduated from traditional institutions of Islamic learning, nor are they situated within these.[36] Most are professional academics in modern universities. Some are self-taught in the Islamic disciplines, but most have engaged in the advanced study of Islam in modern universities, and many have had significant encounters with Islamic studies in the Western academe. Their roles as professional academics converge with their postures as interpreters of Islam. Several consciously adopt and apply contemporary discourses and methods in the academic study of Islam. In contrast with the so-called 'Islamic books' that have flooded markets in many Muslim countries in the course of the last decade or two,[37] certain of the texts discussed here speak to a more elite readership, which is either familiar with these discourses and methods or seeks this familiarity. For some, their appeal lies in their perceived achievement in incorporating these discourses and methods into the Islamic discursive arena, thereby rendering the latter relevant to global intellectual-cultural trends and debates.

The general changes in Muslim contexts sketched above have led some Western observers to note possible parallels with aspects of the Protestant Reformation. The rupture of traditional Islamic intellectual authority, debates concerning intellectual leadership and the authority of the past, the popularisation of access to Islam's primary texts, and the rapid and widespread dissemination of new ideas are all cited, among others, in this regard. Some focus specifically on projects such as those collected in the present volume. For example, one scholar has suggested that the Syrian engineer Mohamed Shahrour's *al-Kitab wal-Qur'an: qira'a mu'asira* may one day be seen as a 'Muslim equivalent' of Martin Luther's *95 Theses*.[38] Dismissive Muslim reactions to such analogies point to the lack of appropriate credentials among Shahrour and his likes. They also emphasise widespread perceptions of their alienation from their own societies, culture and historical traditions.[39]

The Qur'an and the limits of Islamic reform

The lack of consensus concerning Islamic intellectual authority and its requisite credentials is mirrored in the absence of any agreement concerning the purpose, methods and, perhaps most significantly, the limits of Islamic reform. The historical Islamic experience was marked by a continuous tradition of internal revitalisation, encapsulated in concepts of *islah* and *tajdid*.[40] This was conceived as an authentic dimension in the working out of the Islamic revelation in history, and thus went beyond purely practical human needs or ends. Reflecting its inspiration in the vision of the early era of excellence, its ultimate purpose was to bring existing realities into line with the transcendent and universal standard embedded in the Qur'an and Sunna, through a process of restoration. There was neither a spirit of self-conscious innovation, nor dependence on a notion of progress. The tradition of *islah–tajdid* has consistently challenged the Muslim status quo from within the fundamental sources of Islamic inspiration. Its reaffirmation of the status of the Qur'an and Sunna as a unique and complete source of guidance informs a vigilance against anything that might threaten the integrity of the Islamic message, or compromise its distinctiveness. This often finds expression in a call for a return to a strict application of the Qur'an and Sunna, understood through a direct application of *ijtihad*, and rejection of rigid adherence to post-Prophetic elaborations as a source of authority.[41]

While the modern period has witnessed numerous examples of this tradition, the late nineteenth- and early twentieth-century reformist or salafi project is among the most significant. Certain of the thinkers explored in the present volume share with the reformists their interest in Western modernity, their rejection of traditional Islam, and their tendency to repudiate classical Islamic authorities in the endeavour to understand Islam's primary text. However, some of their projects present themselves more as evidence of the internalisation of Western modernity, and thus as a reflection of the problematic of 'Islam and Western modernity' (as suggested above), than as efforts from within to achieve Islamic renewal. In place of the challenge set for subsequent generations by the model of excellence encapsulated in the Sunna and the salaf, some evidently play to the challenge set by the modern West. Responding to global forces and working from within wide-ranging intellectual networks, some of the producers of these projects are hardly rooted in Islamic culture, although they might invoke specific Islamic intellectual traditions in their work.[42] Like the reform project of the turn of the twentieth century, their own projects create a rupture with the traditional intellectual modes of the Islamic past. At the same time, however, some of these projects engender a disruptive conflict with the Islamic present, begging a question concerning their potential contribution to the cultural coherence of their producers' communities of origin, or the broader Muslim community.

Reform necessarily implies a challenge to current – and especially dominant – religious, cultural and intellectual modes. As the most significant form of critical separation from the status quo across Islamic history,[43] the potency of *islah–tajdid* sprang from its operation within the fundamental sources of Islamic guidance and the evolving consensus that set the boundaries of orthodoxy. While animating evolution of the cultural and religious life of the Muslim community, a leading concern of this tradition was to preserve its unity of faith and cohesion. In this spirit, an important aim of the reform project at the turn of the twentieth century had been to restore Muslim consensus. Throughout the century, Muslims moved by the same concerns have endeavoured to engage creatively with the foundational texts of Islam, debating the authority of the past in the service of applying the Islamic message under the changed conditions of modernity, within the broad parameters of the sources of Islamic inspiration. At the same time, however, it must be conceded that Islamic thought as a whole in the twentieth century is no longer internally generated from within Muslim cultural traditions, but is substantially a reaction to extrinsic challenges. In contrast with traditional Islamic epistemology, where divergent opinions and schools of thought (which were tolerated and even celebrated) referred to a common origin, contemporary Muslim thinking reflects both internal and external frames of reference, and is shaped by diverse influences, which may be ideational or structural.[44] The question 'what is Islam?' has come to dominate Muslim debates,[45] and there appear to be as many different responses (and inspirations for such responses) as there are Muslims prepared to reflect seriously upon the question. Shifts in the intellectual-cultural terrain are evidenced by the fact that ways of thinking about 'Islam' which were virtually inconceivable for most Muslims a few generations ago now circulate widely and are enthusiastically advocated by some thinkers.

For many Muslims, some of the thinkers presented here appear occasionally to question the very tenets of Islamic faith, especially in relation to the most sensitive issue: the status and meaning of the Qur'an as God's authentic, uncorrupted and inimitable Word. At the turn of the twentieth century, the reformists were careful to avoid the potential excesses of a rational-historical interrogation of the Qur'an, and would not touch the sanctity of the text. Certain of the thinkers presented here, in contrast, appear to see their own 'return' to an unmediated reading of the Qur'an as an altogether free enterprise, driven exclusively by 'reason' and mediated by the fruits and techniques of Western intellectual life.[46] In some cases, this 'return' is framed in an approach to Islam that appears to reflect a postmodern mood of radical criticism and suspicion, directed at meta-narratives in general, and an interest in the 'hermeneutics of suspicion'. Viewed from the perspective of the Muslim community interpreting its own heritage, even certain of those thinkers who take the principle of God's Word as revealed in the Qur'an as their point of departure are deemed to have exceeded acceptable limits.

Scholarship on the Qur'an in Western universities has recently adopted contemporary schools of literary theory and criticism, and hermeneutical theories.[47] Such approaches demonstrate that the meaning of a text cannot be taken for granted but depends on diverse textual, contextual and inter-textual factors, in addition to the circumstances of textual receptors in creating horizons of meaning.[48] The contribution of Muslim academics to the contemporary field is such that it is now commonly argued that the notion of a 'divide' between 'Muslim' and 'non-Muslim' or 'Western' scholarship on the Qur'an is increasingly irrelevant.[49] When such recent Muslim contributions have become known among a broader Muslim public, general reactions have betrayed a deep-seated unease, with many insisting that specific boundaries be maintained around the text as the authentic repository of God's uncorrupted, inimitable Word, as much in scholarly realms of discourse as in others. The same unease has of course long informed Muslim reactions to 'Western' studies of Islamic sacred literature,[50] but it is particularly acute when such scholarship is of Muslim provenance.[51]

A Muslim scholar has recently characterised the challenge facing colleagues who write for *Muslim* readers, in their attempt to apply discourses such as those on literary theory, deconstruction and hermeneutics to discussions of textuality and determinations of meaning in the Islamic context. Abou El Fadl has pointed to the simple fact that such discourses are alien to the Islamic tradition and its constructs of symbolism and meaning. They reflect a specifically Western historical experience. His recommendation is that Muslim scholars should start with the Muslim experience and consider how such discourses might be utilised in its service. They should be careful not to use categories that reconstruct and remodel it according to Western paradigms, and should not superimpose an epistemology upon Muslims that might not reflect the Muslim experience faithfully. While they are not necessarily to be rejected out of hand, transcultural epistemological transplants should thus be executed 'with measured restraint and a degree of reasonableness so that the receiving body will not violently reject them'.[52]

The pertinence of Abou El Fadl's plea might be illuminated from a somewhat different perspective with an example drawn from the practical experience of a developing Muslim participation in inter-religious dialogue. Reflecting on the 'entrance' of 'Islam' into dialogue based on an assessment of articles appearing in the *Journal of Ecumenical Studies* in the course of the last generation, Leonard Swidler notes that the very first article by a Muslim author, which appeared in 1968, was contributed by Isma'il Ragi al-Faruqi.[53] He writes:

> Faruqi was a traditionally orthodox Muslim ... a highly knowledgeable Islamicist who did an immense amount to break open Islam to dialogue. It was Isma'il's very traditional orthodoxy that allowed him to accomplish this so effectively. His often highly sceptical religious confrères trusted him implicitly not to 'give away' anything Islamic, and hence were open to being coaxed into joining the dialogue, although most often rather defensively.[54]

For most of the thinkers studied in the present volume, their engagement with the Qur'anic text is, of course, far from an exclusively academic or scholarly project. This engagement itself speaks to the continued cultural centrality of this text, and the pivotal place it occupies in the struggles and aspirations of contemporary Muslim societies, as in Muslim politics.[55] In the contemporary world, millions of people refer to the Qur'an daily to justify their aspirations or to explain their actions, reflecting a scale of direct reference unprecedented in the Islamic experience.[56] This can partly be explained in terms of new modes of communication and information technology;[57] it also reflects the impact of the Islamic resurgence on the public arena and the language of politics. Intellectuals from secular backgrounds who are concerned with the future of a fragile civil society are faced with the challenge both of radicalised Islamist forces and the growing successes enjoyed by their moderate counterparts in the democratic process. If they are to find an audience in the discursive arena, they must themselves appeal to the Islamic tradition and its ultimate legitimising text.

Appeals to the Qur'anic text are not only framed in the context of opposition to Islamist discourses, however. As the present volume demonstrates, such appeals also appear in struggles against authoritarian regimes, as in those against dominant patriarchal modes of thought and social structures that marginalise or exclude women, and against traditionalist Islamic culture more generally. They are recruited in addressing concerns over threatening national disintegration and inter-communal strife, as in concerns over cultural impasse, intellectual stagnation, and the absence of material development in Muslim countries.

Like those of the Islamists with which many such appeals to tradition take issue, they can ultimately be interpreted as responses to the ongoing failure in the Muslim world to create a culturally viable, successful modern state. The Islamist reaction to the failure of cultural modernisation and secularisation processes launched by the post-colonial elites is to invoke the self-past, re-imagined in terms of culturally authentic and 'pure' models, and motivated by perceptions of the West (with its agents within the Muslim world) as a threat. In contrast, some of those surveyed in this volume uphold the very same processes of modernisation and secularisation, while dismissing, denying or refuting the issue of their 'alien' cultural provenance and their compatibility with an Islamic commitment to transcendence, through a re-imagining of 'Islam' that itself rivals the Islamist one. This advocating of 'modern' values via a re-imagined Islam nonetheless sets their posture apart from that of the secular intellectuals.

This volume

The three themes discussed above are brought to the fore by the present volume as a whole and, each to a greater or lesser extent, by its individual chapters. The structure of the volume presents a clustering of some chapters, reflecting certain features or tendencies loosely held in common among some of the thinkers considered. The first chapter discusses the project of the late Pakistani scholar Fazlur Rahman, a towering figure of twentieth-century Islamic reform. Although he spent most of his academic life in the West, as **Abdullah Saeed** points out, Rahman remained firmly committed to an Islamic process of knowledge, while at the same time subjecting traditional Islamic thought and methodologies to a profound critique. Rahman emphasised areas that have been neglected in Muslim understandings of the Qur'an, and it is from this that his importance largely derives. Such areas include the socio-historical context of the revelation, the spirit of its message as a whole, and the retrieval of its moral elan, as a basis for elaborating a Qur'an-centred ethics. Rahman's wide-ranging influence is evident in the work of such thinkers as those who form the subject of the two following chapters. These are his former student Nurcholish Madjid, a prominent Indonesian public figure, and the American scholar Amina Wadud.

As **Anthony H. Johns and Abdullah Saeed** demonstrate, Madjid has endeavoured to achieve a pragmatic realisation of Qur'anic values in a manner appropriate to the distinctive character and needs of the Indonesian state. His aim in this is to safeguard Indonesia's integration as a religiously and ethnically plural entity, and to enhance the role of the Pancasila in its capacity as the ideological cornerstone of national unity. His 'contextualist' approach to understanding the Qur'an is informed by a recognition of the pressing need for inter-religious harmony in Indonesia. It is equally motivated by his consciousness of the historically divisive impact of *fiqh* among Muslims there. Also inspired by Rahman and in contrast with Madjid, Amina Wadud's concern, as described by **Asma Barlas**, is with the problematic of Qur'anic interpretation and the marginalisation of women's full human agency within society. Wadud is a pioneer among a growing cluster of Muslim women scholars who are developing a feminist reading of the Islamic tradition and foundational texts. As Barlas, herself a member of this cluster,[58] demonstrates, Wadud highlights the connections between traditional *tafsir* (exegesis) and the means of its production, explaining the genre's masculinist nature, and its resultant biases against women. She calls for a more egalitarian *tafsir*, inclusive of women's voices, and reflecting new, holistic modes of understanding and participation in Muslim religious life. The claim that it upholds the ontological equality of the sexes stands at the core of her own reading of the Qur'an, which thus serves the project of Muslim women's emancipation.

It has been suggested that Rahman never consciously introduced analytic procedures derived from Western thinkers in a major manner, and was not attracted to the ongoing debate in Western intellectual circles, even in those areas that influenced his methodology.[59] In contrast, in the assessment of one scholar, in his employment of 'the categories of post-modernity' to call for a rethinking of the whole Islamic tradition, the Algerian-French scholar Mohammed Arkoun,

> seems to be using the Islamic tradition as a text upon which to continue a debate about Western epistemology. He pays little attention to the specificity of the Islamic condition or tradition, as if the Islamic tradition is expected to serve as a yielding raw material for constructing the epistemological edifice of the West.[60]

Arkoun presents his project as a detached, ideologically neutral and radical perspective on the development of the 'religious phenomenon', and its implications for present and future human concerns. He rejects any link between his own thought and '*islahi* (reformist) thinking'.[61] Questioning the assumptions of the historical-critical method, his own critical reading of 'Islamic reason', his deconstruction of centuries of Islamic thought, and his constructs of revelation and orthodoxy challenge both academic scholarship on Islam, and Muslim self-understandings. As **Ursula Günther** suggests, the 'Arkounian' perspective has had little impact on both potential constituencies thus far.

The Egyptian scholar Nasr Hamid Abu Zayd introduced a linguistic problematisation of the religious discourse to a contemporary Arabic readership in a substantial manner for the first time. As **Navid Kermani** shows, his approach is based on application of the most relevant achievements of contemporary linguistics to the Qur'an, combined with literary study of the text and the adoption of Hans-Georg Gadamer's hermeneutics. Its conclusions are implicitly posited in opposition to contemporary

Islamist discourses with their notion of a single, eternally valid interpretation of the sacred text. This provides the context for understanding postures adopted towards his writings in Egypt, and his trial.

Mohamad Mojtahed Shabestari's project provides an example of the rethinking of the Islamic revolutionary tradition in Iran. It represents one trend among post-revolutionary Iranian Islamic discourses, as they endeavour to address the contradictions inherent in the paradigm of what **Farzin Vahdat** terms 'mediated subjectivity', inherited from the founders of the Islamic Republic. Well-versed in German theological and philosophical scholarship, Shabestari relies on the principle of inter-subjectivity, which he situates within a religious model. He thus adopts a hermeneutic approach to subjectivity, which avoids any direct interpretation of Qur'anic texts. Vahdat sees in his hermeneutic construct of inter-subjectivity a framework in terms of which the discourse of religious modernity in post-revolutionary Iran can be advanced, as compared with the inherited paradigm. Shabestari's critique of the negative side of human subjectivity is accompanied by the suggestion that religion, projected as a source of permanent principles and general values, can help ameliorate the crises that accompany the unavoidable modernisation process in Muslim countries.

The Tunisian scholar Mohamed Talbi is best known for the case he advances from an Islamic perspective for religious pluralism and inter-religious dialogue, and for his work as a historian of North Africa. **Ronald L. Nettler** demonstrates how his progressive, liberal ideas are justified through a historical-contextual approach to the Qur'anic text, which seeks to elucidate God's intention in it. His 'intentional' reading is put forward as a foundation for resolving the current crisis in the Islamic encounter with modernity, and a foil to the literal readings that plague contemporary Muslim understandings.

Osman Taştan points to the pragmatic, utilitarian approach to the Qur'an, and its legal content in particular, developed by the veteran Turkish scholar Hüseyin Atay. Atay's extraction from the Qur'an of practical solutions to specific Islamic issues serves a straightforward understanding and simplified practice of Islam. While this makes it accessible to the general practising public, its rationalist, anti-traditionalist orientation clearly reflects and sits comfortably with the established emphasis on modernity in the Turkish Republican context. This orientation is prominent in the publications of many scholars who, like Atay, are situated in Faculties of Islamic Studies in Turkish universities.

The Syrian engineer Mohamad Shahrour and the Libyan writer Sadiq Nayhum share common features. Both emanate from essentially secular backgrounds, and are self-taught in the area of Islamic learning. Driven onto the discursive arena carved by the Islamic resurgence, their engagement with the Qur'an partly serves a critique of traditional Islamic and Islamist formulations and contemporary political conditions. Shahrour advances his 'contemporary reading' of the Qur'an as the foundation for a comprehensive project of cultural, social, political and material renewal in Arab-Muslim societies. **Andreas Christmann** elucidates his employment of a linguistic analysis to reprogramme Qur'anic terminology, thereby estranging readers from conventional understandings and challenging traditional religious authority. As **Suha Taji-Farouki** demonstrates, Nayhum recruits Qur'anic texts in the context of a call for a culturally rooted form of direct democracy, embedded in 'Islam' reconstructed as a formula for political emancipation. To some extent, his resort to the Qur'an suggests a 'ritualistic' acknowledgement of the Islamic textual tradition. At the same time, it illustrates the appeal of the 'Qur'anic message', however appropriated, among secular-oriented Muslim intellectuals confronting the experience of alienation and fragmentation brought by modernity.

By way of conclusion to this introductory chapter, attention must be drawn to a reform-oriented but Islamically rooted voice, which has become increasingly influential during the late twentieth century, reflecting a certain resonance with a broad public understanding in Muslim societies. This is the voice of reform-minded Muslim intellectuals and academics and a small number of reform-minded ulama, whose diverse contributions, put together, bear witness to important patterns of intellectual development and change in contemporary Islamic thought.

While such reform-oriented thinkers might themselves be subject to various Western influences, having in some cases been trained in Western universities, they work self-consciously from within Islamic cultural and textual traditions, and adhere to an Islamic frame of reference. Often with an eye to invalidating extremist Islamic postures, they address the ongoing challenge of elaborating modern Islamic responses to the modalities and demands of the modern experience, and the profoundly changed realities and novel problems of modern Muslim life. Their interpretive approach to the Qur'an and Sunna is direct and pays attention to social and historical contexts, distinguishing between universal principles and the moral thrust of the revelation on the one hand, and directives that may be bound to its specific circumstances on the other. In determining the meanings and implications of the revelation, they draw on the rich legacy of Islamic tradition in its diverse branches, while carefully probing the complex relation between this tradition and the context of its elaboration, taking into account aspects of its contingency.

Some of these thinkers deconstruct and critique aspects of the project of Western modernity, often sharing common ground in this with the critical discourse of modernity and its post-modern critics. However, they part company with the latter in their Islamic frame of reference, and their concern to offer 'constructive' responses to the human predicament. Refusing to bow to a blanket privileging of the modern over the pre-modern, they maintain that modernity's characteristic sense of superiority must be tempered with a respect for pre-modern sources which, if properly contextualised, can yield much that is of value. Others divest the modern West of its claims to universal validity; their commitment to Islamic cultural resources derives further confidence from an awareness that, at this juncture in history, there is a possibility for other voices to be received with less prejudice. Crucially, their contributions explore and advocate significant contemporary areas of reform within this culture, including democratisation, pluralism, tolerance, openness to other religions, and equality of status for women and minorities in Muslim societies. Their arguments in this regard evince an alertness to the specific worldview upon which concepts and institutions are premised, identifying what may be incompatible with an Islamic cosmology and a commitment to transcendence.[62]

Certain of the thinkers presented in this volume clearly contribute to this reform-oriented, Islamically rooted trend, which is exemplified to varying degrees by such figures as Khaled Abou El Fadl, Muhammad Salim al-'Awwa, Mohammad Hashim Kamali, Taha Jabir al-'Alwani and the 'professional' *'alim* Yusuf al-Qaradawi, to name a few. Relative to them, others studied here create an impression that they are Westernised liberals still under the spell of Western modernity, seeing in it a solution to the needs and problems of Muslim societies. In contrast with both, yet others discussed in this volume appear to have set out on the postmodernist road, which in its extreme form can ultimately lead to nihilism.[63]

The reform-oriented Islamic discourse sketched in these concluding lines remains intimately connected to the reformist discourse of the turn of the twentieth century. Those who contribute to it are perhaps the genuine heirs to the reformists' legacy, while taking this into uncharted waters towards a destination yet unclear, in an unpredictable and rapidly changing context. What is clear is the bid made by such thinkers to avoid the pitfalls and excesses of modernity, and to preserve the moral and cultural integrity of the Islamic worldview, and the special Islamic identity and cohesion of Muslim societies. In the wider world, the contribution of this discourse perhaps lies ultimately in its non-negotiable commitment to applying an ethical dimension to the exercise of reason and power. In Muslim countries, it might respond effectively to pressing concerns for the injection of justice and morality into the political and socio-economic order, while avoiding the problems and excesses inherent in certain Islamist options.[64]

The 'West' is now an omnipresent party to the ongoing process of re-negotiating Islam among Muslims, in which this reform trend represents one of many competing voices.[65] This undeniably complicates the task that confronts it, whether in invalidating extremist Islamic formulations, or galvanising Muslim opinion in the endeavour to establish an effective bridge between the demands of an ever-changing present and a commitment to eternal values and the tradition and culture that embody them. Indeed its foremost challenge perhaps lies in successfully navigating a path between openness to external influences and an enduring faithfulness to the internal cultural map and dynamics of Muslim society, in a world where human interactions are growing dramatically.

It hardly need be pointed out that the Qur'anic text forms the bedrock of any Islamic discourse, reform-oriented or other, worthy of the name. Modernity has focused attention perhaps in an unparalleled way on the complexities of interactions between texts and readers. During the last few decades, Muslims have read the Qur'an in a rich multiplicity of ways, something of which is illustrated by the present volume. It is hoped that the essays collected here will point to some of the challenges, problems and responsibilities contained within this act of reading.

NOTES

1. For a classic discussion of 'the maelstrom of modern life', see Marshall Berman, *All that is Solid Melts into Air: The Experience of Modernity* (London and New York, 1981). For institutional transformations associated with it, see Anthony Giddens, *The Consequences of Modernity* (Oxford, 2000).

2. The uprootings and dynamic of constant change that characterise modernity have been of particular concern to the major religions, as they are rooted in pre-modernity, and endeavour to sustain significant continuity with the past. A 'comparative religions' perspective might thus be valuable. There are evident parallels between Muslim responses and those of modern Christian theology, and between modern Muslim debates concerning approaches to the sacred text and Biblical studies and interpretation. However, a comparative perspective might perhaps more usefully focus on Islamic and Jewish responses to modernity specifically, and on efforts of modern reform within the two traditions.

3. Cf. Daniel Brown, *Rethinking Tradition in Modern Islamic Thought* (Cambridge, 1996), pp. 2–4.

4. Modernity is referred to as 'Western' in this discussion in loose

reference to its largely European origins, and thus to its alien provenance as viewed from a Muslim cultural perspective.

5. Cf. Patrice Broduer, 'Arabic Muslim Writings on Contemporary Religions other than Islam: A Framework for Inquiry', in Jacques Waardenburg, ed., *Muslim Perceptions of Other Religions: A Historical Survey* (New York, 1999), pp. 240–49.

6. For an overview of some relevant ideas, see Gema Martin Muñoz, ed., *Islam, Modernism and the West* (London and New York, 1999), especially pp. 3–21.

7. The preoccupation with 'types' in the study of modern Islamic thought and the use of essentialising formulations to denote them is inherently problematic. Western studies frequently focus on 'Islam' itself, rather than Muslims, as the object of definition and classification. It is approached as an expandable range of ideological constructs, denoted by externally imposed labels that are generally not employed by those concerned to self-define, and often elucidate the concerns of the labeller to a greater extent than the labelled. References to 'radical Islam', 'official Islam' and 'political Islam' are commonplace, for example, while thinkers such as those in the present volume are generally dubbed representatives of 'liberal Islam' or 'modernist Islam'. As expressions of Islamic thought become more diversified and fragmented, it is increasingly difficult to capture this complexity adequately or to do justice to pervasive nuances, admixtures and internal tensions through the application of simple labels, which can be usefully employed only as a heuristic device in academic study.

8. Consistent with this, it must be emphasised that not all comments in this introductory discussion apply at all times to all of those studied in this volume.

9. Amina Wadud is an exception, having converted to Islam as an adult.

10. The term 'intellectual' is employed here to denote 'people who are specialists in ideas, images, and symbols', in accordance with Shils' definition, cited in John L. Esposito and John O. Voll, *Makers of Contemporary Islam* (Oxford, 2001), p. 4. The authors (pp. 3–22) provide a useful discussion of the role of intellectuals in Muslim history and modern Muslim societies.

11. Throughout the twentieth century, works on the Qur'an have enjoyed vast circulation among all sectors of the reading public. These encompass works of *tafsir*, works of *'ulum al-Qur'an* and, more recently, works that draw on more than one Islamic discipline in a broader discussion of the Qur'an, such as Muhammad al-Ghazali's *Kayfa nata'amalu ma'a al-Qur'an* (Herndon, 1991).

12. It is perhaps noteworthy in this regard that some of the contributing authors in this volume are Muslim scholars based in Western universities.

13. As Brown (*Rethinking Tradition*, p. 4) remarks, the tendency among scholars of modern Muslim intellectual history to emphasise ideas that are new, or seem to be the peculiar product of modernity, is a product of cultural bias and a vestige of the Enlightenment idea of progress. Added to this is the tendency to judge an author significant because their ideas are attractive to the scholar who studies them.

14. For a classic discussion of this response, see Albert Hourani, *Arabic*

Thought in the Liberal Age, 1798–1939 (Cambridge, 1989). See also Basheer M. Nafi, *The Rise and Decline of the Arab-Islamic Reform Movement* (London, 2000); idem., 'The Rise of Islamic Reformist Thought and its Challenge to Traditional Islam', in S. Taji-Farouki and B. M. Nafi, eds., *Islamic Thought in the Twentieth Century* (London, forthcoming). The discussion here draws in particular on the latter two sources.

15. See, for example, Ronald L. Nettler, 'Islam, Politics and Democracy: Mohamed Talbi and Islamic Modernism', in David Marquand and Ronald L. Nettler, eds., *Religion and Democracy* (Oxford, 2000), pp. 50 ff; Charles Kurzman, ed., *Liberal Islam: A Sourcebook* and *Modernist Islam, circa 1840–1940: A Sourcebook* (New York and Oxford, 1998; 2002); Seyyed Vali Reza Nasr, 'Religious Modernism in the Arab World, India and Iran: The Perils and Prospects of a Discourse', *The Muslim World*, LXXXIII, 1 (1993), pp. 20–41.

16. On the root notion of *islah* see Hamid Algar, 'Islah', *Encyclopaedia of Islam*, ed. H.A.R. Gibb *et al.*, new edn (Leiden, 1960–), vol. 4, pp. 141 ff. (Hereafter references to this edition of the *Encyclopaedia of Islam* are indicated as *EI²*). In contemporary Islamic literature the term denotes specifically 'reformism of the type that emerges in the doctrinal teachings of Muhammad 'Abduh, in the writings of Rashid Rida, and in the numerous Muslim authors who are influenced by these two masters and, like them, consider themselves disciples of the Salafiyya.' The Qur'an describes *al-muslihun* as engaged in God's work. See John O. Voll, 'Renewal and Reform in Islamic History: *Tajdid* and *Islah*', in John L. Esposito, ed., *Voices of Resurgent Islam* (New York and Oxford, 1983), pp. 32–47.

17. See, for example, Emad Eldin Shahin, 'Salafiyah', *The Oxford Encyclopedia of the Modern Islamic World*, ed. John L. Esposito (New York and Oxford, 1995), vol. 3, p. 463.

18. This is in contrast with the term 'Modernist', which from a contemporary perspective reflects more the preoccupations of Western scholarship or internal Muslim polemics.

19. While the reformist project was undoubtedly a response to the crisis engendered by European dominance, its origins within the intrinsic historical Islamic tradition of renewal and reform must be highlighted. Significant examples of internally generated calls for renewal and reform arose across the Muslim world well before the European colonialist challenge. The Western 'other' was instrumental neither in their appearance nor in their ideas. What set the modern reformists apart from their predecessors was the reality of Western superiority, which presented as the central concern.

20. Their appeal to Islam cannot be reduced to a stratagem for justifying the embrace of modernity, whether for its own sake or as a means to restore the balance of power vis-à-vis Europe. For example, while the positive projection of the West in reformist thought manifested a desire to adopt from it, it was equally employed in the conflict with those who clung to traditional Islam, in the service of what the reformists believed could be the only viable *Islamic* future. See for example Nafi, 'The Rise of Islamic Reformist Thought'. For an alternative view characterising the legacy of 'modernism' in terms of an Islamic tendency divorced from the very foundations of Islamic thought (as a result of its departure from traditional

Islam), see Nasr, 'Religious Modernism'.

21. Postmodernism might be understood to have 'de-centred' the West, by recognising that the claims made by modernity are in many ways 'less like reflections of universal truths and more like narcissistic fantasies'. It has revealed 'the limit of modernity's intellectual, moral and cultural mastery', putting into question the idea that 'West is best'. Moreover, the characteristic postmodern suspicion of meta-narratives has cast doubt on the most powerful narrative of the last two hundred years, which told 'the tale of the West's destiny'. See Bobby Sayyid, *Association of Muslim Social Scientists (UK) Newsletter*, 4 (2001).

22. Certain reformist elements indeed diverted their attention to defending Muslim freedom from the West by force. From 1920 onwards, for example, the great reformist Rashid Rida became actively involved in the Syrian revolt, the Palestinian struggle, and the Moroccan anti-Spanish and anti-French resistance.

23. Nafi, *The Rise and Decline*, p. 63.

24. Ibid., pp. 55–6.

25. As Sadri and Sadri note, 'Those who are quick to point out that... Islamic liberalism has borrowed from mainstream Western liberal theories, forget that the Islamic fundamentalists have also borrowed from Western countercurrents of populism, fascism, anarchism, Jacobinism, and Marxism.' Mahmoud Sadri and Ahmad Sadri, trs. and eds., *Reason, Freedom and Democracy in Islam: Essential Writings of 'Abdolkarim Soroush* (Oxford and New York, 2000), p. xvi. For his part, Nasr ('Religious Modernism', p. 29) argues that Islamic revivalism, which he projects as linked causally with 'modernism', shares in common with it 'the assimilation and absorption of Western ideas and worldviews'.

26. It is common among Islamists in particular to refer to a process of 'cultural invasion' (*al-ghazw al-thaqafi*) as a major consequence of Western imperialism, aimed at weakening Islam and Muslims by transferring Western ideas into Muslim culture, thus creating an ideological battle within the latter. For an example from the writings of Muhammad al-Ghazali see Ibrahim Abu Rabi', 'The Concept of the 'Other' in Modern Arab Thought: From Muhammad 'Abdu to Abdallah Laroui', *Islam and Christian-Muslim Relations*, 8, 1 (1997), pp. 90–1.

27. At the same time, of course, large sectors of Muslim populations have an appetite for the material, political and cultural trappings of Western modernity, created by expanding mass education and communications, and the impact of processes of globalisation.

28. Nafi, *The Rise and Decline*, pp. 38, 44.

29. Cf. Esposito and Voll, *Makers of Contemporary Islam*, pp. 14–17; Nafi and Taji-Farouki, 'Introduction' in Taji-Farouki and Nafi, eds., *Islamic Thought in the Twentieth Century*.

30. Francis Robinson, 'Technology and Religious Change: Islam and the Impact of Print', *Modern Asian Studies* 27, 1 (1993), pp. 245–6. As the author demonstrates, this in turn made possible 'radical leaps forward' in religious thinking, typically among Muslims who were not graduates of seminaries or formally trained ulama, and whose thinking has been partly

shaped by access to sources on Western civilisation. The link between new technologies and new interpreters must be underlined. See for example Jon W. Anderson, 'The Internet and Islam's New Interpreters', in Dale F. Eickelman and Jon W. Anderson, eds., *New Media in the Muslim World: The Emerging Public Sphere* (Bloomington, IN, 2000), p. 43.

31. Dale F. Eickelman, 'The Art of Memory: Islamic Education and its Social Reproduction', in Juan R. I. Cole, ed., *Comparing Muslim Societies: Knowledge and the State in a World Civilisation* (Ann Arbor, 1992), pp. 97–132; Dale F. Eickelman, 'Mass Higher Education and the Religious Imagination in Contemporary Arab Societies', in George N. Atiyeh, ed., *The Book in the Islamic World: The Written Word and Communication in the Middle East* (New York, 1995), pp. 255–72.

32. Augustus Richard Norton, 'The New Media, Civic Pluralism, and the Slowly Retreating State' in Eickelman and Anderson, eds., *New Media*, pp. 19–20; Nafi and Taji-Farouki, 'Introduction'.

33. Dale F. Eickelman and Jon W. Anderson, 'Redefining Muslim Publics', in Eickelman and Anderson, eds., *New Media*, p. 11.

34. See for example Anderson, 'The Internet and Islam's New Interpreters', p. 41 ff.

35. Fazlur Rahman, 'Approaches to Islam in Religious Studies: Review Essay', in Richard C. Martin, ed., *Approaches to Islam in Religious Studies* (Oxford, 2001), p. 195.

36. For this reason, such intellectuals are sometimes described as 'secular', while it is pointed out that they nevertheless believe Islam has an important role in the contemporary world. See for example Abdou Filali-Ansari, 'Can Modern Rationality Shape a New Religiosity? Mohamed Abed Jabri and the Paradox of Islam and Modernity', in John Cooper, Ronald Nettler and Mohamed Mahmoud, eds., *Islam and Modernity: Muslim Intellectuals Respond* (London, 2000), p. 169.

37. That is, popular Islamic publications conveying a 'vernacularised' Islamic discourse addressed to the new readership created by mass education. See Dale F. Eickelman and Jon W. Anderson, 'Print, Islam and the Prospects for Civic Pluralism: New Religious Writings and their Audiences', *Journal of Islamic Studies* 8, 1 (1997), p. 49; Eickelman and Anderson, 'Redefining Muslim Publics', pp. 12–13.

38. Eickelman, 'Inside the Islamic Reformation', *Wilson Quarterly* (Winter, 1998), p. 84. In addition to its approach and conclusions, he considers this book important because it has sold 'tens of thousands of copies', in spite of being banned in many Arab countries. Eickelman argues with some confidence that the 'Islamic Reformation' is underway. For a less sanguine reading of the current situation in Muslim countries see Abdou Filali-Ansari, 'Islam and Secularism', in Martin Muñoz, ed., *Islam, Modernism and the West*, pp. 133–4.

Eickelman is not alone in his opinion concerning Shahrour specifically. See for example Michael Jansen, 'Syria's Islamic Reformer Outsells Mullah', *The Irish Times*, 13 Aug 1993. Similar arguments have been advanced in relation to the Iranian pharmacologist-intellectual Abdolkarim Soroush, also dubbed the 'Luther of Islam'. See for example

Robin Wright, cited in Sadri and Sadri, *Reason, Freedom and Democracy*, p. xv.

39. The debate concerning the reality or possibility of change in Muslim societies amounting to an 'Islamic Reformation' might revisit the highly influential salafi intellectual tradition, and its impact, which has found very broad expression during the twentieth century. Its characteristic bid to recover the foundational texts of Islam from the accumulated weight of classical Islamic tradition through a direct reading finds expression, in certain of its more radical articulations, in an attitude towards received authority reflected in the following dictum, concerning the producers of the legacy of historical learning: 'We are men, and they are men'.

For discussion of parallels between sixteenth-century Protestant reformers and contemporary Islamist movements specifically relating to the direct reading of scripture and implications for views concerning the socialisation required for its authoritative interpretation see Ellis Goldberg, 'Smashing Idols and the State: The Protestant Ethic and Egyptian Sunni Radicalism', *Comparative Studies in Society and History*, 33, 1 (1991), pp. 3–35. The author points out that Shukri Mustafa (radical salafi leader of the 1970s Egyptian Islamist group Jama'at al-Muslimin) argued that the only tool that may be needed to explain some of the terms of the 'clear, Arabic Qur'an' was a good Arabic dictionary. This argument was in open defiance of the control of the ulama elite over scripture and its authoritative interpretation; ibid., p. 28.

40. The notion of *tajdid* is generally referred to a hadith encapsulating God's promise to send renewers of the faith to the Muslim community at the head of each century. On *islah*, see n. 16.

41. This paragraph draws on Voll, 'Renewal and Reform', pp. 32 ff.

42. The Mu'tazili tradition is a case in point, including what has been termed the 'spirit of the Mu'tazili discourse' with its emphasis on 'reason, dialogue with others and a rational basis of ethics'. See Richard C. Martin and Mark Woodward with Dwi S. Atmaja, *Defenders of Reason in Islam: Mu'tazilism from Medieval School to Modern Symbol* (Oxford, 1997), p. 7. A good part of the historical assumptions and worldview of this tradition, held in common with its theological opponents, has of course been quietly abandoned.

43. Esposito and Voll, *Makers of Contemporary Islam*, pp. 10–11.

44. See further Taji-Farouki and Nafi, 'Introduction'.

45. On the 'objectification' of Islam in Muslim consciousness and the impact of 'objectified understandings', see Dale F. Eickelman and James Piscatori, *Muslim Politics* (Princeton, NJ, 1996), pp. 37–45; Eickelman, 'Inside the Islamic Reformation', p. 85; Dale F. Eickelman, 'Islamic Religious Commentary and Lesson Circles: Is there a Copernican revolution?', in G. W. Most, ed., *Commentaries - Kommentare* (Gottingen, 1999), pp. 144–5.

46. They either dismiss the Sunna, or show little interest in it. Early modern architects of *islah–tajdid* emphasised the Sunna as the best model for Islamic life. Rashid Rida, for example, referred to the historical *mujaddidun* as regenerators of the faith and the Sunna: by safeguarding the latter, they protected the continuity of the original values of Islam. Algar, 'Islah',

p. 142. For modern debates over Sunna see Brown, *Rethinking Tradition*.

47.   Stefan Wild, ed., *The Qur'an as Text* (Leiden, 1996), p. ix. The author suggests that there has been a shift of attention away from the preoccupation with the constitution of the text characteristic of much Western scholarship of the last 150 years. Recent decades have marked the rise of a new interest in the Qur'an as textual corpus, regardless of its scriptural history, while the history of its reception, interpretation and aesthetic role is becoming an important new focus of research. This development is linked to 'a general hermeneutical awareness, to a new interest in literary forms and structures, to the development of semantics, semiotics, and textual linguistics, to the theory of discourse, and possibly to other international currents'. For an overview of methodology in contemporary Qur'anic studies (displaying the author's characteristically radical, critical approach), see Mohamed Arkoun, 'Contemporary Critical Practices and the Qur'an', *Encyclopaedia of the Qur'an*, ed. Jane Dammen McAuliffe (Leiden, 2001), vol. 1, pp. 412–31. For an example of the application of 'the languages of late twentieth century critical discourses' to the field, see Jane Dammen McAuliffe, 'Text and Textuality: Q. 3: 7 as a Point of Intersection', in Issa J. Boullata, ed., *Literary Structures of Religious Meaning in the Qur'an* (London, 2000), pp. 56–76.

48.   Boullata, ed., *Literary Structures*, p. xi.

49.   Many point to the ongoing collaborative project of the *Encyclopaedia of the Qur'an* by way of illustration.

50.   See for example Muhammad Abdul-Rauf, 'Outsiders' Interpretations of Islam: A Muslim's Point of View', in Martin, ed., *Approaches to Islam*, p. 185. The author argues that: 'The given truths accepted and upheld by all Muslims for the past fourteen centuries – the life of the Prophet, his Sunna, the text of the Holy Qur'an, virtually the entire sacred content of the faith of Muslims – have been subjected to misguided critical analysis, sometimes ruthless and usually insensitive.' S. Parvez Manzoor projects the 'Orientalist' enterprise of Qur'anic studies as 'an unholy conspiracy to dislodge the Muslim Scripture from its firmly entrenched position as the epitome of historic authenticity and moral unassailability.' Thus: 'The ultimate trophy that the Western man sought ... was the Muslim mind itself. In order to rid the West forever of the "problem" of Islam, he reasoned, Muslim consciousness must be made to despair of the cognitive certainty of the Divine message revealed to the Prophet. Only a Muslim confounded of the historical authenticity or doctrinal autonomy of the Qur'anic revelation would abdicate his universal mission and hence pose no challenge to the global domination of the West. Such, at least, seems to have been the tacit, if not the explicit, rationale of the Orientalist assault on the Qur'an.' Cited in Toby Lester, 'What is the Koran?', *The Atlantic Monthly*, January 1999.

51.   The following comment by a reform-oriented Egyptian salafi intellectual echoes this unease: 'Tinkering with the ... texts ... of the Qur'an and Sunna ... is unacceptable. They ought to remain beyond the reach of those who claim freedom of expression and research, and advance arguments aimed at undermining...[them].' Fahmi Huwaydi in relation to the

Abu Zayd affair, cited in Fauzi M. Najjar, 'Islamic Fundamentalism and the
Intellectuals: The Case of Nasr Hamid Abu Zayd', *BRISMES Journal*, 27, 2
(2000), p. 184. As one Western scholar puts it, Muslims, who have 'the
benefit of hindsight of the European experience', know very well that 'once
you start questioning the holy scriptures, you don't know where it will stop.'
Christoph Luxenberg, cited in Alexander Still, 'Radical New Views of Islam
and the Origins of the Koran', *The New York Times*, 2 March 2002.

52. Khaled Abou El Fadl, *Speaking in God's Name: Islamic Law, Authority
and Women* (Oxford, 2001), pp. 99–100. See also pp. 119 and 125. Referring
specifically to conceptual frameworks and categories of analysis in the field
of hermeneutics as this developed in the West, the author suggests that the
important consideration is to apply these 'with the requisite degree of
sensitivity to the specificity of the Islamic context and also with a certain
amount of deference to established Muslim systems of belief'.

53. The journal was launched in 1964. In 1969, al-Faruqi joined as an
associate editor.

54. Leonard Swidler, ed., *Muslims in Dialogue: The Evolution of a Dialogue*
(Lewiston, NY, 1992), p. v.

55. Characterised as 'an engagement to argue over correct interpretations'; see Eickelman and Anderson, 'Redefining Muslim Publics', p. 6.

56. Cf. comments by Arkoun, cited in Lester, 'What is the Koran?'

57. For example, it has been pointed out that the 'democratisation of
tafsir' has begun, thanks partly to the presence on the world wide web of
thousands of references to the Qur'an, and the absence of scholars or
ulama to police or censor web sites. See Herbert Berg, 'Computers and the
Qur'an', *Encyclopaedia of the Qur'an*, vol. 1, pp. 391–4.

58. In *Believing Women in Islam: Unreading Patriarchal Interpretations of the
Qur'an* (Austin, TX, 2002), Asma Barlas (whose work Wadud describes as a
continuation of her own) claims to derive a method of reading the Qur'an
from the Qur'an itself, both in its theological and its hermeneutic aspects.
Through a historical analysis of religious authority and knowledge, she
demonstrates how Muslims came to read inequality and patriarchy into the
Qur'an in order to justify existing religious and social structures. Her own
rereading points to a Qur'anic affirmation of the complete equality of the
sexes, providing a basis for theorising radical sexual equality from within
the framework of its teachings.

59. Earle H. Waugh, 'The Legacies of Fazlur Rahman for Islam in
America', *American Journal of Islamic Social Sciences* 16, 3 (1999), p. 31. Cited by
Abdullah Saeed, chapter 2. Compare with Farid Esack, *Qur'an, Liberation
and Pluralism: An Islamic Perspective of Interreligious Solidarity against Oppression*
(Oxford, 1998), p. 64 ff.

60. Abou El Fadl, *Speaking in God's Name*, p. 133. The author refers to
Mohammed Arkoun, *Rethinking Islam: Common Questions, Uncommon
Answers*, tr. and ed., Robert D. Lee (Boulder, CO, 1994). He attributes to
this the fact that the book finds little resonance in the Islamic context.

61. Esack, *Qur'an, Liberation and Pluralism*, p. 69.

62. The fundamental point here is summed up by Parvez Manzoor:
'The ultimate conflict between Islam and modernity...is neither over

governance, nor over technology, not even over society and social engineering, but over *transcendence* and the nature of ultimate reality. As against the immanentist claim of modernity, Islam holds that the ultimate reality is transcendent.' S. Parvez Manzoor, 'Modernity, Transcendence and Political Theory', *Encounters*, 5, 1 (1999), p. 56.

63. Reflecting on the 'postmodern mind', for example, Tarnas refers to its 'quasi-nihilistic' rejection of all forms of 'totalization' and 'metanarrative'. By virtue of its own 'self-relativising critical awareness', however, the 'postmodern mind' recognises that its position in this respect is itself not beyond questioning. This underlies what Tarnas describes as 'the unstable paradox that permeates the postmodern mind'. Thus: 'On its own terms, the assertion of the historical relativity and cultural-linguistic bondage of all truth and knowledge must itself be regarded as reflecting but one more local and temporal perspective having no necessarily universal, extrahistorical value. Everything could change tomorrow. Implicitly, the one postmodern absolute is critical consciousness, which, by deconstructing all, seems compelled by its own logic to do so to itself as well.' Richard Tarnas, *The Passion of the Western Mind: Understanding the Ideas that have shaped our Worldview* (London, 1991), pp. 401–2. For differing Muslim views of Postmodernism, see Tomas Gerholm, 'Two Muslim Intellectuals in the Postmodern West: Akbar Ahmed and Ziauddin Sardar', in Akbar S. Ahmed and Hastings Donnan, eds., *Islam, Globalization and Postmodernity* (London and New York, 1994), pp. 190–212, esp. pp. 209–10. See further Ziauddin Sardar, 'Deconstructing Postmodernism', *Encounters*, 5, 1 (1999), pp. 111–18.

64. Such concerns for justice and morality constitute a reaction to the corruption and marginalisation generated by the modern state. Cf. Martin Muñoz, *Islam, Modernism and the West*, p. 10.

65. For example, particularly since the events of 11 September 2001, American and European statesmen have publicly underlined the essential compatibility of Islam with American and European values. Some Muslims in Europe and the USA have self-consciously echoed their sentiments. For example, American Muslim activists recently underlined the consistency of the goals of the shari'a with the constitution of the USA. For their part, some second-generation educated European Muslims project their Islamic affiliation (in terms of universal values such as justice, democracy and tolerance) as a nexus with the European societies in which they live. See Salam al-Maryati, 'The Rising Voice of Moderate Muslims', text of speech delivered to US State Department Open Forum, January 2002, and Fouad Imarraine, cited in *Time Magazine*, 24 December 2001.

2

Fazlur Rahman: a framework for interpreting the ethico-legal content of the Qur'an

ABDULLAH SAEED

T HE Pakistani-American thinker and scholar Fazlur Rahman (1919-1988) was one of the most daring and original contributors to the discussion on the reform of Islamic thought in the twentieth century. As the Qur'an is central to any such discussion, innovative approaches to its interpretation are part of any reform agenda. Given the importance of the ethico-legal content of the Qur'an in the debate on renewal and reform, Rahman's work in this area is the focus of this chapter.

Fazlur Rahman was born on 21 September 1919 in Hazara district, in what is now Pakistan,[1] in an area with strong connections to Islamic religious education. His father, Mawlana Shihab al-Din, was an *'alim*, a graduate of Deoband Seminary in India. Under his tutorship, rather than in a seminary, Rahman received his religious education in *tafsir*, hadith and law, theology and philosophy. He attended Punjab University in Lahore, and obtained Bachelor's and Master's degrees in Arabic. He then went to Oxford, where he wrote his dissertation on Ibn Sina's philosophy.[2] Though his primary interest early in his academic career was Islamic philosophy, he was widely read in Islamic law and history, and in ethics, *tafsir* and hadith. Having completed his studies at Oxford, Rahman moved to Durham University (UK), where he taught Islamic philosophy from 1950 to 1958. He then left to take up the position of associate professor at the Institute of

Islamic Studies at McGill University in Canada, where he remained for three years.

At that time, General Ayyub Khan, the then president of Pakistan, was searching for a liberal reform-minded Muslim intellectual to head the Islamic Research Institute which was established by Ayyub Khan, in Rahman's words, 'to advise the government on religious policies that would be true to the principles of Islam, interpreted by us for application in the changing context of the modern world'.[3] Thus the Institute was to provide intellectual support for Ayyub Khan's modernisation program. Pakistan, a nation founded as a 'homeland for Muslims', had from independence been torn between the traditionalist Islam of the general population and a 'modernist' Islam espoused largely by the intellectual and secular elite of the country. For political reasons, Ayyub Khan needed to steer a path of modernisation that would not offend tradition. With his extensive training in traditional Islamic scholarship and his contact with the West, Rahman was one of the few Pakistani intellectuals at the time with the breadth of knowledge and intellect for the task. At the invitation of Ayyub Khan, Rahman returned to Pakistan to take up, first, a visiting professor's position and, later, the directorship of the Institute, where he remained from 1961 to 1968.

In taking up this position, Rahman saw an opportunity to help reform the Pakistani religious establishment and in particular its educational system. At the Institute he began training young Pakistani scholars to approach the Islamic tradition from a critical perspective. At the same time he provided policy advice and recommendations on matters related to Islamic issues from family law reform to bank interest and *zakat*. In this, his views were 'liberal' and often at odds with those of the traditionalist religious establishment. According to Rahman, the stiffest resistance he faced was 'from religious conservatives, and it centered mainly on the question of the rights of women and the reform of family law'.[4] The discontent of Ayyub Khan's political opponents, led by influential political and religious figures, found an ideal target in Rahman, who symbolised for them the worst aspects of the modernisation project – religious and social reform.

Thus Rahman's ideas, combined with a certain degree of idealism and political naivety, not only put him on a collision course with Pakistan's powerful religious establishment, but also made him a pawn in the establishment's power struggle with Ayyub Khan. The country's deep-rooted traditionalism and mass illiteracy exacerbated the problem. In an atmosphere of hysteria, threats were made against Rahman's life and he finally had to resign and leave Pakistan. He returned to his academic life in the West, in the United States. He was appointed Professor of Islamic Thought at the University of Chicago in 1968, and he remained there until his death in 1988.

At Chicago, Rahman played a significant role in training a number of postgraduate students from countries such as Indonesia and Turkey. While his thought is not generally known in the Arab world or in traditionalist religious circles elsewhere, it is in Turkey and Indonesia where Rahman is most influential. Many of his students occupy senior academic positions in Islamic Studies in those countries. In Indonesia, for instance, Nurcholish Madjid, one of the most influential public intellectuals, studied under Rahman at Chicago. In the United States, where Rahman spent the final twenty years of his life, several students of Islam took up his ideas and attempted to reinterpret specific areas of the ethico-legal content of the Qur'an. A good example is Amina Wadud, whose work *Qur'an and Woman* is an excellent example of an application of Rahman's ideas to the interpretation of the Qur'an.

Although he spent most of his academic life in the West, Rahman's primary engagement was with the Islamic tradition, which he felt it was his mission to explain to a largely Muslim audience. As Waugh comments:

> [F]or all his sojourn in the West, and his importance at the University of Chicago, Fazlur Rahman never consciously introduced analytic procedures derived from Western thinkers in a major manner. Even in those areas that influenced his methodology ... he was not attracted to the ongoing debate. He felt very deeply his Islamic origins, remained committed to an Islamic process of knowledge, and rested within an essentially traditional framework in his theoretical underpinnings.[5]

Rahman's writings are extensive and much broader than his primary field of Islamic philosophy. His writings include reform of Islamic education, Qur'anic hermeneutics, hadith criticism, early development of Islamic intellectual traditions, reform of Islamic law and Islamic ethics. Thus it would be almost impossible to summarise his thought in a short article such as this. His best-known works are *Islam* (1966), *Islam and Modernity: Transformation of an Intellectual Tradition* (1982), *Major Themes of the Qur'an* (1994), and *The Philosophy of Mulla Sadra* (1975). More recently, his *Revival and Reform* (1999) has been edited by Ebrahim Moosa and published posthumously. An extensive array of articles attest to the depth and breadth of his scholarship.[6] One prominent theme in all of his work is reform and renewal, and the importance of method in this reform. Among the most important projects for him was reform of Islamic education. Unlike many reformers of the modern period, Rahman was not involved in a mass movement, and did not seek out political conflict. He eschewed a propagandist approach, avoided activism, and was more comfortable in confining himself to the teaching and research environment of a university.

Rahman's critique of traditional Islam

Rahman saw that the primary reason for the decline of Muslim societies was rooted in the intellectual legacy of Islam. This decline, for him, did not begin with the Western encroachment on Muslim societies from the eighteenth century onwards, as claimed by many a modern reformer, but much earlier. For him it was the intellectual ossification and the replacement of scholarship based on original thought by one based on commentaries and super-commentaries, the closing of the gate of *ijtihad*, and the basing of Islamic method solely on *taqlid* (blind imitation) which led to the decline.[7] Given this, from his point of view, any hope for revival should be based on addressing this intellectual problem, and giving it top priority.

For Rahman, then, the first step in the renewal of Islamic thought was a historical critique of the legal, theological and mystical developments in Islam. It was essential to his project to reveal the dislocation between the worldview of the Qur'an and areas such as theology, interpretation and law:

> A historical critique of theological developments in Islam is the first step toward a reconstruction of Islamic theology. This critique ... should reveal the extent of the dislocation between the world view of the Qur'an and various schools of theological speculation in Islam and point the way toward a new theology.[8]

Rahman relentlessly argued that pristine Islam as reflected in the message of the Qur'an had been lost with the formation of orthodoxy, that is, what later came to be known as Sunnism. Although Sunnism claims to represent the 'original' Islam, Sunnism in Rahman's assessment announced a departure from the pristine faith. It 'owes itself largely to earlier sectarian developments',[9] and 'had in certain fundamental ways, undergone a radical change, indeed a metamorphosis, vis-à-vis its "original" state and the teachings of the Qur'an'.[10] Thus, he dated the 'traumatic departure from the Qur'an' to the period that saw the formation of 'Sunni Orthodoxy': namely, the advent of the Umayyad rule. He believed that the appearance of 'dynastic rule' had the most negative impact on the development of Islam.

For Rahman, Sunnism coincided with the break between politics and law in the nascent Muslim community and the ethics of the Qur'an. Only through the later discourses of Sufism was this break questioned. The stress on Sufi piety by figures such as al-Ghazali (d. 1111) represented relief from the legal rivalries that were often motivated by base political agendas, although Rahman pointed out that al-Ghazali 'did not call for social or community virtues that would once again prepare the community as such to play the role in the world that the Qur'an required of it'.[11] Rahman deplored *zuhd* (renunciation of this world), and even its great figures like Hasan al-Basri, for holding such a negative view of this world.[12] He also criticised 'cognitive Sufism' for disparaging reason and giving the seat of honour to *kashf* as a means of true knowledge. In his view, this stance bolstered an already strong anti-rationalism movement.[13]

Rahman admired the Mu'tazili theories of prophecy and the nature of revelation, which, after history, formed the most important component of his own general hermeneutic of the Qur'an.[14] The Mu'tazila had built a theory of rational ethics on the grounds that good and bad are knowable by natural reason without the aid of revelation. According to this theory, 'primary' or general ethical truths about right and wrong are rationally discoverable by intuitive reason, but for actual obligations of 'secondary ethical truths, humanity needs revelation'. Rahman also had firm affinities with the Mu'tazili ideas on the 'createdness' of the Qur'an. This did not prevent Rahman, however, from being critical of the Mu'tazila's more extreme rationalist positions.

Rahman's severest criticism in the area of the history of Islamic thought was perhaps reserved for Ash'arism. It was plagued, according to him, by a theology of pre-destination and the ethics of *irja'*.[15] This was in addition to its anti-rational outlook, which assumed that human beings could only act metaphorically, an idea that left them, in a sense, stripped of responsibility for their actions. This to Rahman was a grave misrepresentation of the message of the Qur'an: 'This attitude was bound to do severe damage to the human self-image as a repository of initiatives and originality and harmed the assumptions underlying law, which considered human beings as free and responsible agents.'[16]

Rahman's framework for interpretation

Rahman praised modern reformers such as Muhammad Abduh and Ahmad Khan for recognising the need for reform and change, and also key figures such as Hasan al-Banna and Abul A'la al-Mawdudi for countering the excesses of Islamic modernism and for defending Islam against secularism. On the other hand, he criticised them for not having a 'method' and for the *ad hoc* nature of the solutions they proposed. In the case of al-Banna and al-Mawdudi, Rahman was of the view that they substituted cliché mongering for serious intellectual endeavour.[17] Against this, Rahman devoted most of his intellectual energies towards elaborating a new Islamic methodology, because he believed that traditional methods were not able to bring Muslim thought into the intellectual framework of the modern age.[18] His goal was to reassess the Islamic intellectual tradition and provide a way forward for Muslims. In his view, a re-examination of Islamic methodology in the light of the Qur'an itself was a prerequisite for any reform in Islamic thought.

The Qur'an thus remained at the centre of Rahman's thought. He was critical of an *ad hoc* decontextualised approach that treated the Qur'an as a series of isolated verses and failed to 'yield insight into the cohesive outlook on the universe and life'.[19] If different fields of intellectual endeavour in Islam were to cohere, one of the tasks was to formulate an Islamic metaphysics firmly based on the Qur'an.[20] Only if the metaphysical part was clearly understood, could a coherent rethinking of the moral, social and legal message of the Qur'an be possible.

Rahman was, as a result, preoccupied with 'the correct method of interpreting the Qur'an',[21] the most important religious document and most comprehensive guide for humankind.[22] In his view, despite the importance of the method in interpretation, 'the basic questions of method and hermeneutics were not squarely addressed by Muslims'.[23] Rahman criticised Muslims for their failure to 'understand the underlying unity of the Qur'an' and for their adoption of an 'atomistic approach'.[24] He also felt that in the modern period, the piecemeal treatment of the Qur'an had worsened,[25] and that the formulation of an 'adequate hermeneutical method' was 'imperative'.[26] This was also a project to which both Muslims and some non-Muslims could contribute, as it was 'exclusively concerned with the cognitive aspect of the revelation'.[27]

Rahman's mission may be summed up as an endeavour to retrieve the moral elan of the Qur'an in order to formulate a Qur'an-centred ethics. Failing to find a work on ethics that was based solely on the Qur'an, he sought 'to elaborate an ethics on the basis of the Qur'an, for without an explicitly formulated ethical system, one can never do justice to Islamic law'.[28] Rahman emphasises the importance of the ethical dimension in the Qur'an:

Muslim scholars have never attempted an ethics of the Qur'an, systematically or otherwise. Yet no one who has done any careful study of the Qur'an can fail to be impressed by its ethical fervor. Its ethics, indeed, is its essence, and is also the necessary link between theology and law. It is true that the Qur'an tends to concretize the ethical, to clothe the general in a particular paradigm, and to trans-late the ethical into legal or quasi-legal commands. But it is precisely a sign of its moral fervor that it is not content only with generalizable ethical propositions but is keen on translating them into actual paradigms. However ... the Qur'an always explicates the objectives or principles that are the essence of its laws. [29]

It was Rahman's opinion that the Qur'an and the Sunna were mediated by certain historical realities, and that no claim of 'immutability' should be made to the understandings of either. For him, all religious traditions are in constant revitalisation and reform.

One of the most important of Rahman's interests was a frame-work for the interpretation of the ethico-legal content of the Qur'an. He attempted to emphasise the close relationship between the concerns of present-day Muslims and those of the earliest Muslim community. He took a particular interest in using the Qur'an for providing guidance for Muslims in different times, places and circumstances. Lessons were to be learned from the way the Prophet and the earliest Muslim community (i.e., the 'immediate community') used the Qur'an, an approach which, transposed to the modern period, could not only be practical but also retain a high degree of authenticity.

To Rahman, the methodology of the jurists was not based systematically on the broad socio-moral theory that he believed should underlie the law. Indeed, the jurists, in their quest to develop a highly structured legal system, had avoided the fluidity that would have been the result of such a theory. Rahman argued that, even though a system based on socio-moral theory had never been attempted in the past, Muslims in the modern period were in urgent need of one. In emphasising his approach to the interpretation and construction of law and to its application, Rahman also accepted that differences in interpretation would result: 'However they will become more systematically and consciously controlled by the systematic methodology proposed.'[30]

Although Rahman's interest in the Qur'an was broader than its ethico-legal content, this area occupied an important place in his writing, because it was central to his concern with the need for rethinking the interpretation of the Qur'an. In his view, the rigidity of the jurists' interpretations, and their denial of an historical context to the revelation, had resulted in archaic laws that not only prevented Muslims from dealing with modern problems, but also placed stress on the vibrancy of Islam itself. In the following, specific aspects of his approach will be brought together, based on six key elements: revelation and its socio-historical context; ideal/contingent; social justice; moral principles; cautious use of hadith; and, linking the past and present.

Revelation and its socio-historical context

Rahman began with a critique of the 'dictation theory' of revelation accepted by most Muslims, which rejects the possibility of any role for the Prophet except that of receiver of the message from God. The Prophet is reduced to a channel for the transmission of God's word, much like an audio-recording instrument such as a tape-recorder, which simply records the message exactly as it is given in sounds, words and sentences, and then transmits the 'text' as received. Rahman saw revelation as more complex.

First, his position on prophecy was that he believed that the Prophet was the recipient of the final, verbal revelation of God: 'Without this belief no Muslim can be a Muslim even in name.'[31] Yet, despite this statement, Rahman's position did cause a stir when it first appeared in his book *Islam* (1966), and continues to do so today.[32] According to Rahman, for the Qur'an itself, and for Muslims, the Qur'an is the Word of God (*kalam Allah*): [33]

> This 'Other' through some channel, 'dictated' the Qur'an with an absolute authority. The voice from the depths of life spoke distinctly, unmistakably and imperiously. Not only does the word '*qur'an*', meaning 'recitation', clearly indicate this, but the text of the Qur'an itself states in several places that the Qur'an is *verbally revealed*, and not merely in its 'meaning' and ideas.[34]

Next, Rahman attempts to show the psychology of the creative process of the mind of the Prophet, and to show that 'the source and the origin of this creative process lies beyond the ordinary reach of the human agency',[35] while maintaining at the same time that 'this process occurs, in some definite sense, as an integral part of the agent's mind'.[36] He arrives at the conclusion that: 'If the entire process occurs in [the Prophet's] mind, then, in an ordinary sense, it is his word, insofar as the psychological process is concerned, but is *Revealed Word* insofar as its source lies beyond his reach.'[37] Since for Rahman 'word' does not mean 'sound'[38] there is no real contradiction between the Qur'an being the word of God and also the word of the Prophet. He emphasises that there exists, indeed, an organic relationship between feelings, ideas and words. In inspiration, even in poetic inspiration, this relationship is so complete that feeling–idea–word is a total complex with a life of its own.[39]

According to Rahman, during the process of revelation 'the ideas and the words are born in the mind of the Prophet'.[40] But the Qur'an asserts that their source cannot possibly lie in the mind of the Prophet by virtue of their 'novelty'.[41] In this sense, '[they] must be traced and referred to a source beyond'.[42] Rahman's account, which he felt made an appreciable contribution to the debate, sought to distinguish the character of the divine revelation from other forms of inspiration, be they poetic, mystic, artistic or otherwise. For although his account acknowledges that the divine revelation is 'psychologically similar and forms ascending degrees of the same phenomena of creative inspiration',[43] it asserts that 'in terms of religious and moral import and valuation the Qur'an is something entirely *sui generis* and separate from any other form of creative thinking or creative art'.[44]

In this way, revelation for Rahman was the result of an encounter between two realms: the uncreated world and the created world. In this encounter, the Prophet was 'inspired' by the Divine but, in Rahman's view, the dimension of the created world, the world of the Prophet and his immediate community, was allowed to feature prominently in the linguistic product resulting from the 'revelation'. The expectations, anxieties, challenges and interests of the Prophet and his immediate community were reflected in the Qur'an, an aspect that Rahman believed should have been given substantial emphasis in Islamic theology and accommodated in the principles of Islamic jurisprudence. Its relegation was, in Rahman's view, a fatal mistake.[45]

Rahman further asserted that revelation was not a 'book' given at one time, but a process that continued with the prophetic mission over a twenty-two year period, reflecting, throughout the mission's vicissitudes, the mood of the Prophet and the community. This indicated that the Qur'an was not a book sent from the uncreated world to the created world, with no context in the created world. Its concerns, interests and guidance were directly connected with and organically related to the linguistic, cultural, political, economic and religious life, primarily of the people of Hijaz, and more broadly the people of Arabia. Without this connection, revelation would not have made much sense even to the immediate community, let alone as a meaningful guide to humankind.

For Rahman, this close connection between the revelation and its context was disrupted later in the process of the development of Islamic theology and law, creating an ever-widening gap. The unworldly origin of the Qur'an was emphasised in the elevation of the text to an 'aspect' of the Divine, as evidenced in the debate on the 'creation of the Qur'an' (*khalq al-qur'an*), particularly by the Hanbali traditionalists, and was also later included in a modified form in the influential Ash'ari theology. The transcendence of the Divine thus came to be attributed to the Qur'an (as speech of God, *kalam Allah*) itself, reinforcing the total 'otherness' of the revelation. Rahman demonstrated this problematic nature of the revelation as defined by later Islamic theology and law, in which revelation came to be seen as ahistorical, beyond the reach of humankind. According to Rahman, revelation does not function outside history, and we must recognise this if we are to make a strong connection between the Qur'an and the community to which it was initially addressed.

A corollary of the traditional juristic notion of the revelation as without socio-historical context is that the Qur'an is applicable in all times and places. God has absolute knowledge of the past, present and future and, since the Qur'an is from God, whatever it contains must also be suitable for all times, places and circumstances. Revelation is thus to be considered an event precipitated by the All-Knowing God, and not necessarily related to the concerns of the people to whom it was addressed. Also related is the view that the Qur'an originally existed in the Preserved Tablet (*al-lawh al-mahfuz*) well before the creation of humankind, and was thus not necessarily a result of certain distortions and problems that emerged at a particular time in the created world. From this standpoint it became relatively easy to suggest that revelation is transcendent. This 'otherness' of the Qur'an as a cardinal principle of Islamic theology was established in the post-Mu'tazili period. Islamic law conformed, and the two exerted influence on other Islamic disciplines, such as *tafsir,* to adopt the same position that the socio-legal content of the text was without historical or temporal limitations.

In the early Islamic disciplines, the only aspect that Rahman considered supportive, albeit in a very limited way, of a close relationship between the revelation and the socio-historical context was the *asbab al-nuzul* (occasions of revelation) literature, which found its way into the *tafsir* tradition. This, however, did not occur in order to relate the Qur'an to its socio-historical context. In *tafsir,* the *asbab al-nuzul* served to better explicate certain texts, particularly where the Qur'an avoided specific references to particular people, times and places. In *fiqh,* the *asbab al-nuzul* were mainly a way of explaining the chronological sequence of related texts or of better understanding certain texts where the Qur'an avoided specific references. Of these two, chronology was perhaps the more important and came to be used primarily to understand when a particular text (related to law) was revealed, and, where conflict arose between two texts, to determine which text 'abrogated' the other.

The relatively minor interest *fiqh* had in this literature can be seen from the general principle of *usul al-fiqh* (principles of jurisprudence), according to which, if a command or prohibition is given in the Qur'an and the wording of it is general, one should not attempt to restrict it to the specific circumstances in which it was revealed. Rather its application should be general.[46] This de-emphasises the occasion and the specific circumstances of the revelation in favour of the general application of the text. In their quest to construct a comprehensive legal system, the jurists were driven by the idea that the Qur'anic instruction had to be extended to as many situations as possible, and that it should not be limited by any one concrete condition. Thus, texts were read with as little reference as possible to their context, a practice that Rahman criticised and saw as even more prevalent in the modern period.

The ideal and the contingent

Rahman was highly critical of the view prevalent among Muslims that the Qur'an was a book of law. For him, the Qur'an neither was, nor did it purport to be, a book of law; it called itself a guide for humankind (*hudan li al-nas*) and demanded that believers live by its commands, which were, for the most part, not legal, but ethical or quasi-legal.[47] Rahman pointed out that the Prophet himself was a 'moral reformer of mankind' who 'seldom resorted to general legislation as a means of furthering the Islamic cause'.[48] In the Qur'an itself 'general legislation forms a very tiny part of Islamic teaching'.[49] According to Rahman, even the

> legal or quasi-legal part of the Qur'an itself clearly displays a *situational* character. Quite situational, for example are the Qur'anic pronunciations on war and peace between the Muslims and their opponents – pronouncements which do express a certain general character about the ideal behaviour of the community *vis-à-vis* an enemy in a grim struggle but which are so situational that they can be regarded only as quasi-legal and not strictly and specifically legal.[50]

Rahman believed that the ethico-legal Qur'anic instructions functioned at two levels: the 'ideal' and the 'contingent'. The ideal was the goal that believers were to aim for. This ideal might or might not be achieved during the time of the revelation. The contingent, on the other hand, meant what was possible at the time of the revelation, given the structural constraints within the immediate community and the conditions of the time. The close affinity of the Qur'an to the situation at hand, that is at the time of revelation, required that its instructions address problems of the time in *their* specific circumstances, while highlighting or alluding to the ideal to which Muslims should aspire as they moved from one situation to another, from one time to another.

Rahman argued that, in order to understand the ideal and the contingent in Qur'anic pronouncements, the best tool available was 'historical criticism', which could clarify the context and the rationale of the guidance, and distinguish the ideal from the contingent. To demonstrate this point, Rahman used the example of polygamy. The Qur'an undoubtedly improved the rights and status of women compared with their pre-Islamic condition in Hijaz. One of its instructions was that a man should not marry more than one wife if he could not do justice to all of them, adding categorically that, no matter how he tried, just treatment would be impossible. However, it was equally true that the Qur'an gave permission to marry up to four wives. How then could these two sets of instructions be understood? One way was to say that the Qur'an wanted to promote the maximum happiness of family life and that, to this end, a monogamous marriage would be the ideal, but that this declared moral purpose had to be compromised in the reality of seventh-century Arabian society, in which polygamy was too deeply entrenched for it to be removed without defeating the moral purpose itself. The Qur'an therefore accepted polygamy at the legal level, but restricted it and placed as many safeguards as possible, while at the same time enunciating the ideal of the monogamous society towards which the Prophet wanted Muslims to move.[51]

The distinction between the ideal and the contingent, Rahman argued, was given little importance, if any, in the construction of Islamic law and in the interpretation of the Qur'an. Yet, if Muslims were to bring about reform in the modern period, this had to change. According to Rahman, jurists had mistakenly taken much of the Qur'anic content, for example *hudud*, family law, *mu'amalat*, to be ideal and had allowed it to be firmly embedded in Islamic law. If the ideal and the contingent, and the historical context of the text, could be accepted, laws stemming from legal or quasi-legal content in the Qur'an that was really related directly to the immediate community could be rethought or reformed.

Social justice as the primary objective

Rahman believed that the ethico-legal content of the Qur'an was to be read in the light of the 'social justice' objectives of the Qur'an, which for him were the basis of this content. In any understanding of the Qur'an at any period, therefore, important concepts associated with social justice, such as 'cooperation, brotherhood and self-sacrifice for the sake of the common good'[52] were to be considered of primary importance. Further emphasising this, he said that the entire Islamic movement and the teachings of the Qur'an could be seen as 'directed towards the creation of a meaningful and positive equality among human beings. As such the Islamic purpose cannot be realised until genuine freedom to human beings is restored and freedom from all forms of exploitation – social, spiritual, political and economic – assured.'[53]

For Rahman, freedom from all forms of exploitation was essential in order for meaningful moral choices to be made. At the social level, distinctions between rich and poor, powerful and weak, higher 'castes' and lower 'castes' were antithetical to his idea of social justice. He found confirmation of his belief in the Qur'an, which seeks to minimise, if not eliminate, those distinctions that it sees as invalid among human beings. Further, there is an obligation on the part of those who are able to do so to make a difference at political, economic, social and spiritual levels. For Rahman, a primary task of the Prophet was social reform in the context of strengthening the position of the socio-economically weak and depressed classes in the prosperous mercantile Meccan society, including orphans, women and the elderly.[54] Rahman says:

> What emerges most clearly from the entire drift of the Qur'an and the Prophet's actions from this point is that no moral or spiritual welfare is possible without a sound and just socio-economic base.

Indeed, one may correctly assert that the rectitude of moral life in Islam is to be tested by, and is finally realized in, this society-building activity.[55]

As an example, Rahman highlights the social justice objectives in the ethico-legal content of the Qur'an relating to women:

> The Qur'an insistently forbids the male to exploit the female on the strength of his stronger position in society, and Islam set into motion the whole complex of measures – legal and moral – whereby sex exploitation would be completely eradicated. It forbade the recourse to polygamy under normal circumstances, allowed the woman to own and earn wealth, declared her to be an equal partner in the society: noting and allowing for the disadvantages she had in the society of that age. It laid down the basis of matrimonial life to be mutual love and affection, and that spouses were like garments unto each other. It strictly regulated the law of divorce.[56]

Later Muslim history, however, had not done 'full justice to the objective of the Qur'an on the subject and, consequently, due to unregulated polygamy and divorce and their baneful effects on children, Muslim society deteriorated in the Middle Ages. This trend has to be sternly and quickly checked.'[57]

Identification of moral principles

Rahman lamented the almost total neglect of ethics as a discipline in Islam.[58] Any writings on ethics were developed outside the shari'a disciplines and were explicitly based on Greek and Persian sources. It was extraordinary that ethics, so prevalent throughout the Qur'an, should have developed independently of the Qur'an and shari'a disciplines. Rahman found this distance, between ethics on one hand and law and theology on the other, extremely problematic.[59]

For Rahman, ethically-acting individuals preceded the formulation of laws. At the basis of Islamic ethics is *taqwa*, that quality of mind whereby a person becomes capable of discerning between right and wrong and makes the effort to do so.[60] *Taqwa* (also seen as 'God-consciousness') enjoys the most prominent position among the Qur'anic moral principles. The essential aim of the

Qur'an is to create proper conscience, to maximise moral energy and use that energy through appropriate channels'.[61]

In order to read the Qur'an from a 'moral' perspective centred on *taqwa*, Rahman said that Muslims were not to treat the Qur'an as a legal manual documenting minutely what they should or should not do. It was to be considered essentially a text concerned with moral and ethical issues, and turning it into a technical legal text was fraught with danger. In the construction of law on the basis of the Qur'an, Rahman believed the correct approach would be to arrive at the moral principles of the Qur'an first, and then derive law from them. Rahman argued that the Qur'an often gave explicit reasons for its legal or quasi-legal pronouncements, and that where the reasons were not explicit, they could be arrived at by studying the background material. What was required was a systematic identification of rationales or objectives of the Qur'an in terms of its principles and values, which would define the ethics of the Qur'an. Rahman commented on the procedure for this:

> The really effective procedure would have been to erect a system of universal ethical values on the basis of an analysis of the moral objectives of the Qur'an. But did the Sunni jurists do that? This could have been achieved through developing a systematic ethical system derived from the Qur'anic values, which are either there explicitly in the Qur'an or could be extracted from its *rationes legis*. Instead the jurists were content to apply their legal principle of analogical reasoning (*qiyas*) quite unsystematically and in an *ad hoc* manner. The result is that today Muslims wishing to derive workable Islamic law from the Qur'an have to make a fresh start by working out a genuine ethical value-system from the Qur'an.[62]

In Rahman's view, the atomistic approach largely led to the disorder in the interpretation of the ethico-legal content of the Qur'an, as it stands in the form of laws in Islamic legal texts.[63] Instead of developing a system of law based on 'higher non-legal specially moral principles',[64] Islamic law opted for juxtaposing the moral propositions of the Qur'an with the legal and, in doing so, failed to do 'justice to the moral principles of the Qur'an. The principles of the Qur'an deserve systemisation and then from these, law should be systematically derived.'[65]

Again, Rahman's emphasis on historical background informs his thoughts on systematisation, in particular in relation to moral objectives. Given the status of critical tools available in traditional Islamic education, Rahman considered that historical study could be conducted as well by non-Muslims, as long as they had the necessary preparation for such an undertaking.[66] Based on critical historical study, a hierarchy of moral values, or what he called 'general principles'[67] for the interpretation of the Qur'an, could be developed. Rahman, however, did not provide a detailed framework for developing this hierarchy of moral values apart from stating that one should first elicit general principles from specific rulings in the Qur'an by giving full consideration to their socio-historical context. He went on to argue that, on the basis of these general principles, Muslims should develop what he called a 'unified and comprehensive socio-moral theory'.[68] Rahman cautioned that this task had never been attempted before and would present challenges:

> The various purposes and principles of the Qur'an must, therefore, be brought together to yield a unified and comprehensive socio-moral theory squarely based upon the Qur'an and its *sunna* [sic] counterparts. It must be frankly admitted that this task has not been attempted in the past and, although the Qur'anic teaching on socio-moral questions has a definite character, this teaching has never been formulated as a comprehensive and cohesive doctrine.[69]

This was a significantly different concept to *qiyas* (analogy) in *usul al-fiqh*, which jurists used extensively to extend the legal or quasi-legal material of the Qur'an to other situations or problems through the medium of *'illa* (efficient cause). For Rahman, this extension through *qiyas* was too limiting and artificial. He was more interested in utilising 'socio-moral theory', not *'illa*, as a basis for extending or restricting the application of a particular text.

Cautious use of the hadith

An essential element of Rahman's framework was his emphasis on the 'overall patterns of practice' of the Prophet and the immediate community, which could be seen as consistent with broader

Qur'anic guidance while demythologising key aspects of Sunna and hadith. Rahman did not define Sunna in the way it is defined by jurists or hadith critics. For him Sunna can be either the 'prophetic Sunna' or the 'living Sunna'. The prophetic Sunna is what he called 'the ideal legacy of the Prophetic activity',[70] while the living Sunna is the prophetic Sunna creatively elaborated and interpreted to meet new changes, challenges and circumstances faced by the Muslim community.[71] For Rahman in the early period of Islam the concept of the Sunna was fluid, and referred not necessarily to a body of specific *texts* but to the normative behaviour of the Prophet and the early Muslim community, and included both types of Sunna.

Emphasising the importance of Sunna to the Qur'an, Rahman maintained that the Sunna of the Prophet was a valid operative concept from the beginning of Islam, and that the Qur'an was organically related to this Sunna. He criticised those who argued for interpreting the Qur'an without any reference to Sunna; both the Qur'an and Sunna needed each other:

> It would be utterly *irrational* to suppose that the Qur'an was taught without involving in fact the activity of the Prophet as the central background-activity which included policy, commands, decisions etc. Nothing can give coherence to the Qur'anic teaching except the actual life of the Prophet and the environment in which he moved, and it would be a great childishness of the twentieth century to suppose that people immediately around the Prophet distinguished so radically between the Qur'an and its exemplification in the Prophet that they retained one but ignored the other, i.e., saw the one as divorced from the other.[72]

Rahman argued, however, that the Sunna content left by the Prophet (prophetic Sunna) was neither extensive nor meant to be absolutely specific. In the post-prophetic period, this limited material was further added to by the early Muslim communities through the 'living Sunna'. However, in order to maintain the link to the prophetic legacy, this living Sunna was legitimised by the *ijma'* of the community. This function of *ijma'* thus kept isolated hadith outside the boundary of Sunna, giving the living Sunna a certain degree of cohesiveness. Following the mass hadith movement, however, the organic relationship between Sunna and *ijma'* was destroyed. Similarly, the distinction between the 'prophetic Sunna' and 'living Sunna' became blurred. All was subsumed in the broad category of hadith, which became synonymous with the Sunna of the prophet, a gross distortion of the concepts. Much of this distortion took place over the second and third centuries AH, and in particular in the work of al-Shafi'i.

While Rahman saw a close connection between the Qur'an and the prophetic Sunna, he argued that hadith material should be used advisedly, particularly as the hadith came to include many superstitions that developed in the post-prophetic period, such as the Prophet's ascension or *mi'raj*, which, for Rahman, had virtually no support in the Qur'an but appeared often in the hadith. Nonetheless, Rahman thought that the hadith, even though they might not necessarily reflect 'prophetic Sunna', could be useful if subjected to historical criticism. If the study of early hadith material were carried out under the canons of historical criticism in relation to historical and sociological background, even an isolated hadith could become meaningful for now. [73]

In keeping with his belief and his education, Rahman always gave priority to what the Qur'an said, and in particular to its overall message, on any given issue. Where that message conflicted with the hadith, Rahman was in no doubt that the Qur'an was to be preferred over the hadith as representing the actual legacy of the Prophet. In any interpretation of the ethico-legal content of the Qur'an, the actual, explicit and overall message of the Qur'an, in his view, should be given priority. [74] Rahman saw the two main problems for Muslims in rethinking the interpretation of the Qur'an in order to relate it to present needs as the historical belief that the hadith contained the Sunna of the Prophet, and that the Qur'anic rulings on social behaviour had to be literally implemented in all times: 'This stood like a rock in the way of any substantial rethinking of the social content of Islam.' [75] Both beliefs thus had to be challenged and rethought.

Linking past and present: the 'double movement theory'

Rahman brought together the six elements of his framework for interpreting the ethico-legal content of the Qur'an and relating it to the needs of Muslims in the modern period in what is referred to as his 'double movement theory'. He summarises this as follows:

> In building any genuine and viable Islamic set of laws and institutions, there has to be a twofold movement. First one must move from the concrete case treatments of the Qur'an – taking the necessary and relevant social conditions of that time into account – to the general principles upon which the entire teaching converges. Second, from this general level there must be a movement back to specific legislation, taking into account the necessary and relevant conditions now obtaining.[76]

For Rahman, this involved two movements of juristic thought: the first from the particular to the general and the second from the general to the particular. The first requires an understanding of the Qur'anic principles, to which the Sunna is organic. In the first movement, the socio-historical context of the Qur'an is considered in exploring specific Qur'anic cases in order to arrive at general principles like justice, equality, and freedom. In line with his interest in developing a socio-moral theory, Rahman spoke of a set of principles. Since the Qur'anic imperatives had a situational background and came as solutions to actual problems, the texts of 'occasions of revelation', despite their historical and contextual problems, should be studied to understand the reasons behind the ethico-legal content. The reasons, which he referred to as *hikam* (purposes that constitute the essence of Qur'anic teaching in society), form the basis for the general principles.[77]

The second movement in juristic thought referred to the method of reasoning from the general to the particular. Here, the general principles arrived at under the first movement are to be used as a basis for formulating laws relevant to the modern period. It must be noted also that anyone formulating such laws must be thoroughly familiar with the conditions of the modern period.[78] Just as the background of the Qur'anic teaching should be studied to obtain the general principles, so must the contemporary situation be studied in order for the law to be formulated and applied.[79] The importance of Rahman's 'double movement' approach is that he takes into account both the conditions of the time of the revelation and those of the modern period in relating the text to the community. In utilising this double movement theory, it is expected that not only the traditional ulama, who should determine what is Islamically acceptable and what is not, will be involved, but that it will also involve other 'specialists' of relevance from fields as diverse as history, philosophy, law, ethics, sociology, and anthropology to assist in the process of deriving Islamic law that is meaningful, relevant and appropriate.

An assessment of Rahman's contribution

Despite his interest in a systematic approach to the ethico-legal content of the Qur'an, Rahman did not hold that there was one single authoritative interpretation of the text. He saw multiple interpretations as not only necessary but also essential for the survival of the religion as well as for the relevance of the Qur'an. Though he did not openly say so, his position seemed to be that the followers of a religious tradition read various meanings into the text in different times, places and circumstances. This, for him, was a natural and perhaps necessary phenomenon. The multiplicity of interpretations did not in any way detract from the 'sacredness' of the text originating from God. Rather, the text, as a linguistic phenomenon and as a message to all humankind, requires multiple interpretations if it is to remain valid. Sacredness and immutability are to be attributed to the text itself, not to its interpretations, which are merely the human understandings. Rahman stressed that this reading of meanings into the text was to be *guided* by certain principles and a socio-moral set of values of a hierarchical nature in order to avoid unnecessary arbitrariness, or unprincipled and forced readings of the text, and to prevent the Qur'an from being thoughtlessly dipped into to find answers to any question.

Rahman knew that criticism could be levelled at his proposed framework and in particular his 'double-movement' method, because it could be seen to have 'excessive subjectivity' in its process. He was prepared with two responses. The first was that the Qur'an was not silent about its objectives and purposes, either implicitly or explicitly, and that those objectives that were not apparent could be identified by consideration of the background and the context of the rules. Rahman claimed that this procedure would minimise subjectivity, if not eliminate it altogether. His second response was that differences in interpretation had always existed among jurists, and that there was great value in such differences as long as they were sincerely advanced for thoughtful rather than arbitrary reasons.[80]

In providing an alternative framework for the interpretation of the ethico-legal content of the Qur'an, Rahman made a major contribution by emphasising something previously neglected in Qur'anic interpretation, and by providing clear guidelines on how to achieve it. His work was not complete, for the principles he gave at times lacked specific examples of application. But he believed in the potential of the principles to provide answers to contemporary problems and questions; any mismatch between the principle and the specific represented an opportunity, not a barrier to reaching flexible solutions. Rahman noted that if any incompatibility existed between the normative principles of Islam and the new situation, the problem lay with the interpretive approach: 'As for the methodology itself, there is nothing wrong or inherently or insuperably difficult, or un-Islamic about it; on the contrary Islam would have come more truly and effectively into its own through this methodology than it has actually done.'[81] Rahman's words from the late 1960s are still relevant and stand as a summary of his interests in the area of Qur'anic interpretation:

> [T]he implementation of the Qur'an cannot be carried out *literally* in the context of today because this may result in thwarting the very purposes of the Qur'an, and that, although the findings of the *fuqaha'* or the *ulama'* of Islam during the past thirteen centuries or so should be seriously studied and given due weight, it may well be

found that in many cases their findings were either mistaken or sufficed for the needs of that society but not for today. This approach is so revolutionary and so radically different from the approaches generally adopted so far in that it seeks to bring under strictly historical study not only *fiqh* and *sunnah* of the Prophet but the Qur'an as well, that not only the traditionalists but even most of the modernists seriously hesitated to accept. But this would seem to be the only honest method of appraising the historic performance of the Muslims and of genuinely implementing the purposes of the Qur'an and the Prophet. There would be naturally bitter opposition to this kind of approach and particularly the results reached through it. But there is reason to believe that in a span of a decade or so the larger part of the liberals will come round to some such view. Failing this, this writer does not see any alternative for Islam except, in course of time, to be reduced to a set of rites which will claim emotional attachment for some time to come.[82]

Rahman's approach to the Qur'an and its interpretation attracted criticism from several quarters. For many a critic, Rahman's arguments were 'radical' by any measure, and contained major errors.[83] Apart from the traditionalist critique of Rahman's understanding of prophecy and revelation, and of his 'demythologisation' of key aspects of early Islamic intellectual history such as the concept of Sunna, there have been other more recent evaluations of Rahman's methodology. Farid Esack, for example, argues that: 'Rahman shows a lack of appreciation for the complexity of the hermeneutical task and the intellectual pluralism intrinsic to it.'[84] He finds 'this absence of grey areas is the most serious inadequacy in his approach'.[85]

Though Rahman does not elaborate on the philosophical nature of understanding, interpretation, or meaning, he emphasises throughout his writings the inadequacy of classical approaches to the Qur'an that tended to reduce the task of interpretation to a linguistic dimension. While it is true that he argues for a more 'objectivist' approach to the Qur'an in line with the work of Emilio Betti,[86] and in opposition to Gadamer's 'subjectivist' approach, Rahman cannot be said to have ignored the complexity of the hermeneutical task, as Esack claims; he simply was not interested in it for its own sake. Although he was certainly familiar with modern hermeneutical debates (as evidenced in his critique of Gadamer, for instance),[87] he felt that his primary responsibility was to address the specific problems he thought needed attention from the perspective of a Muslim who was struggling to be a relevant participant in a fast changing environment. Given his interest in rethinking Islamic law and the close relationship this has with the interpretation of the Qur'an, he sought to demonstrate the close relationship between the Qur'an and its socio-historical environment, and how this environment facilitated and provided a basis for the understanding of the Scripture. He stresses the need to understand the Qur'an against the background of its revelation and also allows for a multiplicity of perspectives, which is hardly a 'black and white' approach. His understanding of 'axiology', which is constructed on the basis of the Qur'an, also requires historical reconstruction, and even here multiplicity is allowed for. In addition, the double movement theory, which Rahman advances in order to connect past and present, does not assume a black and white view of history. Instead, it assesses available pieces of evidence, both textual *and* contextual, to arrive at both ends of the movement. It is always assumed that this assessment will function within a given intellectual, social, political and religious milieu, which again highlights the connection between text, context, understanding and meaning.

Rahman's double-movement theory and other ideas related to the interpretation of the ethico-legal content of the Qur'an (as highlighted above) were not meant to be a formulaic set of rules. They were intended as a guide to the interpreter of the Qur'an. While recognising the subjectivity associated with the task of interpretation, Rahman attempted to guide Muslims in their approach to the Qur'an away from the classical decontextualised and reductionist approaches, providing instead a wider contextual basis by recognising the environmental and broader linguistic context of the Qur'an. His theory of revelation also takes this into account by his emphasis on the role of the Prophet in the process of revelation and by emphasising the psychological and contextual place of the Prophet himself vis-à-vis his community, needs, concerns and aspirations. On balance, Rahman's approach to the

Qur'an was among the most original, daring and systematic of the mid to late twentieth century. His emphasis on the context of the revelation has had far reaching influence on the debate among Muslims of questions such as human rights, women's rights and social justice. Rahman's approach has been utilised by an increasing number of Muslims to relate the Qur'an to contemporary needs; it will likely continue to be influential among the younger generation of Muslim intellectuals.

NOTES

1. Fazlur Rahman, *Revival and Reform in Islam: A Study of Islamic Fundamentalism*, ed. Ebrahim Moosa (Oxford, 1999), p. 1. The biographical section relies heavily on this work, as well as Rahman's own statements about his life and work. For example, see Fazlur Rahman, 'My Belief in Action', in Phillip L. Berman, ed., *The Courage of Conviction* (New York, 1985), pp. 153–9.

2. Rahman, *Revival and Reform in Islam*, pp. 1–2.

3. Rahman, 'My Belief in Action', p. 157.

4. Ibid., p. 158.

5. Earle H. Waugh, 'The Legacies of Fazlur Rahman for Islam in America', *The American Journal of Islamic Social Sciences*, 16, 3 (1999), p. 31.

6. See bibliography for details.

7. Basit B. Koshul, 'Fazlur Rahman's *Islam and Modernity* Revisited', *Islamic Studies*, 33, 4 (1994), pp. 403–6.

8. Fazlur Rahman, *Islam and Modernity* (Chicago, 1982), pp. 151–2.

9. Rahman, *Revival and Reform in Islam*, p. 30.

10. Ibid., p. 30.

11. Ibid., p. 131.

12. Ibid., p. 111.

13. Ibid., p. 106.

14. Ibid., p. 11.

15. *Irja'*, 'postponement', refers primarily to the idea that one should suspend judgement on what happens to the grave sinner; it is God on the Day of Judgement who will determine the fate of such a person.

16. Rahman, *Revival and Reform in Islam*, pp. 67–8.

17. Rahman, *Islam and Modernity*, p. 137.

18. Ibid., p. 86.

19. Fazlur Rahman, *Major Themes of the Qur'an* (Minneapolis, 1980), p. xi.

20. Rahman, *Islam and Modernity*, p. 133.

21. Ibid., p. 1.

22. Ibid., p. 2.

23. Ibid., p. 2.

24. Ibid., p. 2.

25. Ibid., p. 4.

26. Ibid., p. 4.

27. Ibid., p. 4.

28. Fazlur Rahman, *Islam* (Chicago, 1979), p. 256.

29. Rahman, *Islam and Modernity*, p. 154.

30. Fazlur Rahman, 'Towards Reformulating the Methodology of Islamic Law', *New York University Journal of International Law and Politics*, 12, 2 (1979), p. 223.

31. Fazlur Rahman, 'Divine Revelation and the Prophet', *Hamdard Islamicus*, 1, 2 (1978), p. 72.

32. This attempt to clarify his stance on the 'nature' of prophecy is largely based on his views on revelation as outlined in ibid., pp. 66–72.

33. Rahman, 'Divine Revelation and the Prophet', p. 110.

34. Rahman, *Islam*, pp. 30–31.

35. Rahman, 'Divine Revelation and the Prophet', p. 111.

36. Ibid., p. 111.

37. Ibid., p. 111.

38. Ibid., p. 111.

39. Rahman, *Islam*, p. 33.

40. Rahman, 'Divine Revelation and the Prophet', p. 113.

41. Ibid., p. 113.

42. Ibid., p. 114.

43. Ibid., p. 114.

44. Ibid., p. 114.

45. Fazlur Rahman, 'Concepts Sunnah, Ijtihad and Ijma' in the Early Period', *Islamic Studies*, 1, 1 (1962), p. 10.

46. This is expressed in the principle *al-'ibratu bi-'umum al-lafz la bi-khusus al-sabab*.

47. Fazlur Rahman, 'Islamic Studies and the Future of Islam', in Malcolm Kerr, ed., *Islamic Studies: Tradition and its Problems* (Malibu, 1980), pp. 128–9.

48. Rahman, 'Concepts Sunnah, Ijtihad and Ijma'', pp. 10–11.

49. Ibid., pp. 10–11.

50. Fazlur Rahman, *Islamic Methodology in History* (Karachi, 1965), p. 10.

51. Fazlur Rahman, 'The Impact of Modernity on Islam', *Islamic Studies*, 5, 2 (1966), pp. 121–2.

52. Fazlur Rahman, 'Some Reflections on the Reconstruction of Muslim Society in Pakistan', *Islamic Studies*, 6, 9 (1967), pp. 103–20.

53. Ibid., p. 103.

54. Fazlur Rahman, 'Islam and Political Action: Politics in the Service of Religion' in Nigel Biggar, J.S. Scott and W. Schweiker, eds., *Cities of God: Faith, Politics and Pluralism in Judaism, Christianity and Islam* (London, 1986), p. 153.

55. Rahman, 'Some Reflections', p. 106.

56. Rahman, 'The Impact of Modernity on Islam', p. 111.

57. Ibid., p. 111.

58. Rahman, 'Islamic Studies and the Future of Islam', pp. 126–7.

59. Ibid., p. 127.

60. Rahman, 'Islam and Political Action', p. 155.
61. Ibid., p. 162.
62. Rahman, *Revival and Reform in Islam*, p. 61.
63. Ibid., pp. 98–9.
64. Ibid., p. 98.
65. Ibid., pp. 98–9.
66. Rahman., 'Islamic Studies and the Future of Islam', pp. 131–3.
67. Rahman, *Islam and Modernity*, p. 20.
68. Rahman, 'Towards Reformulating', p. 221.
69. Ibid., p. 221.
70. Fazlur Rahman, 'Social Change and Early Sunnah', *Islamic Studies*, 2, 2 (1963), p. 206.
71. Ibid., p. 206.
72. Rahman, 'Concepts Sunnah, Ijtihad and Ijma'', p. 10.
73. Ibid., pp. 5–21.
74. Rahman, 'The Impact of Modernity on Islam', p. 122.
75. Fazlur Rahman, 'Revival and Reform in Islam: The Tradition', in P.M. Holt, Ann K.S. Lambton and Bernard Lewis, eds., *The Cambridge History of Islam* (Cambridge, 1970), vol. 2, p. 640.
76. Rahman, *Islam and Modernity*, p. 20.
77. Rahman, 'Towards Reformulating', p. 221.
78. Rahman, *Islam and Modernity*, pp. 13–22.
79. Rahman, 'Towards Reformulating', pp. 222–3.
80. Ibid., p. 219.
81. Rahman, 'Islamic Studies and the Future of Islam', p. 130.
82. Rahman, 'The Impact of Modernity on Islam', p. 127.
83. Koshul, 'Fazlur Rahman's *Islam and Modernity* Revisited', p. 403.
84. Farid Esack, *Qur'an, Liberation and Pluralism: An Islamic Perspective of Interreligious Solidarity Against Oppression* (Oxford, c.1997), p. 67.
85. Ibid., p. 67.
86. For Rahman's reference to Betti's views see *Islam and Modernity*, pp. 8–9. For a more detailed discussion of Betti's approach, see Hans-Georg Gadamer, *Truth and Method* (London, 1975), pp. 276, 290–95, 470.
87. For Rahman's critique of Gadamer, see *Islam and Modernity*, pp. 8–11.

BIBLIOGRAPHY

Works by Fazlur Rahman

——. 'Internal Religious Developments in the present Century Islam', *Journal of World History*, 2 (1954–55), pp. 862–79.
——. 'Concepts Sunnah, Ijtihad and Ijma' in the Early Period', *Islamic Studies*, 1, 1 (1962), pp. 5–21.
——. 'Iqbal's Idea of Muslim', *Islamic Studies*, 2, 4 (1963), pp. 439–45.
——. 'Social Change and Early Sunnah', *Islamic Studies* 2, 2 (1963), pp. 206–16.

——. 'The Concept of Hadd in Islamic Law', *Islamic Studies*, 4, 3 (1965), pp. 237–51.

——. 'The Impact of Modernity on Islam', *Journal of Islamic Studies*, 5, 2 (1966), pp. 113–28.

——. 'The Status of the Individual in Islam', *Islamic Studies*, 5, 4 (1966), pp. 319–30.

——. 'Some Reflections on the Reconstruction of Muslim Society in Pakistan', *Journal of Islamic Studies*, 6, 9 (1967), pp. 103–20.

——. 'The Qur'anic Concept of God, the Universe and Man', *Islamic Studies*, VI, 1 (1967), pp. 1–19.

——. 'The Qur'anic Solution of Pakistan's Educational Problems', *Islamic Studies*, 6, 4 (1967), pp. 315–326.

——. 'Economic Principles of Islam', *Islamic Studies*, 8, 1 (1969), pp. 1–8.

——. 'Islamic Modernism: Its Scope, Method and Alternatives', *International Journal of Middle East Studies*, 1 (1970), pp. 317–33.

——. 'Revival and Reform in Islam: The Tradition', in *The Cambridge History of Islam, Volume 2B: History and Civilization.* Cambridge, 1970, pp. 632–56.

——. 'Pre-Foundations of the Muslim Community in Mecca', *Studia Islamica*, 43 (1976), pp. 5–24.

——. 'Divine Revelation and the Prophet', *Hamdard Islamicus*, 1, 2 (1978), pp. 66–72.

——. *Islam.* Chicago, 1966; 1979.

——. 'Islam: Challenges and Opportunities', in A.T. Welch and P. Cachia, eds., *Islam: Past Influence and Present Challenge.* Edinburgh, 1979, pp. 315–30.

——. 'Towards Reformulating the Methodology of Islamic Law', *New York University Journal of International Law and Politics*, 12, 2 (1979), pp. 205–22.

——. 'Islam: Legacy and Contemporary Challenge', *Islamic Studies*, 19, 4 (1980), pp. 235–46.

——. 'Islamic Studies and the Future of Islam', in Malcolm H. Kerr, ed., *Islamic Studies: A Tradition and its Problems.* Malibu, 1980, pp. 125–33.

——. *Major Themes of the Qur'an.* Minneapolis, 1980.

——. 'Islam's Attitude Toward Judaism', *The Muslim World*, LXXII, 1 (1982), pp. 1–13.

——. *Islam and Modernity: Transformation of an Intellectual Tradition.* Chicago, 1982.

——. 'Some Key Ethical Concepts of the Qur'an', *The Journal of Religious Ethics*, II, 2 (1983), pp. 170–85.

——. 'Approaches to Islam in Religious Studies: Review Essay', in Richard C. Martin, ed., *Approaches to Islam in Religious Studies.* Oxford, 1985, pp. 189–202.

——. 'My Belief in Action', in Phillip L. Berman, ed., *The Courage of Conviction.* New York, 1985, pp. 153–59.

——. 'Islam and Political Action: Politics in the Service of Religion' in Nigel Biggar, Jamie Scott and William Schweiker, eds., *Cities of Gods: Faith, Politics and Pluralism in Judaism, Christianity and Islam.* New York, 1986.

——. 'Translating the Qur'an', *Religion and Literature*, 20, 1 (1988), pp. 23–30.

———. *Revival and Reform in Islam: A Study of Islamic Fundamentalism*, ed. Ebrahim Moosa. Oxford, 1999.

Secondary sources:

Esack, Farid. *Qur'an, Liberation and Pluralism: An Islamic Perspective of Interreligious Solidarity Against Oppression*. Oxford, 1997.

Gadamer, Hans-Georg. *Truth and Method*. London, 1975.

Koshul, Basit B. 'Fazlur Rahman's *Islam and Modernity* Revisited', *Islamic Studies* 33, 4 (1994), pp. 403–6.

Sonn, Tamara. 'Fazlur Rahman's Islamic Methodology', *The Muslim World*, LXXXI, 3–4 (1991), pp. 212–230.

Waugh, Earle H. 'The Legacies of Fazlur Rahman for Islam in America', *The American Journal of Islamic Social Sciences*, 16, 3 (1999), pp. 27–44.

3

Nurcholish Madjid and the interpretation of the Qur'an: religious pluralism and tolerance

ANTHONY H. JOHNS AND ABDULLAH SAEED

Introduction

INDONESIA is an archipelago nation with the largest population of Muslims in the world, but with significant minorities of adherents of other religions, including Christianity, Buddhism and Hinduism. It is nevertheless not an Islamic state, and all citizens are equal before the law. It represents a confluence of diverse peoples and cultural traditions brought together by the arbitrary boundaries of the former Dutch East Indies. The Islamic traditions represented within it range from the radical to the latitudinarian. In the early years of the Republic, proclaimed in 1945, the issue of the ideological basis of the state was deeply divisive. There were regional revolts in favour of an Islamic state, and the principal Islamic parties had the achievement of Indonesia as an Islamic state as their long term objective. The ethnic and religious pluralism of Indonesia however gave cause for caution, particularly since there were from time to time sectarian clashes between Muslims and the Christian minorities in certain areas.

The continuing complexity of the situation prompted many Muslims to think about the nature of the state and the position of minorities in a way that went beyond the classical formulations of *fiqh*, alongside the more general issues of how Islam was to play a role in the modern world, and remain true to its identity.

Nurcholish Madjid[1] is one of those taking part in this quest. Born in 1939, he is one of the best known Muslim public figures in Indonesia. He grew up during a critical period in the evolution of the Indonesian state. He was certainly aware of the privations of the period of the Japanese occupation, of the euphoria created by the proclamation of Indonesian Independence in 1945, and the anguish resulting both from the attempts of the Dutch to reclaim their former colony, and political infighting among the Indonesians themselves. During the years of his adolescence, he was able to see how divisions between Muslims had been exacerbated by leaders of different tendencies – reformist, traditionalist, call them what you will – forming political parties to present their conflicting views at the local and national levels. He also took note of their failure to make any effective contribution to the public good in Indonesia from the date of the first Parliamentary elections in 1955 to the end of the traumatic decade of the sixties. It was against this background that he made a speech on 3 January 1970, in which he gave dramatic utterance to the slogan 'Islam Yes, Partai Islam No' (Islam Yes! Islamic Parties, No!).[2] In subsequent lectures and writings, he has proceeded to formulate a significant structure of ideas concerning the position and role of Islam in Indonesia, a state predominantly Muslim, though ethnically and religiously plural.

Nurcholish regards himself as a 'neo-modernist', although it must be conceded that this term, no less than 'modern', is inherently troublesome. He regards modernity as a synonym for rationalism, and Islam par excellence as a religion based on rationality, and argues these views on the basis of the Qur'an and hadith. He has not written any formal work on *tafsir*, however, and in his writings has shown little specialist concern with the other traditional Islamic disciplines.

His ideas and motivations derive from four overlapping contexts: his family background, his education, the events of the period in which he grew up, and the distinctive character and experience of Indonesia as a new nation in the modern world.

Family background and education

Nurcholish was born in Jombang, a small town in the plains of East Java on 17 March 1939. His father was director of a *pesantren* (the common Javanese term for *madrasa*), Madrasa al-Wathaniya.[3] He attended both it and the local government secular school (displaying early a penchant for the combination of religious with secular studies) until 1953. He then enrolled in another local *pesantren*, Darul 'Ulum. Differences within the local Islamic community rendered his presence there unwelcome. His father was a member of the traditionalist Nahdatul Ulama (NU), but gave his political allegiance to the Masyumi, a political party which after 1952 was often associated with a number of the ideas and attitudes of the reformist educational and social welfare organisation, Muhammadiyah, though broader in its appeal and support base.[4] Thus, after two painful years, he moved to another small town about 120 kilometres from Jombang where he enrolled in the Pesantren Darussalam Gontor, also known as Pondok Modern Gontor (Modern Religious Study House of Gontor). This institution was distinguished from other rural *pesantren* by a number of features: it replaced the traditional *halaqa* system of instruction by class room teaching; it taught 'modern' subjects such as history, geography and economics alongside the Islamic disciplines, and Arabic was presented as a language of modern communication and discourse. In fact for some subjects English and Arabic were the languages of instruction. It was an institution open in its sympathies, and did not define itself by an exclusive allegiance to any one of the four *madhahib*. Thus it represented a new development in rural religious education in Java, and was to set a trend. Its modernising curricula was a response to social changes taking place in the wake of Indonesian independence, rising expectations and aspirations of an emerging middle class, and parental expectations for their children extending beyond the roles expected for those who chose a religious rather than secular emphasis in their education. Enrolment at this *pesantren* represented the same combination of religious and secular education that had characterised Nurcholish's early education. He was a successful student there, and in his senior years took part in its teaching programme.[5]

Like many able and ambitious students in the provinces, Nurcholish went to Jakarta for tertiary study. He was determined to continue the combination of religious and secular studies he had already begun, and so enrolled at the Institut Agama Islam Negeri (IAIN: State Institute of Islamic Studies) Syarif Hidayatullah in Jakarta.[6] It was one of a number of such institutes established in each of the major centres of Indonesia, designed to teach religious along with secular subjects using the same modern academic methods, in a way designed to produce graduates with a well-rounded education qualified to serve in the various institutions related to religious administration in the country.

Political events

1960, the year in which Nurcholish entered the IAIN, saw the virtual end to the Darul Islam revolts against the central government in West Java, Aceh and the South Celebes.[7] These had been provoked in part at the end of 1949 by the establishment of Indonesia, not as an Islamic state, but on the non-confessional ideology of the Pancasila, or 'Five Principles'. These are: belief in God (God being designated by the indigenous word *Tuhan*, not the Arabic-Islamic 'Allah'), nationalism, humanitarianism, social justice and democracy.[8] In other words, to be an Indonesian was to profess a religion, but not necessarily to be a Muslim. The goal of these three regional revolts, which were in part coordinated, had been to transform Indonesia into an Islamic republic.

1960 was also a year in which the instruments and ideals of parliamentary democracy in Indonesia were in terminal decline, if not worse. The first parliamentary elections had been held in 1955 and the principal parties emerging with significant representation were the *Partai Nasionalis Indonesia* (the Indonesian Nationalist Party: PNI); the *Partai Komunis Indonesia* (the Indonesian Communist Party: PKI); the Masyumi, an Islamic political party based on reformist religious ideas and principles; and the NU representing traditionalist Islam, traditionalism being understood as adherence to the jurisprudence of the Shafiʻi *madhhab*. Both Islamic parties had as part of their platform the ideal of Indonesia as an Islamic state, to be achieved by parliamentary means. The Nationalists and Communists, and a large number of minor parties, on the other hand, gave their allegiance to the Pancasila as the defining ideology of the new nation.

Notwithstanding the fact that the voting population of Indonesia at the time was about 90 per cent Muslim, the two principal Muslim parties together won only 42 per cent of the total vote. Moreover, although both had as a common goal Indonesia as an Islamic state, they were divided by profound disagreements on a number of issues. These included the need to accept the authority of one or another of the traditional schools of law (not necessarily the Shafiʻi), their regional distribution, which had cultural concomitants – the NU being largely, but by no means exclusively, Java based, and the Masyumi being largely, but again by no means exclusively, Outer Islands based – and by their political policies. The Masyumi was uncompromisingly anti-communist and pro-western, and had little confidence in the personality and policies of the then President Soekarno. The NU, on the other hand, was sympathetic to Soekarno, and prepared to enter into parliamentary coalitions that included both Nationalists and Communists (in which the Masyumi refused to participate), if only to secure political leverage not available to the Masyumi, and thereby have control over the Ministry of Religion. As a result, although both were Islamic parties, there was no basis for political cooperation between them.[9]

Nurcholish began his tertiary studies in Jakarta aware of the failure of the Darul Islam movements to establish an Islamic state in Indonesia by armed rebellion, and of the inability of the Islamic parties even to work together in pursuit of common goals, let alone to gain a majority of parliamentary seats. He had, moreover, suffered personally from his father's attempt to break the nexus between membership of the NU, with all that it entailed in respect of *fiqh* (that is, the authority of the Shafi'i *madhhab*), and accepting the political policies of the Masyumi.

The final collapse of the parliamentary structure set up in 1955 came with an attempted coup in 1965. In its wake, Soekarno lost power, and General Suharto became effective ruler of the country. The effects were widespread and traumatic. Upwards of half a million communists or suspected communist sympathisers were killed, a large proportion of them in Nurcholish's home region of East Java, and many by NU militias. The personal trauma this caused him must have been very profound.[10]

The resulting so-called New Order did not open any new windows of opportunity to Islamic political parties, not even to the Masyumi, which had been consistently anti-communist, and whose leaders had been victimised by both extreme nationalists and leftist sympathisers. Rather, the reverse was the case. In the aftermath of the attempted coup, for the first time in a generation, there had been an outbreak of Muslim violence against Christians in South Sulawesi and West Java. Memories of the Darul Islam revolts were still fresh, and militant Islam was regarded as being as much of a danger to the development of Indonesia as a unitary state as communism; in fact it was regarded as constituting the main political threat to the government. As a result the government took a number of steps to exclude parties identified by religion or a religious ideology from the political process. The Islamic faith was to have full expression as a complex of religious, cultural and social ideas and values, but not to present itself as a political ideology that might challenge the status of the Pancasila. The government's goal was finally achieved in 1973, when the political parties permitted to participate in elections were reduced to three, with names that did not indicate a religious identity. There was the *Partai Persatuan Pembangunan* (the United Development Party: PPP), which subsumed the Muslim parties; the *Partai Demokrasi Indonesia* (the Indonesian Democratic Party: PDI), which subsumed a number of other parties, including non-Islamic religious parties, the former Indonesian (democratic) Socialist Party and the secular nationalists; and, finally, there was Golkar (Golongan Karyawan: the

Association of Functional Groups), a government sponsored and supported association of functional groups based on the power and authority of public service administrators. This was in fact the party of the government, through which Suharto, with the support of the Armed Forces, exercised power.[11]

Tertiary studies

Such were the events that unfolded throughout the years during which Nurcholish was a student at the IAIN. He had enrolled in the Faculty of Arts in the Department of Arabic Literature and the History of Islamic Thought, and followed a broad-based humanities programme, completed in 1968. He graduated in that year with the submission of a thesis entitled *al-Qur'an: 'arabiyyun lughatan wa 'alamiyyun ma'nan.* The title – *The Qur'an: Arabic in Language, Universal in Significance* – should be noted. It indicates a significant stage in his intellectual development: a perception of the tension between the role of a single language given unique status by divine revelation, and the plural world in which this one language and the religion revealed through it were destined to play a universalistic role.

This choice of title shows that his thesis is not simply the conclusion of an academic programme, but a stage in his continuing engagement with issues and ideas about which leading Muslim figures of the time, whether 'modernists' or 'traditionalists', were already contending. These included Muslim identity, inter-religious relations, and the role of religion in politics and in economic and social development.

These debates were enriched at the end of the decade by the return of a number of highly gifted individuals – educationalists, administrators, and scholars – from courses of study at the Institute of Islamic Studies at McGill University in Montreal. Among them were Harun Nasution and Mukti Ali. Harun Nasution was to reorganise the academic programme of the IAIN[12] and establish a seminal post-graduate programme there; and Mukti Ali was to serve as Minister of Religion in 1973, and subsequently become Rector of the IAIN Sunan Kalijaga in Yogyakarta. These and others became leaders in a movement that took the attitudes and thinking of many Indonesian Muslims, Nurcholish among them, beyond the neo-Hanbalism (the intellectual legacy of Rashid Rida) which had dominated the thinking of the self-styled Indonesian reformists during the 1950s.[13] They had not provided clearer answers to the challenges presented by modernity than those offered by the traditionalists they had set out to displace, and the Masyumi, the political party by which they tried to realise their ideals, had limited success.

Just as he had served as a teacher at the Gontor *madrasa* on the conclusion of his studies there, after graduating from the IAIN Nurcholish joined its staff. At the same time, he worked as a researcher at the Lembaga Ilmu Pengetahuan Indonesia (LIPI: The Indonesian Academy of Science).

As a student and academic activist

However, between 1960 and the year of his graduation, Nurcholish was not only a student but emerged as a leader in student religio-political organisations. He joined the Jakarta branch of the *Himpunun Mahasiswa Islam* (the Islamic Student Association: HMI) in 1963, and soon began to play a major active role in its activities. He must therefore have been acutely aware of the events that were taking place around the IAIN campus, which was not insulated from the tensions and oppressive atmosphere that pervaded Jakarta during these years. In 1966 (the year after the attempted coup), he was nominated to attend the national congress of the HMI in Solo, where he was elected General Chairman of its National Executive for a three year term, (1966–1969). He was later re-elected for a second term (1969–1971). Throughout his years there he had been a keen participant in the debate on renewal and reform in Islamic thought, necessary if Islam was to meet the challenges posed by modernity, particularly during his second term as president of the HMI.

The Muslim Student movement in Indonesia had international affiliations in which Nurcholish also played a role. He served as president of Persatuan Mahasiswa Islam Asia Tenggara (the Union of Islamic Students of Southeast Asia: PEMIAT), from 1967 to 1969. From 1968 to 1971, he was Assistant Secretary General and a founder member of the International Islamic Federation of Students' Organisations (IIFSO). He became general editor of the journal *Mimbar Jakarta,* and organised or belonged to a number of study clubs.[14]

By the end of the decade he had realised that the struggle for Indonesia as an Islamic state through the efforts of political parties had come to a dead end. Thus his goal became Indonesia as a state that was Islamic, and he attempted to achieve this by seeking a meaning of 'Islamic' that could take into account the essential ethnic and religious pluralism of Indonesia, which would make it genuinely inclusive of all the diversity within the state. And it is this experience which lies behind the dramatic challenge referred to earlier, 'Islam Yes, Partai Islam No'.

By the time the new decade began, Nurcholish had participated in, and continued to take part in, debates on the ways in which Islam and Muslims could respond to the challenges of modernity. The questions discussed were various, and they were raised in different forms: What kind of rethinking of the interpretation and authority of the Qur'an and hadith was necessary if these foundation texts were to be relevant to the modern world? How could Islam play its role in the modern world and retain its authenticity? Was Islam an ideology in competition with other ideologies? Was an Islamic state a necessary or even a desirable goal? Did Islam have the right or even the need for a privileged position in the apparatus of the state? How could Islam play its role in a civil society, in a religiously plural society, and how should it see its position vis-à-vis other religions?

All these were matters of concern to an emerging generation of Muslims in Indonesia no longer content with the 'classical' traditionalist world view. The questions raised were radical. But paradoxically, despite the increasingly authoritarian attitudes of the government, the kinds of answers proposed – which in fact questioned the value of Islamic political parties – coincided with government policy, thus the debates and proposals deriving from them did not attract government interference, and in fact won its support. Nevertheless Nurcholish was aware that the government had its own ideological agenda and realised that answers to these questions would have to come about within the framework of the Pancasila, the state ideology. By 1972, at least one aspect of his thought was firmly established:

> The concept of 'Islamic state' is a distortion of the [properly] proportioned relationship between state and religion. The state is one of the aspects of worldly life whose dimension is rational and collective, while religion is an aspect of another kind of life whose dimension is spiritual and personal.[15]

In America

A new stage in Nurcholish's life began in 1978 when he went to the University of Chicago. After a false start in sociology, he transferred to philosophy in an Islamic studies programme,[16] working under the late Professor Fazlur Rahman. There he specialised in the thought of Ibn Taymiyya (1263–1328), who was the inspiration for a number of radical reform and revival movements through subsequent Islamic history. He submitted a successful doctoral thesis, entitled *Ibn Taimiya on Kalam and Falsafa: problems of reason and revelation in Islam,* in 1984.

These six years were an important part of his life. The years in America opened up new intellectual horizons for him. Fazlur Rahman was at that time the doyen of a new wave of Islamic thinkers. He was concerned with problems of how to interpret the Qur'an in the modern world, alongside other difficult and sensitive questions. Examples of these included the modality of prophetic inspiration, the centrality of Qur'anic teachings to the achievement of social justice, and the authority of traditional formulations of *fiqh* (particularly those concerning relations between Muslims and the adherents of other religions) in the modern world. He argued that the meaning and message of the

Qur'an and the basis for its continuing relevance lies not in any single verse, but in the book as a whole. This led him to develop a contextual approach to the interpretation of the Qur'an.[17]

Nurcholish did not take up all of Rahman's concerns. He has written little if anything on the modality of prophetic inspiration, for example. However, he was to take up vigorously the notion of 'contextuality' as a heuristic device in Qur'anic interpretation, particularly in the way in which legal rulings were to be applied, and in determining the authority of the *fiqh* of previous centuries in modern times.

Return to Indonesia

Nurcholish returned to Indonesia in 1984, coincidentally the year in which the NU (by then solely a religious educational and social welfare organization, and not a political party) bowed to govern-ment pressure, and became the first major Islamic organisation to accept the Pancasila as its sole ideological basis. It is in the numerous media articles, lectures, interviews and a constant stream of publications after his return that one can see how, in light of his experience, he interprets and uses the Qur'an and hadith to discover appropriate responses to challenges facing the Muslim community in Indonesia. This was a community within the circumstances of a country with a particular identity and at a particular point in its history, under a government determined to enforce particular policies.

His encounter with Fazlur Rahman had given Nurcholish a broader perspective on the problems facing the Islamic world. He had already concluded that political parties could provide no solution. Thus he began to look behind legal rulings to the values enshrined in the Islamic revelation.[18] His aim was to see these values realised in a way appropriate to the distinctive character of the Indonesian state, in a way that would safe-guard the integra-tion of Indonesia as a political entity, and enhance the role of the Pancasila as the cornerstone of national unity.

Nurcholish has written widely on this issue, taking 'contextualism' as the core of his approach.[19] He and others who shared these concerns, likewise inspired by Fazlur Rahman, came to be given various names – 'contextualists', 'liberals', 'substantialists', 'transformationists' or 'neo-modernists' – all reflecting their interest in a more open, more inclusive understanding of Islam. They cannot all be associated with a single identifiable group and are to be found, not only among 'traditionalists', but also within 'modernist' and other 'liberal-minded' groups. Among the latter are Abdurrahman Wahid, Chairman of the NU before his brief period as President of the Republic, Mukti Ali and Munawir Sjadzali, both of whom were Ministers of Religion under Soeharto. Among a younger generation are Azyumardi Azra, now Rector of IAIN Syarif Hidayatullah, who studied at Columbia University, and Budhy Munawar-Rachman of Paramadina University, who are both developing similar ideas.

Nurcholish and the Qur'an

Nurcholish, then, encounters the Qur'an and the Islamic tradition as an individual responding to the social and ideological turbulence of his time, but with neither the constraints nor the insights of the traditional Islamic disciplines of *fiqh* and *tafsir.* Since he has not written any dedicated work of *tafsir,* the principles governing his interpretation of the Book need to be inferred from his writings on other topics, particularly those published after his return from the USA. His approach is pragmatic, as he comes face to face with divisions among Muslims over issues of *fiqh,* and the need for inter-religious harmony in Indonesia. It is far removed from the cerebral concerns with literary theory of a scholar like Nasr Hamid Abu Zayd.[20]

His love, reverence for and acceptance of the Qur'an as a revealed Book, and the authority it commands, is simple and uncomplicated. Its status is unique. It is authentic, existing today in exactly the form it had when revealed to the Prophet. It is the word of God, divinely given and error-free. It is accessible to all in this form. The authority to interpret it is not restricted to any priestly class.

It is, moreover, a revelation totally compatible with reason, and bases its appeal on reason. It proclaims that God did not create the world *'abathan* (in an arbitrary manner), and calls on humankind to make use of its capacity to reason to appreciate the coherence of God's design. The Qur'an then is perfectly compatible with modernity. Modernity is equivalent to rationality, and rationality is integral to Islam. Rationality is not the exclusive monopoly of 'the West', nor is it to be identified with westernisation. The challenge facing Muslims in the modern world is to recover the rational dimension of Islam that has, over the centuries, become overlaid with habit and custom.

Reason and revelation are interdependent. Reason by itself cannot provide adequate guidance for humankind without the support of revelation (the Qur'an). Revelation, however, is necessarily in a human language, and reason is the instrument by which revelation may be properly understood and put to good effect. The use of reason in understanding and applying the message of the Qur'an goes beyond discovering or ascertaining the meaning of individual words or verses. An interpreter has to reflect on every issue touched on in the context of the Qur'an as a whole and, in the light of such an understanding, establish the relevance of its message to the modern world. For Nurcholish, therefore, reason goes hand in hand with faith (*iman*). They cannot be separated.

Contextualist ideas

Up to this point, Nurcholish's acceptance of, and approach to the Qur'an is uncomplicated – even simplistic. It is contextuality that provides the hermeneutic principle which is the starting point for the more radical aspects of his approach to it as he follows in the footsteps of Fazlur Rahman.

Contextualisation involves relating Qur'anic logia to two contexts: one is the time and circumstances of the Prophet when it was revealed, the other is the contemporary situation for which its guidance is needed, the situation in which today's 'receptors' of the text encounter it. Nurcholish uses this principle extensively, and it lies behind most of his ideas, although he does not situate it in any broader theoretical framework.

His starting point is that the Qur'an is closely bound to a place and a time. It is intrinsically related to the world of seventh-century Hijaz. Its content includes the challenges faced by the Prophet, his concerns and aspirations, and those of the Muslim community with him at that time. Although it is the word of God, it cannot be fully understood outside of this context. Nevertheless, it transcends it.

Everything in the Qur'an is part of a divine plan. At a practical level, this means that the laws given in the Qur'an had a purpose for the time and circumstances in which they were revealed. There is a seamless relationship between them, although the classical jurists did not appreciate this relationship, or explore its implications. This principle determines his approach to the Qur'an, for he is aware of the differences between that time and those circumstances, and the world of the late twentieth century. In studying the legal prescriptions it sets out, he considers them in the light of the social context in which they were revealed, and sees the application of them first in the time of the Prophet, and then by successive generations of the 'receptors' of the text and various stages in the interaction of Islam with history at specific times and places.

This is a significant shift away from the traditional understanding of the Qur'anic revelation. Even though classical *tafsir* and *fiqh* scholars were equally aware that the Qur'an was revealed in Arabic in Arabia to an Arab prophet, they did not recognise the corollary that the Qur'an had to be understood as a historical text. They largely disregarded this fact, and stressed the gulf between the Qur'an as word of God and the historical context in which it had been revealed. The closest they came to a recognition of such a relationship was through *asbab al-nuzul* (compilations of hadith setting out the circumstances of revelation of particular Qur'anic verses). Yet even these they regarded as little more than footnotes to revelation itself. In fact, the jurists, in formulating their rulings, often overlooked the association between revelation and context provided by the *asbab al-nuzul* and argued that a ruling should not be regarded as 'specific' in application simply because a circumstance of revelation related it to a particular situation. It was tacitly understood that a ruling was general, and the onus of proof was on establishing that it was not.

For Nurcholish this distinction was of central importance. For him, such rulings were specific to place and time, and the onus of proof was on establishing that they were general. Rather, it was the values behind them that endured, for lying behind these legal prescriptions are values that transcend time and place, even though the particular legal prescriptions themselves need no longer be put into effect. Re-examination of many of them was required, and appropriate methodologies for doing so must be devised.

He was impelled to do so by his awareness that many of the divisions between Muslim communities in Indonesia were caused by disagreement over points of *fiqh*, which were in themselves trifling; such as, whether the formulation of intention before the performance of the ritual prayer should be made orally, or mentally, which was among the issues so bitterly contested between the traditionalists and the reformists. It was differences over jurisprudential matters of this kind that were in part responsible for the pain Nurcholish and his family suffered during the two years that he was at an NU *pesantren* referred to earlier, because his father was politically pro-Masyumi: differences that rendered the Islamic parties politically ineffective, and as a result of which Islam ceased to command respect.

Contextualism was his weapon of choice to put an end to such absurdities, as well as to tackle more serious issues such as the relations between Islam and other religions, and death as the penalty for apostasy. It had to be recognised that the traditional formulations of *fiqh* were essentially contingent, its rulings conditioned by time and place. He proceeded by what he called 'contextualised *ijtihad*', and argues that, although modern as a term, contextualised *ijtihad* was exercised during the earliest period of Islamic history, even though it had not been incorporated into jurisprudence.

Examples of his use and justification of it – involving what he called 'reactualisation' – are included in an anthology of interviews published in 1998.[21] These interviews included responses to criticism. Among them is an answer to an attack on him by the Malaysian scholar Syed Naquib al-Attas. Al-Attas took the view that every law created in the history of Islam had the status of Islam itself. It was therefore improper to contextualise such laws, to 'reactualise' the situation in which they were first applied in order to assess whether they were still binding, or how their application might be modified in the light of changing circumstances.[22]

Nurcholish replied that such a 'reactualisation' had been applied by the second Caliph 'Umar (*r*.634–644). He gave as an example 'Umar's decree forbidding the distribution of conquered land as part of the spoils of war after the conquest of Syria. At first sight, this appears to be counter to the explicit teaching of the Qur'an. Qur'an 8: 41 gives a general rule for the distribution of the spoils of war: one-fifth is for God, the Messenger, his kin, orphans, the poor and travellers; the remaining four-fifths are to be distributed equally among those taking part in the action in question. 'Umar, however, refused to allow Arab soldiers or clans to treat land or landed property as part of the spoils of war, although the Qur'an does not distinguish land from other forms of booty. He ruled that property was to be considered the permanent possession of the conquered community. The revenue it generated might be distributed, but not the land that produced this revenue. The historian Lapidus remarks that this ruling not only ensured a fairer distribution of the spoils of victory, but protected cultivated land from pillage.[23]

Nurcholish explains that 'Umar based his judgement on the sense of the Qur'an as a whole. The Qur'an is fundamentally concerned with social justice, and the public good. This concern overrides the individual rights of those who, on the authority of this verse [Qur'an 8: 41], believed they could claim a share of the conquered land, a claim that would have wreaked havoc with social and economic life. Nurcholish points out that 'Umar showed his awareness that the community he ruled had an ethical sense that lay deeper than any ad hoc legal prescription, and was composed of individuals who had a profound understanding of the spirit of religion.[24]

Another example of Nurcholish's reasoning is his comment on Munawir Sjadzili's suggested 'reactualisation' of a Qur'anic law of inheritance, in that a female with an equal degree of kinship should receive half the share of a male of a deceased's estate [Qur'an 4: 11]. Munawir remarked that the education of his son had involved him in far more expense than that of his daughter, and raised the question as to why should the son, who had received so much from his father already, be entitled to double the share of his estate than that of his daughter?[25]

Nurcholish does not commit himself to a definitive answer but draws from the question a reflection on the appropriateness in such a case of applying a law on the basis of *'ilal al-hukm* (the efficient causes of the ruling), rather than *ma'nat al-hukm* (the reasoning behind the judgment). He suggests that a possible reason (*'illa*) for this Qur'anic ruling is that the male is given a greater share of the estate because of his responsibility as bread winner. But, he continues, the application of a law is determined by the reason for which it was prescribed. If this reason changes, then the application of the law changes. And he cites the appearance of the relatively recent phenomenon of the house-husband in American society, the woman in this situation being the breadwinner, a circumstance which would remove the reason for this ruling. He argues then that legal provisions in the Qur'an, such as the double share of an estate for a male, are themselves an 'event' deriving from the intersection of Islam with history at the moment of the Qur'anic revelation. Legal provisions cannot be considered in isolation from the purpose for which they were revealed, and the values they were intended to enshrine. Not to do so would be unfaithful to the general value-oriented message of the revelation, which was relevant for every time, place and circumstance.

A third example is his rejection of the traditional rule of *fiqh* which states that an individual who abandons Islam for another religion should be punished by death. On the occasion of an international conference, he challenged a delegate from Saudi

Arabia who spoke in defence of the death penalty. In particular he asked why the evidence the delegate adduced in support of his argument was at the level of *fiqh*, which, as Nurcholish argues, is tightly bound to time and place, and not at the level of the Qur'an.

Nurcholish points out that there is no authority for such a penalty for apostasy in the Qur'an, and he cites a number of relevant verses. Of one who turns aside from Islam, the Qur'an says:

> One who seeks other than Islam as a religion, it will not be accepted from him, and in the hereafter he will be among the losers.
> [Q. 3: 85][26]

The Qur'an further declares that a human being is free to accept or reject belief in God and His Prophet:

> Whoever believes, let him believe, and whoever rejects belief, let him reject it. We have prepared for those who do evil a fire that envelops them. [Q. 18: 29]

Nurcholish then draws the conclusion: It is God, not the state that will pass judgement on apostasy, and this judgement will come in a time of God's choosing. That there was at one time a death penalty for apostasy is due to historical circumstances. The death penalty may at one time have been appropriate. During the early period of Islamic history every Muslim was, in some, sense a soldier. The community was under threat from armed enemies and its primary duty was to defend itself. In such a state of war the punishment for desertion is death. This is not now the case. In other words, the ruling according to *fiqh* that apostasy should be punished by death was the result of a specific interaction of event, circumstance, place and time. That interaction was in the past, and the ruling is no longer applicable.[27] The tradition of *fiqh*, then, represents the experience of the 'receptors' of the Qur'anic message at particular points in time. Many other formulations of *fiqh*, representing as they do human responses to the fact of divine revelation, have no permanent, sacral authority.

In his approach to such questions, Nurcholish recognises that in the last resort, God alone is not subject to change. Accordingly, Muslims as members of human society – a plural society, undergoing rapid change – should not attach too much importance to the *fiqh* rulings made in the past beyond learning from them.

In the light of these considerations, Nurcholish, liberated from the impedimenta of history, feels free to discount the traditions of *fiqh* that justify or entail discrimination against the adherents of religions other than Islam, in order to explore without prejudice what the Qur'an itself has to say on the matter.

He insists that the Qur'an recognises these religions as valid instruments of salvation, and adduces a number of proof texts. There are several verses that establish that prophecy is universal, and so all peoples have knowledge of God. Among them,

> Every people has a messenger.
> So when their messenger comes,
> Judgement will be made between them with justice.
> They shall not be wronged. [Q. 10: 47]

And,

> Messengers, some of whom We have already told of to you
> and Messengers of whom We have not yet told you. [Q. 4: 164]

The salvific validity of the religions preached by these prophets is guaranteed:

> Those who believe, those who follow Judaism,
> those who are Christians, those who are Sabaens,
> who believe in God and the Last Day,
> and do good Deeds,
> they have their reward with God.
> No fear shall fall upon them, they shall not grieve. [Q. 2: 62]

This is reiterated elsewhere:

> Among the people of the Book are those who have integrity,
> they recite the verses of God at set times during the night,
> they prostrate themselves [in prayer];
> they believe in God and in the Last Day,
> they summon to what is right and prohibit what is wicked;
> they hasten to do what is right;
> they are included among those who are righteous.
> Any good they do, they will not be deprived of the merit
> they have acquired for it.
> God knows that they are devout. [Q. 3: 113–115]

These verses, Nurcholish argues, should be understood as enjoining the Islamic community not to define itself by narrow and exclusivist interpretations of the Qur'an in relation to other religions which had been formulated in the light of particular historical situations.

He underpins his argument with a reification of four Qur'anic words, *din, Muslim, Islam* and *Allah*. He sees in each of them a dual significance, one specific to the Muslim community and exclusive, the other generic and inclusive.

Thus *din*, in its traditional sense, means the structure and prescriptions of a specific faith, Islam. But the word may, and indeed should also, be understood as having a universalistic dimension, and include the modalities of any and every submission to a divinity. The word *Allah* likewise is to be understood not simply as the personal name of God, as acknowledged by Muslims, but as having the generic sense of Absolute Truth (*Haqq*). *Al-Haqq* however is one of the most beautiful names of God. Thus it is only a short step for *Haqq*, and so Allah, to be understood as a word inclusive of any name of God in any and every religious tradition.

Such a universalistic, inclusive understanding of the two words *din* and *Allah*, he continues, is at the heart of the following Qur'anic verse, in which he clearly understands *Din Allah* as service of the Ultimate Truth,

> Do they seek other than the *Din* of Allah
> when to Him submits everything in heaven and on earth,
> whether willingly or unwillingly? [Q. 3: 83–85]

Islam, likewise, is in one sense the exclusive name for the religion revealed to the Prophet Muhammad. But Islam is also the primal religion first preached by Adam, father of humankind, to all his posterity, who before time began accepted God as their Lord in response to the divine question, *a lastu bi rabbikum?* (Am I not your Lord?) [Q. 7: 172]. All humankind then, before time began, had professed Islam in the widest possible sense of the word. They had indicated their submission, i.e. their humility before the Ultimate Truth.

Understood in this way, the verse *inna al-din 'inda Allah al-Islam* [Q. 3: 19] recognises and confirms the validity of every religion that can be included in these extended definitions of these key words. This even extends to those formally outside the house of Islam: whether Judaism, Christianity, Buddhism or Hinduism. With the Qur'anic words understood in this way, all religions are on an equal footing. And this has a legal consequence: the state has no justification in putting one religion in a privileged position over any other.

This being so, the Qur'anic condemnation of 'whoever seeks a religion other than Islam' [Q. 3: 85] that most of the traditional commentators consider to abrogate the verses, 'Whatever good they do, they will not be deprived of the merit they acquire for it' [Q. 3: 113–115] and 'they have their reward from God' [Q. 2: 62], does not apply to the followers of any religion sincerely held, but only to whoever 'embraces and follows a way of life other than one of obedience and submission to God; one who opposes the divine design, goes counter to the universal law that dominates all the world.'[28] It may be noted that in this Nurcholish neatly sidesteps the whole issue of abrogating (*nasikh*) and abrogated verses (*mansukh*).

If other religions are valid instruments of salvation, it follows that their scriptures too must have an effective authenticity. This is in spite of the argument of many Muslims based on the concept of *tahrif,* developed from the Qur'an [Q. 4: 46 and 5: 13 and 41], that the extant forms of Jewish and Christian scriptures are 'distorted', or else lack authenticity and authority since they are not accessible in the original language of revelation. Nurcholish states that the existing scriptures of these two religions should be considered as having, for those who accept them, the authority of valid revelations. In this, in one way or another, he may be drawing on Ibn Taymiyya's views on the authenticity or otherwise of the Jewish and Christian scriptures. In any case, Nurcholish is giving more weight to content than form. This view is consistent with his basic ideas on religious pluralism. It is, in fact, integral to it.

Nurcholish finds the cornerstone to the structure of his ideas on religious tolerance in the Qur'anic verse in which Muhammad is commanded,

Say, People of the Book, come to a word that is just *(kalima sawa')* between us and you, that we worship none but God alone. [It is] that we associate no partners with Him, and that none of us shall treat others as lords alongside Allah. [Q. 3: 64]

On the basis that *Allah* here is to be understood as the Ultimate Truth, Nurcholish sees in this verse a call to adherents of every religious persuasion to meet each other with mutual respect, while yet remaining true to their own identity. He reifies *kalima sawa'* to mean a 'meeting point' between members of different religious communities. The significance and value implicit in the phrase he sees as fully realised in the Pancasila. The words *kalima sawa'* then are the ultimate authority for the Pancasila, the formula by which Indonesia establishes a meeting point between the state and the various religious traditions at home within it.

Nurcholish's ideas provoked bitter opposition in some Islamic circles. He was accused of either being influenced by Jews or Orientalists or both. On one occasion he was put 'on trial' at the Taman Ismail Marzuki, the principal cultural centre in Jakarta, an event to which he was not invited, but nevertheless attended.[29] His opponents claimed that his interpretation of the words *din, Muslim, Islam* and *Allah* lacked authority. A prominent scholar, Daud Rasyid, denounced him, saying, 'He attempts to find a meeting point between religions by manipulating the meanings of verses, by misunderstanding the hadith of the Prophet, and defiling the words of the ulama'.[30] A number of those making such accusations against him are associated with radical Muslim fringe movements in Indonesia,[31] but it would be an exaggeration to suggest that these were his only opponents. He moves into paths along which many cautious and reflective mainstream Muslims would hesitate to follow him, at least without serious qualification.

His defence against these charges is not based directly on Qur'anic exegesis but on what he regards as a general concern of the Qur'an, one overriding every individual legal ruling, that of *maslaha* (public interest). For Nurcholish, it is *maslaha* which is preponderant in the matter of which interpretation of Qur'anic logia is to be followed, after a contextual analysis of the relevant verses. It is *maslaha* that is the crucial consideration in his plea for acceptance of pluralism and religious tolerance, and it is on the basis of *maslaha* that he gives preponderance to those Qur'anic verses that project tolerance and inclusiveness. If the earlier interpretations in classical Islamic law were to be followed, it would be difficult to justify the total equality of Muslim and non-Muslim within the framework of the state which Nurcholish urges. But public interest demands that this be so. Therefore he argues that Muslims and non-Muslims as human beings must be seen as equals: as citizens of a modern nation state, and as followers of valid religions. This was not the view of the classical formulations of *fiqh*, but Nurcholish argues that the essential flexibility and pragmatism of early Islam has been largely lost in these. Some of the philosophers however had preserved it, and he cites Ibn Rushd, who maintained that all religions were equal, and all were valid paths to God.

Essentially, then, he is emphasizing another hermeneutical principle of central importance to him: that in many cases it is the circumstances of the interpreter and the interpretive community that determines how a text should be understood. The difficulties that many, even mainstream, Muslims have with this principle can be readily understood, and their accusations that he is selective in his choice of texts and distorts the meaning of Qur'anic logia are by no means frivolous.

His reply is that secondary sources in the post-Prophetic period have been accorded a sacral status that puts them virtually on a par with the foundation texts of Islam, and these sources obfuscate the true meanings of these texts. Such interpretations and rulings have to be desacralised through contextual analysis, so that the Qur'an and the Sunna can speak clearly and without any intermediary. In this, the general tendency and ethos of the Qur'an should be accorded more authority than individual verses taken out of their context. As opposed to the neo-Hanbalism of the earlier generation of the reformists – whose aim was to disengage authentic Qur'anic teachings from the views of interpreters, and then apply them with a puritanical literalness – his goal was to go further. His intention was to situate the Qur'anic teachings and establish the reasons for them in the socio-historical context of the revelation, to disclose the value that a particular ruling was intended to present, and then to search out the best means of achieving its realisation in contemporary Indonesia.

Conclusion

Nurcholish has no monopoly of such ideas. *Mutatis mutandis* they are widely scattered across the Muslim world, even though they nowhere command majority status. Yet his presentation of them is distinctive in the Indonesian environment. Even so, there are questions to be raised in any broader assessment of his achievement and its status in the larger panorama of the Islamic tradition. He justifies his ideas on pluralism by the Qur'an, but he has not arrived at them as a Qur'anic exegete. One could even question whether his interpretations of the Qur'an are exegesis at all in the proper sense of the word. Certainly his approach is not based on a word-by-word study of the Qur'an, making use of the established procedures, the checks and balances and qualifications of exegesis as an intellectually based discipline. Rather, it derives from a personal experience of the Qur'an as a whole in the situation of place and time that he is, and a reflection on the significance of particular words and phrases which he then highlights.

It is in this sense that his political and writing career may be seen as an interpretation of the Qur'an. He has attempted to discover in it significances that meet the needs of the contemporary 'receptors' of the revelation, in the light of their current circumstances, and the community in which they live, an effort which finds its apogee in the discovery of a Qur'anic authority for the Pancasila in the phrase *kalima sawa'*. The results of his encounter with the Qur'an seem to match with his perception of the needs of Indonesia, and the political realities of Indonesia. That is one aspect of his vision.

There are however other aspects of his intellectual positions that merit exploration. It has already been noted that he is not an exegete, and that his treatment of the Qur'an does not derive directly from any one stream in the diverse traditions of Qur'anic exegesis. His references to Qur'an interpretation in general do not extend beyond the mystically tinged translation and commentary of Abdullah Yusuf Ali, or the more bleakly rationalist rendering and notes of Muhammad Asad.[32]

Siti Nadroh attempts to situate Nurcholish in a postmodernist context. She suggests that elements of a postmodernist approach are implicit in his understanding of the Qur'an, since he modifies the traditional Muslim view of it as a single reference point, a unique and exclusive meta-paradigm, by seeing it as establishing a variety of complementary reference points, each with its own validity. As she puts it, he concedes that in a pluralist world there is no place for the view, prevalent under modernism, that any one structure can speak with authority for all times and places. The reality of human diversity in a global village[33] does not permit this. He recognises then, that postmodernism has a liberating potential. He is aware, however, of the danger of lapsing into relativism, and thus recognises that postmodernism is not a valid or complete discourse that can give an adequate answer to the problems engendered by modernism. The solution to the problem is to set the paradigm of *tawhid* (the declaration and recognition of the divine unity) over postmodernism. Once *tawhid* is understood as an inclusive, overarching concept, within which every religion has a place, there is no scope for any one religion to claim superiority over another, let alone wage war in defence of its unique claim to truth. In other words, *tawhid* completes and guarantees the ideals implicit in postmodernism, and prevents any excess in the development of it that could lead to relativism. Thus, thanks to the enlightenment it brings, the misuse of religion that renders it a cause of wars is eliminated.[34]

Another approach to his interpretation of the Qur'an is to assess it in the light of more recent theories about the relation of a text to its readers. Madigan, in a recent study on the Qur'an, writes:

It is a brave, some might say foolhardy, person who proposes to tackle the question of the nature of texts in the present intellectual climate, where the very notion of text seems to have become the none-too-stable hinge on which virtually everything else hangs. Nothing is more elusive these days than a text and scriptural religion arguably stands in urgent need of a more sophisticated understanding of the nature of texts.[35]

Nurcholish's plea that it is the circumstances of readers of the Qur'an that play a critical role in determining its meaning for them raises basic questions about the relation of text to reader, and the semiotics of Qur'an interpretation. Up to the present, however, his writings reveal no more explicit concern with semiotics at a theoretical level than with postmodernism.

Thus we return to the political and social context of Indonesia as the dominant element in shaping his work, and come to the tentative conclusion that he is not directly developing any intellectual tradition but responding to the political environment in which he lives, for which the guidance of the late Fazlur Rahman has provided him with a road-map. Certainly his definition of the Pancasila as the Qur'anic *kalima sawa'* – a meeting point of pluralisms – shows the completeness of his immersion in the concerns of Indonesia.

This contextualism (for he too is a contextual being), and the conviction that members of the Muslim community of any place or age have rights over the meanings assigned to the Qur'anic text, are central to his approach. In his writings there is an evident tension between the traditional beliefs concerning the inspiration, authority and authenticity of the Qur'an with which he has grown up, and the demands of the contemporary world in which he lives. This tension is a primary energy source and motivation for him to discover ways of opening up and displaying its relevance to modern issues for Muslims and non-Muslims alike – to strengthen the faith of Muslims, and demonstrate to non-Muslims that in Islam is the best hope for the continuing relevance of religion as a guide to life and moral values in the future.[36]

But, from another perspective, it may be asked how far his journey has really taken him for, although his political aims and ideals are clearly articulated, everything is set within the framework of the Qur'anic revelation, and based on the authority of Qur'anic words. Other religious communities are shown as having a place and rights guaranteed by this revelation, but implicitly need to recognise that the justification they enjoy is accorded them by the Qur'an, over which the traditions to which they belong can claim no authority. In other words, they are participants in an arena established by the Qur'an. It is the Qur'an that sets the terms of their acceptance, and their place in society is justified by the concept of *maslaha*, or public good. This being so, Islamic political parties would have nothing additional to contribute. Incidentally, it may be observed that in Nurcholish's writings, there is little evidence of any genuine encounter with the internal dynamics and spirituality of any of the non-Islamic religious traditions that he accepts as part of Indonesian life, and that his remarks on the course of religious and intellectual history in the West from time to time lack nuance.[37]

However this may be, Nurcholish's approach to the Qur'an is important and distinctive in the Indonesian context. It is a voice that recognises the status quo of a pluralistic society, and is concerned for the public good. It evolves out of and alongside his political activities, and his patriotism. Its primary goal is not a theoretical construct of ideas, but an attempt to contribute to the public good. His hope is that as Indonesia as a nation grows in historical depth, and thus at a higher organizational level of integration, there is evolving with it an articulation of Islam, wedded to Indonesia as a nation, that can serve as a model for inter-religious harmony in other areas of the Muslim world.[38]

NOTES

1. Subsequently Nurcholish only; except on official documents, Indonesians are usually known and referred to by a single personal name.

2. For a succinct account of his career and synopses of some of his works see Peter G. Riddell, *Islam and the Malay-Indonesian World* (London, 2001), pp. 231–237.

3. These and other proper names are spelt according to the conventional Indonesian transliteration of Arabic words.

4. For a background to relations between Masyumi and the NU during

this period, see Anthony H. Johns, 'Indonesia: Islam and Cultural Pluralism' in John L. Esposito, ed., *Islam in Asia: Religion, Politics and Society* (New York and Oxford, 1987), p. 213.

5. The biographical information presented here is taken from Siti Nadroh, *Wacana Keagamaan & Politik Nurcholish Madjid* (Jakarta, 1999), pp. 21–23. This is a useful introduction to Nurcholish and surveys his intellectual development. It had its origin in a thesis submitted to the IAIN Syarif Hidayatullah under the title *Pandangan Keagamaan NurcholishMadjid dalam perspetif Paham Keagamaan Postmodernism.*

6. This institution has a history dating back to July 1945, involving a number of changes in name and even location, but 1 June 1957 is regarded as the date of its foundation. The authors thank Dr. Salman Harun, currently Dean of the Faculty of Arts, for this information (*Pedoman Akademik IAIN Syarif Hidayatullah* [Jakarta, 2001], pp. 1–6).

7. For a full account of these regional revolts, and the threat they presented to the new republic, see C. van Dijk, *Rebellion Under the Banner of Islam* (The Hague, 1981). See especially on West Java pp. 68–91; South Sulawesi, pp.187–94, and on Aceh, pp. 306–29.

8. Merle C. Ricklefs, *A History of Modern Indonesia since c.1300*, 2nd edn (Basingstoke, 1993), p.197.

9. Ibid., pp. 225–44.

10. A standard work on this catastrophic aftermath of the attempted coup is Robert Cribb, ed., *The Indonesian Killings 1965–66* (Melbourne, 1990).

11. For an account of this, see Johns, 'Indonesia', pp. 202–29.

12. For biodata on Harun Nasution, see Riddell, *Islam*, pp. 231–33.

13. Ibid., pp. 231–37.

14. Nadroh, *Wacana Keagamaan*, p. 25.

15. Quoted by Riddell, *Islam*, p. 239.

16. Nadroh, *Wacana Keagamaan*, p. 25.

17. The clearest overview of his approach to and understanding of the Qur'an is in the seminal work Fazlur Rahman, *Major Themes of the Qur'an* (Chicago and Minneapolis, 1980).

18. An outstanding figure in this search for values is the late Ahmad Wahib; see Anthony H. Johns, 'An Islamic System or Islamic Values', in William R. Roff, ed., *Islam and the Political Economy of Meaning* (London and Sydney, 1987), pp. 254–80.

19. Nurcholish is a prolific author. Riddell, *Islam*, p. 239 refers to English renderings of his work in C. Kurzman, ed., *Liberal Islam: A Sourcebook* (New York, 1998). The authors are grateful to Dr. Eko Alvares, who sent from Jakarta a number of volumes from his personal collection of Nurcholish Madjid's works not otherwise accessible to them.

20. Among them Nasr Hamid Abu Zayd, notably in his article 'Ihdar al-siyaq fi ta'wilat al-khitab al-dini' in *al-Qahira*, 122 (1993), pp. 87–115.

21. Nurcholish Madjid, *Islam Doktrin dan Peradaban* (Jakarta, 1998).

22. Ibid., pp. 243–44.

23. Ira M. Lapidus, *A History of Islamic Societies* (Cambridge, 1990), p. 45.

24. Nurcholis Madjid, *Dialog Keterbukaan Artikulasi Nilai Islam dalam Wacana Social Politik Kontemporer* (Jakarta, 1998), p. 244.

25. Ibid., p. 246.

26. This and all subsequent renderings of the Qur'an are by Anthony H. Johns.

27. Komaruddin Hidayat and Ahmad Gaus, *Passing Over - Melintasi Batas Agama* (Jakarta, 1998), p. xxix.

28. Nadroh, *Wacana Keagamaan*, p. 143. Nurcholish discusses these issues at length in Hidayat and Gaus, *Passing Over*, pp. 5–33.

29. This event occurred on 13 December 1992. A report of an interview with Nurcholish concerning it can be found in Madjid, *Dialog Keterbukaan*, pp. 297–300.

30. Nadroh, *Wacana Keagamaan*, p.50.

31. James T. Siegal, 'Kiblat and the Mediatic Jew', *Indonesia*, 69 (2002), pp. 9–40.

32. Abdullah Yusuf Ali, *The Holy Qur'an* (Lahore, 1985), and Muhammad Asad, *The Message of the Qur'an* (Gibraltar, 1984).

33. Nadroh, *Wacana Keagamaan*, pp. 89–93 quotes extensively from Nurcholish outlining this element in his thinking.

34. Ibid., p. 93.

35. Daniel A. Madigan, *The Qur'an's Self-Image: Writing and Authority in Islam's Scripture* (Princeton and Oxford, 2001), p. 69.

36. Madjid, *Doktrin dan Peradaban*, pp. 466–90.

37. Consider for example the section 'Islam dan Negara, serta Masalah Sekularism' ('Islam and the State and the issue of Secularism'), in ibid., pp. ci–cxxi.

38. We are appreciative of the comments of Greg Fealy (Department of Political and Social Change, RSPAS, the Australian National University) on a draft of this chapter.

BIBLIOGRAPHY

Works by Nurcholish Madjid

——. *Islam Doktrin dan Peradaban*. Jakarta, 1992.

——. *Kaki Langit Peradaban Islam*. Jakarta, 1997.

——. *Dialog Keterbukaan Artikulasi Nilai Islam dalam Wacana Sosial Politik Kontemporer*. Jakarta, 1998.

——. *Pintu-Pintu Menuju Tuhan*. Jakarta, 1999.

——. *Cita-Cita Politik Islam Era Reformasi*. Jakarta, 1999.

Other sources

Abu Zayd, Nasr Hamid. 'Ihdar al-siyaq fi ta'wilat al-khitab al-dini', *al-Qahira*, 122 (1993), pp. 87–115.

Boland, B.J. *The Struggle of Islam in Modern Indonesia*. The Hague, 1971.

Cribb, Robert, ed. *The Indonesian Killings 1965–66*. Melbourne, 1990.

Dijk, C. van. *Rebellion Under the Banner of Islam*. The Hague, 1981.

Hidayat, K. and A. Gaus, eds. *Passing Over–Melintasi Batas Agama*. Jakarta, 1988.

Johns, A.H. 'Indonesia: Islam and Cultural Pluralism', in John L. Esposito, ed., *Islam in Asia: Religion Politics and Society*. New York and Oxford, 1987, pp. 202–29.

——. 'An Islamic System or Islamic Values? Nucleus of a Debate in Contemporary Indonesia', in William R. Roff, ed., *Islam and the Political Economy of Meaning*. London and Sydney, 1987.

Kurzman, C., ed. *Liberal Islam: A Sourcebook*. New York, 1998.

Lapidus, Ira M. *A History of Islamic Societies*. Cambridge, 1988.

Madigan, Daniel A. *The Qur'an's Self-Image: Writing and Authority in Islam's Scripture*. Princeton and Oxford, 2001.

Nadroh, Siti. *Wacana Keagamaan & Politik Nurcholish Madjid*. Jakarta, 1999.

Rahman, Fazlur. *Major Themes of the Qur'an*. Chicago and Minneapolis, 1980.

Ricklefs, Merle C. *A History of Modern Indonesia since c. 1300*. Basingstoke, 2nd edn, 1993.

Riddell, Peter G. *Islam and the Malay–Indonesian World*. London, 2001.

Siegal, James T. 'Kiblat and the Mediatic Jew', *Indonesia*, 69 (2002), pp. 9–40.

4

Amina Wadud's hermeneutics of the Qur'an: women rereading sacred texts

ASMA BARLAS

THE inclusion of Amina Wadud in this book on contemporary Muslim intellectuals and the Qur'an is fitting for several reasons. Firstly, her work conclusively establishes the Qur'anic basis of gender equality in Islam, and thus raises questions about patriarchal (mis)readings of the scripture. This has garnered her not only acclaim, but also criticism from those who have been unsettled by her work. Secondly, Wadud is the only woman in this group, a fact that powerfully illustrates her own achievements in a male-dominated field and her charge that, historically, women have been excluded from Muslim interpretive communities and, consequently, from the field of Qur'anic exegesis, or *tafsir*. This exclusion, she believes, explains why traditional *tafsir* is restrictive to women. Lastly, of the scholars included in this volume, Wadud is the only (African-American/Western) convert to Islam. She thus brings to her engagement with the religion not only a specific consciousness shaped by her identity, but also a spirit of critical inquiry that leads her to raise questions about Islam that people who are born Muslim often do not consider asking. As a result, she is often able to offer fresh insights into the Qur'an's teachings.

Since Wadud is the first to acknowledge that people always read from specific sites and that they always bring specific forms of subjectivity into their readings[1] – reading for her is an interpretive activity while interpretation is always subjective – it is appropriate to begin an analysis of her work by first situating her as a reading subject. This is followed by an overview of the salient features of her thought, analytical framework and methodology, and, finally, her *tafsir* of the Qur'an. Throughout this discussion, the aim is to identify the possibilities inherent in her work for re-theorising sex/gender[2] relationships in Islam in light of the Qur'an's own radically egalitarian ethos and teachings.

'On Belonging as a Muslim Woman'

For Wadud, born in 1952 in Bethesda, Maryland to a compassionate but 'disillusioned' Methodist minister and his young and eventually itinerant wife, the spiritual journey that brought her to Islam began as a search for 'transcendent tranquillity in the midst of storm',[3] conducted in the initial stages under her father's guidance. Of 'storms' Wadud has indeed had many, on account of being born Black in a society based on assumptions of White supremacy, poor in a society that confuses value with material wealth, and female in a society that, in spite of its sexual revolution, continues to objectify and discriminate against women.

Wadud's childhood was short-lived. It was marred by poverty, and her mother's early abandonment of the family and the foreclosure of their family home propelled them into a brief period of homelessness. It is, therefore, understandable why Wadud speaks of this phase of her life as one of displacement, loneliness, and above all, of 'betrayal'. Yet she says that she managed to survive it, albeit only through playing the right sorts of 'games' demanded by social conventions, and at the cost of learning to mask her 'inner' self.

Notwithstanding the lack of intellectual support from her family, Wadud's precocious talent for reading – for creating meanings out of words – sparked her initial interest in education. Bright enough to be placed above the 95th percentile in national tests, she nonetheless did badly in elementary school on account of having internalised the idea that 'learning was not important'.

While her grades improved dramatically at her mostly White high school, her self-worth plummeted proportionally as she discovered what it meant to be 'Black and female in America'.[4] If race is what defined her in the eyes of her White peers, gender is what seems to have defined her in the eyes of her Black ones, especially males, when she joined college. For a while, she sought to fit in with the Black community, at first assuming that it meant 'belong[ing] to a Black man'. However, as she was soon to discover, this form of belonging was not for her.[5]

Wadud came to Islam during her university career but how exactly is unclear; all she will say is that one of the doors into Islam for African-American women is 'Muslim men' and that this door opened for her by accident.[6] This does not mean, however, that she passed through it unthinkingly. Not only was her passage enabled by a religious upbringing that had cultivated in her a yearning to seek the Divine, but equally important is the fact that she came to Islam by asking critical questions of it about the purpose of life and her own role in it. Happily, she found the answers she had been looking for. Of course, as Wadud admits herself, this does not suggest that her questions were answered literally; rather she found in the Qur'an 'a vision of the world, and beyond, with meanings and possibilities for self that lead to certainty'.[7] Since 1972, when she took the *shahada* (the declaration of faith), Wadud has been studying the meanings and possibilities inherent in the Qur'an for the self, in particular, the female self. Some three decades later, she can testify that what she has found in the Qur'an is an overwhelming 'confirmation of women's equality' which is, however, at odds with Muslim practices. This realisation has deepened Wadud's commitment to what she calls the 'gender jihad', a moral struggle that, for her, means retrieving the Qur'an's egalitarianism as a means of challenging and reforming Muslim attitudes towards women.[8]

Wadud's endeavours have been warmly received for the most part, particularly by women, who realise the liberatory potential of her work and hence its significance for their own lives. However, perhaps because of its very ability to dislocate existing notions of gender and, along with these, unequal gender relationships,

Wadud's work also has been sharply criticised. She has found that 'disagreement with the status quo is treated as though it were disagreement with Islam', and while her critics have not branded her a heretic, many have reacted to her work by 'name calling and character assassinations' rather than by offering a 'substantive, critical, or coherent refutation of [its] limitations'. She finds this singularly troubling in light of Islam's call to all believers, both men and women, to seek knowledge. Perhaps 'as a woman, of African origin, and an American convert to Islam, I was not supposed to seek beyond what others hand[ed] down to me', she says candidly, referring to her ostracisation by conservative segments of the Muslim community.[9]

The hardest lesson Wadud has had to learn as a Muslim, then, is that as long as she continues to engage in her gender jihad, there will be no place for her in mainstream Muslim communities. However, rather than being discouraged by this realisation, she has come to appreciate the differences between Islam and Muslims on the one hand, and the rectitude of her own ethical and intellectual choices on the other. She now knows that tranquillity and belonging can only be found in God, and that strength lies in recognising that as God's *khalifa*, or vice-regent on earth, a person 'cannot stand on the sidelines in the face of injustice and still be recognised as fully Muslim'.[10] She has chosen to claim a fully actualised Muslim identity by arguing against the injustice of projecting sexual oppression and inequality into the Qur'an, regardless of the personal cost to herself.

Wadud's career, works, and thought

Wadud completed her Ph.D. in Islamic Studies and Arabic at the University of Michigan in 1988, having previously obtained a Master's degree in Near Eastern Studies at that institution. She also has a B.Sc. in Education from the University of Pennsylvania. Wadud's first appointment after graduating was in the Department of Islamic Revealed Knowledge and Heritage in the International Islamic University in Malaysia, where she taught until 1992. It was here that she became involved with the Sisters in Islam[11] and published several pamphlets underscoring the Qur'an's support for sexual equality. It was also here that she published her seminal work, *Qur'an and Woman,* currently in its fifth printing and second edition, as *Qur'an and Woman: Rereading the Sacred Text from a Woman's Perspective* (the book has to date been translated into Turkish, Persian, and Indonesian). Since returning from Malaysia, Wadud has been teaching in the Department of Philosophy and Religious Studies at the Virginia Commonwealth University (where she is an associate professor), having spent a year in between on a fellowship at the Harvard Divinity School.

Although her writings are extensive, Wadud's scholarship has a common thematic and hermeneutic focus. The theme she has most consistently explored is the Qur'an's conceptualisation of gender and gender relationships, while her hermeneutic focus has been on how best to read the text itself, in particular in order to discover 'a woman's voice' therein. In fact, one of Wadud's most crucial contributions to Muslim religious discourse has been to show the connections between the theoretical and method-ological questions, specifically between Qur'anic exegesis (what we understand the Qur'an to be saying) and the means of its production (who reads the Qur'an, and how). Thus, she has concentrated on examining *'what* the Qur'an says, *how* it says it, *what* is said about the Qur'an, and *who* is doing the saying'. These concerns have been supplemented in recent years by an interest in 'what is left *unsaid:* the ellipses and silences [in the Qur'anic text]'.[12] Thus, instead of confusing the Qur'an with its (patriar-chal) exegesis and viewing certain exegetical practices as sacro-sanct and hence beyond criticism, Wadud has opened up to enquiry both Muslim exegesis of the Qur'an, and the textual strategies used to generate it. Of necessity, this has meant critiquing traditional *tafsir* as the first step in moving beyond it. In that context, she has endeavoured to show, first, that the method Muslims traditionally have employed to read the Qur'an is, by nature, 'atomistic'.[13] As she notes in this context, most exegetes of the classical era (whose methodology and *tafsir* Muslims generally consider canonical), 'begin with the first verse of the first chapter and proceed to the second verse of the first chapter – one verse at a time – until the end of the Book. Little or no effort is made to recognise themes and to discuss the relationship of the Qur'an to itself thematically'. Even when some exegetes do refer to the relationship of two *aya*s (verses) to one another, they do so, she contends, without applying any 'hermeneutical principle' since a method for 'linking similar Qur'anic ideas, syntactical structures, principles, or themes together is almost nonexistent'.[14]

Wadud believes that reading the Qur'an piecemeal and in a decontextualised way not only ignores its internal coherence, or *nazm*,[15] but it also fails to recover the broad principles that underlie its teachings, as Fazlur Rahman[16] also argues. As a result, most exegetes end up generalising specific Qur'anic injunctions, a practice Wadud believes is particularly oppressive to women in that some of the most harmful restrictions against them result 'from interpreting Qur'anic solutions for particular problems as if they were universal principles'.[17] She gives several examples of this, including the example of how exegetes have interpreted the Qur'anic provisions on dress(ing). As she clarifies,

> the Qur'an establishes a universal notion regarding matters of dress and asserts that 'the dress of piety is best'. However, shari'ah (Islamic law) uses the Qur'anic references to particular 7th century Arabian styles of dress as the basis of its legal conclusion regarding modesty. Consequently wearing a particular item of dress (for example, the headcovering) is deemed an appropriate demonstration of modesty.[18]

Universalising the veil, argues Wadud, thus also universalises the 'culturally and economically determined demonstrations of modesty' in seventh-century Arab society, thereby imparting a cultural specificity to the Qur'an's teachings. To her, this actually limits the application of these teachings inasmuch as cultures do not necessarily have identical ideas about modesty. Wadud thus believes that we need to understand that what the Qur'an teaches is the 'principle of modesty ... not the veiling and seclusion which were manifestations particular to [the Arab] context'.[19] After all, she argues, even though the Qur'an offers universal moral guidance, the 'mere fact that [it] was revealed in seventh-century Arabia when the Arabs held certain perceptions and misconceptions about women and were involved in certain specific lewd practices against them resulted in some injunctions specific to that culture'.[20]

Wadud, of course, is not alone in emphasising the relationship between the Qur'an (text) and the circumstances of its revelation (contexts). As Faruq Sherif also notes, many *aya*s 'relate to a particular time and place' and several of the Qur'an's penal provisions were aimed at the conditions of seventh-century Arabia such that it would be 'a lamentable anachronism' to treat them as binding today.[21] Thus, the challenge for every new generation of Muslims is to 'understand the principles intended by the particulars [since the] principles are eternal and can be applied in various social contexts'.[22] In fact, the Qur'an itself 'provides, either explicitly or implicitly, the rationales behind [its] solutions and rulings, from which one *can deduce general principles*'.[23] Yet, historically, exegetes have not attempted to do so in part because of their failure to read the Qur'an as a textual unity, and in part because they do not recognise that, in the Qur'an, content and context possess one another.[24] Wadud, on the other hand, favours reading the Qur'an as a textual whole, while also historicising/contextualising its teachings (see below).

Although conservative Muslims balk at any attempt to contextualise the Qur'an on the grounds that such an approach undermines its universalism by historicising it, this is not really so.[25] For one, the Qur'an itself acknowledges the 'necessarily periodic and contextual nature of its contents'.[26] For another, as Rahman argues, the Qur'an 'occurred in the light of history and against a social-historical background [and is] a response' to it.[27] In fact, it is 'God's response through Muhammad's mind (this latter factor has been radically underplayed by the Islamic orthodoxy) to a historical situation (a factor likewise drastically restricted by the Islamic orthodoxy in a real understanding of the Qur'an)'.[28] As such, 'to make the Qur'an immune from history would be to make its own history irrelevant', and would also impede the process of its 'creative repossession' by later generations of Muslims.[29]

If traditional *tafsir* fails to take the Qur'an historically, as Wadud shows, it also fails to consider the role of language in creating gendered meanings, often in ways not intended by the Qur'an itself. As a speaker of both classical and standard Arabic, she knows that every term 'whether referring to inanimate or animate things, physical or metaphysical realms or dimensions – is expressed in gendered terms'. But how, she asks, can 'ideas that transcend gender be expressed in a gendered language?'[30] For instance, Muslim references to God as 'He' linguistically masculinise God even although, as Wadud argues, language cannot express 'what cannot be uttered in language', and even though the Qur'an expressly forbids using similitudes for God.[31] At the very least, therefore, she says, Muslims should realise that language about God 'cannot be interpreted empirically and literally'.[32] (As scholars argue in other contexts, masculinising God also underwrites theories of male privilege in religious patriarchies in so far as it allows men to posit a false affinity between themselves and God.)[33]

Wadud's third criticism of traditional *tafsir* thus has to do with how the Qur'an's teachings are reframed through the lens of sex/gender, both in terms of *how* we interpret its language about sex/gender (see below), and in terms of *who* interprets it. The fact that historically men have interpreted the Qur'an, she believes, explains both the masculinist nature of *tafsir* and its anti-woman bias. As she notes, missing from the 'basic paradigms through which we examine and discuss the Qur'an and Qur'anic interpretation', are women and their experiences, which either have been excluded, or interpreted 'through the male vision, perspective, desire, or needs'.[34] This tendency, of course, is not specific to Muslims since men have interpreted the foundational texts of all religions; nor is it hard to explain given that the Qur'an 'happens against a long background of patriarchal precedent'.[35] Nevertheless, the gaps that result in *tafsir* from excluding women's voices cannot be overcome by resorting to the 'rhetoric of equality in Islam', counters Wadud.[36] Moreover, silencing women's voices not only prevents them, but also the men, from developing a 'holistic understanding of what it means to be Muslim',[37] thereby keeping both from experiencing the full breadth of 'Islamic potentiality' since it allows only men to 'determine legitimacy'.[38] As she points out, just as 'women and men are equal in Islam, so are they distinct from one another'; hence their experiences also are distinct. Yet, this unique experiential component is missing from *tafsir* because men have usurped the right to 'tell women how to be women! Men have evaluated what it means to be Muslim not only for the Muslim male but also for the Muslim female'.[39] While Muslims generally do not protest this practice, Wadud can find no justification for it in the Qur'an or the traditions (hadith) of the Prophet's life and praxis. On the contrary, she argues, not only does silencing women's voices and treating them as taboo, or '*awra*, violate their own dignity as human beings, but it also undermines the Qur'an's designation of men and women equally as God's *khalifa*. As she clarifies, the purpose of

> human creation was revealed when God said, 'Verily, I am going to create a *khalifah* (caretaker, viceregent, or trustee) on the earth' [Q. 2: 38]. *Khilafah* (trusteeship) on the planet is the responsibility of each human. In the Qur'anic worldview, fulfillment of this trust constitutes the *raison d'être* of human existence. [Hence, to] deny full personhood to women is to deny them the full capacity of *khilafah* and to thwart the possibility of their fulfilling the basic responsibility decreed by God for all of humankind.[40]

Given this Qur'anic view of human creation and agency, how – asks Wadud[41] – can the 'Islamic intellectual ethos develop without giving clear and resounding attention to the female voice, both as a part of the text and in response to it?' [42]

Wadud's critique of traditional *tafsir* is meant not only to reveal the flaws in patriarchal readings of the Qur'an, but also to get Muslims to realise what is at stake in rethinking their textual strategies, in devising new interpretive methods, and in including women in the processes of knowledge creation. She believes this will not only allow the women to develop a more authentic Muslim identity, but also will reflect 'new levels of understanding and human participation' in religious life.[43] She remains hopeful that, as Muslims come to appreciate the need continually to reread the Qur'an – after all, a 'key hypothesis of hermeneutical philosophy is that interpretation is an open process which no single vision can conclude'[44] – they also will come to accept a more egalitarian *tafsir* and certainly one that is inclusive of women's voices.

Towards a hermeneutics of equality

What might such a *tafsir* entail? Even more significantly – given that the content of knowledge is never independent of the methods by which it is produced – what kind of a hermeneutic approach might generate it? Before considering Wadud's *tafsir*, therefore, it would be useful to examine her conceptual and methodological framework more closely.

Wadud begins her critique of traditional *tafsir*, as well as her own exegesis of the Qur'an, by clarifying that what 'proceeds from the text … in the name of *tafsir*, is not one and the same as the divine will'.[45] This distinction between 'divine speech and its earthly realisation'[46] is an old one in Muslim theology and one that the Qur'an also makes.[47] Yet, over the course of time, Muslim interpretive communities have come to see their own *tafsir*, hence their own interpretive authority, as being on a par with revelation. For example, the Hanafi legal school – which trains its adherents in the time-honoured method of reading '"backward" through the scholarship of previous generations in an attempt to ensure "continuity with the past"' – holds that 'the authority of the practice defined by later generations [is equivalent to] the authority of revelation'.[48] While equating their own authority with that of revelation allows legal and interpretive schools to claim legitimacy, it also collapses divine discourse with its human interpretations, thus permitting the displacement of biases onto the Divine. This confusion of the Qur'an with its *tafsir* also discourages new readings of the Qur'an since it allows interpretive communities to misrepresent critiques of *tafsir* as critiques of the Qur'an and to marginalise new readings in the name of adhering to a religiously sanctioned tradition. They then are able to protect not only their own hegemony, but also the hegemony of the religious knowledge (on which they draw) produced by a small number of male scholars in the early years of Islam. While not all these scholars were misogynists of course, the sexual ethos of the times in which they wrote (the Middle Ages) was, and they could not but be influenced by it to varying degrees.[49] This is why Wadud's distinction between God's Speech and human renditions of it is so crucial.

If adhering to this distinction marks Wadud as a traditionalist, it also allows her to embrace the modern hermeneutic insight that reading is subjective and incomplete, a fact Muslims overlook when it comes to traditional *tafsir*. This view allows her to free the Qur'an of its (anti-women) misreadings while also permitting her to argue in favour of some readings and against others. Thus, recognising the role of subjectivity in reading does not keep Wadud from arguing that some interpretations are in fact better than others. This is not a contradictory position in that the Qur'an itself recommends reading it for its best meanings (and also specifies some principles for doing so),[50] establishing both that it is open to multiple readings and that not all readings may be equally good. Hermeneutics as a discipline also rests on the premise that while 'multiple readings are not per se mutually exclusive, not all interpretations are thereby equal'.[51] Belief in textual polysemy thus does not render one a moral relativist; nor does embracing monosemy (the idea that there is only one correct reading of a text) signify great virtue.

Secondly, although Wadud does not put it in these terms, she reads the Qur'an as both a 'historically situated'[52] text and as a 'complex hermeneutic totality'.[53] That is, she explains the Qur'an's teachings in terms of the social and historical contexts Islam sought to reform and also in terms of the linguistic, grammatical, and syntactical structures of the text itself. Although, as noted, conservatives reject a 'historicising understanding' of the Qur'an,[54] many contemporary Muslim scholars argue in favour of it. Mahmud Mohamed Taha, for instance, held that such an approach was essential for deriving general principles from the Qur'an. The difference is that Taha held that the distinction between the universal and the particular was built into revelation itself, specifically, into its historical periodisation into two phases:

the Meccan and the Medinan. To him, the Meccan *sura*s embodied the more universal and egalitarian aspects of Islam's message, and the Medinan its more specific and restrictive one (since according to him the Medinans were not ready to live by the higher ideals encoded in the Meccan *sura*s). And yet, Muslim jurists, who believed that the Meccan *sura*s had been abrogated by the Medinan, drew on the latter in drafting the shari'a (law). The solution as Taha saw it, therefore, was to shift some aspects of the shari'a 'from one class of texts [the Medinan] to another [the Meccan, by] examining the rationale of abrogation' itself. In effect, what was needed, argued Taha, was a second message of Islam generated by means of new critical reasoning, or *ijtihad*.[55]

However, while Wadud also favours *ijtihad*, she rejects the tendency, as Rahman puts it, to view the 'career of the Prophet and the Qur'an in two neatly discrete and separate "periods" – the Medinan and the Meccan – to which most modern scholars have become addicted'.[56] Instead, she regards revelation as being both historically and textually continuous. Further, as she notes, not all the Meccan *sura*s are universal in nature, or the Medinan specific. To her, the indecidability of the universal and the particular can be resolved only *hermeneutically*, by means of a 'model which derives basic ethical principles for further developments and legal considerations by giving precedence to general statements rather than particulars'.[57] If this seems like a contradictory view – given Wadud's emphasis on the need to historicise the Qur'an – it is not, since she rejects a historicist approach to it as implicit, for instance, in a certain interpretation of the concept of the *asbab al-nuzul*. Although exegetes translate this term as 'reason(s) for revealing (a particular verse or verses)', she says, the more accurate rendition is 'occasions upon which (or, sometimes, because of which) a certain verse was revealed'. This is a crucial distinction because it 'broadens the application of underlying principles' in the Qur'an inasmuch as viewing certain events as the 'reason for' a verse undermines the doctrine of the Qur'an's trans-historicity and turns it into 'a history book in the limited sense of a record of events'. To Wadud, the aim of recalling the historical contexts of the revelation of an *aya* is to understand the context itself and not to imply 'a restriction of the Qur'anic principles to that context'.[58]

Wadud's position thus is a complex one. On the one hand, she holds that Muslims need to contextualise (historicise) the Qur'an in order to recontextualise it, suggesting that, to her (and to Rahman, on whose work she draws), what makes revelation pertinent to humans is its location *within* history. At the same time, and on the other hand, however, she also refuses to treat the Qur'an as a record *of* history. As she states, the Qur'an is a 'moral history' whose purposes are 'extrahistorical and transcendental' such that their location in time does not exhaust their impact or meaning. Indeed, she believes that it is the Qur'an's goal of providing 'universal guidance' that accounts for the brevity of 'historical details' in it. As such, 'if the reader assumes he is reading a record, what he reads may be insignificant to his own life'. But if readers understand that the historical details, of which the 'Qur'an gives just enough – but not too [many]', are meant to illuminate universal precepts, then they can see its relevance to their own lives.[59]

If the idea of a text's historical situatedness is essential to Wadud's reading of the Qur'an, so too is her view of the text itself as a 'cumulative, holistic process' rather than as 'a linear succession of sentences'.[60] Respect for the Qur'an's textual holism thus leads her to read it intratextually, that is to interpret the Qur'an by the Qur'an, *tafsir al-Qur'an bi al-Qur'an* – a method the Qur'an itself recommends[61] and one that exegetes also have favoured historically. However, as Wadud points out, not only do intratextual approaches to the Qur'an remain 'rare', but not all intratextual readings of it are in fact holistic.[62] Instead, this method is often 'reduced to using a single term or verse to interpret another term or verse' rather than to determine the 'Qur'anic ethos or spirit'. Wadud believes that such narrow literalism not only serves no hermeneutic purpose, but that it undermines the Qur'an's ethos, and she draws on historical precedent to argue against it. She recalls that following a war campaign, the second Caliph, 'Umar ibn al-Khattab, refused to take 'the booty explicitly prescribed in the Qur'an, citing that to do so would violate the spirit of the Qur'an in the existing situation of hardship'. As she says, if anyone were to depart from the Qur'an's letter in order to adhere to its spirit today, they 'would be considered a heretic', and she believes this is because Muslims 'lack faith in the possibility that the Qur'anic whole could yield something greater than its parts'.[63] Wadud's own reading of the Qur'an, then, is meant to arrive at an understanding of its ethos and spirit and not merely its letter.

That Wadud regards the Qur'an as the 'primary arbiter'[64] of its own meanings, confirms that she views revelation as being self-sufficient. Although this doctrine is rooted in Muslim tradition, she nonetheless has been criticised by those who interpret the Qur'an by way of the Prophet's Sunna or praxis, and therefore by way of secondary religious texts like the hadith (which record the Sunna). The criticism has been severe enough to elicit a defence from her in the second edition of her book. She clarifies that, unlike the hadith, the Qur'an is inerrant, that she cannot believe that the Prophet would have removed its stipulation of 'equality between women and men', and that even if she were faced with contrary evidence, she 'would choose in favor of the Qur'an' because it is of 'greater significance'.[65]

Although Wadud also adheres to the doctrine of the Qur'an's invariability, she believes that our understanding of its teachings can, and indeed must, remain subject to change. As she argues, what changes in its readings is not the Qur'an itself, but how it is understood within and by a community, and – like other modern scholars – she views this changing understanding as a function of how Muslims engage the text itself, specifically, of the kinds of questions they ask of it. Referring to the disciplines generated by *tafsir,* she argues that 'they satisfied particular needs or answered particular questions that had arisen' at a particular point in time. However, 'certain questions did not arise. Consequently, the answers to these were not sought out. Obviously, the answers to these were not found'.[66] The implication is that Muslims also have not asked certain questions of the Qur'an thus far, in particular about its position on equality and gender – perhaps because the need to do so has not arisen, or perhaps because they have not risen to the level of the Qur'an. As such, they also have not found answers to some questions. In this way Wadud not only justifies her own rereading of the Qur'an, but she also leaves open the possibility for Muslims continually to ask new questions of it, a practice that is integral to all interpretive processes but which conservative Muslims regard with distrust.

However, many Muslim scholars now admit that our understanding of the Qur'an depends on our faculties and methodologies and must therefore always be a changing and incomplete one. For instance, Abdolkarim Soroush also holds that while 'the last religion is already here … the last understanding of religion has not yet arrived'.[67] As he argues, Islam may be complete and perfect but our knowledge of it is not. Indeed, religious knowledge 'as a branch of human knowledge [is bound to be] incomplete, impure, insufficient and culture-bound'.[68] This is why 'revivalists' periodically need to rehabilitate religious thought, correct misreadings, and redirect 'religion towards its essence'.[69] However, in spite of his support for such processes Soroush does not examine women's role in them, while Wadud regards it as being crucial inasmuch as gender is 'a category of thought' and not just a subject of discourse.[70] She thus sees as one of her own tasks 'to articulate ways of reading for gender and then to advocate how such a reading is central to comprehensive Qur'anic analysis'.[71]

Wadud's concern with sex/gender manifests itself at two levels. At the first level, as noted, she argues in favour of including women in interpretive processes on the grounds that the Qur'an advocates sexual equality, that only women can represent themselves, and that their participation is essential for developing a holistic knowledge of Islam. At the second level, she emphasises the need to examine the Qur'an's language, especially in view of the absence of a neuter in Arabic. As she says, while this means that every word is 'designated as masculine or feminine, it does not follow that each use of masculine or feminine persons is necessarily restricted to the mentioned gender'. To her, therefore, it is only possible to discover the Qur'an's meanings accurately by studying the 'language act, syntactical structures, and

textual context' in which a specific term is used, both the immediate contexts of its usage and also its 'larger textual development'.[72]

In sum, Wadud reads the Qur'an as a discursive unity and in
terms of its own truth claims, paying attention to both the historical contexts of its teachings as well as to its linguistic and syntactical structures. Underlying these conceptual and methodological
principles is an ethical and moral concern that Muslims learn to
read the Qur'an for its best meanings, even though she does not
frame it in these terms. Wadud herself chooses to do so in order
both to claim a fully authentic Muslim identity and also 'to challenge the arrogance of those men' who, while demanding respect
and dignity for themselves deny it to women simply because they
are women. She particularly rejects 'the false justification of such
arrogance through narrow interpretations or misinterpretations
of the Qur'anic text, namely interpretations which ignore the
basic social principles of justice, equality, and common humanity'
that the Qur'an teaches.[73] As she notes, rather than being
elevated by the Qur'an, many interpreters bring it 'down to their
level when they project [into it] narrow or negative meanings
which suit their individual whims, perceptions, and prejudices
about women. This is most often done on the basis of a single
word! Some of these words do not even exist in the text'.[74]
Unfortunately, such tendencies have fostered a 'witch-hunting
mentality' among Muslims that 'looks for "inherent" evil in
woman, and then justifies constraints on her every move'.[75]
Wadud finds this execrable not only because the Qur'an rejects
such notions, but because it commands respect and equality
between the sexes. Had Muslims learned to extend such Qur'anic
principles to their lives, she observes, they could 'have evolved
into leading examples of humane and just social systems'.[76]
Perhaps, in the end, it is this ethical vision – that justice, equality,
and dignity are the God-given right of every human being – that
most clearly sets apart Wadud's hermeneutics from those of many
other scholars.

'Rereading the Sacred Text from a Woman's Perspective'

If one half of Wadud's project is to lay 'the groundwork for non-traditional *tafsir* from a scripturally legitimate perspective',[77] the other half of it is to offer an egalitarian exegesis of the Qur'an itself. (In view of the complexity of her *tafsir* and also constraints of space, it is only possible to consider it in broad outline here.)

At the core of Wadud's reading of the Qur'an is the claim that it does not teach the concept of male ontological superiority and of female inferiority or subordination to men. Contrary to what most Muslims claim, she argues, the Qur'an does not teach that there are '*essential* distinctions between men and women reflected in creation, capacity and function in society, accessibility to guidance (particularly to Qur'anic guidance), and in the rewards due to them in the Hereafter'.[78] Nor, remarkably – given the rigidity of gender roles in Muslim societies – does the Qur'an 'propose or support a singular role or single definition of a set of roles, exclusively for each gender across every culture'.[79] Specifying such roles, she believes, would have reduced it 'from a universal text to a culturally specific text – a claim that many have erroneously made'.[80] In fact, Wadud believes that the Qur'an itself overcomes 'gender distinction ... in order to fulfill its intention of universal guidance'.

In this context, Wadud's most profound insight is that the Qur'an does not use the category of sex/gender to differentiate between humans, much less to discriminate against women. Indeed, there is no '*concept* of woman' or of 'gendered man' in the Qur'an.[81] Hence, while the Qur'an recognises 'anatomical' (sexual/ biological) differences, it does not endow these differences, or sex itself, with symbolic meaning (it does not confuse sex with gender, as this author has argued elsewhere).[82] However, if sex/gender is not a meaningful category in the Qur'an, then the Qur'an cannot advocate sex/gender differentiation, and if it does not advocate sex/gender differentiation, then the Qur'an also cannot sanction sex/gender hierarchies or inequalities, inasmuch as such hierarchies and inequalities presuppose the idea of sexual differentiation.[83]

113

In fact, not only does the Qur'an *not* teach a theory of sexual differentiation, it actually teaches the idea of the ontological equality of the sexes. As both Wadud's reading and that of Riffat Hassan shows, in Islam, women and men are related to one another ontologically and this relationship is based on equality and not on differentiation or hierarchy. Thus, for instance, the Qur'an does not teach that women and men were created from different substances, or that woman was created from man, or even that woman was created *after* man,[84] which are claims that religious patriarchies make in justifying sexual hierarchy /inequality. Rather, as Wadud and Hassan, and other scholars, point out, the Qur'an teaches that humans originated in a single self, or *nafs,* and are endowed with the same nature, capacities, and abilities. Not only does the Qur'an not 'state that Allah began the creation of humankind with the *nafs* of Adam, the man', argues Wadud, but by using words like *nafs* and *zawj* (spouse) in its account of creation [Q. 4: 1], it confirms that 'the original parents [are] irrevocably and primordially linked; thus, the two are equally essential' and essentially similar. Hence, even though God created humans 'in the male/female pair', the Qur'an 'does not attribute explicit characteristics to either one or the other, exclusively'.[85] Nor, for instance, does it assign the responsibility for the expulsion of this pair from Paradise to the woman, a claim made to justify representations of women as naturally lax and given to sin. Instead, 'with one exception, the Qur'an always uses the Arabic dual form to tell how Satan tempted both Adam and Eve[86] and how they both disobeyed [God]'.[87] Hence, even though Muslims represent man as the norm and woman as 'less than men', the Qur'an itself never alludes to them in this way.[88] The only basis on which it distinguishes between humans is on the basis of their moral personality – their ability, that is, to acquire *taqwa,* or God-consciousness – and it is in terms of their moral praxis that individuals will be judged and recompensed in the Hereafter. What matters in and to the Qur'an, then, is not sex/gender, but an individual's 'faith and deeds'.[89]

Although conservative Muslims reject any exegesis that claims simultaneity of creation – since that irrevocably undermines theories of male ontological superiority – they readily admit that in the realms of faith and worship (*'ibada*), men and women are equal. However, they argue that in the legal and social realms they are not, a claim that is tantamount to asserting that even though women and men are equal before God, they are not so in the sight of men. Such ideas derive in part from those *ayas* in the Qur'an that are read as stating that God has preferred (*faddala*) men to women, given them a degree (*daraja*) over women, and made them women's guardians (*qawwamun 'ala*). They also derive from assuming that the Qur'an's different treatment of women and men with regard to such issues as polygyny, evidence-giving, inheritance, and so on, establishes their inherent inequality.[90] Wadud, however, undermines such claims with a contextualised reading of the relevant *ayas*. She shows, for instance, that the 'degree' refers to a husband's rights in a divorce and not to male ontological superiority, or to men's rights in general, that the 'preference' refers to (some) men's greater share in inheritance (determined by their greater financial responsibilities vis-à-vis women) and not to the idea that God prefers men because they are biologically males, and the term *qawwamun 'ala* to the husband's role as a breadwinner (that is, his obligation to provide for his household) and not to the idea of men's guardianship or rulership over women.[91]

In much the same way, Wadud also challenges customary *tafsir* of other *ayas* that are read as establishing men's dominion over women, including the crucial *aya*, Q. 4: 34, interpreted as mandating a wife's obedience (*qanitat*) to her husband and giving the latter the right to beat (*daraba*) disobedient (*nushuz*) wives. On her reading, however, *qanitat* refers to a moral attitude of obedience on the part of both women and men to God, *nushuz* to a state of marital discord and not to a wife's disloyalty, and *daraba* to a restriction on spousal abuse, not a license for it. Similarly, with respect to polygyny [Q. 4: 3] – which also is seen as a sign of male privilege and superiority – Wadud points out that the Qur'anic reference to the practice occurs in the context of a discussion about the just 'treatment of orphans' and is contingent on a man's ability to deal justly with more than one wife. In effect, the *aya* is 'concerned with *justice*: dealing justly, managing funds justly, justice to the orphans, and justice to the wives, etc.'.[92] At no point does the Qur'an recommend polygyny as a way to deal with a wife's inability to conceive, or to pander to male sexual needs, or as a right for those men who can afford to have multiple wives, all reasons that Muslims use in justifying polygyny. Wadud similarly contests *tafsir* of Qur'an 2: 282 which counsels taking two women instead of one man as witnesses, thus establishing a 'two-for-one formula' (the idea that two women equal one man). If this were the Qur'an's intent, she argues, 'four female witnesses could replace two male witnesses. Yet, the Qur'an does not provide for this alternative'.[93] Furthermore, she argues, this two-for-one formula also has been 'reinforced through oversimplification of the Qur'anic discussion regarding inheritance' which is interpreted as always giving a woman half the share of a man. But, as she clarifies, 'if there is one female child, her share is half the inheritance' and the principle that women get half of what men do 'is not the sole mode of property division, but *one* of several proportional arrangements possible'.[94] Finally, Wadud also rereads the Qur'an's provisions for divorce and shows them to be protective of women's rights. The *tafsir* of each *aya* involves a careful reading of language, grammar, and syntax and as well as an analysis of its historical contexts so as to help readers understand the logic of the Qur'an's teachings and also the universal precepts they seek to convey, even by means of 'particulars'.

Although the purpose of Wadud's *tafsir* is to establish the scriptural basis of sexual equality in Islam, she reminds her readers that there are many different meanings of 'equal' and 'equality'. She rejects those theories of equality that imply that women and men are the same. However, she also rejects those theories that view women and men as being unequal because they are biologically different. As she continually emphasises, the Qur'an does not locate human creation, agency, morality, or individuality in sex, and, to the contrary, affirms the equal humanity of women and men, in addition to advocating mutual love, honour, and guardianship between them. It is these principles – embodied in the totality of its teachings – that Wadud believes continue to make the Qur'an so relevant to Muslim women's (and men's) lives today. As she states, the Qur'an can guide us 'in whatever era, *if* the Qur'anic interpretation continues to be rendered by each generation in a manner which reflects its whole intent'.[95]

Conclusion

Increasing numbers of Muslims around the world have begun to realise that the privileges accruing to men in Muslim societies are a function not of the Qur'an's support for sexual inequality, but of the power that men enjoy in actually existing patriarchies, which Islam has had no hand in creating and which, in fact, it censures in different ways.[96] Muslim women thus also are gradually coming to accept that they do not need to reconcile their own oppression with the edicts of their faith because discrimination is not divinely ordained. On the contrary, as Wadud's work demonstrates, the denial of autonomy and equality to women subverts the Qur'an's intent of 'full equality'.[97]

As other Muslim women scholars – notably Leila Ahmed and Fatima Mernissi – also have shown, the persistence of sexual inequality and misogyny in Muslim societies has more to do with political, social, cultural, and historical factors than with religious. However, even though sexism and misogyny exist in all societies, and not simply those that are religious, and even though Muslims are not the only people who discriminate against women, one of the most powerful ideological sources of oppression in Muslim societies today is religious knowledge, or, more accurately, knowledge about religion. Thus, it is in their capacity as 'official interpreters of divine will'[98] that men have been able so profoundly to influence Muslim attitudes and practices towards women. That may be why Muslim women scholars are becoming increasingly interested in Qur'anic hermeneutics (Azizah al-Hibri and Riffat Hassan being among the better known). Even those scholars, like Ahmed, who do not themselves focus on reading the Qur'an, underscore the need for women to do so in view of the fact that different readings of the same (religious) text can yield fundamentally different understandings of Islam.

117

Amina Wadud remains a pioneer in this field, and the most influential. Her work, of which this essay has provided only an indicative account, goes the farthest both in challenging oppressive readings of the Qur'an and in showing the relevance of a Qur'anic hermeneutics to the project of Muslim women's emancipation. Of course, whether or not Muslims take up the challenge to retheorise their understanding of sexual equality and relationships in light of her *tafsir* remains open to question. So far, as noted and as should be expected, she has attracted both acclaim and criticism. However, if she has succeeded in anything, it is in showing that the responsibility for misreading the Qur'an in oppressive and anti-women modes lies with its readers, not with the text itself. Even those who excoriate her reading can no longer find easy refuge for their own sexism in the Qur'an after she has shown us in such caring and promising detail the possibilities inherent in it for a truly liberatory view of human equality and dignity.

NOTES

1. I depart from Wadud in not putting 'reading' in one category and 'exegesis' in another. She seems to hold that while reading is shaped by pre-understanding and hence is subjective, exegesis relies on 'scientific' methodologies and is objective. But, her own work shows that this is not always so. Also, by her own admission, 'no exegete is able to remove the significance of the personal reading and the force of the prior text from interpretation'. I thus use the words reading/interpretation and exegesis/*tafsir* interchangeably. Amina Wadud, *Qur'an and Woman: Rereading the Sacred Text from a Woman's Perspective* (New York, 1999), p. 94.

2. Although sex (biology) is distinct from gender (its social constructions), I use the term sex/gender to indicate the close relationship between them and because it is not always clear that Wadud means only gender when she uses that term, since a great deal of her argument also is about sex (biology). For a discussion of the Qur'an's position on sex/gender as I understand it, see Asma Barlas, *'Believing Women' in Islam: Unreading Patriarchal Interpretations of the Qur'an* (Austin, TX, 2002).

3. Amina Wadud, 'On Belonging as a Muslim Woman,' in Gloria Wade-Gayles, ed., *My Soul is a Witness: African-American Women's Spirituality* (Boston, 1995), p. 253.

4. Wadud, 'On Belonging', p. 258.

5. Ibid., p. 260.

6. Ibid., p. 263.

7. Ibid., p. 265.

8. Wadud, *Qur'an and Woman*, p. x.

9. Ibid., p. xviii.

10. Ibid., p. xix.

11. Sisters in Islam (SIS) 'is a group of Muslim professional women committed to promoting the rights of women within the framework of Islam. Our efforts to promote the rights of Muslim women are based on the principles of equality, justice and freedom enjoined by the Qur'an as made evident during our study of the holy text.' See http://www.sisters inislam.org.my/

12. Wadud, *Qur'an and Woman*, p. xiii; her emphases.

13. Mustansir Mir, *Coherence in the Quran: A Study of Islahi's Concept of Nazm in Tadabbur-i-Quran* (Plainfield, IN, 1986).

14. Wadud, *Qur'an and Woman*, p. 2.

15. Mir, *Coherence in the Quran*.

16. Fazlur Rahman, *Islam and Modernity: Transformation of an Intellectual Tradition* (Chicago, 1982).

17. Wadud, *Qur'an and Woman*, p. 99.

18. Amina Wadud, 'Towards a Qur'anic Hermeneutics of Social Justice: Race, Class and Gender', *Journal of Law and Religion*, 7, 1 (1995–96), p. 44.

19. Wadud, *Qur'an and Woman*, p. 10.

20. Ibid., p. 9.

21. Faruq Sherif, *A Guide to the Contents of the Qur'an* (London, 1985), pp. 3–4.

22. Wadud, *Qur'an and Woman*, p. 9.

23. Rahman, *Islam and Modernity*, p. 20; his emphasis.

24. Kenneth Cragg, *The Event of the Quran: Islam in its Scripture* (Oxford, 1994), p. 116.

25. I discuss the conservative position at length in *'Believing Women'*.

26. Cragg, *The Event of the Quran*, p. 115.

27. Rahman, *Islam and Modernity*, p. 5.

28. Ibid., p. 8.

29. Cragg, *The Event of the Quran*, pp. 114, 123.

30. Wadud, *Qur'an and Woman*, p. xii.

31. Qur'an 16: 74 in Abdullah Yusuf Ali, *The Holy Quran: Text, Translation and Commentary* (New York, 1988), p. 676.

32. Wadud, *Qur'an and Woman*, p. 11.

33. See, for instance, C. Bynum, S. Harrell and P. Richman, eds., *Gender and Religion: On the Complexity of Symbol* (Boston, 1986).

34. Wadud, *Qur'an and Woman*, p. 2.

35. Cragg, *The Event of the Quran*, p. 14.

36. Amina Wadud, 'Alternative Qur'anic Interpretation and the Status of Women', in Gisela Webb, ed., *Windows of Faith: Muslim Women Scholar-Activists in North America* (Syracuse, NY, 2000), p. 13.

37. Ibid., p. 19.

38. Ibid., pp. 14, 19.

39. Ibid., p. 18.

40. Ibid., p. 48.

41. Wadud, *Qur'an and Woman*, p. x.

42. Wadud does not fully explain, or perhaps I do not fully understand, what she means by 'part of the text' inasmuch as the Qur'an is not a dual-gendered text, i.e. it does not have female and male voices in it since it was not written by humans. It does seem to be the case, of course, that women and men tend to read it differently.

43. Wadud, 'Alternative Qur'anic Interpretation', p. 4.

44. Paul Ricoeur, *Hermeneutics and the Human Sciences: Essays on Language, Action and Interpretation*, trans. John B. Thompson (Cambridge, 1981), p. 109.

45. Wadud, 'Alternative Qur'anic Interpretation', p. 11.

46. Josef van Ess, 'Verbal Inspiration? Language and Revelation in Classical Islamic Theology' in Stefan Wild, ed., *The Quran as Text* (Leiden, 1996), p. 189.

47. I discuss the Qur'an's auto-hermeneutics in '*Believing Women*'. My argument is that the concept of God's Unity, *tawhid*, suggests that we need to interpret God's Speech (the Qur'an) in light of what we know about God (Divine Ontology). Since what we know about God derives from how God describes God (the nature of Divine Self-Disclosure) in the Qur'an, we must begin an exegesis of the Qur'an by examining the nature of God's Self-Disclosure in it. I argue that this Self-Disclosure militates against reading the Qur'an as a patriarchal text, as do the methodological principles that the Qur'an specifies for its own reading.

48. Brandon Wheeler, *Applying the Canon in Islam: The Authorization and Maintenance of Interpretive Reasoning in Hanafi Scholarship* (Albany, NY, 1996), pp. 14, 88, 239.

49. See, for instance, Leila Ahmed, *Women and Gender in Islam: The Historical Roots of a Modern Debate* (Connecticut, 1992), and Barbara Stowasser, *Women in the Quran: Traditions and Interpretation* (New York, 1994).

50. See ibid.

51. Trible in Gerald O. West, ed., *Biblical Hermeneutics of Liberation: Modes of Reading the Bible in the South African Context* (Pietermaritzburg, South Africa, 1995), p. 149.

52. I borrow this term from Nicholas Wolterstorff who uses it in another context. Nicholas Wolterstorff, *Divine Discourse: Philosophical Reflections on the Claim that God Speaks* (Cambridge, 1995).

53. This is from a reference to the Bible, but is no less applicable to the Qur'an or other sacred texts. C. Boff, 'Hermeneutics: Constitution of Theological Pertinency', in R.S. Sugirtharajah, ed., *Voices from the Margin: Interpreting the Bible in the Third World* (New York, 1991), p. 34.

54. Abdelwahab Bouhdiba, *Sexuality in Islam*, trans. Alan Sheridan (London, 1985), p. 3.

55. Mahmud Mohamed Taha, *The Second Message of Islam* (Syracuse, NY, 1987), pp. 23–24.

56. Fazlur Rahman, *Major Themes of the Quran* (Minneapolis, MN, 1980), p. 133.

57. Wadud, *Qur'an and Woman*, p. 30.

58. Ibid., pp. 30–31.

59. Ibid., p. 30.

60. This is Paul Ricoeur's definition of a text. *Hermeneutics and Human Sciences*, p. 212.

61. See '*Believing Women*'.

62. Wadud, 'Alternative Qur'anic Interpretation', p. 44.

63. Ibid., p. 43.

64. Mustansir Mir, 'The Sura as a Unity: A Twentieth Century Development in Quran Exegesis', in G.R. Hawting and Abdul-Kader A. Shareef, eds, *Approaches to the Qur'an* (New York, 1993), p. 218.

65. Wadud, *Qur'an and Woman*, pp. xvii–xviii.

66. Ibid., pp. xx–xxi.

67. Abdolkarim Soroush, *Reason, Freedom, and Democracy in Islam: Essential Writings of 'Abdolkarim Soroush*, ed. and tr., Mahmoud Sadri and Ahmad Sadri (Oxford, 2000), p. 37.

68. Ibid., p. 32.

69. Ibid., p. 86.

70. Wadud, *Qur'an and Woman*, p. xi.

71. Ibid., p. xiv.

72. Ibid., p. xiii.

73. Ibid., p. 96.

74. Ibid., p. 97.

75. Ibid., p. 99.

76. Ibid., p. 101.

77. Vincent J. Cornell, 'The Qur'an as Scripture,' *The Oxford Encyclopedia of the Modern Islamic World*, ed. John L. Esposito (New York, 1995), vol. 3, p. 392.

78. Wadud, *Qur'an and Woman*, p. 7; her emphasis.

79. Ibid., p. 8.

80. Ibid., p. 9.

81. Ibid., p. xxi; her emphasis.

82. Ibid., loc. cit.

83. See, for instance, Thomas Laqueur, *Making Sex: Body and Gender from the Greeks to Freud* (Boston, 1990); and Marshall Sahlins, *The Use and Abuse of Biology: An Anthropological Critique of Sociobiology* (Ann Arbor, MI, 1976).

84. Riffat Hassan, 'An Islamic Perspective', in Karen Lebacqz, ed., *Sexuality: A Reader* (Cleveland, 1999), p. 342.

85. Wadud, *Qur'an and Woman*, pp. 20, 21.

86. For the record, of course, the Qur'an does not use the name 'Eve' for Adam's spouse.

87. Wadud, *Qur'an and Woman*, pp. 24–25.

88. Ibid., p. 35.

89. Ibid., p. 58.

90. For a critique of the confusion of difference with inequality, see '*Believing Women*'.

91. Wadud, *Qur'an and Woman*, pp. 66–74.

92. Ibid., p. 83; her emphasis.

93. Ibid., p. 86.

94. Ibid., p. 87; her emphasis.
95. Ibid., p. 104; her emphasis.
96. See '*Believing Women*'.
97. Wadud, 'Alternative Qur'anic Interpretation', p. 47.
98. Ibid., p. 47.

BIBLIOGRAPHY

Works by Amina Wadud

——. 'Alternative Qur'anic Interpretation and the Status of Women', in Gisela Webb, ed., *Windows of Faith: Muslim Women Scholar-Activists in North America*. Syracuse, NY, 2000.

——. *Qur'an and Woman: Rereading the Sacred Text from a Woman's Perspective*. New York, 1999.

——. 'Towards a Qur'anic Hermeneutics of Social Justice: Race, Class and Gender', *Journal of Law and Religion*, XII, 1 (1995–96), pp. 37–50.

——. 'On Belonging as a Muslim Woman', in Gloria Wade-Gayles, ed., *My Soul is a Witness: African-American Women's Spirituality*. Boston, 1995, pp. 253–265.

Other sources

Ahmed, Leila. *Women and Gender in Islam: The Historical Roots of a Modern Debate*. Connecticut, 1992.

Ali, Abdullah Yusuf. *The Holy Quran: Text, Translation and Commentary*. New York, 1988.

Barlas, Asma. '*Believing Women' in Islam: Unreading Patriarchal Interpretations of the Qur'an*. Austin, TX, 2002.

Boff, C. 'Hermeneutics: Constitution of Theological Pertinency', in R.S. Sugirtharajah, ed., *Voices from the Margin: Interpreting the Bible in the Third World*. New York, 1991.

Bouhdiba, Abdelwahab. *Sexuality in Islam*, trans. Alan Sheridan. London, 1985.

Bynum, C., S. Harrell and P. Richman, eds, *Gender and Religion: On the Complexity of Symbols*. Boston, 1986.

Cornell, Vincent J. 'The Qur'an as Scripture', *The Oxford Encyclopedia of the Modern Islamic World*, ed. John Esposito. New York, 1995, vol. 3, pp. 387–94.

Cragg, Kenneth. *The Event of the Quran: Islam in its Scripture*. Oxford, 1994.

Ess, Josef van. 'Verbal Inspiration? Language and Revelation in Classical Islamic Theology', in Stefan Wild, ed., *The Quran as Text*. Leiden, 1996.

Hassan, Riffat. 'An Islamic Perspective', in Karen Lebacqz, ed., *Sexuality: A Reader*. Cleveland, OH, 1999.

Laqueur, Thomas. *Making Sex: Body and Gender from the Greeks to Freud*. Boston, 1990.

Mir, Mustansir. 'The Sura as a Unity: A Twentieth Century Development in Quran Exegesis', in G.R. Hawting and Abdul-Kader A. Shareef, eds,

Approaches to the Quran. New York, 1993.

——. *Coherence in the Quran: A Study of Islahi's Concept of Nazm in Tadabbur-i-Quran*. Plainfield, IN, 1986.

Rahman, Fazlur. *Islam and Modernity: Transformation of an Intellectual Tradition*. Chicago, 1982.

——. *Major Themes of the Quran*. Minneapolis, MN, 1980.

Ricoeur, Paul. *Hermeneutics and the Human Sciences: Essays on Language, Action and Interpretation*, ed. and tr., John B. Thompson. Cambridge, 1981.

Sahlins, Marshall. *The Use and Abuse of Biology: An Anthropological Critique of Sociobiology*. Ann Arbor, MI, 1976.

Sherif, F. *A Guide to the Contents of the Qur'an*. London, 1985.

Soroush, Abdolkarim. *Reason, Freedom, and Democracy in Islam*, ed. and tr., Mahmoud Sadri and Ahmad Sadri. Oxford, 2000.

Stowasser, Barbara. *Women in the Quran: Traditions and Interpretations*. New York, 1994.

Taha, Mahmud Mohamed. *The Second Message of Islam*. Syracuse, 1987.

West, Gerald O., ed. *Biblical Hermeneutics of Liberation: Modes of Reading the Bible in the South African Context*. 2nd rev. edn, Pietermaritzburg, South Africa, 1995.

Wheeler, Brannon M. *Applying the Canon in Islam: The Authorization and Maintenance of Interpretive Reasoning in Hanafi Scholarship*. Albany, NY, 1996.

Wolterstorff, Nicholas. *Divine Discourse: Philosophical Reflections on the Claim that God Speaks*. Cambridge, 1995.

5

Mohammed Arkoun: towards a radical rethinking of Islamic thought

URSULA GÜNTHER

Introduction

MOHAMMED ARKOUN is one of the pioneers amongst contemporary scholars and thinkers in the field of Islamic Studies, challenging both Muslim and non-Muslim perceptions and approaches to Islam. He confronts the field of Islamic Studies – as well as Islamic thought within the orthodox framework – with the *unthought* or *unthinkable*, by calling into question putative certainties and by going beyond the limits established and defended by orthodoxy (and that includes the kind of orthodoxy produced by and within Islamic Studies).[1] He goes beyond the boundaries of Islamic Studies by appropriating methods that traditionally are not part of what is considered to be Islamic Studies or the study of Islam. In this sense, he moves beyond the methodological framework usually ascribed to the field. Furthermore, he strives for a radical change of paradigm by coming out against the established symbolic and semantic system of how to approach Islam, at the same time as calling it into question and outlining counter-strategies. The reactions and the silences – as a particular form of response – concerning Arkoun's contribution to Islamic thought reflect the significance of his critique.

Of particular interest for this essay[2] is Arkoun's project of a critical reading of Islamic reason, and the consequences it has for new approaches to the Qur'an. The pillars of Arkoun's edifice of ideas are several concepts that emerged in the course of his search for an alternative, that is, a new, understanding of Islamic thought as a counterpoint to the orthodox version. Apart from the concept of the *imaginaire* whose origin goes back to the French Annales school of historians, other concepts such as *Qur'anic* and *Islamic fact/event* (*fait coranique* and *fait islamique*),[3] *societies of the Book/book*,[4] the *unthought* and the *unthinkable*, all bear Arkoun's mark. He has applied all of them to Islamic Studies with ever-increasing sophistication and has enlarged them over the course of time.

These concepts portray the structure of Arkoun's thought, which might be described through the metaphor of an infinite pattern of stars on the Moorish faïence, especially when seen in relation to the broader context of his vision of a religious anthropology, and his intention to give Islamic Studies in general new impetus. At the same time, they also provide the necessary tools for comprehending Arkoun's approach.

The complex dynamics of and correlation between the different concepts he describes make some introductory remarks necessary, all the more so considering that Arkoun himself has not systematised his thought. Instead, he develops one concept out of another, refers regularly to his earlier work, and completes propositions made elsewhere without explanation and without reiterating the central points thoroughly. Nevertheless, an in-depth analysis of his writings brings to light the fact that Arkoun creates a complex network of thought and concepts which become even more important when they are explicitly related to each other and applied as a synthesis. With some exceptions, Arkoun develops his ideas largely on a theoretical level[5] although, regrettably, he does not provide the necessary systematisation for his readers to enable them to apply his ideas to other contexts. Consequently his readers are confronted with several difficulties: a detailed analysis of his thought firstly demands the management of a large body of literature, and secondly, enough time in which to establish a systematic overview.[6] Furthermore, the majority of Arkoun's articles and books are published only in French with only a small number of English translations available, and translations into Arabic are easier to obtain in Paris or London than in Arabic-speaking countries.

This essay brings together the interconnected concepts of Arkoun's thought within the context of his approach to the Qur'an. After an overview of his life and career, his main works are introduced and their significance discussed. The main part of the essay then focuses on the impact of Arkoun's thought with regard to the Qur'an.

Biographical considerations

Mohammed Arkoun is a Berber. He was born in 1928 in Taourit Mimoun in Algeria and grew up in an extended family with a rather poor background and almost no influence within the structures of the village.[7] His family led a traditional and religious life. During his first years of primary school the nine-year-old left Kabylia in order to join his father who owned a grocery shop in Aïn-el-Arba, a wealthy village of French settlers east of Oran. He was meant to follow in his father's footsteps while continuing at primary school. The move to where his father now lived encapsulated aspects of a culture shock and was a formative experience in his life. For the first time he was confronted with the marginalisation and contempt concerning the Berber population in Algeria for being neither Arabophone nor Francophone. Simultaneously he had to resolve the inner conflict of making a distinction as to whether the rejection arose from the colonial system and therefore affected the entire 'indigenous' population or whether it arose from the conflict of different social statuses between Arabophone and Berberophone Algerians.[8] Furthermore he had to learn two languages at the same time in order to achieve social status and to be able to communicate outside the Berber regions. Bearing in mind Algeria's history one can imagine that this is but one example amongst many of the experience of being ostracised.

Finally it is thanks to the commitment of an uncle that Arkoun did not become a grocer but received a good education, being one of the few Muslims attending a French school. Thanks to a bursary, he completed his graduating examination and went on to study Arabic literature in Algiers. In comparison with the stimulating classes at grammar school with the White Fathers, the university seemed to him something of an intellectual desert, leaving his thirst for knowledge unsatiated. Therefore in addition he attended classes in law, philosophy and geography and entered the field of Arabic philosophy. Two factors during his university years in Algeria were decisive for his intellectual and academic development: firstly, there were the bad conditions for students and limitations of the prevailing structures of knowledge and research; and, secondly, there were serious difficulties with Henri Pérès, the general inspector for the study of Arabic in Algeria, who constantly tried to place obstructions in Arkoun's way. He was strictly opposed to Arkoun's plans to leave for Paris in order to finish his studies in France. Both factors nurtured a rebellious attitude and the desire for different academic approaches.

On the eve of the war of independence Arkoun left Algeria for Paris to register for study at the Sorbonne University under Régis Blachère, Charles Pellat, Evariste Lévi-Provençal, Robert Brunschvig and Henri Laoust, for the Agrégation-diploma in Arabic language and literature.[9] In 1956 he passed the examination and left for Strasbourg to teach at both school and university. It was Claude Cahen, also teaching at Strasbourg University, who made him familiar with the ideas and concepts of the Annales School of Historians and their innovative approach to the history of the Muslim Orient. Furthermore, Arkoun's intellectual formation and motivation were shaped by the general climate of new departures in the 1950s and 1960s in France. The field of humanities at the time was characterised by a search for new perspectives and approaches, which led either to the creation of new intellectual movements and schools, or to the consolidation of existing theoretical and methodological approaches (for example, structuralism, structural anthropology, critical discourse analysis or the school of Annales). In 1970 Arkoun submitted his Doctoral dissertation on Miskawayh and Arab humanism in the tenth century.[10] After having been *maître assistant* at Sorbonne University and *maître de conférences* in Lyon he held a chair of Islamic History of Ideas at the University of Vincennes (Paris VIII), then at the Sorbonne. In 1980 he was offered a professorship at Sorbonne Nouvelle (Paris III), including the Deanship of Arabic and Islamic History of Ideas. Since 1993 he has been Professor Emeritus. As well as various fellowships and lectureships abroad he is visiting professor at the Institute of Ismaili Studies in London. He has been awarded the highest French honours (the Chevalier de la Légion d'Honneur and the Officier des Palmes Académiques) and he recently received the prize of Levi della Vida.

The research on Miskawayh made Arkoun familiar with the field of medieval studies and philosophy and changed his perspective because he gradually realised that it was not only in the field of Islamic studies that Islam was mostly reduced to Sunnism and Arabism. On the one hand, he was impressed by the openness and receptiveness of Miskawayh and his contemporaries to other traditions like the Greek and the Persian ones. On the other hand, he discovered that within *adab* religious reason could integrate parts of philosophical knowledge without provoking disapproval amongst theologians and jurisconsults/legal scholars.[11] Miskawayh represents a formative impulse in Arkoun's thought: the correlation of socio-cultural and socio-political circumstances, and the success or failure of intellectual currents, all of which corresponds to the reflection on modalities of mental structures at a certain time in a certain place. Therefore the study of Miskawayh, in the context of the history of Arabic and Islamic thought, provided impetus for undertaking the long-term project of a critique of Islamic reason embedded in the generic context of religious thought. This critique is at the heart of Arkoun's approach and reveals his self-assessment as a scholar. He describes himself as the combination of a researcher and thinker or a 'reflective researcher' (*chercheur penseur*), that is, a critical thinker applying modern methods of humanities and social sciences in order to analyse Islamic thought according to a philosophical critique.[12]

Arkoun focuses on the hermeneutics of sacred texts – that is, texts declared to be sacred and, as such, providing meaning and

transcendency. His approach is simultaneously historical, philosophical and anthropological and should not be confused with a
general critique of religion as such. Instead he tries to unravel the
unthought and *unthinkable* within Islamic thought in order to open
up new horizons, while leaving the fixed scope of revelation and
religious dogmatics undisturbed but, at the same time, pleading
for a rethinking. Thus he analyses and deconstructs the different
epistemes, while still remaining in effect within various discourses.
Arkoun assumes that any historical analysis should be preceded by
a critical assessment of the prevailing epistemes because this
analytical category facilitates the emergence of implicit postulates
shaping the creation of a discourse.[13]

If one glances at Arkoun's life it seems almost obvious that
biographical factors set the pattern for his thought. One might
even be encouraged to go further in assuming that the continuity
in his approach towards Islam can be put down to these early
experiences. From early on he continually traversed the borders
between Berber, Arabic and French cultures, languages and
traditions. This explains how a varied and complex understanding of Islam was always part of his reality, and how, at the
same time, his experience of the oral tradition within the Berber
culture was an important element of his cultural heritage.
However, he did not encounter in other contexts the self-
evidence of the coexisting forms of Islam (considered to be equal
to each other), associated with his Berber origins. On the
contrary, as a student he was confronted with orthodoxy and thus
with the priorities set by the custodians of orthodoxy, whose
judgement served as the basis for the creation of the 'other'.
Being of Berber origin he became part of the 'other'. These
experiences account for his commitment both to contribute to an
archaeology of the hidden, repressed and marginalised spheres
regarding Islam, and to analyse both the reasons and the
processes of their disappearance or marginalisation, in order to
integrate them while emphasising the importance of what he calls
exhaustive tradition.[14] Being sensitive, because of the colonial
experience, to the phenomenon of Eurocentrism and Western
hegemony, he searched for an endogenous way, but without

taking up the ideas of Muslim reformers like Muhammad Abduh, Rashid Rida or others. He pursued a more radical approach in departing from orthodox delimitations and dogmatic enclosure (*clôture dogmatique*). Finally, it should be mentioned that Arkoun himself insists on the fact that existential experiences shaped his intellectual development.[15]

Reflections upon Arkoun's main works

On closer examination of Arkoun's publications it is obvious that he is a versatile and exceptional scholar making his way despite numerous difficulties and mixed responses to his ideas and concepts.[16] The list of books and essays is overwhelming.[17] A thorough introduction to the entirety of his work is beyond the scope of this essay, especially since it consists mainly of collections of essays partly published in periodicals and journals that are not readily available. For reasons of clarity, the concepts and premises of Arkoun's Qur'anic approach will be presented separately because they cannot be identified with one single collection or essay. They will be seen in relation to a general view of Arkoun's thought. Therefore only those collections which serve to elucidate his approach in dealing with the Qur'an are referred to here.[18]

Although Arkoun never composed a specific *muqaddima* or prologue to his critique, our reflections on his work here begin with some general remarks concerning the project of a critical reading of Islamic reason. This is both the kernel of his approach and the connecting theme for the different concepts, running like a *leitmotif* throughout his work. This critique includes a radical rethinking of Islam as a cultural and religious system. In addition it gives rise to a general critique of epistemology. Hence it necessarily follows that a philosophical perspective should be adopted in combination with an anthropological and historical approach. Such a framework provides the possibility of leaving aside theological and dogmatic 'a priories', and enables the scholar to focus on philosophical and mental structures regarding Islamic reason.

This constitutes a first step; the second is to embed these in the corresponding social, historical and socio-cultural context, in order to provide documentation of a dialectic interrelationship. The latter is alive likewise on the level of religious reason, revelation, truth, history and orthodoxy, scriptural or literate culture (in contrast to oral tradition) and the established power.[19]

Arkoun considers Islamic reason as a specific manifestation of reason in general and a branch of religious reason in particular. The framework for reason in general is set up by the cultural and social context and its inherent systems and visions:

> One shall insist that the modifiers *occidental* and *Islamic* appended to reason refer to particular rationalities that construct themselves and succeed in imposing themselves more or less permanently under changing linguistic, social, cultural, historical and anthropological conditions.[20]

Needless to say, the different forms of reason interact.[21] Islamic reason emerged in the context of the *Qur'anic* and *Islamic fact/event* and in the course of what Arkoun calls 'the experience of Medina', that is, concrete historical events that were transformed into 'the model of Medina', in other words, into a history of salvation.[22] Hence Islamic reason (or the dogmatic reason of Islam) is a form of reason which

> accepts to function within religious postulates. That means that it will agree not to discuss the latter but rather to take them as starting points for all constructions and to work at their most fundamental level.[23]

The premise of a logocentric and dogmatic enclosure (*clôture dogmatique*), in existence since the tenth/eleventh century, underlies Arkoun's thought.[24] It defines the sphere of Islamic reason, Islamic thought and Islamic discourse and cannot be separated from the phenomenon of orthodoxy. Dogmatic enclosure is a decisive break within the history of Islamic thought putting an end to the innovative period of philosophical thought while contributing to the closing of the *bab al-ijtihad*.[25]

> The term 'dogmatic enclosure' applies to the totality of the articles of faith, representations, tenets and themes which allow a system of

belief and unbelief (q.v.) to operate freely without any competing action from inside or outside. A strategy of refusal, consisting of an arsenal of discursive constraints and procedures, permits the protection and, if necessary, the mobilisation of what is presumptuously called faith (q.v.). ... No green light has ever been given to a deconstruction of the axioms, tenets and themes that hold together and establish the adventurous cohesion of every faith.[26]

Dogmatic enclosure guarantees consistency and coherence of the corresponding tradition or orthodoxy because the group members share the same framework of perception and representation/expression. Furthermore, it explains the fact that discontinuities within Islamic thought and history have not been picked out as a theme but rather disappeared in the sphere of the *unthought* and *unthinkable*. That is exactly what needs to be deconstructed in order to establish the prerequisite for a reassessment. Moreover a deconstruction of the putative continuity explains the variety within Islamic thought and brings to light the need for the apparently unbroken lines within Islamic thought to be considered as constructs and projections.

The generic focus of Arkoun's interest is expounded in his first anthology *Essais sur la pensée islamique* (*Essays on Islamic Thought*),[27] namely, the above mentioned critique within the field of *Applied Islamology*[28] outlining the fundamental principles of his approach in terms of the chosen perspective, methodology and hypotheses. Furthermore, Arkoun emphasises the necessity of a meta-level for topics in the field of history of ideas. He considers a meta-level indispensable for the reassessment of cultural actions, their meaning and implications. Reassessing or rethinking Islamic thought requires analysis of the way in which discourses are integrated within the logocentric and dogmatic enclosure, and thus the modalities of how reason was put into the service of religious truth and used in order to consolidate the monopoly of interpretation held by the representatives and supporters of orthodoxy.

Further details about Arkoun's perspective regarding the Qur'an are set out in *La pensée arabe* (*Arab Thought*), a small volume addressed to a wider public.[29] He approaches the Qur'an by including both the written word and the liturgical speech, while stressing the transition from speech to text. Therefore he introduces the concepts *Qur'anic* and *Islamic fact/event* firstly in order to comprehend the process of this transition, and secondly to provide further analytical tools for the critique of Islamic reason.

Lectures du Coran (*Readings of the Qur'an*) is probably his most challenging and inspiring collection of essays although it met with only little response.[30] It must be stressed that the innovative aspects unfold even further if one combines the theses and findings here with *Pour une critique de la raison islamique* (*For a Critique of Islamic Reason*) and *Essais sur la pensée islamique*. These three collections complement each other as well as clarify and illustrate the critique of Islamic reason, which must be regarded as the starting point of Arkoun's approach.[31] The title *Lectures du Coran* itself points out the focus of his interest: a pluralistic approach and a rereading of the Qur'anic text, including forgotten or marginalised traditions and the application of new findings within social sciences and humanities to the field of Islamic studies. Analyses making use of the methodological tools and the theoretical background of linguistics and semiotics bring to light the implicit and inter-textual level. Such analyses also illuminate the development and transformation of mental structures with regard to changing socio-political contexts which in turn contributes to the creation and consolidation of a new *imaginaire* within the community.[32] The findings further an anthropology of revelation, that is, of the holy scriptures of Judaism, Christianity and Islam, and thus a religious anthropology. This takes into account the necessity of a comparative approach in order to emphasise the generic category of the *religious fact/event* (*fait religieux*) inherent to a philosophical perspective on the three monotheistic religions.

Pour une critique de la raison islamique provides further insights into Arkoun's thought, aspects of which can only be comprehended while bearing in mind the content of *Essais sur la pensée islamique,* and *Lectures du Coran.*[33] The unifying element of this compilation of essays is the following guiding question: 'Under what verifiable conditions does the idea of truth acquire such strength as to command the destiny of an individual or produce a collective history?'[34] This question can be regarded as one of the central *leitmotifs* of Arkoun's entire work. It is based on the thesis that Islamic thought developed under the premise of belief in a type of reason with divine origin, which manifests itself in the Qur'an. Thus Islamic reason corresponds to the claim on the part of the Muslims that this reason is superior to any other form of reason, because it is visible in the Qur'an and yet transcendent. Therefore Islamic thought and Islamic reason cannot be separated.[35] Reason came under the influence of the *Islamic fact/event* and the orthodox variant gained general acceptance. According to Arkoun, the deconstruction of the creation of Islamic reason and its influence on Islamic thought and the *imaginaire* of the Muslim community is a prerequisite for rethinking Islamic thought, while simultaneously disclosing the realm of the *unthought* and the *unthinkable.*

Despite increasing interest in Arkoun's work, only one translation into English exists to date: *Rethinking Islam: Common Questions, Uncommon Answers.*[36] In the form of questions and answers, Arkoun unfolds his thought along the lines of basic information about the nature of Islam. He points out his holistic approach to the reformulation of the *exhaustive tradition*, the disclosure of the *unthought* and *unthinkable,* and thus the breaking down of the monopoly of definition and interpretation on the part of the custodians of orthodoxy. His generic *leitmotif* of a 'transhistorical, transcultural and simultaneously historical, sociological and anthropological approach to the *religious phenomenon* with the example of Islam' is highly visible.[37]

Arkoun impresses through his diversity and his extensive knowledge of both the Arab-Muslim and the Occidental-Christian culture and history of thought including recent discourses in social sciences and humanities, all coupled with a sharp awareness of overlapping and comprehensive correlations. Furthermore, he is talented at forging exceptional links which at times are daring and radically challenging. Finally, he has courageously pursued his visionary ideas about how to approach Islam beyond the borders established and defended by any kind of orthodoxy. In this, he has disregarded the serious consequences for his position as a scholar, being attacked or ignored both by his colleagues within Islamic Studies and by the representatives of orthodoxy in the Muslim world. It is only in the course of the last decade that he received acknowledgement and recognition and is now regarded not only as challenging but also as an innovative vanguard in the field of the study of Islam.[38]

Arkoun's pluralistic approach combines multi- and inter-disciplinarity with a wide range of methods borrowed from social sciences and humanities and rearranged in a creative synthesis. It is encouraging because everything seems to be possible, and all receive a chance to speak. He pleads for the dissolving of dichotomies (such as margin and centre, superior and inferior, orthodoxy and heterodoxy), and for focusing on the equal coex-istence of putative differences without levelling them out. At the same time his approach is daunting and maybe even alienating because of the inherent risk of eclecticism, and because of the requirement that a scholar be well-versed in Arkoun's termi-nology, the achievements of social sciences and Islamic history. In addition, there is the problem of the lack of explicit systematisa-tion of his thought in general and his concepts in particular.

Reactions and responses to Arkoun's work

Although many of Arkoun's articles and anthologies conveying his major concepts were already available during the 1980s, reac-tions appeared only from the 1990s onwards.[39] Indeed only three monographs have been devoted to analysing Arkoun's work,[40] although there are some essays and chapters that discuss Arkoun as a representative of intellectual trends or critics of the Muslim world in general, and North Africa in particular.[41] Of these, there is only one thorough introduction to Arkoun's thought and critique. This is Ayadi's essay 'Mohammed Arkoun ou l'ambition d'une modernité intellectuelle' (Mohammed Arkoun or the ambition of an intellectual modernity), in an anthology presenting contemporary North African thinkers.[42] Lee operates on a generic level, homogenising Arkoun's approaches according to the thesis that he is a representative of Islamic authenticity. Although Lee does not present Arkoun's concepts in detail, this essay (like Ayadi's) is suitable for a first impression of Arkoun's thought. Haleber focuses on the impact of other thinkers and philosophers on Arkoun's thought, while asking whether Arkoun applies correctly the theoretical models or methodologies he has adopted, instead of analysing the content of his work. The reader's curiosity (aroused by the title 'Arkoun's world') is left unsatisfied because, according to Haleber, the features of this world are borrowed from Derrida, Baudrillard, Foucault and other intellectuals.[43]

The above-mentioned authors agree as to the difficulty in classifying Arkoun's thought due to its impressive variety on the level of theory, methodology and content, which illustrates why Arkoun is considered an innovative and original scholar. While they pay special attention to the concepts of the *Qur'anic* and *Islamic fact/event,* they do not necessarily link these to the category of the *societies of the Book/book* (this is Arkoun's basis for a meta-level guarantee of comparative analysis of the monotheistic religions in the context of the *religious fact/event* respective to the *religious phenomenon*).[44] Although Arkoun's critical remarks concerning the field of Islamic Studies meet general approval, his project of *applied Islamology* is rarely explained.[45]

The majority of the authors criticise Arkoun's complex and elusive expressions, the abundant terminology and the lack of systematisation. Added to this is the fact that a profound knowledge of recent discourses and innovations in the field of social sciences and humanities are indispensable to a full appreciation of Arkoun's work. This is not to mention the additional difficulties arising from Arkoun's failure to provide a systematic overview for his readers, which means that they must acquire the relevant knowledge by consulting further articles. One of the sharpest reproaches is that, instead of putting already formulated concepts and suggestions in concrete form and applying them, Arkoun elaborates his theses and adds more questions without providing answers.[46]

Despite this critique the authors are not ungenerous in their praise. The assessments of Arkoun's significance are impressive and show a considerable approval. For example, he is described as a pioneer in the deconstruction of political Islam and for the reconciliation of a hermeneutics of Islam with the political discourse of modernity;[47] a liberal interpreter of Islam, a critic of orientalism searching for a modern *ijtihad*;[48] the most important Francophone Muslim scholar in the field of Islamic Studies;[49] a liberal thinker contributing to a different image of Islam,[50] and as someone who breaks 'the monopoly of traditional and neopatriarchal interpretation of Islamic history and the Qur'an'.[51] Robert D. Lee writes:

> He pushed to the very frontiers of Western social science in an effort to free Islam not just from Western misperceptions and misconceptions but also from the grips of many of its most fervent advocates. In so doing, he put himself on the cutting edge of Islamic discourse, or beyond it.[52]

Armando Salvatore adds:

> In particular, reading Arkoun is helpful to situate the modern construction of Islam at the crossroads between processes of subjectification–interiorization, which are the complex and creative sources of any social distinction while taking them for granted.[53]

In summary one should stress that although Arkoun's contribution is regarded as innovative, important and challenging (numerous honours, invitations and conferences on his thought testify to this)[54] the scholarly community has not really taken up the challenge inherent in his approach, including his critique of Islamic Studies. His concepts have not found their way into Islamic Studies or been applied in other contexts, nor has his critique been taken up seriously and discussed in order to initiate change.[55]

Concepts shaping Arkoun's readings of the Qur'an

According to Arkoun the notion of orthodoxy is 'one of the keys to rethink the whole theology of Islam'.[56] Therefore a thorough analysis of orthodoxy is a prerequisite for an approach beyond dogmatic enclosure.

> Orthodoxy – in its Sunni or Shi'i version – is no more than the offi-
> cial religion resulting from the collaboration of a majority of the so-
> called 'ulama' [sic] with the state. This is very obvious with the
> Umayyads and 'Abbasids; but we depend more on the historians and
> jurists who worked under the 'Abbasids.[57]

Arkoun also elaborates elsewhere:

> *Orthodoxy* is defined as the system of beliefs and mythological repre-
> sentations through which, and with which, a given social group
> perceives and constructs its own history. ... In this context, ortho-
> doxy can also be defined as the *system of values which functions prima-
> rily to guarantee the protection and the security of the group.* That is why
> any orthodoxy is necessarily an ideological vision overwhelmingly
> oriented toward the subjective interest of the group to which it
> belongs. But the group considered as a 'collective consciousness' is
> *never* aware of its subjective, biased use of history; it sees its 'ortho-
> doxy' as a genuine expression of its identity.[58]

Orthodoxy is one of the most important and influential factors
for development and change within a given society. Social groups
thus perceive and construct history by means of the system of
belief and non-belief and imaginations established by orthodoxy.
This is effected by excluding other social groups who, for their
part, create their own orthodoxy. The group in power condemns
any deviant opinion as heretical, claiming to represent the only
possible expression of religion and the only authentic one.[59]

> Thus the notion of orthodoxy is always used in a theological sense,
> yet has never been *thought* in a historical sense; however, it is daring
> to point out that it is the result of a slow historical process of selec-
> tion, elimination and diffusion of names, works, schools, ideas
> according to the objectives aimed at in each case by the group,
> community and power in place. This is how tradition is formed that
> works like a security system for the religious or national
> community.[60]

Diagram 1 explains the implications of orthodoxy. These are
crucial for Arkoun's critique of Islamic reason, providing on the
one hand the necessary conceptual tools and, on the other,
setting the agenda for a departure from the fixed framework of
theological 'a priories' established by orthodoxy.

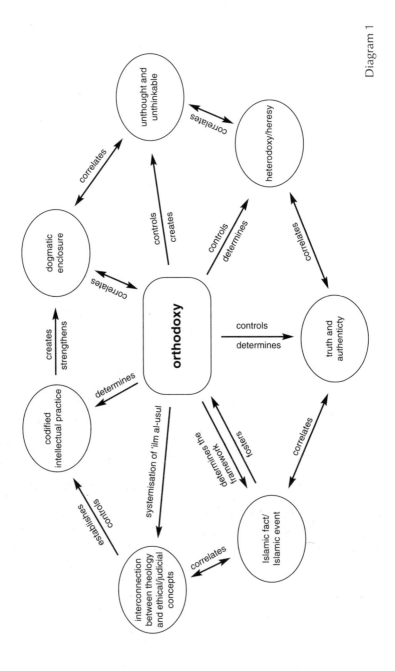

Diagram 1

140

Arkoun emphasises that the phenomenon of orthodoxy – and this is true for any kind of orthodoxy – is equivalent to an ideological, and therefore a historical, process.[61]

Needless to say, this perception of orthodoxy goes hand in hand with a reconsideration of the notion of revelation. The socio-political and historical context of the formation and consolidation of orthodoxy, in combination with the shifts of discourses that illustrate this formative process (see below), provide the necessary analytical framework and categories for a critical and radical rethinking of Islam (at least as described by Arkoun). Revelation then needs to be perceived as a phenomenon which cannot be separated from orthodoxy and its societal implications. Such a perspective opens up new space for thought and interpretation and prepares the way for an open interpretation of the Qur'an, that is, a plurality of readings. At the same time, it lays the basis for a religious anthropology, including a comparative approach between the three monotheistic religions, having regard to the concepts of the *Qur'anic* and *Islamic fact/event* and the *societies of the Book/book* (see below).

> Revelation is not a normative speech (*parole*) that came down from heaven compelling man to reproduce indefinitely the same rituals of obedience and action; it is an offer of meaning for existence and can be revised (see the abrogating and abrogated verses in the Qur'an). It can be interpreted within the scope of the freely consented Alliance between man and God.[62]

Diagram 2 shows the correlation between orthodoxy and other societal forces, co-operating in solidarity with forces sharing the same political and ideological interest (i.e. upper horizontal line); linked by a dialectic interaction (i.e. horizontal arrows). Simultaneously, the societal forces resist (i.e. vertical arrows) the counter-forces (i.e. lower horizontal line) which, in turn, co-operate with forces of the same orientation to which they are linked by a dialectic interaction:[63]

Diagram 2

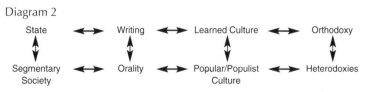

The power in place (that is, the state) is based on a unified culture of writing that is fixed and legitimised by the representatives of learned culture. This lays the foundation for fostering the impression of social unity. In this way orthodoxy is formed and embraces the cause of securing and preserving the powers that be. The respective forces mutually legitimise and strengthen their position of power. It is important to recognise that orthodoxy is a phenomenon that occurs not only in the field of religion but also in other fields, for instance in language, literature or historiography. However, religious orthodoxy plays a prominent role; firstly, for holding the monopoly of definition and interpretation with regard to the sacred texts; and, secondly, for establishing the interconnection of theology with ethical-judicial concepts through the systematisation of '*ilm al-usul.* This in turn results in intensifying the dogmatic enclosure and in defining the sphere of Islamic reason and its limits.[64] Additionally, orthodoxy plays a central role in the shaping of the *imaginaire* in relation to the Qur'an and Sunna.

Arkoun's notion of revelation is associated with the concept of the *Qur'anic fact/event* and the discourse attributed to it. It takes into consideration the historical, cultural and linguistic transformation in the *Islamic fact/event* that corresponds to the shift from an oral discourse into an *official closed corpus* of the sacred text and its corresponding discourse, that is, the transition from speech to text. *Qur'anic fact/event* and *Islamic fact/event* are concepts and analytical categories providing a superior framework in order to contribute to a historical, linguistic, hermeneutical and anthropological analysis which neither criticises religion as such nor adopts theological or orthodox postulates. For Arkoun, religion is 'a way proposed to man to discover the Absolute'.[65] The assumption that religion is a societal/social phenomenon is set against the orthodox and dogmatic a priori that religion is an extra-societal and transcendent phenomenon. In addition, Arkoun postulates an open perspective with regard to the potential meaning inherent to any religion. However, this open perspective was to be lost in the course of time in the context of a community where specific systems of belief and non-belief and interpretations were imposed in the form of theologies and/or orthodoxies. From this philosophical point of view, disregarding the commitment to any religious denomination, it follows that Islam is one specific expression of the *religious fact/event* that is the *religious phenomenon*.[66]

> Let us start out from a heuristic definition: the religious fact/event is the totality of distinctive features that allow identification of the *specificity of the religious instance* (*instance religieuse*) with regard to political, cultural, judicial, ethical, aesthetic and economic instances.[67]

It goes without saying that Arkoun's interest lies neither in questions of faith nor in criticising the truth of one particular faith or faith as such, nor in defending it. He seeks rather to put an end to the hierarchical and polarising perceptions of religion(s) or systems of belief, while accepting faith as *one* potential truth.[68] Hence, according to Arkoun, any analysis of religion and the religious question needs to be embedded in the superior context of the question of meaning.[69] This reflects his vision of a philosophy of theology respective of a religious anthropology which is not content with exclusive theological positions but rather takes up a position beyond dogmatic fixations and theological 'a priories'.

Qur'anic and *Islamic fact/event* allow a differentiation between a linguistic event and the consolidation of the new religion, that is, between the period of revelation shaped by the Qur'anic or prophetic discourse which ended with the death of Muhammad in 632, and the fixation of revelation as a written document resulting in a determination of the reading which is supposed to have been effected from 661 on. Thus these concepts describe the historical process of the coming into being of a new religion, effected and supported by social, political and cultural actors.[70] Furthermore, the concept of the *Islamic fact/event* takes into account that Islam, as a system of belief, has been used for ideological and political purposes in order to legitimise and maintain power. Such an approach to Islamic history or Islamic thought is not conceivable without taking up a position beyond theological and orthodox postulates.

The characteristic features of each fact/event are compared
and confronted as follows.

Qur'anic fact/event[71]	Islamic fact/event[72]
Occurred in the seventh century due to political, economic and moral experiences on the Arabian peninsula.	It is the concrete historical projection of the *Qur'anic fact/event* and the more recent event from a historical point of view.
Can be interpreted as God's appeal to human consciousness.	The Qur'an as a closed corpus of text is the axis of the *Islamic fact/event*.
It is of existential meaning and linked to a language, namely Arabic.	In the course of the formation of orthodoxy meaning and implications of the *Qur'anic fact/event* were usurped through arbitrary dissemination of selected meaning. The Qur'an as a text in a linguistic and historical understanding was used as a pretext, i.e. it was exploited for the cause of the social actors in power.
It belongs to the sphere of oral tradition.	Orthodoxy used the symbolic capital of the Qur'an in order to create an official and orthodox Islam and to impose this variant of Islam.[73]
Although the discourse as such has been concluded with the death of Muhammad, it is transhistorical, i.e. it has not lost its character as an appeal to men who are preoccupied with the question of meaning.	Ranges between the Arabic language and revelation.
Revelation in this kind of reality opens up horizons and is open with regard to its meaning; it is not systematised, there is no discontinuity between the mythical and the rational.	In this kind of reality revelation no longer has an open meaning.
Corresponds to the Qur'anic or prophetic discourse.	Corresponds to the Islamic discourse.

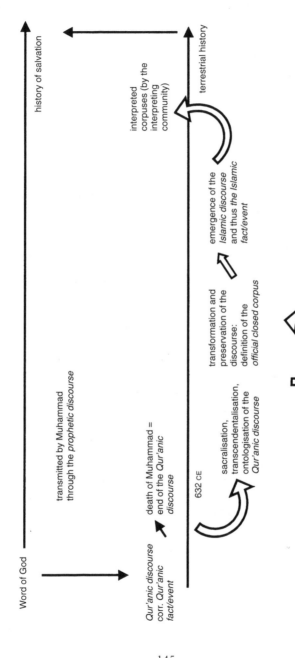

Diagram 3

145

The process of transformation and the societal forces supporting the latter are illustrated and clarified in Diagram 3 (p. 145).[74]

The transformation of the *Qur'anic fact/event* into the *Islamic fact/event* manifested itself on two different but interrelated levels: firstly, the level of state and institutions, namely with regard to the necessity to integrate the conquered groups and societies ideologically into the Islamic realm; and, secondly, the level of confirmation of the doctrine. The linguistic, semiotic and historical conditions of the genesis of the *Qur'anic fact/event* elucidate the differences between the *Qur'anic* and *Islamic fact/event*.[75] These concepts set up the analytical framework necessary for approaching the Qur'an as a reflective thinker (*chercheur penseur*), that is, as a scholar who simultaneously takes into consideration

> ... the theological requirement of the believers, the philological imperative of the positive (but not positivistic) historian, the explanatory perspective of the anthropologist and the critical control of the philosopher.[76]

Synchronically, this synthesis of perspectives allows the Qur'an to be read on different levels, while at the same time the cognitive bounds established by orthodoxy have ceased to be in force. Firstly, the Qur'an is considered to be a document of revelation, and thus the expression and source of universal consciousness. This corresponds to the full recognition of its religious meaning. Secondly, it is an historical and literary document. As such, and beyond the spiritual dimension, it reflects cultural and historical phenomena, the correlation of socio-political forces, currents within the history of thought and new or changing epistemes of the Qur'anic and Islamic discourse and mental structures.[77]

> It is necessary to open up the Qur'anic fact by situating it in a comparative approach not only within the three monotheistic religions but also within a historical anthropology of the religious event ... .[78]

In fact the broader context of the *religious phenomenon* or the *religious fact/event* provides a meta-level for pursuing the long-term project of a comparative approach that includes all monotheistic religions. Therefore the concepts *Qur'anic* and *Islamic fact/event* must be completed by the analytical and historical category of the *societies of the Book/book*. It is the combination of these concepts that contributes to elucidating the process of the construction of history by means of revelation, and the corresponding orthodox interpretations. Thus the relationship revelation–truth–history is picked out as a central theme.[79] Additionally, this concept discloses a psychological and cultural process within the respective monotheistic societies that is beyond the theological and ideological differences of the respective communities. This illustrates how the idea of revelation as providing meaning was to become the central idea and was (rather, *is*) crucial for the perception of history. This is because the mental image of the revelation as a book was formative for the communities' *imaginaire*.

Before considering the implications of Arkoun's concepts for a rereading of the Qur'an (and thus a rethinking of Islamic thought), the conceptual framework must be completed by introducing the historical categories of the *unthought* and *unthinkable* (and by implication the *thinkable*). These are inextricably linked with the *Qur'anic* and *Islamic fact/event* on the one hand (and therefore with the notion of orthodoxy), and on the other with the universally applicable historical category of the *imaginaire*.[80]

Two premises are crucial for an understanding of *unthought* and *unthinkable*: firstly, any thought reveals at a given time a positive and negative part; and, secondly any tradition of thought comes into being by means of selection inwards and outwards while excluding and marginalising other trends.[81] Therefore the *unthought* and the *unthinkable* (and by implication the *thinkable*) cannot be comprehended without taking into account the dogmatic enclosure and the orthodox understanding of truth. This is because orthodox discourses lay down the limits of the domain of the *thinkable,* fixing simultaneously the domain of the *unthought* and *unthinkable*. On closer examination, it is obvious that the *thinkable* corresponds to the contents within dogmatic enclosure.[82]

The transformation of the *Qur'anic fact/event* into the *Islamic fact/event* (including the creation of an official closed corpus and

the definition of the limits of interpretation effected by the custodians of orthodoxy) allows deeper insight into a domain that has
not been taken into account within the study of Islam, whether by
Muslim or non-Muslim scholars. The transformation hides three
turning points with regard to the development of the Qur'an,
altering the boundaries between the *thinkable, unthought* and
unthinkable. Firstly, revelation, i.e. *Qur'anic fact/event* or rather
Qur'anic discourse (610-623 CE). Secondly, collection and
canonisation of the *mushaf* (632-936), i.e. official closed corpus
and beginning of the *Islamic fact/event* or rather the Islamic
discourse. Thirdly, the period of orthodoxy (936-...), i.e., the
formation of a new *imaginaire* within the Muslim community and
the shaping of the *thinkable*, the *unthinkable* and *unthought* as well
as Islamic reason.[83] In the long term this shift resulted in the
formation of a new *imaginaire.*

To sum up, one can say that the *thinkable* of a linguistic community covers all that one is able to think and to express with regard
to the historical circumstances and in connection with their intellectual possibilities.[84] It shapes the discourse. Classical exegesis or,
rather, its approach and functioning, was decisive for the formation of the *thinkable* and the *Islamic fact/event.* Beyond the bounds
of the *thinkable* is the *unthinkable*, a further feature of a system of
thought and a particular time. It contains all that is forbidden
historically or politically to be thought or expressed. This ban
ensues in the name of the truth determining Islamic thought. The
unthinkable corresponds to a storage tank of taboos that might be
explained in terms of the cognitive bounds of the respective
socio-cultural system, or the fact that, by means of self-censor-
ship, the regulations of the dominant ideology have been internalised. With regard to Islamic thought, both historiography and
usul widened the sphere of the *unthinkable* by selection and exclusion. This resulted in a construct of history that could be
controlled and channelled within the fixed bounds of
orthodoxy.[85]

The *unthought* is the equivalent to the total of the *unthinkable.*
Furthermore it embraces all that is at a particular time beyond the
bounds of knowledge (for example the idea of a heliocentric

system in the medieval ages). The assumption of the historicity of a discourse that became an official closed corpus is still part of the *unthought*. All that has been rejected and marginalized, as well as forgotten, is likewise part of the *unthought*.[86]

According to Arkoun, the following taboos, rejected, suppressed and forgotten topics should be located in the storage tank of the *unthought* and *unthinkable*: the history of the text of the Qur'an and the hadith, the historical and cultural conditions of the formulation of the shari'a, the phenomenon of revelation, the question of the creation of the Qur'an, the transformation of religious symbolism into state-power, the legal codex, the status of the person, the legal status of women, tradition, orthodoxy. If these issues are discussed at all, it is in an apologetic way. Beyond the field of religion, Arkoun mentions the concepts of state, civil society, and individual liberties or laicism.[87] Furthermore, one might add 'all the cultures and systems of thought related to pagan, polytheistic, *jahili* (pre-Islamic), or modern secularized societies'.[88]

To conclude, the *unthinkable* and the *unthought* may be regarded as the 'negative' of the concept episteme. These concepts complement the concept of the *Qur'anic* and *Islamic fact/event*. At the same time, they open up an additional perspective with regard to the long-term project of Arkoun's critique of Islamic reason, as well as stimulating the investigation and discovery of a mental space beyond the fixed orthodox settings and bans (in the sense of an archaeology of the *exhaustive tradition*).[89] Furthermore, these categories not only stretch the cognitive bounds of Muslim orthodoxy and theology but also those of orientalism. They are suitable for bringing out deeper underlying structures. The latter might contribute to a changing viewpoint concerning Muslim societies and in the long-term maybe even to a liberation of Islamic thought.

The last pillar of Arkoun's edifice of ideas (that is, the concepts and theoretical framework that shape his approach to the Qur'an in particular, and his thought in general) corresponds to the *imaginaire*. This is another historical category of analysis introducing an additional concept in order to assess societal phenomena on the level of symbolic structures which refer to the construction and perception of reality in a given society.[90] *Imaginaire* completes the concepts of the *Qur'anic* and *Islamic fact/event* as well as the *unthought* and *unthinkable*. Like those concepts it is not only effectively beyond the definitions and bounds established by orthodoxy, and thus beyond the Islamic discourse, but it also deconstructs these as cognitive boundaries.

> Thus the imaginaire becomes an essential key for an appropriate reading of societies; it allows explanation of the usual operations of mythologisation, sacralisation, mystification, ideologisation, even transcendentalisation that social actors support according to their positions and roles within society. [...] The imaginaire is associated in the usual language with the unreal, the imagination (affabulation), the fictitious, the legend, the mythical: all notions deviating from the *real*, the constant object of rational search.[91]

Hence the *imaginaire* describes the realm of reception and combination of images and imaginations with regard to reality, that are accepted in a given social group sharing the same historical context. Arkoun distinguishes between three forms of *imaginaire*. Firstly, there is the religious *imaginaire* containing all convictions within faith that are accepted, thought and expressed as being true, and therefore do not allow critical reason to interfere. It is possible that the religious *imaginaire* dominates all fields of life. Secondly, there is the social *imaginaire*, a dynamic combination of ideas, forces, perceptions, interpretation and expression of reality linked with specific associations. It emerges from the ideological discourses and plays an important role for the idea of unity within a social group, society or nation. Thirdly, there is the individual *imaginaire* that is involved in creating the social *imaginaire*.[92]

The Qur'an provides the axis and the basis for the *imaginaire*; it gives it shape, renders it dynamic and defines the values indispensable to Islamic ethics.[93] Real historical events were transformed into paradigms and became an essential reference for human existence and therefore are embedded in the *imaginaire* of a society or a group. Religious consciousness is shaped by the paradigm of the ideal society, as perceived in the historical experience of Medina, which in turn underwent interpretations on the part of orthodoxy.[94] The roots of this *imaginaire* go back to the past to an extent that it does not make any difference whether the imagination of the ideal society corresponds to reality at the time or not. The meaning attributed to the model of Medina may be more real than reality itself. The *imaginaire*'s contribution as an analytical category becomes obvious since it provides the necessary tools to deconstruct perceptions of reality. As long as the *imaginaire* is taken for reality and not identified as imaginations about reality there is a risk of its becoming an instrument of politics.[95]

Arkoun describes the impact of the *imaginaire* for a rethinking of Islamic history and Islamic thought as follows:

> To elucidate how the working of the imaginaire, in the present and in the past, gets the better of positivistic reason of the historian philologist, to follow the recurrent operations this imaginaire reproduces itself with and continues to be crucial to the historical stages of societies, to introduce a requirement for intelligibility in a domain that is abandoned to the blind forces of the collective psyche. These are in my opinion the new, innovative and liberating tasks of the historian of Islam.[96]

The implications of Arkoun's conceptual framework with regard to methodology and its application to the study of Islam, including the study of the Qur'an, are challenging since his project of a rethinking of Islamic thought requires a considerable versatility and flexibility on the part of the scholar. The conventional approaches of philology and history are neither adequate nor suitable methods for deconstructing the pillars of Islamic thought or sifting out ideological elements and demystifying its constructs.

Diagram 4 (p. 152) illustrates the different levels of Arkoun's approach and the mutual correlations that can be characterised as pluralistic in every respect.

There is no doubt that Arkoun's pluralism is challenging. It exposes omissions and deficiencies regarding the study of Islam and is directed both at Muslim and non-Muslim scholars. Arkoun gives the study of Islam in general and the study of the Qur'an in particular new impetus. His broader project of a critique of

Ursula Günther

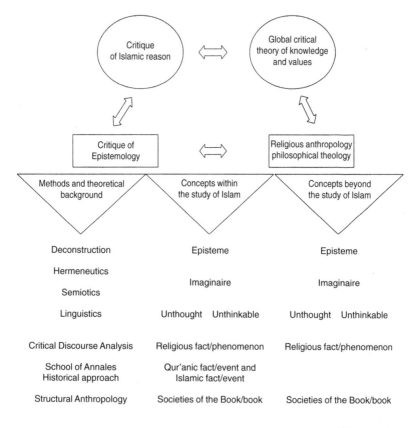

Diagram 4

Islamic reason (which is inextricably linked to a rethinking of Islamic thought) confronts any scholar with a dilemma that is difficult to resolve. This is the deconstruction of centuries of Islamic thought, at the same time bearing in mind the entire conceptual and methodological framework referring to a meta-level, in order to avoid the trap of any cognitive boundary. This demands a considerable expenditure of energy, time and familiarity with both Islamic and Occidental-Christian history as well as recent developments and discourses in the field of humanities and social sciences. Thus attention must be given to the application of linguistics, semiotics and critical discourse analysis while

152

interpreting the Qur'an.[97] Classical exegesis must be revisited in order to disclose its contribution to the formation and consolidation of the *imaginaire* and the *unthought* and *unthinkable.*[98] Furthermore, an approach comparable to Tillich, Bultmann or Barth should also be adopted by Muslim theologians.[99] And the comparative potential of, for example, the *societies of the Book/book,* must be taken into consideration. These are but a few examples of the challenges and opportunities awaiting scholars who wish to take up Arkoun's concepts.[100]

Concluding remarks

Arkoun's contribution to the study of Islam is unique for several reasons. First is its holistic approach that replaces conventional analyses, while at the same time refraining from employing polarising analytical categories, and focusing on a radical plurality of meaning and complexity. Second is its radical call for a departure from the cognitive bounds established by any kind of orthodoxy. Third, it includes a critical revision of reason as such, and calls into question the achievements of modernity and its hegemonic character. Fourth, it aims at an integration of 'Islam and Muslim culture into a global critical theory of knowledge and values'.[101]

The metaphor of the rhizome might in different respects throw light on Arkoun's approach.[102] It symbolises a shift of paradigm that has already occurred at different levels of modern life. It stands for integrity, wholeness and plurality in contrast to dualism, decomposition and particularism. A rhizome is a system without centre and without hierarchies; it is defined by correlation, mutual completions and inner dynamics through a constant expansion in complexity. In this respect Arkoun's approach bears features of postmodernism.

Although Arkoun provides some examples of how to apply his concepts, the importance of his work consists in offering an outstanding conceptual and theoretical framework with regard to the study of Islam. Although many questions remain unanswered, and in fact even generate further questions, one would not do

justice to Arkoun by expecting him to be as productive on the
level of application as he is on a theoretical and conceptual
level.[103] His kind of approach can only be assessed in the fullness
of time, especially if one takes into consideration that Arkoun
regards himself as somebody kindling fire,[104] hoping that the vital
spark will be spread. The extent to which the persistence and the
potential of his critique will stimulate ongoing enquiry and reformulation remains to be seen.

NOTES

1. In the following, Arkoun's specific concepts appear in italics, in
addition to the concept of *imaginaire*. Arkoun did not create this category of
historical analysis yet he was among the first (if not the first) to apply it
systematically to Islamic Studies and he still advocates fervently its integration into any kind of study of Islam.

2. Thanks are due to Gordon Mitchell for his kind comments on an
earlier version of this paper.

3. The translation of the concepts *fait islamique, fait coranique* and *fait
religieux* presents some difficulties, especially because they are not consistently translated in English texts: sometimes we find *Islamic fact*, sometimes
Islamic event and sometimes *Islamic phenomenon* (the latter's correspondent
in French is often used synonymously by Arkoun himself). See e.g.
Mohammed Arkoun, 'Contemporary Critical Practices and the Qur'an', in
Encyclopaedia of the Qur'an, ed. Jane Dammen McAuliffe (Leiden, 2001), vol.
1, p. 415 (*event*); Arkoun, 'Islamic Studies: Methodologies', in *The Oxford
Encyclopaedia of the Modern Islamic World*, ed. John L. Esposito (New York,
1995), vol. 2, p. 337 (*phenomenon*); Robert D. Lee, 'Arkoun and Authenticity',
Peuples Méditerranéens, 50 (1990), p. 91 (*fact*). This discussion uses *fact/event*
in referring to Arkoun's synonymous employment of *fact* and *phenomenon* in
order to emphasise the association of a dynamic character, in contrast to
the character of a fait accompli (that might be associated with *fact*). With
regard to the concept *imaginaire* the French term is retained since it can be
regarded as a technical one, used in the context of the School of Annales as
an epistemological category.

4. Arkoun uses an orthographic trick to illustrate the ambiguity of
book: Holy Book vs. book in the sense of a cultural product. For detailed
explanations concerning this concept, see below.

5. See e.g. the essays 'Lecture de la Fatiha' and 'Lecture de la Sourate
18' in Arkoun, Mohamed [sic]. *Lectures du Coran*, 2nd edn (Tunis, 1991), pp.
77–101, 103–25. See also Arkoun, Mohammed. *L'Islam. Morale et Politique*
(Paris, 1986; 2nd edn, 1990). This clarifies the concept of the *imaginaire*.

6. This might explain the small number of detailed or systematic
studies on his thought.

7. The following paragraph refers to several conversations with Arkoun and to correspondence with him. It also refers to Hassan Arfaoui, 'Entretien avec Mohammed Arkoun' *M.A.R.S.: Le Monde Arabe dans la Recherche Scientifique (The Arab World in Scientific Research;* al-'Alam al-'Arabi fi al-bahth al-'ilmi), 5 (1995), pp. 7–32; Arkoun, 'Avec Mouloud Mammeri à Taourit Mimoun', *Awal, Cahier d'Etudes Berbères* (Alger, 1990), pp. 9–13; Arkoun, *Rethinking Islam Today* (Washington, 1987), and 'Le cheminement d'une critique. Entretien'. *Revue Intersignes*, 10 (1995), pp. 217–27. The author thanks Arkoun for providing unpublished manuscripts and for generously giving his time.

8. See Arkoun, 'Avec Mouloud Mammeri', pp. 9–12; Arkoun, *Rethinking Islam Today*, pp. 1–2. The quotation marks used for the term 'indigenous' are intentional. It is the French and therefore synonymously the colonial expression for the Algerian population, i.e. Arabs and Berbers.

9. On 1 November 1954, all Algerians were called to armed resistance. This was the beginning of the struggle for liberation. See e.g. the chronology and documents in Sigrid Faath, *Algerien. Gesellschaftliche Strukturen und politische Reformen zu Beginn der neunziger Jahre* (Hamburg, 1990).

10. Arkoun, *L'humanisme arabe au IVe/Xe siècle: Miskawayh, philosophe et historien* (Paris, 1970; 2nd revised edn, 1982).

11. See Arkoun's article on Miskawayh in *EI²*, vol. 7, pp. 143–4 and 'Le cheminement d'une critique', pp. 217–218. In the context of Miskawayh, the meaning of *adab* includes a philosophical component and means culture in the sense of humanitas and the literature connected with this, i.e., it is more than belles lettres.

12. Correspondence with author in which Arkoun confirmed that it is the very first time he used this term.

13. See e.g. Arkoun, 'Réflexions sur la notion de "raison islamique" ', *Archives des Sciences Sociales des Religions,* 63, 1 (1987), pp. 125–32, here p. 127; Arkoun, *Rethinking Islam Today*, p. 5.

14. *Exhaustive tradition* is another term established by Arkoun. It stands for a holistic and inclusive view of traditions within Islamic thought, taking into account the parts characterised by orthodoxy (or the official religion) as heterodox, and therefore marginalised and repressed. It is another example of Arkoun's way of creating space beyond the scope of orthodox definitions. The notion of *exhaustive tradition* explains inner discontinuities within Islamic thought, such as with regard to a pluralism of doctrines, or a cosmopolitan attitude on the basis of a great cultural variety within the Islamic realm. Simultaneously, it detects external discontinuities in being connected with Europe and/or the Western world and intellectual modernity. See e.g. the manuscript *L'Islam actuel devant sa tradition et mondialisation*, p. 19; also the slightly modified version Arkoun, 'L'islam actuel devant sa tradition', in Joseph Doré, ed., *Christianisme, Judaïsme et Islam. Fidélité et ouverture*, pp. 103–51. See further Ursula Günther, *Mohammed Arkoun: ein moderner Kritiker der islamischen Vernunft* (Würzburg, forthcoming), especially the glossary of Arkounian terms.

15. See Arfaoui, 'Entretien', p. 7; Arkoun, *Rethinking Islam Today*, p. 1.

16.　It is only since the very late 1980s and clearly since the 1990s that his work has been seriously taken into account.

17.　For a complete bibliography, see Günther, *Mohammed Arkoun*.

18.　For a detailed introduction to Arkoun's works, see ibid.

19.　For further details, see below.

20.　Arkoun, 'Du dialogue inter-religieux à la reconnaissance du fait religieux', *Diogène*, 182 (1998), p. 106, italics in the original; author's translation.

21.　Arkoun introduces three forms of reason: 'religious reason', 'scientific (teletechnical) reason' and 'philosophical reason'. As soon as one restricts the development of free and critical thought while setting cognitive limits and claiming the sole representation it is a matter of a specific feature of reason, namely hegemonic reason. Both Islamic and Occidental reason need to be classified as hegemonic. See Arkoun, '"Westliche" Vernunft kontra "islamische" Vernunft? Versuch einer kritischen Annäherung', in Michael Lüders, ed., *Der Islam im Aufbruch? Perspektiven der arabischen Welt*, 2nd edn (Munich, 1992), pp. 265–66, 269; Arkoun, 'Du dialogue inter-religieux', p. 106. Recently Arkoun has introduced a fourth category of reason, namely 'emerging reason' (*raison émergente*), emphasising that this form of reason needs to be situated on a meta-level. See Günther, *Mohammed Arkoun*, especially the chapter *Darstellung und Analyse der wesentlichen Thesen und Konzepte Mohammed Arkouns*. This refers to interviews conducted with Arkoun in Paris, and to the manuscript *Toleration, Intolerance, Intolerable: A Comparative Approach of Religious Reason and Modern Reason*; Arkoun, 'Du dialogue inter-religieux', p. 104 where *emerging reason* is mentioned for the first time. A thorough reading leads to the conclusion that *emerging reason* is the sophistication of critical reason which takes into account the challenges of intellectual modernity.

22.　See Arkoun, *Lectures*, pp. 128, 223; Arkoun, *Pour une critique de la raison islamique* (Paris, 1984), p. 6; Jean-Pierre Chagnollaud, Bassma Kodmani-Darwish and Abderrahim Lamchici, 'Le fait islamique: "Vers un nouvel espace d'intelligibilité"', *Confluences Méditerranée*, 12 (1994), pp. 13–31, pp. 16, 21.

23.　'Le cheminement d'une critique', p. 219, author's translation. The analytical category of episteme applied to the history of Islamic thought reveals that Islamic reason, and simultaneously Islamic thought and Islamic consciousness, may be characterised as a closed cognitive system. For further details see Arkoun, *Lectures*, p. 70; Arkoun, *Pour une critique*, pp. 136, 304–5; Arkoun, *Penser l'Islam aujourd'hui* (Algiers, 1993), p. 279; Arkoun and Louis Gardet, *L'Islam, hier-demain* (Paris, 1978), pp. 169–71.

24.　See Arkoun, *Essays sur la pensée islamique*, 3rd edn (Paris, 1984), especially chapter V, 'Logocentrisme et Vérité religieuse dans la pensée islamique', pp. 185–231.

25.　See e.g. *Pour une critique*, p. 21, Arkoun, 'The Concept of "Islamic Reformation"', in Tore Lindholm and Kari Vogt, eds, *Islamic Law Reform and Human Rights: Challenges and Rejoinders* (Copenhagen, 1993), pp. 11–24, here p. 12; Arkoun, *Penser l'Islam aujourd'hui*, p. 21. The closure of the *bab al-ijtihad* reduced the intellectual activities of scholars to a re-cognition (*re-*

connaissance) and acceptance of revelation, since the existence of an official closed corpus of the Qur'an implied the existence of *the truth*. According to Arkoun this form of reductionism is equivalent to the end of intellectual independence; see ibid. Along with several other Arabic intellectuals, Arkoun regards Ibn Rushd's death (1198) as marking the failure/break-down of Arabic philosophy and the end of Arabic rationalism. See e.g. Arkoun, *L'Islam. Morale et Politique*, p. 112; 'Mohamed [sic] Arkoun: Passer au crible de la pensée islamique', interview produced by Paul Balta, *Arabies*, 13 (1988), p. 69; Arkoun, '"Westliche" Vernunft kontra "islamische" Vernunft?' p. 273.

26.   Arkoun, 'Contemporary Critical Practices' p. 427. Arkoun's critique with regard to the dogmatic enclosure does not exclude orientalist scholar-ship from operating within the borders established and defended by Muslim orthodoxy. According to him, orientalist scholarship does not question the hegemony of orthodoxy concerning the discourse on Islam. On the contrary, it is almost tantamount to the reproach that the scholarly position of the majority within the field of Islamic Studies fosters the intel-lectual imprisonment created by dogmatic enclosure on the one hand, and the persistence of the taboos laid by orthodoxy with respect to the discourses on Islam or Qur'anic studies, on the other; see ibid. See also Arkoun, 'Islamic Studies', p. 337. Scholars working in the field of the study of Islam contribute 'to consolidating and spreading the *unthinkable* and the *unthought* in the scientific discourse of Islam beyond Muslim discourse itself' because they restrict themselves solely to transferring various Muslim discourses into European languages without calling it into question or trying to rethink it; ibid.

27.   *Essais sur la pensée islamique* is a collection of ten essays partly devel-oped from the context of his Ph.D. on Miskawayh and the tenth century. At the time of its publication all essays had already appeared in different jour-nals.

28.   The concept of *Applied Islamology* arises from the fact that Arkoun's critique of Islamic reason leads necessarily to a calling into question of conventional approaches within Islamic Studies because his innovative perspectives bring to light the methodological deficiencies of the field. *Applied Islamology* can be regarded as a counter-strategy and completion to the predominantly philological and historical methods within Islamic Studies. For details, see the introduction in Arkoun, *Essais sur la pensée islamique*, pp. 7–12; 'Pour une islamologie appliquée' in Arkoun, *Pour une critique*, pp. 43–63.

29.   *La pensée arabe* is part of the encyclopaedic collection *Que sais-je?* published by Presses universitaires de France.

30.   One might offer several reasons for this lack of interest. Firstly, Arkoun's multi- and inter-disciplinary approach demands detailed knowl-edge of the discourses within social sciences especially with regard to theo-retical settings and methodology (semiotics, deconstruction, discourse-analysis, structural and cultural anthropology and the approaches of the School of Annales are not common practice in the field of Islamic Studies). Secondly, one has to bear in mind that the innovative

aspect of Arkoun's thought – especially on the level of theory, methodology and epistemology – includes a sharp critique of the established approaches within Islamic Studies which exposes the deficiencies and omissions of the field. Thus working on Arkoun, or rather, applying his concepts, inevitably implies further investigation with regard to the self-restrictions of the field. This kind of challenge is not always welcomed within Islamic Studies, which has established its own kind of orthodoxy. Thirdly, as a consequence of the fact that Arkoun has not worked out a systematic overview of his thought, it is incumbent upon the reader to break down the correlations of the inter-linked and interlaced concepts. This is a task requiring so much time and energy that it often will not be undertaken.

31. Arkoun himself emphasises the correlation between *Lectures du Coran* and *Pour une critique de la raison islamique* and recommends that his readers consider them as a complementary pair. See Arkoun, *Lectures*, p. 32. The first edition being out of print, references here are to the second one, where two important essays have been added: *De l'Ijtihad à la critique de la raison islamique* and *The Notion of Revelation*, pp. 127–151, 257–81.

32. This is illustrated for example in the essay, 'Le problème de l'au-thenticité divine du Coran', pp. 63–76 and the analysis of the first and eigh-teenth *sura*, pp. 77–101 and pp. 103–25.

33. Arkoun's readers are confronted with the dilemma created by his implicit assumption of their familiarity with his concepts and other writings. This might explain the fact that he refers to other essays without additional explanation. Furthermore, one has to bear in mind that he has been continuously refining his critique over the course of decades.

34. Arkoun, *Pour une critique*, p. 33; Robert D. Lee's translation in 'Arkoun and Authenticity', p. 89.

35. See e.g. Arkoun, *Pour une critique*, pp. 311f. and 369f.

36. That is, excluding his articles published in English anthologies. Robert D. Lee translated and edited the second edition of *Ouvertures sur l'Islam* (Paris, 1992). *Penser l'Islam aujourd'hui* is an expanded version of *Ouvertures sur l'Islam*, including eleven additional essays which convey his approach and illustrate his concepts thoroughly. Meanwhile, a third revised edition with the title *L'Islam: Approche critique* was published in Paris in 1998, but unfortunately without incorporating the additional articles of the Algerian edition. Lee stresses in the foreword to the English version that this book 'constitutes his most concerted effort to reach a wider audience'. See *Rethinking Islam: Common Questions, Uncommon Answers*, p. xii. The collection of essays in English entitled *The Unthought in Contemporary Islamic Thought* (London, 2002) was still in press at the time of writing this article.

37. See Arkoun, *Der Islam: Annäherung an eine Religion* (Heidelberg, 1999), p. 12, Arkoun's emphasis. This is the translation into German of *Ouvertures sur l'Islam*.

38. The relative silence or lack of attention concerning Arkoun's thought in the 1970s and the early 1980s, and the sudden and gradually increasing interest from the late 1980s on, might be explained by means of the general shift of paradigm due to the fall of the Iron Curtain and the sudden focus on Islam as a new threat and new enemy for the Western

world, as Islamic fundamentalism also gained ground. The consequence of this was that contemporary expressions of Islam became a special focus of attention and critical voices were heard as a counterbalance to the one-sided representation in the media. If one glances at publications of the very late 1980s and the 1990s it is obvious that new intellectual trends among Muslims, e.g. regarding the discourses on heritage and modernity etc., took an important place in research. See e.g. Halim Barakat, *The Arab World: Society, Culture and State* (Berkeley, 1993); Issa J. Boullata, *Trends and Issues in Contemporary Arab Thought* (New York, 1990); Collectif, ed., *Penseurs maghrébins contemporains* (Casablanca, 1993); Richard C. Martin and Mark R. Woodward with Dwi S. Atmaja, *Defenders of Reason in Islam: Mu'tazilism from Medieval School to Modern Symbol* (Oxford, 1997); Armando Salvatore, *Islam and the Political Discourse of Modernity* (Reading, 1997); Hisham Sharabi, 'Cultural Critics of Contemporary Arab Society', *Arab Studies Quarterly*, 9, 1 (1987), pp. 1–19; idem., ed., *The Next Arab Decade: Alternative Futures* (Boulder, 1988); idem., ed., *Theory, Politics and the Arab World: Critical Responses* (London, 1990).

39. Two exceptions must be mentioned: Christine Souriau, 'La conscience islamique dans quelques oeuvres récentes d'intellectuels du Maghreb', *Revue de l'occident musulman et de la Méditerranée*, 29 (1980), pp. 69–107, and W. Montgomery Watt, 'A Contemporary Muslim Thinker', *Scottish Journal of Religious Studies*, 6, 1 (1985), pp. 5–10. Souriau discusses several North African thinkers dedicating only three pages to Arkoun (pp. 95–98). She refers solely to Arkoun and Louis Gardet, *L'Islam, hier-demain* (Paris, 1978), although *Essais sur la pensée islamique* and *L'humanisme arabe au IVe/Xe siècle: Miskawayh, philosophe et historien* and *La pensée arabe* were already published. Watt's article is based on *Pour une critique de la raison islamique, Essais sur la pensée islamique, L'humanisme arabe au IVe/Xe siècle: Miskawayh, philosophe et historien, Lectures du Coran* and *La pensée arabe*. He focuses on ten hypotheses concerning the concept of *Applied Islamology*. Neither Souriau nor Watt introduce Arkoun's central theses and concepts.

40. Ron Haleber (with P.S. van Koningsveld), *Islam en humanisme: De wereld van (Mohammed) Arkoun* (Amsterdam, 1991); the doctoral dissertation of Suadi Putro, *Mohammed Arkoun Tentang Islam & Modernitas* (Jakarta, 1998); and Günther, *Mohammed Arkoun*. Arkoun alerted the author to the Indonesian thesis: it is not referred to here. Haleber strives in the joint study with van Koningsveld for a complementary perspective, combining his own sociological and philosophical approach with van Koningsveld's perspective of theology and Islamic Studies. Finally, it should be pointed out in passing that some unpublished MA theses on Arkoun's thought have been submitted at American, African and Asian universities.

41. Regarding the essays on Arkoun, see Ursula Günther, 'Weder Modernismus noch Fundamentalismus: Karl-Jaspers-Vorlesungen zu Fragen der Zeit an der Universität Oldenburg vom 9.11. bis 19.11.1994', *Verfassung und Recht in Übersee*, 28, 4 (1995), pp. 550–58; Robert D. Lee, 'Arkoun and Authenticity'; and Watt, 'A Contemporary Muslim Thinker'. For chapters in anthologies see Mohammed el-Ayadi, 'Mohammed Arkoun ou l'ambition d'une modernité intellectuelle', in Collectif, ed., *Penseurs*

maghrébins contemporains, pp. 43–71; Sharabi, 'Cultural Critics' and the revised version in Sharabi, *Neopatriarchy: A Theory of Distorted Change in Arab Society* (New York, 1988). For chapters or sections see Boullata, *Trends and Issues*; Leonard Binder, *Islamic Liberalism: A Critique of Development Ideologies* (Chicago, 1988); Abdallah Labdaoui, *Les nouveaux intellectuels arabes* (Paris, 1993); Martin *et al.*, *Defenders of Reason in Islam: Mu'tazilism from Medieval School to Modern Symbol*; and Salvatore, *Islam and the Political Discourse*. The few available studies in Arabic are mostly of a polemic nature and do not contribute to deeper insights into Arkoun's thought (quite the contrary: the argumentation is dubious and references are missing). See e.g. Nu'man 'Abd al-Razzaq al-Samarra'i, *Al-Fikr al-'Arabi wal-fikr al-istishraqi bayna Dr. Muhammad Arkun wa Dr. Edward Sa'id* (Riyad, 1989); Ma'ruf al-Dawalbi, 'Kitab Arkun 'an naqd al-fikr al-Islami yatadammanu ara' munkara waqi'an wa ta'rikhiyyan!! Limadha yatadayaq Arkun min intishar al-Islam fi al-gharb?!', *Akhbar al-'alam al-Islami*, 1092 (17–10–1988/7; Rabi' al-awwal 1409), p. 4.

42. See above.

43. A detailed analysis of Haleber and van Koningsveld's study is beyond the scope of this essay, principally because it does not contribute to a better understanding of Arkoun's approach as the latter deals with the Qur'an. For further details see the chapter 'Stimmen zu Mohammed Arkoun' in Günther, *Mohammed Arkoun*. A few remarks should suffice. Haleber's approach is descriptive rather than analytical. It lacks a central theme; he often deviates by discussing for example the controversy between Levinas and Derrida or comparing Levinas with Spinoza. It is not clear why he emphasises supposed models or impulses in Arkoun's thought instead of analysing whether his approach can be considered a creative synthesis of already existing trends or a new creation and whether Arkoun's originality lies in this. Van Koningsveld regrets the missing systematisation in Arkoun's work without contributing to changing this. He presents some of Arkoun's concepts without leaving the established settings of Islamic Studies. He even suspects Arkoun of being 'a modern apologist for Islam', see p. 213.

44. Regarding the concept of the *Qur'anic* and *Islamic fact/event* see Ayadi, *Mohammed Arkoun ou l'ambition d'une modernité intellectuelle*, pp. 59ff, 65; Haleber, *Islam en humanisme*, pp. 20ff, 27f, 213ff; Lee, 'Arkoun and Authenticity', pp. 90–91; Martin *et al.*, *Defenders of Reason in Islam*, p. 217; Sharabi, 'Cultural Critics', pp. 4, 6; Souriau, *La conscience islamique dans quelques oeuvres récentes d'intellectuels du Maghreb*, p. 96. Only Ayadi outlines the conditions of a meta-level and the context of the *religious fact/event*; see Ayadi, *Mohammed Arkoun ou l'ambition d'une modernité intellectuelle*, p. 56. He also stresses the importance of the analytical category *imaginaire*, mostly neglected or not mentioned at all.

45. For references to Arkoun's critique with regard to Islamic Studies, see Ayadi, *Mohammed Arkoun ou l'ambition d'une modernité intellectuelle*, pp. 44–45; Boullata, *Trends and Issues*, p. 79ff; Haleber, *Islam en humanisme*, pp. 20 and 136f; Lee, 'Arkoun and Authenticity', p. 87; and Martin *et al.*, *Defenders of Reason in Islam*, p. 204. For references to *Applied Islamology*, see Ayadi, *Mohammed Arkoun ou l'ambition d'une modernité intellectuelle*, p. 48;

Boullata, *Trends and Issues*, p. 84; Sharabi, *Theory, Politics and the Arab World*, p. 24; and Watt, 'A Contemporary Muslim Thinker', p. 68.

46. See e.g. Haleber, *Islam en humanisme*, pp. 201, 239; Sharabi 'Cultural Critics', p. 12; Watt, 'A Contemporary Muslim Thinker', p. 10. With regard to the reproach of missing concretisation, see e.g. Lee, 'Arkoun and Authenticity', pp. 96–98; Haleber, *Islam en humanisme*, p. 33; and Boullata, *Trends and Issues*, p. 84.

47. Salvatore, *Islam and the Political Discourse*, pp. 248–9.

48. Boullata, *Trends and Issues*, pp. 57, 79, 81.

49. Luc Barbulesco and Philippe Cardinal, 'Mohammed Arkoun', in Barbulesco and Cardinal, *L'Islam en questions: Vingt-quatre écrivains arabes répondent* (Paris, 1986), p. 176.

50. Watt, 'A Contemporary Muslim Thinker', pp. 5, 7, and Montgomery W. Watt, *Islamic Fundamentalism and Modernity* (London, 1989), pp. 69, 123.

51. Sharabi, *Theory, Politics and the Arab World*, p. 24; Sharabi, 'Cultural Critics', pp. 5–6.

52. Robert D. Lee, 'Foreword', in Arkoun, *Rethinking Islam: Common Questions, Uncommon Answers* (Boulder, 1994), p. viii.

53. Salvatore, *Islam and the Political Discourse*, p. 252.

54. E.g. the international conference entitled *Rencontre autour de l'Oeuvre de Mohammed Arkoun*, 17–18 December, 1993 in Carthage, or a recent conference in Amman on his thought.

55. It is beyond the scope of this essay to discuss this in greater detail: see the chapter *Impulse für die Islamforschung* in Günther, *Mohammed Arkoun*.

56. Arkoun, 'Algeria', in S. Hunter, ed., *The Politics of Islamic Revivalism*, p. 186, footnote 6. This article fails to provide further explanations concerning his understanding of orthodoxy.

57. Arkoun, 'The Concept of Authority in Islamic Thought', in Klaus Ferdinand and Mehdi Mozaffari, eds, *Islam: State and Society* (London, 1988), p. 38.

58. Arkoun, *Lectures*, pp. 258–9, italics in the original.

59. See e.g. ibid; Arkoun, *Rethinking Islam Today*, p. 7. Arkoun assumes (as does Bourdieu) that orthodox systems operate on the basis of mutual exclusion, reflected in the polarities orthodoxy vs. heterodoxy and orthodoxy vs. heresy. Literature classified as being heretical provides an impressive documentation of currents existing besides orthodoxy. See also Arkoun, *Essais sur la pensée islamique*, p. 34; and Arkoun, *Pour une critique*, p. 307. Regarding the dichotomy orthodoxy vs. heterodoxy see also Bourdieu, Pierre, *Entwurf einer Theorie der Praxis* (Frankfurt, 1979) and the diagrams in this chapter.

60. Arkoun, *Penser l'Islam aujourd'hui*, p. 290, footnote 1, author's translation. With regard to orthodoxy Arkoun stresses the important contribution of the *usul*; see also Arkoun, 'La place et les fonctions de l'histoire dans la culture arabe', in UNESCO, ed., *Histoire et diversité des cultures: Etudes préparées pour l'UNESCO* (Paris, 1984), p. 273.

61. See Arkoun, 'Islamic Studies', p. 337.

62. Arkoun, 'Le concept de sociétés du Livre-livre', in Jean-Pierre Jossua and Nicholas-Jean Séd, eds, *Interpréter: hommage à Claude Geffré* (Paris, 1992), p. 217, author's translation.

63. Concerning the diagram and comments on it, see Arkoun, 'Islamic Studies', pp. 337–8, Günther, 'Weder Modernismus noch Fundamentalismus', pp. 554–5. For further explanations with regard to the balance of power, see Arkoun, *L'Islam: Morale et politique*, p. 31. Bearing in mind the general approach of Islamic Studies, the diagram also points out that referring primarily to written sources is equivalent to repeating the hierarchical structures established by orthodoxy, as well as working within the fixed framework and borders of dogmatic enclosure. Thus the field of Islamic Studies contributes to the construction of a certain image of Islam. This is one of Arkoun's sharpest points of critique with regard to Islamic Studies: see e.g. Arkoun, 'Discours islamiques, discours orientalistes et pensée scientifique', in Lewis, Leites and Case, eds, *As Others See Us: Mutual Perceptions, East and West*, p. 109, endnote 25. See also the chapter *Impulse für die Islamforschung* in Günther, *Mohammed Arkoun*.

64. See e.g. Arkoun, *Penser l'Islam aujourd'hui*, pp. 20–21. See also Bourdieu, *Entwurf einer Theorie der Praxis*, who stresses the same dialectic interaction.

65. Arkoun, *Rethinking Islam Today*, p. 7.

66. See e.g. Arkoun, 'The Concept of "Islamic Reformation"', p. 14; Arkoun, *Rethinking Islam Today*, pp. 7, 10; Arkoun and Maurice Borrmans, *L'Islam, religion et société*, interviews conducted by Mario Arioso (Paris, 1982), p. 48; Arkoun, 'Réflexions sur la notion de 'raison islamique', pp. 129–130.

67. Arkoun, 'Du dialogue inter-religieux', p. 117, italics in the original, author's translation; see also Arkoun, *Pour une critique*, p. 51.

68. Arkoun, *Lectures*, pp. 54–55. This philosophical point of view could result in a changing assessment of the Qur'an as being regarded as a document of universal consciousness. This is equivalent to the vision of a philosophy of theology. The Qur'an would no longer be considered as the ultimate revelation on the one hand and a brilliant construction on the other; see ibid., p. 55. A believer would obviously have serious difficulties in accepting this point of view.

69. Arkoun, 'Du dialogue inter-religieux', p. 104.

70. Arkoun, *La pensée arabe*, pp. 7–11.

71. See e.g. Arkoun, *Essais sur la pensée islamique*, p. 311; Arkoun and Gardet, *L'Islam, hier-demain*, p. 142; Arkoun, *Lectures*, p. 274.

72. See e.g. Arkoun, *Lectures*, pp. 270–71; *Essais sur la pensée islamique*, p. 311; *L'Islam: Morale et Politique*, p. 23; *Penser l'Islam aujourd'hui*, p. 48;

73. The notion 'official' refers to the assumption that a political decision on the part of the powers that be favours one interpretation and tries to eliminate deviant forms. The notion 'orthodox' refers to the assumption that political power designates experts as being responsible for a correct interpretation, i.e. in line with the powers that be. The issue of sacralisation and transcendentalisation of law and institutions must be highlighted as a theme in this context.

74. It attempts to integrate the diagrams in Arkoun, *Lectures*, p. 270 and in Arkoun, *Pour une critique*, p. 221 with the author's readings and understanding of Arkoun's concepts.

75. See e.g. Arkoun, *Penser l'Islam aujourd'hui*, pp. 287–8 where he explains this in more detail.

76. Arkoun, *Lectures*, p. 20, author's translation.

77. See ibid., p. 12.

78. Arkoun, 'Contemporary Critical Practices', p. 429. He emphasises the concept of the closed official corpus [sic] providing the necessary tools for a comparative approach of the *religious fact/event* since Christian and Jewish tradition went through similar developments with regard to the genesis of a closed official corpus.

79. See e.g. Arkoun, *Lectures*, pp. 73, 224, 257–81; Arkoun, 'Le concept de sociétés du Livre-livre'.

80. Arkoun stresses that the *unthought* and *unthinkable* are historical categories rather than philosophical ones since they are subject to changes according to historical or socio-political circumstances; see e.g. Arkoun, *Rethinking Islam Today*, p. 13.

81. Arkoun, *Pour une critique*, p. 307.

82. See e.g. Arkoun, *Lectures*, pp. 23, 116 and Arkoun, *Der Islam: Annäherung an eine Religion*, p. 196.

83. Arkoun, *Lectures*, p. 10.

84. Ibid., p. 11.

85. Arkoun, 'La place et les fonctions', p. 273.

86. See Arkoun, *Lectures*, p. 14; Arkoun, *Pour une critique*, pp. 307–8.

87. Arkoun, *Penser l'Islam aujourd'hui*, p. 28.

88. Arkoun, *Rethinking Islam Today*, p. 5.

89. Arkoun, *Penser l'Islam aujourd'hui*, p. 250.

90. As already mentioned, this concept or analytical category goes back to the School of Annales. Arkoun has consistently applied it to Islamic Studies; he emphasises the innovative aspect of the concept for a rethinking of Islamic thought. He refers especially to Georges Duby and Cornelius Castoriadis, who rendered outstanding services to the elucidation of the *imaginaire*. See e.g. Arkoun, *Penser l'Islam aujourd'hui*, pp. 290–1 or the manuscript *L'Islam actuel devant sa tradition et mondialisation*. Arkoun stressed these references during a conversation with the author (2000).

91. Arkoun, *Penser l'Islam aujourd' hui*, p. 224, italics in the original, author's translation.

92. See e.g. Arkoun, *L'Islam: Morale et Politique*, pp. 13–14 and Arkoun, *Pour une critique*, p. 10.

93. Arkoun, *Pour une critique*, p. 196.

94. Arkoun emphasises that in the course of the formation of the *Islamic fact/event* the concrete experience of Medina was transformed into the model of Medina and thus became crucial for the history of salvation. This transformation is almost equivalent to a transcendentalisation. See Arkoun, *Pour une critique*, pp. 15, 222, 225. The construct of the 'golden age' is another example of the Muslim *imaginaire*. See Arkoun, *Penser l'Islam aujourd'hui*, pp. 290–1. *L'Islam: Morale et Politique* elucidates thoroughly the concept while applying it to concrete historical and/or socio-political circumstances. See ibid., pp. 55ff.

95. It is hardly necessary to mention the impact of the *imaginaire* on

Islamic fundamentalism and on the mobilisation of the collective *imaginaire*.

96. Arkoun, *Discours islamiques, discours orientalistes et pensée scientifique*, pp. 100, 109, n. 25.

97. Arkoun illustrates this reading of the Qu'ran impressively in *Lectures du Coran*, e.g. pp. 77–101, 103–125.

98. See e.g. Arkoun's articles in *Essais sur la pensée islamique* and *Lectures du Coran*.

99. See Arkoun, 'Islamic Studies', p. 334, where he complains of the deficiency in this development within Muslim theology.

100. For a discussion of the impact on believers of plural readings of the Qur'an in the sense of Roland Barth see Günther, *Mohammed Arkoun*.

101. Arkoun, 'Islamic Studies', pp. 333, 228.

102. Gilles Deleuze and Félix Guattari, *Rhizom* (Berlin, 1977) inspired this comparison.

103. This does not mean that he does not provide any illustration of his concepts.

104. Conversation with author (1994).

BIBLIOGRAPHY

Works by Arkoun

———. *Lectures du Coran*. Paris, 1982; 2nd edn, Tunis, 1991 (2nd edition contains two more essays: *De l'ijtihad à la critique de la raison islamique* and *The Notion of Revelation*).

———. *L'humanisme arabe au IVe/X^c siècle: Miskwayh, philosophe et historien*. 2nd rev. edn, Paris, 1982.

———. *Essais sur la pensée islamique*. Paris, 1973; 3rd edn, 1984.

———. 'La place et les fonctions de l'histoire dans la culture arabe', in UNESCO, ed., *Histoire et diversité des cultures. Etudes préparées pour l'UNESCO*. Paris, 1984, pp. 259–80.

———. *Pour une critique de la raison islamique*. Paris, 1984.

———. 'Discours islamiques, discours orientalistes et pensée scientifique', in Lewis, Bernard, Edmund Leites and Margaret Case, eds, *As Others See Us: Mutual Perceptions, East and West*. New York, 1985, pp. 90–110.

———. 'Réflexions sur la notion de "raison islamique"', *Archives des Sciences Sociales des Religions*, 63, 1 (1987), pp. 125–32.

———. 'Algeria', in Hunter, ed., *The Politics of Islamic Revivalism: Diversity and Unity*. Bloomington, IN, 1988, pp. 171–86.

———. 'The Concept of Authority in Islamic Thought', in Ferdinand, Klaus and Mehdi Mozaffari, eds, *Islam: State and Society*. London, 1988, pp. 53–73.

———. *Ouvertures sur l'Islam*. Paris, 1989.

———. *L'Islam : Morale et politique*. Paris, 1986; 2nd edn, 1990.

———. 'Le concept de sociétés du Livre-livre', in Jossua, Jean-Pierre and Nicholas-Jean Séd, eds, *Interpréter: hommage à Claude Geffré*. Paris, 1992, pp. 211–23.

———. 'The Concept of "Islamic Reformation"', in Lindholm, Tore and Kari Vogt, eds, *Islamic Law Reform and Human Rights: Challenges and Rejoinders.* Copenhagen, 1993, pp. 11–24.

———. '"Westliche" Vernunft kontra "islamische Vernunft?" Versuch einer kritischen Annäherung', in Lüders, Michael, ed., *Der Islam im Aufbruch? Perspektiven der arabischen Welt.* 2nd edn, Zurich, 1993, pp. 261–74.

———. *Penser l'Islam aujourd'hui.* Algiers, 1993 (a revised, considerably extended edition of *Ouvertures sur l'Islam*).

———. *Rethinking Islam: Common Questions, Uncommon Answers,* trans. R.D. Lee. Boulder, CO, 1994.

———. 'Islamic Studies: Methodologies', in *The Oxford Encyclopaedia of the Modern Islamic World,* ed. John L. Esposito. New York, 1995, vol. 2, pp. 332–40.

———. *La pensée arabe.* Paris, 1975; 5th edn, 1995.

———. *L'Islam: Approche critique.* Paris, 1997 (3rd rev., extended edn of *Ouvertures sur l'Islam*).

———. 'Du dialogue inter-religieux à la reconnaissance du fait religieux', *Diogène,* 182 (1998), pp. 103–26.

———. *Rethinking Islam Today.* Washington, 1987; also in Kurzman, Charles ed., *Liberal Islam: A Sourcebook.* New York, 1998, pp. 205–21.

———. *Der Islam: Annäherung an eine Religion.* Heidelberg, 1999.

———. 'L'Islam actuel devant sa tradition', in Doré, Joseph, ed., *Christianisme, Judaïsme et Islam : Fidélité et ouverture.* Paris, 1999, pp. 103–51.

———. 'Contemporary Critical Practices and the Qur'an', in *Encyclopaedia of the Qur'an,* ed. Jane Dammen McAuliffe. Leiden, 2001–, vol. 1, pp. 412–31.

Arkoun, Mohammed and Maurice Borrmans. *L'Islam, religion et société.* Interviews conducted by Mario Arioso. Paris, 1982.

Arkoun, Mohammed and Louis Gardet. *L'Islam, hier-demain.* 2nd edn, Paris 1978, 1982.

Unpublished manuscripts

Penser l'Islam aujourd'hui. La communication impossible. 1997.

Toleration, Intolerance, Intolerable: A Comparative Approach of Religious Reason and Modern Reason. n.d.

Secondary sources on Arkoun

el-Ayadi, Mohammed. 'Mohammed Arkoun ou l'ambition d'une modernité intellectuelle', in Collectif, ed., *Penseurs maghrébins contemporains.* Casablanca, 1993, pp. 43–71.

Boullata, Issa, J. *Trends and Issues in Contemporary Arab Thought.* New York, 1990.

Bourdieu, Pierre. *Entwurf einer Theorie der Praxis.* Frankfurt, 1979.

Collectif, ed., *Penseurs maghrébins contemporains.* Casablanca, 1993.

al-Dawalbi, Ma'ruf. 'Kitab Arkun 'an naqd al-fikr al-Islami yatadammanu ara' munkara waqi'an wa ta'rikhiyyan!! Limadha yatadayaq Arkun min intishar al-Islam fi al-gharb?!', *Akhbar al-'alam al-Islami,* 1092 (17-10-1988/7 rabi' al-awwal 1409), p. 4.

Günther, Ursula. 'Weder Modernismus noch Fundamentalismus. Karl-

Jaspers-Vorlesungen zu Fragen der Zeit an der Universität Oldenburg vom 9.11. bis 19.11.1994.' *Verfassung und Recht in Übersee*, 28, 4 (1995), pp. 550–58.

——. *Mohammed Arkoun: ein moderner Kritiker der islamischen Vernunft.* Würzburg, forthcoming.

Haleber, Ron and P.S. van Koningsveld. *Islam en humanism: De wereld van (Mohammed) Arkoun.* Amsterdam, 1991.

Lee, Robert D. 'Arkoun and Authenticity', *Peuples Méditerranéens*, 50 (1990), pp. 75–106.

——. 'Foreword' in Arkoun, *Rethinking Islam: Common Questions, Uncommon Answers.* Trans. R.D. Lee. Boulder, CO, 1994, pp. vii–xiii.

Malti-Douglas, Fedwa. 'Arkoun, Mohammed', in *The Oxford Encyclopaedia of the Modern Islamic World*, ed. John L. Esposito. New York, 1995, vol. 1, pp. 139–40.

Putro, Suadi. *Mohammed Arkoun Tentang Islam & Modernitas.* Jakarta, 1998.

Al-Samarra'i, Nu'man 'Abd al-Razzaq. *Al-Fikr al-'Arabi wal-fikr al-istishraqi bayna Dr. Muhammad Arkun wa Dr. Edward Sa'id.* Riyad, 1989.

Sharabi, Hisham. 'Cultural Critics of Contemporary Arab Society', *Arab Studies Quarterly*, 9, 1 (1987), pp. 1–19.

Souriau, Christine. 'La conscience islamique dans quelques oeuvres récentes d'intellectuels du Maghreb', *Revue de l'occident musulman et de la Méditerranée*, 29 (1980), pp. 69–107.

Watt, W. Montgomery. 'A Contemporary Muslim Thinker', *Scottish Journal of Religious Studies*, 6, 1 (1985), pp. 5–10.

Interviews and newspaper articles

Arfaoui, Hassan. 'Entretien avec Mohammed Arkoun', MARS: *Le Monde Arabe dans la Recherche Scientifique / The Arab World in Scientific Research/ al-'Alam al-'Arabi fi al-bahth al-'ilmi*, 5 (1995), pp. 7–32.

Barbulesco, Luc and Philippe Cardinal. 'Mohammed Arkoun', in Barbulesco and Cardinal, eds., *L'Islam en question: Vingt-quatre écrivains arabes répondent.* Paris, 1986, pp. 175–83.

Chagnollaud, Jean-Pierre, Bassma Kodmani-Darwish and Abderrahim Lamchici. 'Le fait islamique: "Vers un nouvel espace d'intelligibilité"', *Confluences Méditerranée*, 12 (1994), pp. 13–31.

'Mohamed [sic] Arkoun: Passer au crible de la pensée islamique. Interview produced by Paul Balta', *Arabies*, 13 (1988), pp. 68–73.

'Le cheminement d'une critique. Entretien', *Revue Intersignes*, 10 (1995), pp. 217–27.

General secondary sources

Barakat, Halim. *The Arab World: Society, Culture and State.* Berkeley, 1993.

Binder, Leonard. *Islamic Liberalism: A Critique of Development Ideologies.* Chicago and London, 1988.

Deleuze, Gilles and Félix Guattari. *Rhizom.* Berlin, 1977.

Doré, Joseph. *Christianisme, Judaïsme et Islam: Fidélité et ouverture.* Paris, 1999.

Faath, Sigrid. *Algerien: Gesellschaftliche Strukturen und politische Reformen zu Beginn der neunziger Jahre.* Hamburg, 1990.

Ferdinand, Klaus and Mehdi Mozaffari, eds, *Islam: State and Society*. London, 1988.

Hunter, Shireen, T., ed. *The Politics of Islamic Revivalism: Diversity and Unity*. Bloomington, 1988.

Jossua, Jean-Pierre and Nicholas-Jean Séd, eds. *Interpréter: hommage à Claude Geffré*. Paris, 1992.

Kurzman, Charles, ed. *Liberal Islam: A Sourcebook*. New York, 1998.

Labdaoui, Abdallah. *Les nouveaux intellectuels arabes*. Paris, 1993.

Lewis, Bernard, Edmund Leites and Margaret Case, eds. *As Others See Us: Mutual Perceptions, East and West*. New York, 1985.

Lindholm, Tore and Kari Vogt, eds. *Islamic Law Reform and Human Rights: Challenges and Rejoinders*. Copenhagen, 1993.

Lüders, Michael, ed. *Der Islam im Aufbruch? Perspektiven der arabischen Welt*. Munich, 1992; 2nd edn, 1993.

Martin, Richard C. and Mark R. Woodward with Dwi S. Atmaja. *Defenders of Reason in Islam: Mu'tazilism from Medieval School to Modern Symbol*. Oxford, 1997.

Salvatore, Armando. *Islam and the Political Discourse of Modernity*. Reading, 1997.

Sharabi, Hisham. *Neopatriarchy: A Theory of Distorted Change in Arab Society*. New York, 1988.

——, ed. *The Next Arab Decade: Alternative Futures*. Boulder, CO, 1988.

——, ed. *Theory, Politics and the Arab World: Critical Responses*. New York, 1990.

Watt, Montgomery W. *Islamic Fundamentalism and Modernity*. London, 1988.

6

From revelation to interpretation: Nasr Hamid Abu Zayd and the literary study of the Qur'an[1]

NAVID KERMANI

FUELLED by controversy and aggression, the debate that raged concerning the Egyptian literary scholar Nasr Hamid Abu Zayd soon attracted more attention than the content of his books. The scandal provoked by Cairo University's refusal to appoint him full professor, along with public accusations of heresy, death threats, as well as the 'divorce' proceedings filed against him and his wife, highlighted his case and helped rally support for him at home and abroad. The debate focused more or less on one single issue: who was it who actually violated Islamic doctrine, Abu Zayd or his adversaries? Owing to the volatile political nature of the scandal, the useful insights on how Muslim Qur'anic studies could be reformed and embedded in an international scholarly debate on Islam which were highlighted in Abu Zayd's book 'The Concept of the Text' (Mafhum al-nass) were largely disregarded.

Biographical note

Nothing in Abu Zayd's background pointed to the furore he would cause as a critic of the prevailing theology in Egypt and the Sunni world.[2] Born on 10 July 1943 in the village of Quhafa near the lower Egyptian provincial city of Tanta, Abu Zayd was a devout student of the Qur'an from a young age, a qari' and hafiz, and was able to recite it verbatim by the age of eight. When he was still a child, Abu Zayd joined the Muslim Brotherhood, and was briefly imprisoned at the age of eleven in 1954. After leaving school and up to the 1960s, he worked as a technician to provide for his family following his father's death. Nevertheless, he still maintained his sympathies for the Muslim Brothers, and was influenced by the writings of their charismatic leader, Sayyid Qutb, who was executed in 1966. Set against this religious background, yet already distanced from the ideas of the Muslim Brothers (an organization that was to become even more influential thanks to the wave of Islamisation implemented by Anwar Sadat), Abu Zayd began to study literature at Cairo University, specialising in Islamic studies. In 1976, he received his Master's degree from the Arabic Studies Faculty at Cairo University. He then went on to study and lecture at the American University in Cairo and at the University of Pennsylvania. By 1981, Abu Zayd had completed a doctorate at the University of Cairo, and then, from 1985 to 1989, Abu Zayd worked as a visiting lecturer at Osaka University in Japan. On returning to Egypt, he took up a position as 'Assistant Professor in Islamic and Rhetorical Studies' at Cairo University. However, in Spring 1993, 'Abd al-Sabur Shahin, a professor at the Cairo Dar al-'Ulum, publicly denounced Abu Zayd as an apostate (*murtadd*), effectively blocking his promotion to the post of full professor. Soon after, the mainstream, semi-state press followed with a flood of vitriolic articles accusing him of heresy. In June, a group of Islamists led by the former state official, Muhammad Samida Abu Samada, applied to the family court in Cairo to nullify the marriage between Abu Zayd and his wife, arguing that Islamic law forbids a marriage between a Muslim woman and an apostate. The couple first came to hear about the case in the tabloids. Although the charge was dismissed in the first instance and Abu Zayd was finally declared a full professor at his university, nevertheless the plaintiffs won the case on appeal: on 14 June 1995, judge 'Abd al-'Alim Musa proclaimed Abu Zayd a heretic and announced the dissolution of his marriage. Shortly after, a group of professors at al-Azhar University, the theological centre of Egypt, issued a joint statement calling for Abu Zayd's execution,[3]

170

backed by calls for his assassination by the extremist organisation, al-Jihad al-Islami. As a result of this turmoil, Abu Zayd was forced into exile with his wife and, since the winter of 1995/96, he has been professor of Islamic studies at Leiden University in Holland.

This brief outline of Abu Zayd's education and career shows the striking combination of influences that shaped him intellectually. Firstly, he came from a small village, and proceeded through the stages of a traditional religious school system. Consequently, he was totally at ease in 'popular Islam', and had first-hand experience of traditional Islamic knowledge and popular piety. Secondly, he was a serious scholar of Western literature and studied and taught at international universities. Reflecting his background, his refreshing style – free from solemn rhetoric but at times quite complicated – is a blend of almost antiquated Arabic, neologisms and foreign European phrases. What is even more striking in his writings, however, is the manifestation of an abiding sense of surprise at the way in which certain of the ideas and content of traditional Islamic learning and attitudes are to be found – in different forms and with a different terminology – in Western learning, and that the latter ('alien') knowledge provides a possible key to understanding his 'own' tradition. As a consequence, the categories of 'own' and 'alien' constantly blur and sometimes vanish in Abu Zayd's works.

The other side of the text

In Abu Zayd's view the outstanding civilising role of the Qur'an makes Arab culture 'a culture of the text' (*hadarat al-nass*). Indeed, he goes so far as to describe it as the culture of the text *par excellence*. Arab culture, he argues, was spawned by 'man's confrontation (*jadal*) with reality, and his dialogue (*hiwar*) with the text'.[4] But to define Arab-Islamic civilisation as a culture of the text implies that it is also a culture of interpretation (*hadarat al-ta'wil*);[5] the language of the Qur'an – like any other text – is 'not self-explanatory, since any understanding of the text and its meaning depends on the intellectual and cultural horizon of the reader (*intaj dalalatihi*)'.[6] Hence, the message of the text can only be revealed by its interpreters. If the Qur'an supposes a person who interprets, or, in linguistic terms, 'decodes' it, then text and interpretation, *nass* and *ta'wil*, are bound to be inextricably linked: as Abu Zayd puts it, the interpretation is 'the other side of the text' (*al-wajh al-akhar li al-nass*).[7] Abu Zayd deliberately and consistently uses the term *ta'wil* instead of the more common term *tafsir* ('commentary; explanation'), in order to emphasise the share of the human intellect (*'aql*) in the act of interpretation, as opposed to a hermeneutical approach which gives priority to the narrated traditions (*naql*) in understanding the text.[8] In the first period of Muslim theology *ta'wil* was the *terminus technicus* for the exegesis of the Qur'an, before it became restricted in the realm of religious studies to the allegorical interpretation of the ambiguous verses (*ayat mutashabihat*), or even acquired negative connotations as it became employed with regard to arbitrary readings of the Qur'an. For Abu Zayd the interpretive act goes beyond mere explanation or commentary, for without it the Qur'an would be a meaningless text, simply an 'object with intrinsic value'[9] but devoid of any message for mankind.

> The [Qur'anic] text changed from the very first moment – that is, when the Prophet recited it at the moment of its revelation – from its existence as a divine text (*nass ilahi*), and became something understandable, a human text (*nass insani*), because it changed from revelation to interpretation (*li-annahu tahawwala min al-tanzil ila al-ta'wil*). The Prophet's understanding of the text is one of the first phases of movement resulting from the text's connection with the human intellect.[10]

Following the late Russian semioticist Jurij M. Lotman, Abu Zayd developed a theoretical communication model in which the Qur'an – like any other message (*risala*), be it signs (*ayat*) that are verbal or non-verbal – depicts 'a communicative relationship between the sender (*mursil*) and receiver (*mustaqbil*), based on a code (*shifra*) or linguistic system'.[11] Abu Zayd, who translated two of Lotman's works into Arabic,[12] embraced the Russian semioticist's concept of the text. Lotman contended that art was 'a special means of communication, a language organized in a particular manner'.[13] According to this premise, each work of art conveys information through a system of signs. This places it as a 'text' within a specific language system, despite the fact that works of art include both verbal and non-verbal texts. Hence each artistic text 'behaves as a kind of living organism which has a feedback channel to the reader and thereby instructs him'.[14] It conveys 'different information to different readers in proportion to each one's comprehension'.[15]

Turning to the Qur'an, Abu Zayd points out that if the information conveyed by the text varies according to the reader's personal as well as his cultural and social horizons, then the essence of the message conveyed by the Qur'an to a twentieth-century reader must vary from the information conveyed to a Muslim in the seventh, eighth or eleventh century. Accordingly, any interpretation based on the corpus of classical exegesis, or on the legacy of the Prophet and his companions, which is essentially based on an earlier interpretation (given that the hadith are nothing other than Muhammad's interpretation of the divine message, that is, the Qur'an), cannot trace the specific message of the Qur'an for each age.[16] Abu Zayd strongly condemns belief in one single, precise and valid interpretation of the Qur'an handed down by the Prophet for all times:

> Such a claim [that the Prophet's understanding is sacred] leads to a kind of polytheism, because it equates the Absolute with the relative and the constant with the transient; and, more specifically, because it equates the Divine Intent with the human understanding of this Intent, even in the case of the Messenger's understanding. It is a claim that leads to an idolization of a conferral of sainthood upon the Prophet, by concealing the Truth that he was a human, and by failing to present clearly enough the fact that he was merely a prophet.[17]

In Abu Zayd's view, an individual's interpretation is never absolute (*fahm mutlaq*). It is always relative (*fahm nisbi*), since the 'information' in the divine 'message' varies according to whoever 'receives' it. He vigorously contests any claim that this concept of text, which transcends literal or traditional interpretation and stresses the role of the interpreter, clashes with the Qur'an and

Islamic theology.[18] In fact he argues that the Qur'an itself inherently relies on interpretation through human reason and systematic literary methods, and quotes both verses from the Qur'an and citations from Mu'tazili theologians; in addition, he refers to the canonical disciplines of Qur'anic Studies (*'ulum al-Qur'an*), as established in the classical surveys of al-Zarkashi (d. 1392)[19] or al-Suyuti (d. 1505)[20] to endorse this view. He also argues that any interpretation based on the 'authority of the elders' (*sultat al-qudama'*)[21] would link the meaning of the text to the intellectual horizon and cultural milieu of the first generation of Islam, or the historical circumstances of an Islamic golden age that is long past.[22]

> This connection radically contradicts the understanding, anchored in the culture, that the meaning of the text transcends the limits of space and time. Yet limiting ourselves to the first generation's interpretation, and restricting the role of modern exegetes to that of narrating from the old scholars leads in the end to an even more questionable result. Hence people either cling to the 'literalness' of these interpretations and turn them into a 'professing', which in the end results in limiting them to these 'primally eternal' (in the sense of 'ultimate') truths, and in abandoning the method of the 'experiment' in studying natural scientific and human phenomena; or else results in 'science' turning into 'religion', and religion into superstition, tall tales, and a mere vestige from the past.[23]

The history of interpretation

Three key themes emerge from Abu Zayd's work: (1) to trace the various interpretations and historical settings of the single Qur'anic text from the early days of Islam up to the present; (2) to demonstrate the 'interpretational diversity' (*al-ta'addud al-ta'wili*)[24] that exists within the Islamic tradition; and, (3) to show how this diversity has been increasingly neglected across Islamic history. These concerns date back to his Master's thesis, which examines the rational interpretation of the Qur'an put forward by the Mu'tazila[25] and their attempt to demythologise Qur'anic metaphors within the context of the political, economic, and social conditions of the age. In his doctoral thesis, Abu Zayd explored another classical interpretation of the Qur'an, namely the mystical interpretation by Muhyi al-Din ibn 'Arabi (d. 1240).[26] Ibn 'Arabi's reflections on interpretation and his understanding of existence and the Qur'an as open systems of communication between God and man[27] have substantially shaped Abu Zayd's hermeneutical approach, as he himself demonstrates at length in his autobiography.[28]

Abu Zayd's provocative critical writings on Islamic theology encompass debates with Imam al-Shafi'i (d. 820),[29] and Abu Hamid Muhammad al-Ghazali (d. 1111),[30] but also with Muhammad Abduh (d. 1905) and his salafi legacy.[31] In these works Abu Zayd demonstrates how specific historical, political or ideological motivations originally underpinned certain interpretations that have become canonised within the contemporary range of existing interpretations. Abu Zayd criticises what he describes as 'the hold of reactionary thought over tradition',[32] which has often marginalised or banished critical, rational, heterodox and mystical tendencies from 'the paradise of Islam and the Arabic language',[33] while reducing Islamic cultural history to politically conservative, traditional theology. The aim of this reactionary religious discourse is, according to Abu Zayd, 'to simplify the ancient books'.[34] It advocates pure memorising and repetition, without grasping the deeper levels of meaning in the text. Muslims, he adds, have lost 'their free relationship to the Qur'an',[35] which is now shrouded with an aura of untouchability and inscrutability. Revered as a sacred icon, its actual message is ignored. Abu Zayd scathingly criticises the reduction of the Qur'an to a mere object (he calls this *tashyi'* for which the German *Verdinglichung* would be a precise translation), to 'a trinket for women and a magic charm for children'.[36] He also complains that it has been 'swamped by layers (*tabaqat*) of interpretation, each compromised by some historical ideology, hampering all efforts to appreciate the text and its true role in present-day Arabic society'. In light of this, Abu Zayd describes the intentions of his own work thus: 'My research and writings focus on the following problems: how to achieve a scientific understanding of the Qur'an, and how to brush aside layers of ideological interpretation, in order to unearth the historical reality of the text.'[37]

Revelation and the dialectic of the Qur'an

Abu Zayd argues that it is necessary to focus on the historical context of the revelation if we hope to distinguish between its historical meaning (*ma'na*) and its broader, enduring significance (*maghza*).[38] Since the linguistic system (*nizam lughawi*) of the Qur'an itself focuses on the original addressees (*mukhatabun*), that is, the persons initially addressed, a consciousness of the historicity of the text is especially important if we are to be able to understand its message today.

> Certainly it is a message from Heaven to earth, but it is not a message independent of the rules of reality, with all the structures in which this reality is embedded, the most important of these being the cultural framework. The Absolute reveals Itself to humans by means of Its speech. It 'lowers Itself to them' (*yatanazzalu ilayhim*), by employing their cultural and linguistic system of meaning.[39]

Accordingly, Abu Zayd argues that the revelation adapts itself to the linguistic and intellectual horizon of the first addressees: in order to change the reality, it thus embodies it. This implies that the revelation has some connection – albeit a negative one in the dialectic sense – to reality. Abu Zayd highlights the 'dialectic relationship' (*'alaqa jadaliyya*)[40] that exists between the Qur'an and reality in many aspects of the history of its revelation. An example arises in the way that it dealt with specific ethical, spiritual and ideological concepts of the pre-Islamic tribal era so as to embed these in a monotheistic creed and a value system based on human equality. He describes how the revelation reacted to specific historical events, in addition to the general social and political changes which were already ongoing, even before the rise of Islam. Abu Zayd also discusses at length the extent to which classical Qur'anic Studies ('*ulum al-Qur'an*) – with its several disciplines such as 'the causes of revelation' (*asbab al-nuzul*) and 'the abrogating and the abrogated' (*al-nasikh wal-mansukh*) –

proceeded from a notion of the Qur'anic text that took the historical dimension of the revelation into account. As a scholar of literary studies, his own focus, naturally, is on the language of the revelation. While he analyses the linguistic norms and metaphors of the Qur'an which were taken from the social reality and the literary canon of its place and time and then recast in a form that was hitherto unknown,[41] he starts from a much broader assumption, inspired directly by Toshihiko Izutsu's pioneering work.[42] By transmitting the Qur'an in Arabic, God had adopted a human language and the culture that had produced this language. Hence the Qur'an, Abu Zayd argues, is essentially a product of (a particular) culture (*muntaj thaqafi*).[43] The following passage, which appears in the introduction to *Mafhum al-nass*, spells this out:

> When He revealed the Qur'an to the Messenger (God bless him and keep him), God, the Elevated and Praised, chose the specific linguistic system of the first recipient. The choice of a language is not the choice of an empty vessel, even if the contemporary religious discourse may assert this; for the language is the community's most important instrument for grasping the world, and giving it order in consciousness. It is impossible to speak of a language apart from the (associated) culture and reality. It is thus also impossible to speak of a text apart from the culture and reality, because the text is something located within the linguistic and cultural framework.[44]

God chose Arabic to communicate with man; in order to decipher His message, man must analyse His speech by using the same methods and rules which are applied to any other verbal speech, since, according to Abu Zayd, 'the divine act (*al-fi'l al-ilahi*) in the world takes place in space and time, that is, it takes place within the framework of the laws of this world'.[45] He adds that the widespread reluctance to apply the methods of human reason to divine speech stems from the assumption that 'the relationship between the Divine and the human is based on separation, even opposition and antagonism, an illusion generated by the Ash'ari view of the world'.[46] However,

> Such a complete separation between the Divine and the human fails to recognise an important truth, confirmed by the Divine Revelation

Itself when It designates Itself a 'sending down' (*tanzil*), which means a ring that binds, and a speech through which the Divine and the human are tied to each other. In other words: when the Divine Speech (which points out God's path) by being a 'sending down' makes use of the means of human language, despite God's omniscience, His perfection, power, and wisdom, then human reason, by interpreting, is tied to the Divine Speech, despite all the ignorance of man, his imperfection, weakness, and desires.[47]

Having established that a causal relationship exists between the text and the interpreter, even in the case of purely factual texts, Abu Zayd points out how much more complex this relationship is in the case of literary texts, which he refers to as *al-nusus al-mumtaza*,[48] or 'superior' texts. He cites Shakespeare as an example of the extremely dense (*mukaththafa*) linguistic structure of these texts, which makes it possible to convey a maximum and, at the same time, a variability of information. This also applies to the Qur'an, whose miraculous nature has often been traced in its literary structure.[49] Abu Zayd points out that while the language of the Qur'an 'does not deviate from the general language system, it creates its own code, reconstructing elements of the original semantic system'.[50] He maintains that the particularly complex structure of the language of the Qur'an distinguishes it from natural speech. It thus fluctuates between different linguistic levels, 'between, albeit rarely, the pure transmission of "information" (*i'lam*), and dense "literary" language, which produces its own specific mechanisms'.[51] The tools of literary studies are necessary to analyse these 'specific mechanisms' of literary language (*lugha adabiyya*): these include hermeneutics, literary criticism, semantics, linguistics and linguistic science. Abu Zayd advocates a symbiosis of Qur'anic and literary studies, arguing that only an interpretation which takes into account its specific linguistic mechanisms is capable of analysing the Qur'an, deciphering its code, and unravelling the message that the Qur'an contains for present society. In so doing, such an interpretation transcends the historical meaning of the Qur'an for Arab society at the time of its revelation.

Amin al-Khuli and his 'literary exegesis'

Abu Zayd's literary study of the Qur'an refers to a tradition of classical Muslim scholars like 'Abd al-Jabbar (d. 1025)[52] and, especially, 'Abd al-Qahir al-Jurjani (d. 1078),[53] who took it for granted to study the language of the Qur'an in the light of poetry and its related studies. He also sees himself as a direct successor to the late professor of Qur'an interpretation at the University of Cairo, Amin al-Khuli (d. 1967), who developed the theory of a literary exegesis of the Qur'an (*al-tafsir al-adabi li al-Qur'an*).[54] This theory promoted the use of all accessible scientific methods, irrespective of religious considerations, the view being that the Qur'an's message could only be understood after its historical, literal meaning for the first addressees – and thus the historical and linguistic context of the revelation – had been identified.[55] This requires a precise linguistic analysis of all verses that deal with a specific subject, or contain a word that needs to be interpreted. The interpreter must also consider the sentence structure and the psychological effect that Qur'anic language has on the listener.[56] Like Abu Zayd, Amin al-Khuli also stressed the role of the interpreter:

> The person who interprets a text, especially when it is a literary text, colours it with his interpretation and his understanding. The personality of an individual who seeks to understand an expression limits the conceptual level of that expression. It is he who determines the intellectual horizon and who extends sense and intention to the expression. The interpreter does all this in accordance with his conceptual level and in the framework of his intellectual horizon, for he can never leave behind or step beyond his personality. One will not be able to understand a text without extending one's thoughts and one's intellect to it.[57]

The parallels between Abu Zayd and Amin al-Khuli have to do with their aesthetic interest in the Qur'an. Amin al-Khuli described the Qur'an as 'the greatest book and the most spectacular literary work in the Arabic language. It has immortalised this language and its essence, and has itself become immortal. It became the pride of this language and the jewel of its tradition.

Although Arabs may differ in religion or attitude, all of them sense this attribute of the Qur'an, its Arabness ('*arabiyyatuhu*)'.[58] Arabs, he continues, should study the Qur'an 'as other nations study the literary masterpieces produced in various languages'.[59] For the Qur'an is 'the holiest book of Arabic art, whether or not the observer considers it to have the same status in religion'.[60]

Fifty years later, Abu Zayd reiterates the same views:

> I treat the Qur'an as a text in the Arabic language that the Muslim as well as the Christian or atheist should study, because the Arab culture is united in it, and because it is still able to influence other texts in this culture. It is a text that took up the pre-Islamic texts and that all texts after it have taken up, even those that are produced today. I venerate the Qur'an more than all the salafis. The salafis limit it to the role of prescription (*halal*) and proscription (*haram*). This is in spite of the fact that it is also a text that has been productive for the arts. The visual arts thus arose from the Qur'anic text, for the most important art is the art of calligraphy. The vocal arts arose from the art of reciting the Qur'an – all classical singers in the Arab culture began with Qur'an recitation. How did this diversity of meanings and indications, this presence on all levels, become transformed? I enjoy listening to a recitation of the Qur'an. How much remains hidden because of the limitation to prescription and proscription! In reality, no one enjoys the Qur'an. We read the Qur'an and are afraid, or dream of Paradise. We transform the Qur'an into a text that provides incentives, and intimidates. Into a stick and a carrot. I want to liberate the Qur'an from this prison, so that it is productive again for the essence of the culture and of the arts, which are strangled in our society.[61]

Hermeneutics

Abu Zayd highlights his relationship to Amin al-Khuli as a reference to his own Egyptian roots, but does not conceal the fact that his theories took shape through his engagement and discussion with writers from different times and contexts, including the Iranian grammarian Sibawayhi (d. *c.* 800), the Japanese Islamic scholar Toshihiko Izutsu, who introduced analytical linguistic methods to Islamic studies, and the German philosopher and theoretician of hermeneutics, Hans-Georg Gadamer, author of the influential work *Wahrheit und Methode*. Some of these discussions are documented in his book *Ishkaliyyat al-qira'a wa aliyyat al-ta'wil*, which is a compilation of his main linguistic and literary articles. The work includes an annotated introduction to European philosophical hermeneutics,[62] which was first published as early as 1981, and was one of the first comprehensive surveys on this topic in the Arabic language. The emphasis on Gadamer's hermeneutics links Abu Zayd specifically to the Iranian theologian Mohamad Mojtahed Shabestari,[63] but seems to indicate at the same time a broader trend within contemporary Islamic thinking. The relevance attributed to hermeneutics for the interpretation of religious writings is partly due to the fact that, in contrast to analytical linguistic and positivistic methods, hermeneutics stresses the subjectivity of any kind of understanding of a text. In philosophical hermeneutics, initiated substantially by the theologian and philosopher Friedrich Schleiermacher (d. 1834), the cognitive subject generally reflects his personal circumstances. This is based on the idealistic principle that the subject is instrumental in shaping the world and that knowledge never reflects a reality which is independent of the subject. Applied to the Qur'an, this means that it has no 'objective' meaning which is accessible to individuals (or theologians). It also implies that, unlike logical empiricism, no strict 'natural scientific' distinction exists between the subject (interpreter) and the object (text). Instead, each interpretation is the result of a certain relationship between the text and its interpreter, and reflects the uniqueness of this relationship. It therefore cannot be identical to an interpretation from another era or socio-cultural context. This subject-focused approach is particularly explosive in the light of the current trend throughout the Islamic world to grasp the one and 'true' meaning of the Qur'an (a virtually positivistic approach), the subject's sole task being merely to analyse this unchanging truth.[64]

Critique of religious discourse

Abu Zayd's provocative critique of the dominant Islamic discourse in Egypt, which he puts forward above all in *Naqd al-khitab al-dini* and two books on the status of women,[65] evolves from his concept of the text: arguing for the plurality of exegesis, he rejects claims that link Islam to one, eternally valid interpretation:

> This is a statement that is disproved by the history of Islam, the history that witnessed a diversity of trends, currents and groups that arose for societal, economic, and political reasons, and formed their standpoints by interpreting and trying to understand the texts. Whatever the intentions of one book or the other, this insistence on the existence of a single Islam and the rejection of the plurality that actually exists leads to two results. The first is a single, unchanging understanding of Islam, an understanding impervious to the influence of the movement of history and of the differences between societies, not to mention the influence of the diversity of groups that take form within a single society, due to the differences between their interests. The second result is that this unchanging understanding is possessed by a group of people – the theologians exclusively – and that the members of this group are considered to be free of the arrogance and the natural bias of humans.[66]

Abu Zayd condemns the 'creation of a priesthood' which claims to 'understand true Islam' in order to confine 'the power of interpretation and commentary to this circle'.[67] In their view the theologian has sole right of interpretation, contrary to Islamic doctrine, which rejects a 'sacred power or priesthood'.[68] More inexcusable still, they present their interpretation as the absolute truth, denying any other opinion. This removes the distinction between the text and its interpretation.[69] As Abu Zayd puts it:

> Everyone talks about *the one* Islam, without any of them feeling any trace of uncertainty whether this is in truth *his* (own) understanding of Islam, or of its texts.[70]

Furthermore, Abu Zayd points out that by claiming to recognise the divine intention in the Islamic texts, theologians venture into 'a sensitive area, the area of "speaking in the name of God", which religious discourse throughout its history has avoided, except in a few cases'.[71] Such reasoning, he maintains, 'eventually leads to the appointment of a certain species of human being who claim to have a monopoly on comprehension, explanation, commentary and interpretation, and thus feel that they alone are entitled to speak about God'.[72]

Above all, this monopolisation of interpretation runs parallel with the extension of its social relevance, since the texts or, more precisely, a specific, contemporary interpretation of these determined not least by political interests, are defined as a comprehensive frame of reference (*marja'iyya shamila*): all social or physical phenomena are traced directly to God, and the texts are expected to explain these phenomena. Abu Zayd points out that this understanding of the Qur'an at the same time contradicts the very message of the Qur'an itself, since it negates the importance of human reason, and contradicts the tradition of understanding God's revelation in the Islamic world.

> It gives pause for thought that none of the exegetes or thinkers defends his explanation of natural or human phenomena on the grounds that this is 'Islam'. When the Prophet's companion 'Abd Allah ibn 'Abbas (who bears the title of 'the interpreter of the Qur'an' – *tarjuman al-Qur'an*, and 'scholar of the community' – *habr al-umma*) explained thunder as 'an angel who drives the clouds before him with a silver catapult' (an explanation that can be traced back to statements of the Apostle, may God bless and keep him) in some hadith compilations, none of the Muslims grasped this as an absolute, holy, religious meaning which scientific research must not contradict. The Muslims understood that the religious texts present no explanation for physical and human phenomena, but that their explanation is left to the activity of human reason, which develops continually, in order to discover the horizons of humanity and nature. This understanding precisely is among the most important reasons for the scientific and technical achievements of Muslim scholars – those same scholars whom current religious thought never ceases proudly pointing to – on account of what they gave to Europe in the way of foundations for (and precursors of) the experimental method, at the beginning of the Renaissance.[73]

Abu Zayd criticises the frequent contemporary calls for the Islamisation not only of law, but of literature, art and knowledge in general. According to these, in all fields of culture and science the Qur'an and Sunna should become the 'authority for judgements and analyses',[74] leading ultimately to the domination of all areas of life by 'men of religion (*rijal al-din*)'.[75] He underlines the fact that although the tendency to see the Qur'an as a general frame of reference for all areas of life was not invented by contemporary Islamists and indeed stems from a long tradition whose roots go back to the Kharijis,[76] during the Prophet's lifetime, religious and secular affairs were kept quite separate. Thus:

> From the first moments in the history of Islam – and during the period of the Revelation and the formation (*tashakkul*) of the texts – there was a stable awareness that the texts of the religion have a special area of validity or activity (*majalat fa"aliyyatiha*), and that there are other areas subject to the activity of human reason and experience, which are not connected with the activity of the texts. It often happened that, when presented with a situation, the first Muslims asked the Prophet whether his behaviour was based on a revelation or on his personal experience and reason. And they often had a different opinion than his and suggested a different behaviour, when it had to do with an area of experience and reason.[77]

Abu Zayd's criticism of contemporary phenomena is not a political sub-agenda in an otherwise purely academic debate. On the contrary, the scholarly study of the past as a tool to understand and change the present is a vital aspect of his work. His criticism of leading contemporary theologians and journalists in Egypt and his challenging of their monopoly on the interpretation of the sacred texts is indeed highly political. It is part of the struggle by a number of intellectuals against the mounting influence of religious authorities in all parts of society, and the growing acceptance of Islamist ideas within the state. Abu Zayd frequently attacks government religious policy and the prevalent official religious discourse in Egypt, which is shaped by al-Azhar University, televised religious programmes and the conservative, partly state-owned press. He accuses prominent protagonists of this discourse of abusing religion for political power and, sometimes, financial gain. He also sees no essential difference between their line of thought and that of the extremist religious opposition. In fact he claims that it was precisely the state-controlled religious media, with their immense influence on the largely illiterate Egyptian population, that paved the way for religiously-motivated violence. In his view, the struggle between ruling Islamic representatives and those who oppose the regime is not a conflict between two different ideologies: it is a raw struggle for power. Because his critique of social trends and political decisions appears in the context of an academic study of Islam, it is no surprise that those at the receiving end of his criticism, and their supporters, have reacted on a theological level, and retaliated with accusations of heresy. Abu Zayd described this mechanism in his book *Naqd al-khitab al-dini*, in the following terms: 'We are allowed to challenge the rule of men; one can oppose it through various forms of human combat, and replace it by more just systems. But the struggle against the rule of theologians is subject to accusations of unbelief, atheism and heresy, generally depicted as disobedience and heresy against the power of God'.[78] One year later, in an interview to the *Middle East Times* in the summer of 1993, he could make the ironic comment concerning himself that: 'Every academic is happy to see his ideas become reality'.[79]

A further reason for the indignation triggered by Abu Zayd is the vocabulary and methods he employs to discuss the Qur'an. A book like *Mafhum al-nass* seems from the outset to have no relation to the forms and formulations of traditional Qur'anic exegesis which have survived relatively unchanged for centuries. Abu Zayd does not balk at terms like ideology, historicity, code and dialectics, and discusses God's revelation – influenced by Western hermeneutics and linguistics – using a theoretical communication model, whose terminology he has translated into Arabic. The fact that the contents and findings of the model are less new and spectacular than the model itself is soon overlooked. Bearing in mind the outcry that his work has provoked in Egyptian society, one is perhaps surprised to find that, while undoubtedly scholarly and informative, his writings contain large passages of rather dry explanations from traditional Qur'anic studies, or analyses of these, which neither attempt to redefine

Islam nor to challenge belief in the divine origin of the revelation. In fact, the least productive approach to Abu Zayd's writings is to search for entirely new and, from an Islamic viewpoint, 'heretical' ideas. It is one of the characteristics of his writings that they make mention of religious beliefs, but largely succeed in excluding them from the academic discourse. During a long interview published by the journal *al-Qahira* in November 1993, Abu Zayd himself repeatedly stressed that he did not aim to present a completely new concept or thesis, but simply to rework themes which have already been discussed in classical Qur'anic studies. 'I have not come with any wonder of scholarly discovery (*mu'jiza ma'rifiyya*)', he said to his discussion partner. He proceeded to remark that 'it was the environment, climate and the attempt to politically instrumentalise religion that made it so'. Whoever searches Abu Zayd's writings looking primarily for statements aimed at shaking belief in the foundations of Islam will be disappointed. In fact he is criticised not only for writings that are too 'un-Islamic', but also for the opposite reason. In an article entitled 'A Discourse which challenges Fundamentalism, but shares the same Roots', the secular writer Ali Harb writes: 'The truth is that Abu Zayd's statements are progressive and secular, but his way of thinking is still fundamentalist (*usuli*).'[80]

Perspectives[81]

Abu Zayd's efforts to redefine the social role of religion, his critique of its political instrumentalisation, and his endeavour to stress the individual and the necessarily subjective experience of the believer in prayer, meditation and reading of the sacred scriptures, all link him to reformist thinkers like Mohammed Arkoun, the Algerian who lives and teaches in Paris, or the Iranian Abdolkarim Soroush, and certain other contemporary Muslim writers. Working in widely varying social and intellectual contexts, such thinkers emphasise the fact that the Qur'an provides general ethical guidelines, but does not have the answer to all human and social issues. Earlier Islamic reformist thinkers defended democracy or respect for human rights on the grounds that such principles are supported by Islam. In contrast, such contemporary intellectuals argue that we should not resort to Islam to support such principles: we should rather uphold them on the basis of our own human reason and social will. 'Islam', Abu Zayd argues, 'as a religion acts as a frame of reference, but I can't influence human rights by simply referring to Islam. After all, many human achievements undeniably exist outside of religion.'[82] By rejecting the instrumentalisation of religion irrespective of motivation (including, in other words, its exploitation for politically progressive programmes), such intellectuals have overcome a basic obstacle in Muslim reformist thinking. Earlier generations felt obliged to interpret religious source texts that challenge modern notions of human rights and society to the point where they resolved any contradiction between the two. Abu Zayd and Soroush, to name only two contemporary thinkers, accept the contradiction as a matter of fact but consider it irrelevant because it does not affect the essence of religion.

To conclude, the most interesting aspect of Abu Zayd's work appears to be his attempt – based on a profound knowledge of the traditional religious sciences – to adapt the findings of modern linguistics and the theories of philosophical hermeneutics to his analysis of the Qur'an and Islamic theology. In doing so, he has continued a promising project in literary exegesis initiated by al-Khuli, which views the Qur'an as a poetically structured text, and a literary monument, rather than a list of judgements or a merely legal text. Like al-Khuli and his direct associates (especially his widow 'A'isha 'Abd al-Rahman and his pupil Muhammad Ahmad Khalafallah), Abu Zayd has a deep-seated knowledge of Islamic tradition. However he makes an even more pronounced effort to apply the findings of modern linguistic science and the theories of philosophical hermeneutics to the study of the Qur'an and Islamic theology. This has produced remarkable parallels to concerted efforts within contemporary Western Islamic studies to study the Qur'an as a literary text. The fact that Abu Zayd is not a lone voice but has contemporary Muslim colleagues who hold

similar views indicates that the field of Qur'anic studies in the
Islamic world is becoming increasingly diverse and reflective.

NOTES

1. This article is based on Navid Kermani, *Offenbarung als
Kommunikation. Das Konzept wahy in Nasr Hamid Abu Zayds 'Mafhum al-nass'*
(Frankfurt am Main, 1996).

2. On Abu Zayd's biography cf. his autobiographical *Ein Leben mit dem
Islam.* Narr., Navid Kermani; German trans., Chérifa Magdi (Freiburg,
1999); information also available online: http://msanews.mynet.net/
Scholars/NasrAbu.

3. Statement printed in *al-Tasawwuf al-Islami,* July 1995, p. 47.

4. *Mafhum al-nass: dirasa fi 'ulum al-Qur'an* (Cairo, 1990), p. 11.

5. Ibid., p. 247.

6. *Naqd al-khitab al-dini* (Cairo, 1992), p. 87

7. *Mafhum al-nass,* p. 11; similarly *Naqd al-khitab al-dini,* p. 99.

8. Cf. *Mafhum al-nass,* pp. 247–73.

9. Ibid., p. 337.

10. *Naqd al-khitab al-dini,* p. 93.

11. *Mafhum al-nass,* p. 27; cf. *al-Nass, al-sulta, al-haqiqa: al-fikr al-dini
bayna iradat al-ma'rifa wa iradat al-haymana* (Cairo, 1995), pp. 213–85.

12. 'Nazariyyat hawl al-dirasa al-simiyutiqiyya li al-thaqafat' and
'Mushkilat al-luqta', both published in Nasr Hamid Abu Zayd and Siza
Qasim, eds, *Anzimat al-'alamat. Madkhal ila al-simiyutiqa* (Cairo, 1986).

13. *The Structure of the Artistic Text,* trans. Gail Lenhoff and Ronald
Vroon (University of Michigan, n.d.), p. 6.

14. Ibid., p. 23.

15. Ibid.

16. Cf. *Naqd al-khitab al-dini,* pp. 37 ff. In passages like this it becomes
evident why Muhammad Abduh is among the Muslim scholars to whom
Abu Zayd refers frequently; cf. Muhammad Rashid Rida, ed., *Tafsir al-
Qur'an al-shahir bi tafsir al-Manar.* 12 vols, 4th edn (Cairo, 1954–1961),
commentary on Q. 2: 111.

17. *Naqd al-khitab al-dini,* pp. 93 f.

18. Cf. *Mafhum al-nass,* pp. 28 ff.

19. Badr al-Din Muhammad ibn 'Abd Allah al-Zarkashi, *al-Burhan fi
'ulum al-Qur'an,* 4 vols (Beirut, 1988).

20. Jalal al-Din al-Suyuti, *al-Itqan fi 'ulum al-Qur'an,* ed. Ahmad Sa'd
'Ali (Cairo, 1951).

21. Ibid., p. 250.

22. Cf. ibid., p. 252.

23. Ibid., p. 251.

24. *Mafhum al-nass,* p. 11.

25. *al-Ittijah al-'aqli fi al-tafsir: dirasa fi qadiyyat al-majaz fi al-Qur'an
'inda al-Mu'tazila* (Beirut, 1982).

26. *Falsafat al-ta'wil: dirasa fi ta'wil al-Qur'an 'inda Muhyi al-Din ibn 'Arabi* (Beirut, 1983).

27. Cf. Muhyi al-Din Ibn 'Arabi, *al-Futuhat al-Makkiyya*, 13 vols, ed. Ibrahim Madkur and 'Uthman Yahya (Cairo 1405/1985, 1410/1990).

28. *Ein Leben mit dem Islam*, p. 111 ff.

29. *al-Imam al-Shafi'i wa ta'sis al-idiyulujiyya al-wasatiyya* (Cairo, 1992).

30. *Mafhum al-nass*, pp. 275–350.

31. *al-Nass, al-sulta, al-haqiqa*, pp. 13–66.

32. *Mafhum al-nass*, p. 12.

33. 'Die Befreiung des Korans. Ein Gespräch mit dem ägyptischen Literaturwissenschaftler Nasr Hamid Abu Zaid', interview by the author, published in the German edition of *Naqd al-khitab al-dini: Islam und Politik. Kritik des religiösen Diskurses*, trans. Chérifa Magdi (Frankfurt am Main, 1996), pp. 191–213; this quote, p. 201.

34. *Mafhum al-nass*, p. 13.

35. 'Die Befreiung des Korans', p. 200.

36. *Mafhum al-nass*, p. 337.

37. 'Die Befreiung des Korans', p. 196.

38. Abu Zayd here refers to the distinction between meaning and significance as advanced by the American linguist Eric D. Hirsch Jr. (*Validity in Interpretation*. Yale, 1969, pp. 1–10.). This can be traced back to the German philosopher Gottlieb Frege: 'Über Sinn und Bedeutung', *Zeitschrift für Philosophie und philosophische Kritik*, NF 100 (1892), pp. 25–50.

39. *Mafhum al-nass*, p. 64.

40. Ibid., p. 28.

41. One of Abu Zayd's analyses that address this topic is available in English: 'Divine Attributes in the Qur'an: Some Poetic Aspects', in John Cooper, Ronald L. Nettler and Mohamed Mahmoud, eds, *Islam and Modernity: Muslim Intellectuals Respond* (London, 1998), pp. 190–211.

42. Especially his *God and Man in the Koran: Semantics of the Koranic Weltanschauung* (Tokyo, 1964; repr. New York, 1980).

43. *Mafhum al-nass*, p. 27.

44. Ibid., p. 27.

45. Ibid.

46. *Naqd al-khitab al-dini*, p. 195.

47. Ibid., p. 63.

48. *Mafhum al-nass*, p. 120; cf. ibid., p. 212.

49. Cf. ibid., pp. 173–178.

50. *Naqd al-khitab al-dini*, p. 194. Abu Zayd refers here to the famous distinction between *parole* and *langue*; cf. Ferdinand de Saussure, *Cours linguistique générale* (Paris, 1916).

51. *Mafhum al-nass*, p. 212.

52. Cf. Abul Hasan 'Abd al-Jabbar, *I'jaz al-Qur'an* (vol. 16 of his *Mughni fi abwab al-tawhid wal-'adl*), ed. Amin al-Khuli (Cairo, 1380/1960).

53. Cf. 'Abd al-Qahir al-Jurjani, *Dala'il fi i'jaz al-Qur'an*, ed. Mahmud Muhammad Shakir (Cairo, 1404/1984).

54. Amin al-Khuli's theories on the exegesis of the Qur'an are mainly found in his compilation *Manahij tajdid fi al-nahw wal-balagha wal-tafsir*

wal-adab (Cairo, 1961), cf. in particular the chapter 'al-Tafsir. Ma'alim hayatihi – manhajuhu al-yawm' (pp. 279–336), first published in 1944 in Cairo. On al-Khuli cf. Katrin Speicher, 'Einige Bemerkungen zu al-Khuli's Entwurf eines *tafsir adabi*', in Lutz Edzard and Christian Szyska, *Encounters of Words and Texts: Intercultural Studies in Honour of Stefan Wild on the Occasion of his 60th Birthday, March 2, 1997, Presented by his Pupils in Bonn*. (Hildesheim, New York, 1997), pp. 3–21. A survey can also be found in J.J.G. Jansen, *The Interpretation of the Qur'an in Modern Egypt* (Leiden, 1974), pp. 65–68.

55. al-Khuli, *Manahij tajdid*, p. 304.

56. Amin al-Khuli did not produce a commentary on the Qur'an himself; however his ideas can be found, albeit in a more moderate form, in the writings of his wife 'A'isha 'Abd al-Rahman; cf. her *al-Tafsir al-bayani li al-Qur'an*, 2 vols. (Cairo, 1966); *al-Qur'an wal-tafsir al-'asri* (Cairo, 1970). For another book inspired by al-Khuli's exegetical programme, cf. Muhammad Ahmad Khalafallah's controversial *al-Fann al-qasasi fi al-Qur'an al-karim* (Cairo, 1953).

57. al-Khuli, *Manahij tajdid*, p. 296.

58. Ibid., p. 303.

59. Ibid.

60. Ibid., p. 304.

61. 'Die Befreiung des Korans', p. 204.

62. 'al-Hirminiyutiqa wa mu'dilat tafsir al-nass', first printed in *Fusul*, April, 1981. A valuable analysis of explicit and implicit parameters, sources and underpinnings of Abu Zayd's thought can be found in Charles Hirschkind, 'Heresy or Hermeneutics: The Case of Nasr Hamid Abu Zaid', *The American Journal of Islamic Social Sciences*, 12 (1995), p. 477 ff.

63. Abu Zayd himself stresses his affinity to Shabestari in a long interview to an important Iranian religious journal, which was banned shortly afterwards: Morteza Kariminiya, 'Ta'wil, haqiqat wa nass: Goft-o-gu-ye Kiyan ba Nasr Hamed Abu Zayd', *Kiyan*, 54 (2000), pp. 2–17. His emphasis on the indispensable multiplicity of interpretations connects him, of course, to another Iranian intellectual, Abdolkarim Soroush. It is interesting to note that a well-known Iranian publisher (*Tarh-e nou*) is planning to publish a Persian translation of *Mafhum al-nass* soon.

64. Cf. Navid Kermani, *Gott ist schön. Das ästhetische Erleben des Qur'an* (Munich, 1999), pp. 121–49.

65. *al-Mar'a fi khitab al-azma* (Cairo, 1995); *Dawa'ir al-khawf: qira'a fi khitab al-mar'a* (Casablanca, 1999).

66. *Naqd al-khitab al-dini*, p. 30.

67. Ibid., p. 31.

68. Ibid.

69. Cf. ibid., pp. 28, 37.

70. Ibid., p. 29.

71. Ibid.

72. Ibid., p. 81.

73. Ibid., p. 186 f.; cf. *Mafhum al-nass*, p. 251 f.

74. *Naqd al-khitab al-dini*, p. 187. The call for Islamisation of knowledge has been put forward in the last decades by scholars and institutions in

different Islamic countries, but Abu Zayd refers to only one specific example, an 'International Conference on Islamic Literature' organised by the 'Society of Young Muslims' in January 1990.

75. Ibid., p. 188.
76. Cf. *al-Imam al-Shafi'i*, p. 21 f.
77. *Naqd al-khitab al-dini*, p. 28.
78. Ibid., p. 81.
79. Stefan Negus, 'Professor Charged With Apostasy', *Middle East Times*, 6–12 July 1993.
80. 'Nasr Hamid Abu Zayd. Khitab yunahid al-usuliyya wa lakinnahu yaqifu 'ala ardiha', in Ali Harb, *Naqd al-nass* (Beirut, 1993), pp. 199–220, here, p. 218. Cf. by the same author: *al-Istilab wal-irtidad: al-Islam bayna Rujih Gharudi wa Nasr Hamid Abu Zayd* (Casablanca, 1997).
81. For a more detailed evaluation of Abu Zayd's thought, see Kermani, *Offenbarung als Kommunikation.*
82. Muhammad Husayn Husayn, 'Fahm al-nass. Hiwar ma'a Nasr Hamid Abu Zayd', *Adab wa naqd*, 93 (May 1993), pp. 70–75, here, p. 71.

BIBLIOGRAPHY

Works by Abu Zayd

——. *al-Ittijah al-'aqli fi al-tafsir: dirasa fi qadiyyat al-majaz fi al-Qur'an 'inda al-Mu'tazila.* Beirut, 1982.
——. *Falsafat al-ta'wil: dirasa fi ta'wil al-Qur'an 'inda Muhyi al-Din ibn 'Arabi.* Beirut, 1983.
——. *Anzimat al-'alamat. Madkhal ila al-simiyutiqa* (ed. with Siza Qasim). Cairo, 1986; Casablanca, 1987.
——. *Mafhum al-nass: dirasa fi 'ulum al-Qur'an.* Cairo, 1990.
——. *Ishkaliyyat al-qira'a wa aliyyat al-ta'wil.* Cairo, 1990.
——. *al-Imam al-Shafi'i wa ta'sis al-idiyulujiyya al-wasatiyya.* Cairo, 1992.
——. *al-Khitab al-dini. Ru'ya naqdiyya.* Beirut, 1992.
——. *Naqd al-khitab al-dini.* Cairo, 1992. German trans.: *Islam und Politik: Kritik des religiösen Diskurses*, trans. Chérifa Magdi; intro. Navid Kermani. Frankfurt am Main, 1996.
——. *al-Mar'a fi khitab al-azma.* Cairo, 1995.
——. *al-Tafkir fi zaman al-takfir: didda al-jahl wal-zayf wal-kharafa.* Cairo, 1995.
——. *al-Nass, al-sulta, al-haqiqa: al-fikr al-dini bayna iradat al-ma'rifa wa iradat al-haymana.* Cairo, 1995.
——. *al-Qawl al-mufid fi qissat Abu Zayd.* Cairo, 1995.
——. *Dawa'ir al-khawf: qira'a fi khitab al-mar'a.* Casablanca, 1999.
——. *Ein Leben mit dem Islam.* Narrated by Navid Kermani; German trans., Chérifa Magdi. Freiburg, 1999.

Sources on Abu Zayd

Harb, Ali. *Naqd al-nass.* Beirut, 1993.

——. *al-Istilab wal-irtidad: al-Islam bayna Rujih Gharudi wa Nasr Hamid Abu Zayd*. Casablanca, 1997.

Hirschkind, Charles. 'Heresy or Hermeneutics: The Case of Nasr Hamid Abu Zaid', *The American Journal of Islamic Social Sciences*, 12 (1995), pp. 463–77.

Kariminiya, Morteza. *Ara wa andisheha-ye Doktor Nasr Hamed Abu Zayd*. Tehran, 1998.

Kermani, Navid. 'Rezension von Nasr Hamid Abu Zaid, *Mafhum an-nass*', *Orient*, 36 (1995), pp. 344–46.

——. *Offenbarung als Kommunikation: Das Konzept 'wahy' in Nasr Hamid Abu Zayds 'Mafhum an-nass'*. Frankfurt am Main, 1996.

Wielandt, Rotraud. 'Wurzeln der Schwierigkeit innerislamischen Gesprächs über neue hermeneutische Zugänge zum Korantext', in Stefan Wild, ed., *The Qur'an as Text*. Leiden, 1996, pp. 257–82.

Wild, Stefan. 'Die andere Seite des Textes. Nasr Hamid Abu Zaid und der Koran', *Die Welt des Islams* 33 (1993), pp. 256–61.

Sources on the 'Abu Zayd affair'

Bälz, Kilian. 'Eheauflösung aufgrund von Apostasie durch Popularklage: Der Fall Abu Zayd', *Praxis des Internationalen Privat- und Verfahrensrechts (Iprax)*, 16 (1996), pp. 353–56.

Fawzi, Muhammad, ed. *Nasr Hamid Abu Zayd bayna al-kufr wal-iman*. Cairo, 1995.

Hashim, Muhammad, ed. *Bayna al-takfir wal-tanwir*. Cairo, 1996.

Heilmann, Annette. 'Die Affäre Abu Zayd und der Begriff der "Ethik der Toleranz" in der heutigen politischen Diskussion in Ägypten', in Ferhad Ibrahim, ed., *Staat und Zivilgesellschaft in Ägypten*. Münster and Hamburg, 1995, pp. 145–68.

Kermani, Navid. 'Die Affäre Abu Zayd. Eine Kritik am religiösen Diskurs und ihre Folgen', *Orient*, 35 (1994), pp. 25–49.

Najjar, Fauzi M. 'Islamic Fundamentalism and the Intellectuals: The Case of Nasr Hamid Abu Zayd', *British Journal of Middle Eastern Studies*, 27 (2000), pp. 177–200.

Shahin, 'Abd al-Sabur, ed. *Qissat Abu Zayd wa inhisar al-'almaniyya fi jami'at al-Qahira*. Cairo, 1995.

Sfeir, George N. 'Basic Freedom in a Fractured Legal Culture: Egypt and the case of Nasr Hamid Abu Zayd', *Middle East Journal*, 52 (1998), pp. 402–14.

The magazines *al-Qahira* (125, 1993) and *Adab wa naqd* (93, 1993) have dedicated special issues to Abu Zayd which include important articles, interviews, documents, biographical data, and the controversial university reports on Abu Zayd.

For a comprehensive bibliography including Abu Zayd's articles, interviews, and translations, as well as Arabic articles on Abu Zayd, cf. Kermani, *Offenbarung als Kommunikation*, pp. 121–138.

7

Post-revolutionary Islamic modernity in Iran: the intersubjective hermeneutics of Mohamad Mojtahed Shabestari

FARZIN VAHDAT

P OST - REVOLUTIONARY Islamic thought in Iran is very much characterised by a hermeneutic approach. However, the hermeneutics involved in this thought is of a different nature from that of its predecessors, that is, the Islamic revolutionary discourses of the 1960s and 1970s. The contemporary Islamic discourse in Iran is no longer engaged primarily in a direct inter-pretation of Qur'anic verses, and much less so of the Sunna. The chief reason for this turn of events, it seems, is the peculiar nature of socio-political developments in Iran, particularly the advent of the Islamic Revolution and its complex relations with the forces of the modern world. The Islamic revolutionary discourse of the previous generation undoubtedly advanced serious challenges to the discourse of modernity. Yet, in its own discourse, the Islamic thought of the revolutionary era was itself very much affected by the discourse of modernity, mostly at the philosophical and theo-retical levels. Thus, many of the figures who contributed to the Islamic thought of the 1960s and 1970s were in one way or another involved in the interpretation of the Qur'an, and to a lesser extent the Sunna, in light of what they considered to be the essential elements of modernity. Ali Shariati (1933–1977), Ayat Allah Mahmud Taleqani (1911–1979), Mehdi Bazargan (1907–1995) and

Ayat Allah Morteza Motahhari (1920–1979) were the most prominent of those who were more or less directly involved in their
discourses in reinterpreting Qur'anic verses, in light of what each
believed to be the crucial aspects of the modern civilisation.[1] In
contrast the post-revolutionary Islamic discourses, and especially
those articulated by Mohamad Mojtahed Shabestari and
Abdolkarim Soroush, have, by and large, refrained from interpreting the Qur'anic text directly. It would appear that the post-
revolutionary conditions have led to different sets of interests and
preoccupations among contemporary Islamic thinkers in Iran.

The main reason for this shift from a Qur'anic exegetic
approach to that of a hermeneutics that is not primarily based on
the Qur'an lies in the peculiar nature of the Islamic revolutionary
paradigm of the previous generation. The logic of the revolutionary discourse of the founders of the Islamic state could not
have developed any further because of the particular fashion in
which the metaphysics of the Qur'anic text was interpreted to
construct a notion of human subjectivity and agency which could
not proceed any further, in the context of a deeply religious
society. I use the term 'mediated subjectivity' for the paradigm
that emerged in the process of reinterpreting Islamic thought in
light of modern concepts: it is the result specifically of the interpretation of the Qur'an in light of modern conceptions. Because
of the contradictory nature of this paradigm and the conundrums
it has engendered, the post-revolutionary modernist Islamic
thought in Iran has for the most part avoided direct interpretations of the Qur'an and the Sunna. It has focused instead on an
alternative hermeneutic approach, which is analysed in the
discourse of Mohamad Mojtahed Shabestari in this chapter.[2]

Before discussing the core concept of mediated subjectivity,
some theoretical understanding of the philosophical tenets of
modernity, in interaction with which the Islamic discourses of the
revolutionary era evolved, is necessary.

Two pillars of modernity: subjectivity and universality

Jürgen Habermas has invoked Hegel to understand the normative content of the modern world principally in terms of subjectivity: 'The principle of the modern world is freedom of subjectivity, the principle that all the essential factors present in the intellectual whole are now coming into their right in the course of their development.'[3] In *Philosophy of Right* (e.g., section 124) and elsewhere in his discussion of subjectivity, Hegel seems to be emphasising not only human autonomy but also its beneficiary, the individual. In Hegelian thought, subjectivity is considered as the ontological foundation of the right-bearing individual. As a pillar of modernity, subjectivity in this sense can be viewed as the property characterising the autonomous, self-willing, self-defining, and self-conscious individual agent. Subjectivity, very much rooted in the humanist tradition, tends to view the human individual as the determinant of her or his own life-processes and is related closely to notions such as human freedom, volition, consciousness, reason, individuality, etc., although it is not reducible to any single one of these. An important aspect to keep in mind about subjectivity is that it is simultaneously the repository of emancipation as well as domination. While the Cartesian *cogito* as the modern detached subject is the source of liberation (e.g., the philosophical foundations of the rights of citizenship), it is also responsible for the objectification of nature, the 'other', such as the colonised and women, as well as of the subject itself. From Hegel to Habermas, many social thinkers and philosophers have attempted to reconcile this subject of modernity and its 'other'. Hegel conceptualised this synthesis primarily in terms of universality.

As such, universality, a somewhat more elusive category to analyse, may be perceived as the mutual recognition among the plurality of subjects of each other's subjectivity. Expressed differently and in its historical context, universality refers to elimination of restrictions based on privilege, status and/or other essential considerations. In a more restricted sense, universality could be considered as the bourgeois formal equality before the law. Hegel interpreted the two concepts of subjectivity and universality as epitomised in the notion of civil society, which, according to him, is comprised of 'an association of members as self-sufficient individuals in a universality which because of their self-sufficiency is only formal'.[4] In this passage Hegel seems to be expressing a concern about the diremption from nature and society and the moral 'chaos' that is the result of the process of subjectification and radical human autonomy associated with human subjectivity, which the principle of universality in civil society in Kantian formulation is supposed to heal, but which Hegel finds wanting because of the 'vacuity' and formality of the bourgeois understanding of universality as mere equality before the law. In fact, Hegel was one of the first and most prominent to attempt to address and resolve the contradictions and the close affinity between subjectivity and universality in a substantive (as opposed to formal) synthesis of the two principles.[5]

The principle of subjectivity has given rise to freedom and the notion of individual and collective autonomy in the modern era. The unbridled subjectivity of modernity, however, also has been responsible for moral and political chaos and various types of domination of the 'others'. For this reason, much of the intellectual and political thought since Hegel in one way or another has attempted to address the abstract, monadic, and self-same subject of modernity and has striven to embed it in a larger context.[6] The latest and most comprehensive effort at the synthesis between subjectivity and universality is elaborated in the works of Habermas and his attempt at shifting the ontological foundation of modernity from mere subjectivity to that of intersubjectivity in his theory of communicative action.[7]

Given the historicity of these debates, our concerns here have more to do with the emergence of subjectivity and its path of development in the Islamic revolutionary discourse in Iran than with issues of universality. In the premodern contexts, notions of human subjectivity are embedded in a universality of the divine and the collectivity, and it is only with the emergence of a full-fledged subjectivity in modernity that the 're-embedding' of subjectivity poses a problem.

Islamic revolutionary discourse: the self as mediated subjectivity

The Islamic discourse that developed in the intellectual, political, and social contexts prior to the revolution of 1979 was variegated and nuanced. The thought of Shariati, Ayat Allah Ruh Allah Khumayni (1902–1989) and Motahhari reflect this opalescence. However, the most basic element that connected the discourses of Shariati, Khumayni, and Motahhari was a phenomenon that may be conceptualised as 'mediated subjectivity'. Mediated subjectivity refers to the notion of human subjectivity projected onto the attributes of monotheistic deity – attributes such as omnipotence, omniscience, and volitism – that are then partially re-appropriated by humans. In this scheme, human subjectivity is contingent on God's subjectivity. Thus, while human subjectivity is not denied, it is never independent of the Divine's and in this sense it is 'mediated'. This conceptualisation is usually conducive to a perception of great conflict between the divine subjectivity and human subjectivity, a conflict that gives rise to various other types of conflicts, one of the sharpest of which is the constant and schizophrenic shifting of ground between a confirmation and negation of human subjectivity in general, as well as a constant oscillation between individual subjectivity and a collective notion of subjectivity. In modern Islamic discourses, mediated subjectivity often is expressed in the notion of the human as vicegerent of God on earth (*khalifat Allah*).[8]

The paradigm of mediated subjectivity thus can be considered as a forward movement in the direction of democratic and citizenship rights in a civil society, a movement whose ontological foundation is grounded in the positing of human subjectivity, but which very often is negated almost immediately. During the two decades since the establishment of the Islamic Republic in Iran, the more political and sociological aspects of contradictions of these core sets of conflicts have been revealed. At the more theoretical level these conflicts also have been noticed and much of the post-revolutionary Islamic discourses, in one way or another,

address these issues, in addition to more mundane and immediate matters of everyday political and social concerns. Within
these post-revolutionary Islamic discourses at least two general
trends can be observed.[9]

One trend, closely associated with Abdolkarim Soroush, seems
to be characterised by an attempt to mitigate the contradictions of
the paradigm of mediated subjectivity, and arriving at the thresh-
olds of subjectivity and intersubjectivity, while viewing religion as a
private affair and respecting the religious sensibilities of a Muslim
population.[10] The second trend, the focus of this chapter, is
represented by Mohamad Mojtahed Shabestari. It is best
described as an attempt to overcome the contradictions of mediated subjectivity which it has inherited, by endeavouring to
reconcile the disparate terms of that paradigm. Thus, while
remaining within the paradigm of mediated subjectivity, this
second trend seems to be effecting a significant reduction of the
impact of the fluctuations characteristic of it.

As I will argue below, Shabestari has integrated hermeneutic
and existentialist approaches in his thought, in order to smooth
the contradictions in the discourses of his revolutionary predecessors. As such, he has attempted to achieve an interpretive
formulation of an Islamic orientation that is much more compatible with the exigencies and challenges (as well as addressing
some of the discontents) of the enormous forces of the modern
world. However, because of the peculiar nature of mediated
subjectivity, in which human status as God's vicegerent cannot
develop any further, the Islamic discourses in post-revolutionary
Iran have had to take a detour. This detour, which appears in the
mature discourse of Shabestari, has involved a hermeneutical
approach which, for the most part, avoids any direct interpretation of the Qur'anic text.

Shabestari and the hermeneutics of intersubjectivity

Shabestari is a professor of theology at Tehran University. He was
born in Shabestar, a district of Tabriz, in 1936 and received a

traditional seminary education at Qom, where he lived from 1950 to 1968.[11] During his stay in Qom, Shabestari became interested in modern and non-religious fields of inquiry and attempted to learn English. From 1970 until the revolution of 1979, he was the director of the Islamic Centre at Hamburg, West Germany. While he does not seem to have attained any formal education in Germany, he became fluent in German and well-versed in the German theological and philosophical tradition of scholarship. In Qom, Shabestari served on the editorial board of the *Makatab Islam*, a Shi'i journal which addressed many of the social and political issues of the 1960s and 1970s, and the problems and challenges that Muslims faced in the modern world. By contributing frequently to this journal, Shabestari established a reputation as a progressive cleric, interested in the place of Muslims in the modern world. After the revolution, he published his own liberal-leaning journal called *Andishe Islami* for a while in Tehran. During the chaotic and tumultuous early years of the revolution, *Andishe Islami* created a forum for the more moderate Muslim thinkers and readers, especially among the younger and less dogmatic Islamic intelligentsia. Shabestari was elected to the first Islamic Consultative Assembly after the revolution from his native Shabestar, but after serving his four year term he has devoted most of his time to teaching and writing. Currently, Shabestari enjoys a large reception among the youth in Iran, especially the college students, many of whom come from religious backgrounds and seek a new interpretation of religion that is compatible with the exigencies of the modern society.

Unlike Soroush, who has totally eschewed the theomorphic approach to human subjectivity, Shabestari has upheld the metaphysical assumptions of his predecessors more or less intact.[12] He maintains that 'the Quran recognises the human as the ruler on earth, its developer, employer of other living forms and creators of civilization and culture'.[13] In fact, Shabestari has posited a form of 'journey toward subjectivity' that characterised the discourses of his revolutionary predecessors Shariati, Khumayni, and Motahhari. Referring to existential conditions such as 'history', 'language', 'society', and the '[human] body' as four sources of human unfreedom, Shabestari has called for a migration from a 'self' caught in these 'prisons' toward divinity:

> Islam is a 'total (re)orientation', and when there is a reorientation, there is an emerging from the 'self', a migration from the self, a travel from the self to the Other. It is our self from which we must migrate, the self which constitutes the dimensions of human identity; the historical self, social self and the linguistic self. Humans are limited by four 'dimensions' in which they normally live: history, society, body and language. The role of divine revelation is to open another horizon and, without negating the four [existential] dimensions, to make them transparent, traversing the human toward God. To be certain, this transcendence is always accompanied by dust and is never completely transparent.[14]

Shabestari also paraphrases 'Allama Mohamad Hossein Tabataba'i (1903–1981), to the effect that the idea of prophethood finds its meaning in its role as guiding humans in a movement from nature toward the 'meta-physical' realm and perfection.[15] Very much reminiscent of his intellectual parents in the two decades prior to the Islamic Revolution, Shabestari broaches the notion of human subjectivity in terms of God's vicegerency on earth. He writes:

> Both Islam and Christianity consider man a being whose essence is superior to matter. He is the noblest being and God's successor [*khalifa*] on earth. He is in possession of a God-seeking, free, and independent nature, and carries God's trust. He is responsible for himself and the universe, dominant over nature, the earth and heavens; he is inspired [by knowledge] of good and evil ... his capacity to know and act are limitless.[16]

However, compared to his revolutionary forerunners, Shabestari places less emphasis on a theomorphic approach to human subjectivity. Just like Soroush, and alarmed by the excessive revolutionary zeal that such approaches inspired during the early phases of the revolutionary period, Shabestari has warned against notions of humans becoming God-like (*khoda-guneh shodan*) in the process of historical development.[17] In addition to the concern about the excessive zeal that can result from a theomorphic approach to human subjectivity, there is also another crucial factor involved. The logic of theomorphic subjectivity, albeit deeply rooted in an Islamic metaphysics, cannot further develop in a strongly religious society like Iran, since it inevitably would come into conflict with other, more entrenched, aspects of religiosity, and notions of divine sovereignty.

A hermeneutic approach to subjectivity

Because of the impossibility and undesirability of further extending the logic of theomorphic subjectivity, it seems that Shabestari's discourse has taken an epistemological detour. As early as 1979, and possibly before, Shabestari had insisted that our understanding of revelation must be viewed in terms of a hermeneutic exercise, and that this understanding is not a fixed category.[18] It is, however, his very important book *Hermenutik, Ketab va Sunnat: farayand-e tafsir-e vahy*, published in 1996, that provides the hallmark of Shabestari's mature work. In this book he has posited the act of 'interpretation' as a form of agency that can easily be elevated to the position of subject in the hermeneutic process. In this process, the text cannot but be the object to the subjectivity of the hermeneutic interpretation: 'Every text is a hidden reality that has to be revealed through interpretation. The meaning of the text is produced in the act of interpretation. In reality, the text comes to speak by means of interpretation, and pours out what it contains inside.'[19]

Arguably, it is the silence of the text that leads to the agent and subject of interpretation. This subjectivity of the interpreter vis-à-vis the text is valid even in regard to revelation.[20] As Shabestari has put it:

> Verses do not speak by themselves. It is the interpreter (*mufasser*) who raises a question first, and then seeks its meaning by interpreting different verses. Wherefrom does the interpreter derive his basic assumptions? His question contains basic assumptions that are not derived from the Quran itself, but from various [human] sources of knowledge.[21]

Shabestari's hermeneutic approach is also marked by other unmistakable characteristics of modern subjectivity. He has argued that interpretation is possible only as a result of a critical attitude. First, as he has argued, the very belief in the necessity of interpretation for the text is grounded in the critical attitude,[22] associated, one may add, with the modern subject. Second, the interpretive act involves volition and intention on the part of the interpreter, characteristic attributes of the modern subject. As Shabestari has described it, 'every interpretation of the text' involves a volitional act that is 'derived from interpreters' interests and is implemented in order to achieve a goal'.[23]

Delving into the linguistic theories of the Mu'tazila, Shabestari has argued for the 'conventional' character of signifiers,[24] and the intentionality of the speech acts. The intentionality in Mu'tazili semiotics secures a place for agency, since the subject of speech attaches the signifier to the signified only by intention:

> In the view of the Mu'tazilis, the first condition for [establishing] signification is *muwazia* and pre-agreed human conventions to determine the relation between the signifiers and the signified. The second condition is the knowledge of the circumstances, attributes and intentions of the speaker. In his oeuvre, al-Qadi 'Abd al-Jabbar emphasises the conditions of the speaker, his attributes and his intentions.[25]

One of the radical corollaries of Shabestari's hermeneutic approach is that knowing God is impossible without a body of human-based knowledge. Knowing God and his prophets in all ages has not been possible except through human knowledge and the episteme of the specific period. In every period the intellectual foundations utilised by everyone who engages in understanding and interpreting God or the prophets are derived from the human sources of knowledge available in that period. These bodies of knowledge, whether philosophical or experimental, are the only means that make human conceptualisation and acknowledgment of God and the Prophet possible. Society can only survive with these mundane and human sources of knowledge, and religious thought can only receive nourishment from these sources. Moreover, these types of knowledge are subject to change, since human history changes.[26] Even the efforts of *ijtihad* (the application of individual judgement to the sources of Islamic jurisprudence to derive religious injunctions), based on certain preconceptions and accepted conventions, are all grounded in human knowledge.[27]

This approach inevitably has led Shabestari to make a distinction between what is eternal and fixed, and what is subject to change, in religion.[28] As I will analyse more elaborately below, Shabestari believes that specific precepts and rules, for the most part, belong to the realm of 'change', and only general and broad principles fall into the fixed and eternal category. With regard to the political sphere and the issue of the state and its forms and institutions, for example, Shabestari maintains that there are no given preferences, and all that is emphasised in Islam is the principle of justice.[29] The Qur'an does not consider it within its purview to determine the form of the state and methods of ruling. Rather, the proper task of revelation is to establish the fundamental values involved in governing.[30] In fact, Shabestari has alluded that he concurs with some Islamic theologians and *fuqaha'* that the general and principal purposes established by the Prophet and the shari'a may be confined to the following: 'The protection of persons (*nufus*), intellects (*'uqul*), lineages (*ansab*), properties, and religion.'[31]

Another implication of Shabestari's hermeneutic approach is the need for new bodies of knowledge and human sciences to inform the preconceived notions that Muslim scholars bring to their intellectual activities and understanding of the world. The new bodies of knowledge are necessary because without them it is not feasible to distinguish between the fixed and eternal principles, and the rules and precepts that are subject to change.[32] Contemporary *fuqaha'* need to be conversant with modern human sciences and philosophical approaches in order to be able to renew their preconceptions and areas of interest. Sciences such as modern anthropology, philosophy, sociology, history, economics, political science, and psychology are necessary to inform the foundational assumptions in *fiqh*. Traditional philosophy is not adequate in achieving the task. The fact that the Shi'i seminaries have neglected the modern human sciences is the reason why, 'today, we do not have a proper philosophy of law, neither a philosophy of ethics and politics, nor a philosophy of economics.'[33]

The subtle confirmation of human subjectivity through a hermeneutic approach and its corollaries constitutes only one dimension of Shabestari's mature discourse. The full extent of his thought is evident in his attempt at reconciling the two disparate terms of the Islamic intellectual paradigm that he has inherited *nolens volens.*

Reconciling divine and human subjectivity

Shabestari believes that human knowledge can never penetrate the depth of divine existence; yet, this fact does not mean that human knowledge is to be denied vis-à-vis the ultimate truth. In fact, according to Shabestari's somewhat pantheistic argument, the infinite truth cannot negate the 'finite truth', even though the former subsumes the latter and is in a position of transcendence. Therefore, one must be cautious 'not to set God against the human and make Him deny human existence'.[34] Here again, the conceptual frame that Shabestari draws on consists also of a hermeneutic approach that postulates a dialogue between the two sides of a message, the sender and the receiver – in this case the divine message or revelation – crucial in the understanding of the message. According to Shabestari, every message is addressed to a specific receiver and the meaning of the message transpires in the interplay between both the sender and receiver of the message.[35] Thus, in understanding divine revelation, both sides of the message, God and human, are equally crucial entities.

In a closely related vein, Shabestari has criticised those who claim that *fiqh* can provide the answer for all problems that the Muslim community encounters in modernity. This means the denial of the ability of human knowledge to organise society, and sets religion against reason. Advocates of such views believe that, 'unless the human is denied, no space would be created for God, and until reason is rejected, there cannot be revelation'.[36] Then, in a footnote, Shabestari explains that those who hold such views always consider the relation between God and human in terms of a relation of opposition and domination from above, while in Islamic mystical tradition ('*irfan*), this relation is nothing but 'love'.[37] This means that the Islamic revelation should not be pitted against human achievements in civilisation and culture. As Shabestari has put it:

> In sum, the Qur'an had declared that it did not come to nullify human culture and civilisation. On the contrary, it came to give a new impetus to the existing [human achievements] in the direction of monotheism (*tawhid*). In the early centuries of Islam, a group of fanatic and benighted people appeared who, by denying the entire human knowledge and heritage, claimed all principles and procedures in life must only be derived from the exoteric dimensions of the Book and the Sunna. But the Muslims did not submit to this shortsightedness, and the dignity of human sciences and knowledge was preserved. Had this not happened, there would not be a trace of Islamic culture and civilisation today.[38]

There should be no doubt that Shabestari's positing of human subjectivity and steering clear of any friction with the divine subjectivity is secured by first surrendering to God's sovereignty. Shabestari invoked a central doctrinal concept in the Islamic faith, *tawhid*, which has different layers of meaning but here can be translated as divine unity and profession of the oneness of God. He defined this concept in terms of negation of divinity or sovereignty for all beings except God, and sincere submission to the will of God and surrendering to His law, while living with His love.[39] Yet, Shabestari argues, this will not lead to the negation of human subjectivity:

> This view of *tawhid* is a type of relation between God and man. When this relation is 'lively' (*zendeh*) and 'limpid' (*zolal*), man experiences God ... neither God is negated nor man. In a relation based on pure *tawhid*, God's sovereignty is not competing with man, but gives him meaning and solidifies him.[40]

We can easily distinguish the traces of mediated subjectivity at the core of Shabestari's discourse here. However, what distinguishes Shabestari's discourse is that he tries to avoid the contradictory vacillation of simultaneously positing and negating human subjectivity that characterised the thought of his revolutionary predecessors. In fact, the upshot of Shabestari's discussion of the God–human relation here is not negation of human subjectivity. He has proposed a dialectical scheme in which humans gain consciousness in a perpetual dialogical interaction between divine revelation and human reason. The outcome of this dialogical relation between the human and the Divine is the confirmation of the human. Describing the early human consciousness as 'meager capital', Shabestari wrote:

> The story of [our] understanding of God's word is that of a timeless, wrangling (*jedal amiz*), passionate, and two-sided conversation between man and God. With his meager capital, man [first] turns to God's word and receives a ray [of light] from His word. Man makes sense of what he has received from God's word with his own interpretations. These interpretations ... are given an acceptable form through critique by philosophy and science. This will be man's capital in the next phase, and constitutes his assumptions and predispositions in this phase. A second time man turns to God's word with this [new] capital, and there would be another ray of light. ... This dialogue between man and God, the most incredible story in the universe, continues endlessly. This is how the interpretation of revelation is achieved and there is no end to it. Thus, under these circumstances, as man is never negated vis-à-vis God, he will always remain one party in the dialogue and the addressee of God's revelation.[41]

As mentioned earlier, following other Islamic thinkers before him, including Shariati, Khumayni and Motahhari, Shabestari also employs the notion of a journey from our foundation in matter and nature to a 'spiritual' sphere beyond nature, a process that I have designated as a journey toward subjectivity. Among the previous Islamic thinkers, this journey usually does not culminate in human subjectivity and the modern self-consciousness of the individual, since at the end the 'traveller' is annihilated in God. The usual metaphor that these previous thinkers advanced was that of 'the drop and the ocean', whereby the drop disappears in the ocean at the end of the process of theomorphic journey. In Shabestari's ontology, however, not only is this outcome avoided,

but the result of the movement toward the Absolute is the affirmation of the human. Shabestari has expressed this crucial ontological difference with his predecessors clearly:

> The question is that if man *qua* a fluid, regenerating and self-tran-
> scending, but finite, being of intellect, finds himself at the threshold
> of the Absolute Universal Essence, and experiences himself as a
> drop of the Ocean, would the Absolute negate the human or affirm
> (*qavvam*) him? If the Absolute negates the finite, then God is against
> human freedom. If the Absolute affirms the finite, then God makes
> man into man [i.e., subject]. With deep philosophical reflection it
> becomes apparent that God does not limit and negate man; He does
> not confine or eliminate man. God is the Absolute Universal
> Essence through whom man becomes man.[42]

In fact, the outcome of this journey in Shabestari's account is
freedom and especially freedom of consciousness and thought, a
sine qua non for modern subjectivity. The most important characteristic of the human subject that is the product of this journey, is
that of freedom of consciousness. Shabestari, arguing in an existentialist fashion, believes that freedom of subjectivity is the
necessary result of human contingency and finitude, a finitude
that is in contrast to attributes of the Absolute. Yet, this contingency does not negate freedom and consciousness but is the very
essence of freedom itself.[43] In some instances, Shabestari takes his
position on human freedom to some rather unexpected levels.
The radical freedom of volition that Shabestari has posited seems
to belong to the type of the will that wills itself, that is, human
volition liberated from any force, external or internal, an
autonomous self-foundational will who knows no numen other
than itself.[44] Similarly, Shabestari has declared freedom as the
'authentic identity of humans', and the meaning of authentic
human existence as freedom under all circumstances.[45]

I and Thou

Despite, or perhaps because of, such radical ontological ventures,
Shabestari's notion of subjectivity is, in its larger context,
contained by a notion of 'subject-subject' scheme that is

informed by his hermeneutic and existentialist approaches. The 'philosophy of subject', that of unbridled subjectivity in the modern world, has been criticised as the 'dark' side of modernity from various points of view. Briefly, this critique is in reference to the ontological foundation of modernity that grounds itself in a subject-object relation, where the unbridled freedom of the subject is not delimited by another subject but a relation of domination prevails between the subject and the object.[46]

Drawing on his erudition of European and specifically German hermeneutic theology, Shabestari has proposed an 'I and Thou' design in a subject-subject paradigm. The archetypal sides of the I and Thou relation in Shabestari's discourse are of course none other than the human and the Deity. Yet, the principle actor seems to be the human in this relation. We humans, Shabestari argues, are capable of two types of action. There is action that takes place in reference to objects and there is action that is directed toward another person as a consciousness.[47]

It is only the second type of action that can bring about freedom. We cannot establish an interaction between objects and ourselves. When we direct our volition at an object our will encounters a barrier and rebounds.[48] But it is different in the case of action directed toward another consciousness. The encounter between one person as a consciousness and another also as a consciousness is the only means of guaranteeing freedom for, and the integrity of, both sides.[49] This logic, Shabestari maintains, is true especially in the relation between God and human, where the notion of I and Thou guarantees the highest form of freedom for humans.[50] There is little doubt that Shabestari here is dwelling on an intersubjective paradigm. Yet, owing to his relatively parsimonious treatment of the individual as the carrier of human subjectivity, his notion of intersubjectivity lacks much needed concreteness.

Faith as choosing: individual as the carrier of subjectivity?

To be sure, throughout Shabestari's discourse, one can detect an implicit recognition of the individual as the carrier of human subjectivity. However, this implicit recognition by Shabestari rarely becomes explicit in his writings. It is a cardinal principle in Islam, Shabestari argues, that every Muslim should obtain a rigorous 'conception' (*tasavvor*) of God, the Prophet, the resurrection (*ma'ad*) and the creed (*din*) by herself or himself, without imitating even the highest religious authority.[51] Here the crucial role of the individual subject in making decisions with regard to such solemn tasks needs very little elaboration.

In Shabestari's thought, like that of some other contemporary Islamic thinkers in Iran, any notion of the individual *qua* subject is closely intertwined with that of 'faith'.[52] What makes the subtextual acknowledgement of the individual prevalent in Shabestari's discourse is the grounding of faith in the ability, and in fact the requirement, to choose freely on the part of the individual who comes to believe in the creed. Without the ability to choose freely, faith has no meaning. As Shabestari has put it:

> Faith is an act of choosing, a fateful act. The question is when a human being is facing a dilemma and chooses the type of lifestyle he wants to live by, what path should he take? ... The ideal society for faith [to flourish] and the faithful is one in which [conditions for making] this choice is most widely available. ... The truth of faith is a free act of conscious choice. All of our mystics ('*urafa*') have urged the forsaking of imitated faith and adoption of conscious faith.[53]

Similarly, Shabestari has grounded his understanding of the notion of faith firmly in freedom of thought and free human will. In his recent book, *Iman va azadi*, Shabestari's attempt at reconciling the two conflictual terms in the paradigm of mediated subjectivity is manifested in his effort to harmonise the two categories of faith and freedom. Shabestari has presented four approaches toward the concept of faith in Islamic tradition. According to the first approach, what he refers to as the Ash'ari doctrine, the truth of faith is the profession of belief in God and the prophets as well as divine decrees based on sincere feelings.[54]

In the second approach, espoused by the Mu'tazila, the essence of faith is comprised of 'action based on responsibility'. In this formulation faith stems from innate human rationality that makes us capable of distinguishing between good and evil, and as such charges us with duty and responsibility. The faithful person is one who acts in accordance with this sense of responsibility, and the mere acknowledgement of the prophets is an inadequate measure of faith.[55]

The third approach is that of the Islamic philosophers, for whom the truth of faith is expressed as 'gnosis' (*ma'rifa*) and philosophical knowledge of the 'realities in the sphere of being'. According to the proponents of this view, faith consists of human evolution toward a state of contemplative perfection.[56] Finally, Islamic mystics have interpreted faith as 'embracing (*iqbal*) God and turning away from non-God.[57]

What all these conceptualisations of faith have in common, Shabestari argues, is that they are inseparable from freedom of thought and human free will. The profession of belief as the criterion of faith is only possible through human will, and the latter in its essence belongs to the category of freedom. Since the profession of belief is contingent upon knowledge and 'rational attestation', it cannot be possible without liberation of reason from imitation and unfreedom.[58] The same is true of the Mu'tazilis' view of faith as grounded in the notion of 'natural responsibility'. This responsibility only can be recognised through reason and realised through action. Action that is the principle foundation of faith in this view is in turn the result of human volition, which is again free in its essence.[59]

An analysis of the third conceptualisation of faith as 'philosophical knowledge', Shabestari maintains, demonstrates that this type of knowledge, like other types of knowledge, cannot be possible except through free thought.[60] The mystic's interpretation of faith as 'embracing of God', is possible only if thought is capable of critically transcending itself and liberating itself from any form of dogmatism. Without such a thorough critical attitude, thought cannot be directed toward the embracing of God, while the precondition for a critical attitude is freedom of thought and free human volition.[61]

Throughout *Iman va azadi*, Shabestari's principal aim seems to be the positing of a close link between different interpretations of 'faith' and human freedom, especially freedom of consciousness and free will, in his effort to reconcile modern subjectivity and religion. Yet, he rarely makes any explicit references to the individual as the carrier of modern subjectivity. Only in one passing reference in the entire book does he allude that a collective notion of faith is a vague idea, and it is only individuals who can undergo a religious experience.[62] The rest of Shabestari's discourse seems to be silent on any explicit discussion of the individual as the beneficiary of human subjectivity. Perhaps one of the factors contributing to this phenomenon has to do with Shabestari's familiarity with some of the discontents of modernity, a familiarity which is first and foremost informed not by an 'Islamic' critique of modernity, but by 'Western' critiques of the modern world, expressed in the twentieth century by some Western philosophers and theologians.

Modernity and its discontents

Shabestari thinks that one of the most significant achievements of modernity is the abandoning of dogmatism. Before Muslims encountered modernity, and willingly or unwillingly adopted its epistemological tenets, he argues, Islamic theology and cosmology in general was primarily and obsessively concerned with the question of truth about God, prophecy, and the future of humans in this world and the next. The intellectual atmosphere in which this type of inquiry and pursuit of truth was conducted was that of dogmatism and the search for absolute facts that could corroborate the preconceived notions about religious beliefs.[63] In such an atmosphere 'certitude' was considered the measure for correspondence to truth as well as the salvation of the believers.[64] In our modern era, however, the intellectual and epistemological atmosphere has changed. In this new milieu the philosophical and epistemic dogmatism has been rejected and the certitude of the bygone era is proved fruitless and as a result a form of 'non-dogmatism' pervades in all fields.[65]

The positive consequence of this process, Shabestari seems to suggest, is the prevalence of a critical attitude with regard to all types and facets of knowledge. In the centuries since modernity has taken root, humans have taken a detached attitude toward the mind and its activities, resulting in self-consciousness and a ubiquitous critical approach.[66] As a result, modern humans find themselves in a position that requires constant evaluation, rethinking, and above all constant movement, without having a determined and demarcated goal and destination in view. In such a world, humans always quest after something and always 'face a problem'. Yet, people seek moorings in this world, since all that is solid constantly is deconstructed. This is a world without a definitive 'conception' and meaning and humans lack a definitive conception of themselves.[67] Shabestari suggests that the proper task for modern theology is to address these issues and provide some possible solution to the loss of meaning and 'conception' which is a by-product of the loss of permanence.

Parallel to the loss of meaning and 'conception', Shabestari argues, is the emergence of a 'perplexed self' (*man-e sargardan*, borrowing the notion from Muhammad Iqbal), which has visited the Westerners in modernity because they have abandoned their permanent principles.[68] The Muslims, Shabestari advises, should not be afflicted by a 'perplexed self' and therefore they should not abandon their principles. On the other hand, the rejection and prevention of change in life that caused Muslims' misfortune in the past centuries is neither possible nor desirable. Therefore, the only solution is preserving both, by trying to create a synthesis between what is permanent and what is changeable, a principal goal in Shabestari's discourse.[69]

Shabestari also has criticised the negative side of human subjectivity, domination, and its socio-political consequences. He is rightly cognizant of the darker side of modern subjectivity and its devastating effects, afflicting the victim of the Western subject manifested in such phenomena as colonialism and imperialism, as well as some of the consequences of modern subjectivity affecting the Western subject more directly, for example, domination of humans by technology and consumerism. As Shabestari has put it:

If we ask what is the most prevalent and ubiquitous manner of thought and action of the majority of people in Western societies – the motor of their society – the answer that emerges would be along the following lines: 'empowering of man and making him dominant over the process of everyday life by utilising the three weapons of science, technology and wealth. ... Cardinal evils such as domination of life by machines, old and new colonialism, severe scientific, technological, and even cultural dependence of the countries that are kept underdeveloped on the West ... endangering of human life by nuclear weapons, reducing the meaning of life for the masses to consumerism, the appearance of nihilism and philosophies of nullibicity and other evils of this kind are the consequences of this manner of thought and action.[70]

What Shabestari has described as reification by modern technology (utilising the term 'mashinism', a transliteration from French), seems to be in close parallel to the humanist critiques of the oppressive aspect of modern subjectivity articulated by more than one current of thought in the West in the twentieth century. He has admonished Iranians and other Muslims to be aware of the problems involved in the transfer of technology and act with prudence to achieve a technology that is in 'conformity with humans'.[71] Yet, Shabestari is quick to point out that the modern West cannot be reduced to this reifying aspect. Moreover, there is a growing opposition to this phenomenon in the West itself and the quest for new, as well as old, forms of 'spirituality' remains strong there. Modernity, Shabestari argues, is inevitable and no country, Muslim or otherwise, can escape adjusting itself to its different aspects.[72]

In fact, in the past 150 years the Islamic countries, including Iran, have chosen the modern life-style. The remaining question is how to cope with the darker sides of modernity. Religion can lend its support to ameliorate the crises of meaning, disempowerment, and perplexity that accompany the process of modernisation.[73] It can do so by facilitating the creation of a religious art and literature to provide spiritual nourishment for a society in the process of modernisation.[74] Shabestari, however, does not hesitate to emphasise here that the spiritual support religion can provide in the process of modernisation is totally different from the management of society, political or otherwise, through religion. Shabestari's discourse can be characterised primarily as socio-philosophical; yet, the socio-political aspect of his thought, albeit very subtle and lacking overt polemical and contentious attributes, closely reflects the first aspect, and deserves some examination in itself.

Politics of intersubjective hermeneutics

In *Hermenutik, Ketab va Sunnat,* Shabestari has discussed three types of positions with regard to the encounter of religion and modernity among contemporary religious thinkers in Iran. According to the first approach, Shabestari contends, it is human civilisation that needs to adapt itself to the Qur'an and Sunna. In this context, Shabestari has analogised civilisation and religion to a garment and body. In the view of the proponents of the first approach, according to Shabestari, the body representing civilisation needs to be tailored to fit the garment of religion. Religion in this view is the criterion of a healthy civilisation, and as such all civilisations and forms of social organisation at all times must conform to its dimensions.[75]

Among the proponents of the second approach, the consensus is that only the general values undergirding government and society are fixed, while the form of state is not. When civilisation undergoes change, the political institutions of a Muslim society must assume new forms also.[76] These institutions should be organised in such a way as to secure the maximum possibility for the observance of religious requirements in society. This type of state, however, is the product of Muslims' excogitation and as such is not the institutionalisation of the shari'a itself. It is not uncriticisable, since it is a human institution and unsacred.[77]

The third group believes that the Qur'an and Sunna do not articulate even general values undergirding the political institutions and the state which are fixed and permanent. According to this point of view, Shabestari argues, the normative principles in the Qur'an and Sunna address the 'ethics of the individual' only.

This is the doctrine that advocates the separation between politics and religion. The people, in this view, choose not only the type of state organisation that fits their needs, they also determine their socio-political norms and values by themselves.[78]

Shabestari has rejected the first and the third positions and opted for the second. He rejects the third position because in his view, the complete severance of politics from normative religious principles is untenable among a religious population. It is the second position that is most conducive to a reconciliation between religiosity on the one hand, and change and modernity, on the other. Shabestari seems to endeavour to ensure that, in this reconciliation, human freedom is not sacrificed. Reflecting Shariati's critique of institutionalised religion, Shabestari has maintained that when religion is institutionalised the peril of it negating the human looms large. Shabestari has explained the reason for this phenomenon in his own dialectical-dialogical formulation that views the mutual integrity of God and human as preconditions of each other:

> When religion is institutionalized, the danger appears that man is negated by the institution. Why? Because when religion is institutionalized, God's 'absoluteness' is denied. With the institutionalization of religion, God is confined ... within the enclosure of Church or Mosque. God thus is eclipsed, and when He is eclipsed, man no longer finds himself before an absolute God, but before a God that is confined and reified. Under these circumstances man is negated and when man is negated God is experienced as anti-freedom.[79]

In a radical departure from a religious thinker like Khumayni who considered the act of legislation by humans as blasphemous, Shabestari has alluded, albeit rather subtly, to the possibility of legislation by mortals. In this scheme God's legislation is primarily the enactment of general, but eternal, value systems. God is first and foremost the fountainhead of the ethical principles, which leaves space for human decisions such as 'framing' laws.[80] In this way the possibility of change in divinely inspired laws and regulation is not ruled out, while the divine values themselves do not change. This important premise leads Shabestari to the conclusion that laws themselves are not sacred, even though they might have been legislated in conformity with the general religious values in the first place. The range that Shabestari has allowed for human legislation is considerably large and covers areas that usually are not considered open to change. These areas include legal relations in the family, social relations, politics, the state and its institution-alisation, judicial matters, the punishments and legal sanctions, as well as contracts in general.[81] In this context Shabestari obliquely has criticised the lack of the possibility for women to divorce their husbands in many of the countries that profess to be Islamic. He has referred to the example provided by Iqbal of some Muslim women in Punjab resorting to apostasy to be able to divorce.[82]

In a society in which this type of attempt at reconciliation between religion and modernity constitutes the organisational principle, Shabestari suggests, critical attitude and the concept of critique are of central importance. In this type of society even external critiques of religion, for example those of Marx and Feuerbach, not only are tolerated, but they can help the faithful refine their conceptions of religion and thus achieve purer forms of religiosity.[83] In this type of society, if books against religion are not published and critique of religion is not allowed, faith loses it main characteristic and no longer would be a conscious act of choosing.[84] Furthermore, 'in the society of the faithful there are no 'red lines' to demarcate the limits of critique. The critics must have all the space to engage in critique without any red lines'.[85]

Shabestari has credited development of modernity with the process of transforming despotic polities in the past few centuries. The cultural-political transformation that has characterised modernity is conducive to a 'reflexivity' and detached attitude toward the 'self', which led to a desire for political change that aimed at overthrowing despotic regimes. In this way, issues such as freedom and political participation, equality, and human rights were thematised in the modern period.[86] In a similar vein, Shabestari argues, in order for a society of the faithful to be viable in the modern industrial world, there must exist institutional guarantees for freedom since in 'totalitarian and despotic soci-eties the seeds of faith', which as we saw before he equates with a conscious act of choosing, 'would rot'.[87]

Consequently, in what seems to be an oblique critique of the concept of guardianship of the jurist (*velayat-e faqih*), Shabestari has argued that Islam neither recognises nor recommends any single form of polity.[88] Instead, given the definition of faith that Shabestari has provided, the form of polity in which faith can flourish is none other than one in which, in addition to the institutional guarantees of freedom, there is also distribution of power, provision for checks and balances, and a mechanism for peaceful transition of power.[89] Such a polity, Shabestari argues, is only possible in a society in which a parliamentary system works hand in hand with a 'well-operating' judiciary and a 'healthy' sustainable economy.[90] In this regard, Shabestari has denied that only the ulama and Islamic experts are capable of determining whether the polity is compatible with Islam; it is the right of non-expert citizens to participate in the political affairs of the country.[91]

What seems to be of most significance among Shabestari's political views is that he considers the state and political institutions as 'civil', as opposed to religious, in nature. As marriage and divorce are two civil institutions, and the application of religious measures to them does not strip them of their civil identity, the same is true of the state and political institutions. The fact that religious criteria may be applied to these institutions does not mean that they are not 'civil' by nature. Shabestari even has used the term '*urfi*, which can be translated as 'laicist', to describe the state in this context.[92]

Conclusion

From a theoretical perspective, Shabestari's discourse in general may best be viewed as an attempt to reconcile the contradictions that Islamic revolutionary discourse engendered in the 1960s and 1970s. As such, his discourse is embedded in the paradigm of mediated subjectivity. While Shabestari's thought is a valuable attempt to overcome the contradictions of this paradigm, it is not totally immune from relapsing, albeit very infrequently, into the type of contradictions it tries to heal. For example, while he has advocated political and social freedoms of various types, he has expressed conservative views with regard to personal matters, that is, the affairs of private life regulated by the shari'a, at least on one occasion in his recent writings.[93] Similarly, it may be argued, while Shabestari attempts to drastically reduce the contradictions of religious modernity in Iran, he has not directly tackled the largest of these contradictions, that is the concept and the institution of guardianship of the jurist.

Yet, the most significant achievement of Shabestari's discourse seems to lie in a hermeneutic construction of intersubjectivity in terms of which the discourse of religious modernity in Iran can be advanced. Because of the perceived or real contradiction that the paradigm of mediated subjectivity has engendered between human and divine subjectivity and sovereignty, this paradigm could not have developed further, together with a hermeneutic that involved a direct exegesis of the Qur'an. The result has been the development of a hermeneutic that represents the expansion of the subjectivist elements in mediated subjectivity, without emphasising the theomorphic approach that characterised the thought of the revolutionary predecessors. The further development of the logic of the theomorphic approach could have confronted the process of modernity with serious problems in a profoundly religious society, because human subjectivity could easily be perceived as challenging the divine subjectivity and sovereignty. The subtle detour that Shabestari has taken toward a hermeneutic approach to subjectivity saves him from this possibility. Another significant characteristic of this approach is that it relies upon the principle of intersubjectivity. Shabestari's approach constructs a hermeneutics in which the human assumes a position of subjectivity by treating the text as the 'object' of his subjectivity. However, because the text, sacred or otherwise, always presupposes an author who is a subject, the relationship that exists between two sides of the hermeneutical process is not that of subject-object, but that of subject-subject. The 'I and Thou' principle that Shabestari has introduced into his discourse is very much a model for a religious notion of intersubjectivity. It may serve to deter the positivist form of modernity, based on a subject-object relationship, from dominating the process of modernity in Iran once again.

NOTES

1. For the ideas of such figures representative of the Islamic revolutionary discourses see Hamid Dabashi, *Theology of Discontent: The Ideological Foundation of Islamic Revolution in Iran* (New York, 1993), and Houchang Chehabi, *Iranian Politics and Religious Modernism: The Liberation Movement of Iran under the Shah and Khomeini* (Ithaca, 1990).

2. The following draws partly on two articles that first appeared in *Critique: Journal for Critical Studies of the Middle East*, 14 (1999), pp. 50–73 ('Metaphysical Foundations of Islamic Revolutionary Discourse in Iran: Vacillations on Human Subjectivity'), and 16 (2000), pp. 31–54 ('Post-Revolutionary Discourses of Mohammad Mojtahed Shabestari and Mohsen Kadivar: Reconciling the Terms of Mediated Subjectivity, Part 1: Mojtahed Shabestari'). Thanks are due to the editor of *Critique* for permission for this.

3. G.W.F. Hegel, *Hegel's Philosophy of Right* (Oxford, 1967), p. 286; cited in Jürgen Habermas, *The Philosophical Discourse of Modernity: Twelve Lectures* (Cambridge, 1987), p. 16.

4. Hegel, *Hegel's Philosophy of Right*, p. 110.

5. On the dialectical relations between the two categories of subjectivity and universality, Hegel's objection to Kant's 'formality', and his own attempt at a substantive synthesis between them, see Charles Taylor, *Hegel and Modern Society* (Cambridge, 1979). See also Lawrence E. Cahoone, *The Dilemma of Modernity: Philosophy, Culture and Anti-Culture* (Albany, 1987); David Kolb, *The Critique of Pure Modernity: Hegel, Heidegger and After* (Chicago, 1986); and Fred Dallmayr, *G.W.F Hegel: Modernity and Politics* (Newbury Park, CA, 1993).

6. For a very helpful discussion of contemporary debates regarding efforts to embed the unbridled subject of modernity without compromising the freedom of subjectivity see Seyla Benhabib, *Critique, Norm and Utopia* (New York, 1986); and idem., *Situating the Self: Gender, Community and Postmodernism in Contemporary Ethics* (New York, 1992).

7. See Jürgen Habermas, *The Theory of Communicative Action; Vol. 1, Reason and the Rationalization of Society* (Boston, 1981); and idem., *The Theory of Communicative Action; Vol. 2, Lifeworld and System: Critique of Functionalist Reason* (Boston, 1984).

8. For further elaboration on the notion of 'mediated subjectivity' see Farzin Vahdat, 'Metaphysical Foundations of Islamic Revolutionary Discourse in Iran'. The Qur'anic concept of man as God's vicegerent on earth, which explicitly informs the discourse of Shariati and Motahhari (Khumayni does not refer to it as explicitly and frequently) also appears as

a significant theme in the thought of other Iranian Islamic thinkers, like Mehdi Bazargan and Ayat Allah Taleqani. For a general analysis of their discourse, see Dabashi, *Theology of Discontent*, and Chehabi, *Iranian Politics and Religious Modernism.*

9. A third trend, which has been closely associated with the philosopher Reza Davari Ardakani, has inspired many of the figures within the conservative factions among the ruling Islamic elite. For a discussion of Ardakani's views see Farzin Vahdat, *God and Juggernaut: Iran's Intellectual Encounter with Modernity* (Syracuse, 2002), pp. 186–98; Mehrzad Boroujerdi, *Iranian Intellectuals and the West: The Tormented Triumph of Nativism* (Syracuse, 1996), pp. 156–65.

10. For a sample of Soroush's writing in English, see Abdolkarim Soroush, *Reason, Freedom, and Democracy in Islam: Essential Writings of Abdolkarim Soroush,* ed. and tr. Mahmoud Sadri and Ahmad Sadri (New York, 2000). For an analysis of Soroush's thought and modernity, see Vahdat, *God and Juggernaut.*

11. Most of the biographic data for Shabestari is taken from Hasan Yusefi Eshkvari, *Nougarai dini* (Tehran, 1998), p. 160.

12. Soroush has warned against a human desire to achieve the status of divinity as the first step toward corruption and evil. See Abdolkarim Soroush, *Hekmat va ma'ishat* (Tehran, 1984), p. 62. He has also criticised the notion of humans as a 'becoming-toward-perfection'. Faulting the expectation of moral perfection on the part of citizens, Soroush has blamed the Islamic government for setting unrealistically high moral standards for Iranians. See Abdolkarim Soroush, *Tafarroj-e son'* (Tehran, 1987), p. 263.

13. Mohamad Mojtahed Shabestari, *Hermenutik, Ketab va Sunnat: farayand-e tafsir-e vahy* (Tehran, 1996), p. 56.

14. Mohamad Mojtahed Shabestari, *Iman va azadi* (Tehran, 1997), p. 120.

15. Ibid., p. 95. For a discussion of Tabataba'i's work see Hamid Dabashi, *Theology of Discontent*, pp. 273–323.

16. Ibid., p. 114.

17. Mohamad Mojtahed Shabestari, 'Fetrat-e Khoda joy-e ensan dar Qur'an', *Andishe-ye Eslami* 1, 9 (1358/1979), p. 6.

18. Mohamad Mojtahed Shabestari, 'Fetrat-e Khoda joy-e ensan dar Qur'an', *Andishe-ye Eslami* 1, 7, (1358/1979), pp. 7–9.

19. Shabestari, *Hermenutik*, p. 15.

20. It is the interpreter's task to understand the revelation-in-itself. See ibid., p. 128.

21. Ibid., p. 36. Shabestari has described his understanding of hermeneutics along a Kantian epistemological approach, in that for him the data of revelation constitutes a noumenal ground as the 'revelation-in-itself' (*vahy fi nafse*), from which the subject may derive phenomenal understandings.

22. Ibid., p. 15.

23. Ibid., p. 22.

24. Ibid., p. 104.

25. Ibid., p. 105. The Mu'tazili theologian al-Qadi 'Abd al-Jabbar

(d. 1025), lived in Baghdad and later Rey. The Persian term *muwazia* derives from the Arabic *muwada'a* (the lexical meaning of a word).

26. Ibid., p. 33.
27. Ibid., pp. 36–37.
28. Ibid., p. 40.
29. Ibid., pp. 56–57.
30. Ibid.
31. Ibid., p. 58.
32. Ibid., p. 47.
33. Ibid., pp. 48–49.
34. Shabestari, *Iman va azadi*, p. 112.
35. Shabestari, *Hermenutik*, p. 69.
36. Ibid., p. 52.
37. Ibid.
38. Ibid., p. 57.
39. Ibid., p. 182.
40. Ibid.
41. Ibid., p. 238.
42. Shabestari, *Iman va azadi*, p. 26.
43. Ibid., p. 24.
44. Ibid., p. 33.
45. Ibid. The radical nature of Shabestari's thought on this subject is underscored when one compares other understandings of 'authenticity' in terms of essentialised notions such as religion, tradition, ethnicity, etc.
46. For a discussion of discourse theory on this issue see, for example, Jürgen Habermas, 'Communicative Versus Subject-Centered Reason', in James Faubion, ed., *Rethinking the Subject: An Anthology of Contemporary European Thought* (Boulder, CO, 1995).
47. Shabestari, *Iman va azadi*, p. 34.
48. Ibid.
49. Ibid., pp. 35–36.
50. Ibid., pp. 36–37.
51. Shabestari, *Hermenutik*, pp. 92–93.
52. Soroush, for example, considers freedom of the individual as pivotal for any conception of faith: 'The faith of each individual is the exclusive experience and the "private property" of that individual. Each of us finds faith as an individual, as we die as an individual. There may be collective rituals but there is no collective faith'. Abdolkarim Soroush, 'Modara va modiriyat-e mo'menan: sokhani dar nesbat-e din va demokrasi', *Kiyan* 4, 21 (September–October 1994), p. 7.
53. Shabestari, *Hermenutik*, pp. 184–85.
54. Shabestari, *Iman va azadi*, pp. 12–13.
55. Ibid., pp. 13–14.
56. Ibid., p. 16.
57. Ibid., p. 19.
58. Ibid., p. 21.
59. Ibid.
60. Ibid., p. 22.

61. Ibid.
62. Ibid., p. 124.
63. Shabestari, *Hermenutik*, pp. 171–72.
64. Ibid.
65. Ibid., p. 172.
66. Ibid.
67. Ibid., p. 173. For a now classical discussion of loss of all permanence and fixity in modernity, see Marshal Berman, *All that is Solid Melts into Air: The Experience of Modernity* (New York, 1988).
68. Ibid., p. 203.
69. Ibid.
70. Shabestari, *Iman va azadi*, pp. 149–50.
71. Ibid., p. 155. Interestingly, here Shabestari has exempted modern natural sciences from the reifying effect, and considers them neutral in nature.
72. Mohamad Mojtahed Shabestari, 'Qara'at-e rasmi az din' , *Rah-e Naw*, no. 19 (*Shahrivar* 7, 1377/August 29, 1998), p. 19.
73. Ibid., p. 20.
74. Ibid.
75. Shabestari, *Hermenutik*, pp. 63–64.
76. Ibid., pp. 64–65.
77. Ibid.
78. Ibid., p. 66.
79. Shabestari, *Iman va azadi*, p. 29.
80. Shabestari, *Hermenutik*, p. 78.
81. Shabestari, *Iman va azadi*, pp. 87–88.
82. Shabestari, *Hermenutik*, pp. 207–8.
83. Ibid., p. 186.
84. Ibid.
85. Ibid., p. 187.
86. Ibid., p. 210.
87. Shabestari, *Iman va azadi*, p. 8.
88. Ibid., pp. 74–75.
89. Ibid., p. 79.
90. Ibid., p. 132.
91. Ibid., pp. 75–76.
92. Ibid., p. 68.
93. Shabestari, *Hermenutik*, p. 81. Without elaborating, Shabestari specifies that 'shari'a rules pertaining to individuals' are immutable.

BIBLIOGRAPHY

Works by Mohamad Mojtahed Shabestari

——. 'Fetrat-e Khoda joy-e ensan dar Qur'an', *Andishe-ye Eslami* 1, 7 (1358/1979)
——. 'Fetrat-e Khoda joy-e ensan dar Qur'an', *Andishe-ye Eslami* 1, 9

(1358/1979).

——. *Hermenutik, Ketab va Sunnat: farayand-e tafsir-e vahy.* Tehran, 1996.

——. *Iman va azadi.* Tehran, 1997.

——. 'Qara'at-e rasmi az din', *Rah-e Naw*, 19. *Shahrivar* 7, 1377/August 29, 1998.

Other sources

Benhabib, Seyla. *Situating the Self: Gender, Community and Postmodernism in Contemporary Ethics.* New York, 1992.

——. *Critique, Norm and Utopia.* New York, 1986.

Berman, Marshal. *All that is Solid Melts into Air: The Experience of Modernity.* New York, 1988.

Boroujerdi, Mehrzad. *Iranian Intellectuals and the West: The Tormented Triumph of Nativism.* Syracuse, 1996.

Cahoone, Lawrence E. *The Dilemma of Modernity: Philosophy, Culture and Anti-Culture.* Albany, 1987.

Chehabi, H.E. *Iranian Politics and Religious Modernism: The Liberation Movement of Iran under the Shah and Khomeini.* Ithaca, 1990.

Dabashi, Hamid. *Theology of Discontent: The Ideological Foundation of Islamic Revolution in Iran.* New York, 1993.

Dallmayr, Fred. *G.W.F Hegel: Modernity and Politics.* Newbury Park, CA, 1993.

Habermas, Jürgen. 'Communicative Versus Subject-Centered Reason', in James Faubion, ed., *Rethinking the Subject: An Anthology of Contemporary European Thought.* Boulder, CO, 1995.

——. *The Philosophical Discourse of Modernity: Twelve Lectures.* Cambridge, Mass., 1987.

——. *The Theory of Communicative Action; Vol. 1, Reason and the Rationalization of Society.* Boston, 1981.

——. *The Theory of Communicative Action; Vol. 2, Lifeworld and System: Critique of Functionalist Reason.* Boston, 1984.

Hegel, G. W. F. *Hegel's Philosophy of Right.* Oxford, 1967.

Kolb, David. *The Critique of Pure Modernity: Hegel, Heidegger and After.* Chicago, 1986.

Soroush, Abdolkarim. *Reason, Freedom, and Democracy in Islam: Essential Writings of Abdolkarim Soroush*, ed. and tr. Mahmoud Sadri and Ahmad Sadri. New York, 2000.

——. *Tafarroj-e son'.* Tehran, 1987.

——. *Hekmat va ma'ishat.* Tehran, 1984.

——. 'Modara va modiriyat-e mo'menan: sokhani dar nesbat-e din va demokrasi', *Kiyan* 4, 21 (1994).

Taylor, Charles. *Hegel and Modern Society.* Cambridge, 1979.

Vahdat, Farzin. *God and Juggernaut: Iran's Intellectual Encounter with Modernity.* Syracuse, 2000.

——. 'Metaphysical Foundations of Islamic Revolutionary Discourse in Iran: Vacillations on Human Subjectivity', *Critique: Journal for Critical Studies of the Middle East*, 14 (1999).

——. 'Post-Revolutionary Discourses of Mohammad Mojtahed Shabestari and Mohsen Kadivar: Reconciling the Terms of Mediated Subjectivity.

Part I: Mojtahed Shabestari,' *Critique: Journal for Critical Studies of the Middle East*, 16 (2000).
Yusefi Eshkvari, Hasan. *Nougarai dini.* Tehran, 1998.

8

Mohamed Talbi on understanding the Qur'an

RONALD L. NETTLER

MOHAMED TALBI is one of the most prominent Muslim modernist thinkers of the twentieth century.[1] Born in Tunis in 1921, Talbi received a traditional Islamic education of the *madrasa* type as well as secular studies. He then went to Paris in 1947 for doctoral studies in Islamic history. Recounting his experiences there and assessing his teachers and the impressions made upon him by the vibrant Paris intellectual culture of the time, Talbi waxes positive. He evinces a strong enthusiasm for the variety of new ideas and intellectual methods which came his way and he does so without any apparent defensiveness. On the contrary. In surveying the range of ideologies and intellectual trends on offer in post-war Paris, such as Marxism and Freudianism, and in describing the new (for him) perspectives on Islam encountered in his studies with the great French Islamicists, Talbi expresses his gratitude for this exposure and the value which he found in it. All the new ideas and methods could, in his view, be incorporated in his own thought and historical scholarship, toward deepening and broadening his views. Any elements of the new – ideas which might clash with or otherwise be unassimilable in his prior outlook – could be dealt with in a constructive way, emphasising the positive nature of the challenge, rather than seeing there a deep threat. From his Tunisian tradition-centred and somewhat sufi Islamic background, itself no doubt somewhat influenced by European intellectual trends, Talbi confidently took on Paris and came out all the better for it. In the way he tells the story, it is clear that in combination with his own personality and background, Talbi's European experience was crucial in his later development as historian and modernist thinker.[2]

Mohamed Talbi has had a distinguished dual career as a historian of medieval North Africa and as a Muslim modernist thinker. In the latter role – our main interest here – Talbi has been particularly prominent for his developed conception of a religious pluralism derived from Islamic history and tradition. While obviously reflecting certain modern notions of pluralism, his conception is distinctly Islamic in its formulation, its sources and its author's intent. Talbi's main claim for his pluralism is that it is an integral part of the Qur'an and Islamic tradition. In his presentation and elaboration of pluralism, he is, in his view, merely making explicit what was already a central feature of Islam, if not always made prominent. Pluralism for Talbi basically means respect of all parties for the views of others, in a context of intellectual and religious freedom. This mutual respect (*ihtiram mutabadal*) provides a basis for true dialogue (*hiwar*) which is the cornerstone of religious (and intellectual) pluralism. Dialogue is the implementation of the theory of pluralism: if the theory indicates the sources, ideas and arguments for pluralism, then dialogue breathes life into all this, making pluralism real. In this way, in such direct encounter, would the equal value which Talbi's theory of pluralism attributes to the religions be made manifest, including also intra-Islamic differences in views.[3]

In addition to pluralism, Talbi's thought contains a number of other main ideas which, like pluralism, for him are also prominently and integrally associated with Islam; salient among these are freedom, the notion of Islam as apolitical, and equality of status for women.

Freedom in Talbi's view is an inherent and inalienable right of the individual in society. Essential to Islam, freedom is the absence of human coercive forces which would arbitrarily limit individual decisions and choices. Coercion by either governmental or religious authority would be central, in Talbi's view, as the major potential threats to freedom. Though not organised, directly or precisely, on modern notions of freedom, Talbi's discussions of the subject do reflect such ideas. In the course of discussing various other problems and issues, Talbi reveals various aspects of his notion of freedom.[4]

In politics, Talbi argues against the idea of a particular Islamic governmental form. All such ideas – and attempts to implement them – are, in his view, false. Islam has no intrinsic political principle or organisation. If through Islam's history 'Islamic' political claims have been made on behalf of certain ideologies and governments, these claims have been wrong and misguided. Their proponents may sincerely have believed that their political ideas and institutions were properly and intrinsically Islamic, but they were mistaken. Islam is in the main a revealed system of belief, piety and worship – not a polity. Whichever form of government Muslims adopt in any time or place is, therefore, not Islamic and can make no Islamic claims. Does this, then, mean that Islam, as God's revealed truth, does not distinguish between better and worse forms of government and gives no indication of which form is to be preferred? For Talbi, it seems that, strictly speaking, this would be true. However, in his view Islam does more subtly evince an interest in how Muslims are governed, without justifying, endorsing or promoting one particular government or form of government. In light of Islam's inherent liberal values and practices such as freedom, love, tolerance and pluralism, it may then be inferred that Islam preferred a form of government which exemplified these; as it happens, democracy, in our time, is just that system and thus should it be seen *for now* as the best political system for Muslims, despite its human imperfections. Democracy, however, is still not an *Islamic* governmental form and one day there might well be another type of political system even better suited to the expression of Islam's liberal features.[5]

The status of women is an issue close to Talbi's heart. For him, it would seem to constitute a barometer-reading of a society's level of humanity, measured by the degree of female equality present. Islam, Talbi argues, at its inception greatly ameliorated the previous hardships suffered by women. The Islamic ethos is greatly sympathetic to women and points toward an equal status for them with that of men. Talbi, in one place, attempts to show this through an analysis of Qur'an 3: 34, a verse which seems to sanction husbands' beating of recalcitrant wives, if the women cannot in less severe ways be made obedient. Talbi's interpretation of the verse rejects a literal reading which might for some make this chastisement permissible (nay, obligatory) in all times and places, as certain interpretations have indeed held. For Talbi, this verse must be understood through the historical context of its revelation. Using historical sources in this way, Talbi can then understand God's intentions in revealing this verse as not to provide a continuing divine sanction for striking women, but rather to reduce tensions in Medina around the issue of the treatment of women. For, Talbi says, this issue had threatened to cause civil strife between Muslim parties who differed on it. God's intention in revealing this verse, as Talbi ascertains it, was to provide a *temporary* concession to those who preferred harsher treatment of women. But this was only to prevent the building tensions from seriously shaking the new community's very foundations. Subsequently, the prophet's 'feminist' inclinations would guide the community toward God's true intention concerning this problem: equality and kind treatment for women.[6]

The ideas discussed above are representative of Talbi's conception of Islam. They express values which generally would be identified as liberal and modern and specifically associated with the latter part of the twentieth century. Talbi's identification of Islam with these and related ideas derives from his discovering them within Islamic tradition, particularly in the Qur'an. This discovery involves him in a substantial review of historical sources and religious thought. For him, this process, while necessarily critical of some received trends, amounted to a sort of separating of the good from the bad, the better from the worse. What remain are some essential features and truths of Islam which may provide a sound foundation for the present and future. For Talbi, the similarity of these with their modern counterparts also reflects a deeper integration based on a common humanity. Though different and uneven development of religions and civilisations may manifest different patterns and rhythms of these human universals, they are for Talbi truly universal. This is not simply because of a general common humanity, but, more basically, because that common humanity itself derives from a deep human faculty present in all people. This faculty is an assumed intrinsic human nature containing the universal values and ideas, the *fitra* which Talbi at times invokes.[7] Here the Qur'anic values which Talbi cites toward a true Islam for our time reflect that universality of revelation and human nature as one. The great religions are built on this same foundation, whether or not their adherents all recognise it; it is now their task to rediscover their own true genius in the values which would enable them authentically to enter the modern global world. The pluralism which Talbi sees as being deeply implicit within the religions, despite their sometime exclusivist ethos, is now, more than ever, urgently required, for their own fulfilment and for the good of the world. Islam's own intrinsic pluralist ethos, as Talbi sees it, would here naturally combine with the globalisation which he considers will be our common future.[8]

In elucidating and situating these ideas, Talbi uses certain methods of analysis and interpretation of history and texts. Though varied, these methods generally emphasise historical contexts of ideas, including those in the Qur'an, and the true intentions of texts and their sources or authors. Talbi does employ certain special terms and concepts in developing and applying his methods, though he does not do this in any rigorously systematic way. Through repeated, and sometimes interchangeable, use of such terms, however, some sense of a loosely organised and consistent approach is conveyed.[9]

Talbi's ideas and methods are highly Qur'anic, in origin, conception and application. He locates his main ideas in the Qur'an and his intellectual methods, though conceived and applied over a broad range of subjects, are especially sharpened and focused in confronting the Qur'an. Indeed, with Talbi all intellectual and spiritual roads lead back to the Qur'an. He explicitly discusses and demonstrates his way of understanding the Qur'an in a few writings. In one brief piece, a section of the book

'Iyal Allah, he presents a particularly clear and succinct explanation of his method. A translation of this discussion below will serve as a focus for more detailed treatment of Talbi's method:[10]

Intentional reading of the sacred text

Personally, I have tried, for example, to deal with the question of the beating of women and its relation to Islam. This is a problem which has provoked fierce debate. Indeed, I carried out a historical study of verses 34 and 35 of the Chapter 'Women' [in the Qur'an] which I published in the weekly *al-Maghrib al-'Arabi...* [11] This is a study from which it becomes clear that Islam does not sanction the punishment of woman by beating and abusing her. Though this phenomenon was in the past widespread and remains so, it exists not only in Islamic countries, but in the West as well. I have also treated in the same way the problem of apostasy and its connection with freedom of belief, in an article from which it becomes clear that Islam is a religion [promoting] religious freedom and that there is no trace of the [later, traditional] legal judgement concerning apostasy in the Qur'an itself, and that this legal judgement is the product of historical conditions in which apostasy was considered as treachery against the homeland in time of war...[12]

In the field of Islamic Studies, I have numerous other works, but there is no need here to elaborate on them. All of these are intellectual attempts on my part, while nowhere in them do I impose my opinion on anyone, especially as I am not a religious-legal authority (*faqih*), nor do I want to be described as such an authority. For I am a historian, but [this should not be considered a source of bias] preventing me from believing [as I do] that the historian has a role in resolving crucial religious problems, and that this involvement is important and fundamental. [This is] because [the historian] puts the problems in their historical and human dimensions. Indeed, putting the problems in their historical and human dimensions is what made me, in my work with

Maurice Bucaille, *Reflections on the Qur'an*,[13] announce my determination to follow this earlier book with a second one to which I would give the title *The Qur'an and Life in this World*.[14] This is a book which, like its predecessor, would naturally also be a historical and human reading of the Qur'an.

From within this reading, I shall try – if God will grant me the opportunity – to bring to light the intentions of the Law-Giver, relying on historical development [in the contexts of the revelations, as an approach to the sacred text], as I did in the article devoted to [the subject of] punishing women by beating which was mentioned earlier.

However, the intentional reading of the sacred text is not a hasty new invention, for it had its helpful [intellectual supports] in the past; these today need new momentum and spirit. [The analogical reasoning – *qiyas* – employed by the legal scholars was one such support.] The intentional reading of the sacred text, though, goes beyond this analogical reasoning – which many legal scholars in the past rejected – and I prefer intentional reading to analogical reasoning, without rejecting analogy in all circumstances; indeed, I do not absolutely reject it. But I do consider it to be inappropriate and unable to solve all the problems of modernity and all the issues of our present life. [This is because] analogical reasoning is devoid of a dynamic dimension, approaching the present [as is its wont] by way of analogy with the past. It is a past-orientated understanding of the sacred text, dealing haphazardly with the present, within models of the past, and striving to force the present to conform to those archaic models. This is something which leads to blocking any vision of progress and to a rejection of modernity.

Thus is God 'the Living, the Eternal. Neither slumber nor sleep may take hold of Him' (Q. 2: 255). It follows from that, then, that His word lives forever among us. I must, therefore, heed it in the here-and-now, where I am. What does God say to me at this moment and in this place? I cannot [now] ask the sacred text this question, i.e., from the heart of moder-

nity, unless I first pose it in its historical and temporal dimensions. Indeed, the historical human reading must necessarily
precede any other reading of the text, so that we might, in
equal measure [before asking what does God say to us now]
understand in the text the circumstance of the revealing [of
the particular verse] and the intention of the revelation: in
other words, the starting-point and the intended goal.

I shall cite an example emerging from discussions today,
[discussion of] which is [now] accepted in all Islamic countries, including Mauritania: the example of the abolition of
slavery. Neither Islam nor any other religion prohibited
slavery. And practice of it in Islamic countries remains on a
large scale, in all areas of life and institutions, not excluding
concubinage. But the sacred text, Qur'an and hadith,
ameliorates the situation of the slave in a tangible way and
gives them broad rights and guarantees, so long as they
assume these. [The Qur'an] in particular, and with great
enthusiasm, encourages the freeing of slaves (Q. 2: 177, 4: 92,
5: 89, 58: 2, 90: 13, 9: 60).

I shall here establish two points. The first: the condition of
the slave before the revelation. The second: the condition of
the slave after the revelation and through the kindness of the
revelation. I shall then draw a line whose direction will mark
off the two points. In this way, then, I shall attain an orientation-finder whose direction will clarify for me the intentions
of the Law-Giver. Thus do I take into consideration, in every
understanding of the sacred text, these intentions [of the
Law-Giver] and move in their direction. The intentional
reading, therefore, in a first phase is based on an analysis of
the text's orientation. This is a reading which is at the same
time historical, human and final; it is thus a dynamic reading
of the text which does not stop me at its literal word or what is
by way of analogy to it. [The intentional reading] just moves
me along with the orientation of the [text]. This orientation
with regard to the slaves is the freeing of slaves. Thus though
the abolition of slavery may not be in agreement with the
letter of the text, it is in agreement with its orientation, i.e.,

with the intentions of the Law-Giver. [The text], therefore, works within the Islamic orientation, though no verse seeks to forbid [slavery]. That is because to nullify and prohibit it in the historical and human conditions which accompanied the revelation would have been ahead of its time.

I believe that analysis of [the text's] orientation and the extensive intentional reading which accompanies it participate in a decisive way in the development of Islamic thought and toward removing it from the crisis which has continued to afflict it for more than a century and which feeds strong clashes within society. Intentional reading, proceeding in line with the orientation-finder mentioned above, is to a great extent capable of playing a role in the Islamisation of modernity and the modernisation of Islam. It is possible that we may apply the epistemological method, or, if you will, the hermeneutics, which we have defined, to the problems of social life which today so insistently impose themselves on us. In the forefront of these problems is the issue of women, which is the site of fierce conflicts between the modernists and the Islamists and is the issue of the hour. [We may, then, apply our method] to the solution of this problem, as a solution which would at the same time satisfy both modernity and the Islamic conscience; for fixed in our view is the fate of Islam and its future in the new world whose advent we have now become aware of.

Thus when I find that the Qur'an directs the position of woman toward improving her situation, to the point of equality between her and man and toward her acquiring rights which did not previously exist, then I must of necessity move in the same direction as that indicator ordains [in the Qur'an]: continuous liberation, continuous moderation, continuous justice, in a form which brings me as close as possible – though acknowledging the situation I am in today – to what the Law-Giver intended. I prefer this way to that of analogy. It is possible that one day it will become a point of consensus, with a proliferation of studies which confirm its fidelity to the spirit of Islam.

The Muslim historian, in his relationship with the sacred text, will always and forever begin from a human reading. But that does not mean that he considers the human reading an end in itself; it is only an epistemological, methodological stage in the penetration of the meaning of the text, in its beginning and its end. [That is] with respect to what [the text] specifies by way of revealing solutions and clarifying the path necessary for [the historian] to traverse. It is the way of the straight path. God, glory be to Him, Most High, calls us to the straight path. But how can we ascertain this path? This path is not something limited; it is only a way in which we move always and ever forward. And when I have ascertained the direction, I shall try to move that way and walk in the straight path, in continuous movement, on a track which God's light will illumine, consonant with God's intentions. This is the basic conception which I shall try to be guided by in the [new] book [on reading the Qur'an mentioned above] which I intend to write, if [continued] life should be granted for that.

That, then, in very brief compass, is my involvement, which I shall continue, in [ascertaining] the intentions of the shari'a,[15] without any obligation to [my] ideas [for others] and without inferiority or superiority complexes [on my part]. Indeed, what I am doing and what I shall in future do is no more than simple attempts, not free of error, amenable to debate and argument; that is God's way, that there be debate within the Muslim community. I call for establishing this dialogue within the community, because there is no way out of the intellectual crisis in which we are living without this dialogue. Thus the pressures, in all of their varieties, whether emanating from totalitarian terrorist groups or from political regimes, will not resolve the problem, because the problem is on the level of conscience; and nothing at this level may be resolved except by way of dialogue, persuasion and being convinced. That is the only way.

Talbi's opening recitation of his various writings on Qur'anic issues and social problems slips easily into explication of his method, as was his obvious intention. The interpretive method which Talbi variously defines as an 'intentional' (*maqasidiyya*), 'historical' (*ta'rikhiyya*) or 'human' (*anasiyya*) reading (*qira'a*) of the sacred text (*al-nass al-dini*) possesses a common meaning in all these definitions. The terminological differences allow Talbi to convey certain dimensions of conceptual and operational difference toward his interpretive goal. The historical reading, then, puts Qur'anic passages in their historical contexts to provide the situation of revelation, and the human reading would consider the special human peculiarities seen in that situation. The intentional reading, incorporating the findings of the other two dimensions, brings us to the goal: ascertaining the intentions of the Law-Giver in revealing the particular passage under review. These intentions – *maqasid* – inform us of both God's reasons for the particular revelation and its (related) meanings. In this sense, the intentional reading is the broadest of Talbi's three interpretive dimensions, as his ultimate goal in understanding the Qur'an is to grasp God's revelational purpose and meaning. But as these revert back to and are derived from the historical and human contexts, the unity of these three dimensions is clear: the meaning common to them all is that the Qur'an may best be understood in its context, in order to discern God's true intentions and meaning in his revelations to us. 'Literal meanings', taken out of context and seen as applicable in all times and places, are often inappropriate and may even contradict God's true intentions or misconceive them. Talbi cites here his own previous writings on the issues of women and apostasy in the Qur'an, concluding that the Qur'an itself does not sanction the harsh interpretation given the relevant verses by some later commentators; rather, the Qur'an's meaning is much more liberal. It is only the divine intention which will give true Qur'anic guidance in subsequent times and places, long after the cessation of direct revelation. In this way for Talbi one can hear God's voice anew through the ancient text. That is what is required today and that is what Talbi's interpretive method is meant to do.

Past Islamic understanding and practice were not devoid of elements of this method and supports for it, says Talbi. One such was the analogical reasoning, *qiyas*, mainly associated with Islamic jurisprudence (*fiqh*). However, despite the help which *qiyas* did give in enabling jurists to confront new situations, this method is still 'past-orientated' and lacking the 'dynamic dimension' required for a fully successful adaptation of Qur'anic tradition to changing circumstances. While Talbi still sees some utility in *qiyas*, he sees his own method as being vastly superior in confronting the task at hand. Talbi's notion of *qiyas*, it must be said, seems somewhat different from the traditional legal conception and usage where it would more usually have been applied to hadith rather than to the Qur'an itself; and the interpretation of the Qur'an is, of course, here Talbi's main concern. We must assume that despite his own designation of *qiyas* as a legal method, Talbi uses the term to mean any sort of reasoning which would see close analogies from the past (here in more literal readings of the Qur'an) as being strict guidelines for the present – hence the presumed absence of dynamism which he attributes to *qiyas*.

Talbi's main example here of determining what God says to us now, in our own time, through the Qur'an (his ultimate goal) is the issue of slavery. The structure of his argument remains true to his basic method and conception: Islam (like other religions) did not prohibit slavery, though the Qur'anic pronouncements on slavery serve to ameliorate the condition of slaves, often by reference to freeing them. Using his own terminology and related analysis, Talbi seeks to know about the slave's condition before and after the revelation 'and through the kindness of the revelation'. Thus will he acquire an 'orientation-finder' (*sahm muwajjih*), after drawing a line between the slave's condition before and after the revelation. The 'orientation-finder', then, will show the direction or orientation of the text (*ittijah*), as this plots the change in the slave's condition from pre-revelation to post-revelation. And here God's intentions become clear, in the heart of the intentional reading. It is also an 'analysis of the text's orientation' or its direction (*tahlil ittijahi*), as well as being at the same time a reading which is 'historical, human and final'. This reading, says Talbi, is 'dynamic'; it does not 'stop at the literal word'. Thus with regard to slavery, the orientation of the text is towards amelioration of the slave's condition or even the abolition of slavery itself, though the latter is nowhere to be seen in the Qur'an. However, for Talbi that is God's ultimate intention which may be known through this method of interpretation; included here, of course, is historical information on the circumstances of the revelation, which Talbi has presumably used, but not given to us in detail.[16] But it is this context which enables Talbi to know why God did not simply abolish slavery altogether in His Qur'anic revelations, rather than just mooting abolition; for that 'would have been ahead of its time'. And it is here, in the discovery of God's intentions in His revelations, where God's word lives forever and, as Talbi says, 'I must heed it in the here-and-now, where I am'.

Talbi's understanding of the Qur'an, as illustrated here, for him goes beyond the abiding traditional reasons for such an endeavour: The method which grows out of his attempt is offered as a way of saving Islamic thought from its modern 'crisis'. It is offered as nothing short of the very 'straight path' (*sirat mustaqim*) to which the Qur'an directs the believers. Though Talbi, typically for him, is careful not to claim exclusive interpretative authority for his method, calling for debate and dialogue about it, he clearly considers it the proper way forward. The ongoing 'intellectual crisis' of Islam in the modern era, as Talbi sees and defines this, in his view requires a penetration of the ideas in the Qur'an which will reveal the true intentions of the Law-Giver. This would break the logjam of retrogressive literal reading and the pernicious attempts at their application. Freed in this way, God's intentions in the Qur'an would then provide the (now missing) dynamism forward, toward Islam's successful encounter with modernity and the assertion of its deeper values. 'Both modernity and the Islamic conscience' would then have been satisfied, as Talbi puts it, and progress would have occurred in 'the Islamisation of modernity and the modernisation of Islam'. This for Talbi would represent Islam's 're-discovery' of its own humane truth in integration with the most humane values of modern culture. These, it transpires, appear very much the same.

NOTES

1. Talbi writes in Arabic, French and English, sometimes publishing the same work in more than one language. His writings on Islam and modernity and religious pluralism are extensive. Three works in Arabic represent well Talbi's basic modernist Islamic thought: *'Iyal Allah: afkar jadida fi 'alaqat al-Muslim bi nafsihi wa bi al-akhirin* (Tunis, 1992); *Ummat al-wasat: al-Islam wa tahaddiyyat al-mu'asara* (Tunis, 1996); *Al-Islam: hurriyya wa hiwar* (Beirut, 1999). A specialised book on the Qur'an written with a colleague provides a good general introduction to Talbi's thought on that subject: Mohamed Talbi and Maurice Bucaille, *Reflexions sur le Coran* (Paris, 1989).

2. For autobiographical statements, see Mohamed Talbi, *'Iyal*, pp. 7–45.

3. Ibid., pp. 64–177. Also Ronald L. Nettler, 'Mohammed Talbi: "For Dialogue between all Religions"', in Ronald L. Nettler and Suha Taji-Farouki, eds, *Muslim-Jewish Encounters: Intellectual Traditions and Modern Politics* (Reading, 1998), pp.171–199.

4. See Mohamed Talbi, *al-Islam: hurriyya wa hiwar*, passim.

5. See for example *'Iyal*, pp. 90–92.

6. Mohamed Talbi, *Umma al-wasat*, pp. 115–142. See also Ronald L. Nettler, 'Mohammed Talbi's Commentary on Qur'an IV: 34: A "Historical Reading" of a Verse Concerning the Disciplining of Women', *The Maghreb Review*, 24, 1–2 (1999), pp. 19–34.

7. See, e.g., Talbi, *'Iyal*, p. 77. Found in various derivative forms in the Qur'an (for example, Q. 30: 30) with different shades of meaning, as well as in later theological works, this term is used by Talbi as indicated here. See also, George Hourani, *Islamic Rationalism* (Oxford, 1976).

8. In a frequently reiterated theme, Talbi refers to the continuing evolution of the world toward some global order, culture and integration of peoples. See especially, *al-Islam: hurriyya wa hiwar*, pp. 195–227.

9. Some of Talbi's main terms are dealt with below.

10. Talbi, *'Iyal*, pp. 142–45.

11. *al-Maghrib al-'Arabi*, 182–3, 12 and 29 December 1989.

12. Mohamed Talbi, 'Religious Liberty: A Muslim Perspective', in *Proceedings of the Second World Congress on Religious Liberty* (Michigan, 1985), pp. 156–68.

13. As mentioned in n. 1, above.

14. To the best of my knowledge, this book has not yet been published.

15. Talbi seems to be using the term shari'a here to refer to revelation in general rather than law.

16. Talbi often refers to historical contexts without indicating the sources he has used and the way in which he has treated them.

BIBLIOGRAPHY

Works by Mohamed Talbi

——. 'Religious Liberty: A Muslim Perspective', in *Proceedings of the Second World Congress on Religious Liberty.* Michigan, 1985, pp. 156–168.

——. *'Iyal Allah: afkar jadida fi 'alaqat al-Muslim bi nafsihi wa bi al-akhirin.* Tunis, 1992.

——. *Ummat al-wasat: al-Islam wa tahaddiyyat al-mu'asara.* Tunis, 1996.

——. *al-Islam: hurriyya wa hiwar.* Beirut, 1999.

——. Talbi, Mohamed and Maurice Bucaille, *Reflexions sur le Coran.* Paris, 1989.

Other sources

Hourani, George. *Islamic Rationalism.* Oxford, 1976.

Nettler, Ronald L. 'Mohammed Talbi: "For Dialogue between all Religions"', in Ronald L. Nettler and Suha Taji-Farouki, eds, *Muslim-Jewish Encounters: Intellectual Traditions and Modern Politics.* Reading, 1998, pp. 171-199.

——. 'Mohammed Talbi's Commentary on Qur'an IV: 34: A "Historical Reading"' of a Verse Concerning the Disciplining of Women', *The Maghreb Review*, 24, 1–2, (1999), pp. 19–34.

al-Maghrib al-'Arabi, 182–3, December 12 and 29, 1989.

9

Hüseyin Atay's approach to understanding the Qur'an

OSMAN TAŞTAN

Introduction

The prevailing political circumstances and long-lasting moderni-sation policy of the Turkish establishment from the late Ottoman period through the Republican regime implicitly identify legiti-macy with modernity. This state-led modernist trend has been all encompassing, from the late Ottoman military and constitutional reforms, during the radical changes in the early decades of the Republic, and its continuing ramifications up to the present day.[1] In this respect, religion and religious education were to be seen as part of a new identity and culture, targeted by and through the official modernisation process. While legitimacy became virtually identified by modernity, what was to be recognised as modern could be achieved only through the established institutions of the state. This applied in the case of the Religious Affairs Directorate, responsible for religious information and services via the office of the Muftis, and extending to local mosques. It applied equally to the different levels of religious education, in the İmam-Hatip Lycees (vocational schools with a substantial religious curriculum) or the Faculties of Islamic Studies established at varying stages during the Republican era.[2] Modernisation was intended both in form and in content. Accordingly, use of the official language of the state was to be increased in the sphere of religious practice (the focus of which was, in principle, the

241

Qur'an). A Turkish language commentary on the Qur'an by Elmalı'lı Hamdi Yazır was thus compiled under the patronage of the Republican regime,[3] and the Turkish language gradually came to be included more extensively in Friday sermons.[4] In 1932 the call for prayer was made in Turkish[5] until resumption of Arabic was permitted in 1950.[6] During the early decades of the Republican era there were intermittent discussions about whether the recitation of the Qur'an could be religiously permissible in Turkish language translation in the prayer:[7] perhaps unsurprisingly, this matter has been resurrected in recent years.

In the 1980s, the relation of religion and state had attained some degree of stability and was largely in favour of religion gaining ground within the state. The İmam-Hatip Lycees were very popular, and there were some nine Faculties of Islamic Studies in major cities.[8] Religion was thus receiving much attention. Meanwhile, Turkey was ever more open to the influence of radical Islamism, through translations into Turkish from the rest of the Muslim world of works such as those of Abul A'la Mawdudi, Sayyid Qutb, and Muhammad Qutb. There were two possible lines of approach to the Qur'an, one from outside of the state-sponsored religious educational circles (and resorting mostly to the influential trend of radical Islamism), the other from within the Faculties of Islamic Studies. Both approaches share a common ground in the form of an anti-traditionalist view of Islam, but for different reasons. For the former, the incentive to rid itself of traditional Islam derives from a perception of the veiling of the pristine nature of Islam by centuries of increasingly backward-looking interpretations, particularly through the various schools of law and theology. What was greatly needed was first to highlight a clear Islamic faith and attitude, based on the Qur'an as the plain message of God. Distinctive to this line of thought is its radical commitment to the principles and direct content of the Qur'an, accompanied by a sharply focused political stand for an Islamic identity. The second approach is equally critical of traditional Islam, and has a comparable interest in the close study of the Qur'an. However, it differs from the first in its declared objective of reaching an understanding of the Qur'an for the sake of a viable practice of Islam that is reconcilable with modern contexts. This line of understanding, mostly belonging to scholars of Islamic sciences at universities, such as Hüseyin Atay, Süleyman Ateş and Yaşar Nuri Öztürk, leads to a pragmatic approach.

Of the three aforementioned professors of Islamic studies, Yaşar Nuri Öztürk is closest in style to the discourse of those from outside the Faculties of Islamic Studies. Öztürk is more interested in identifying Islam with the Qur'an in a plain manner, devoid of traditional, 'non-Qur'anic', culture. However, the incentive behind his position is relatively more practical, that is, to guide people to a simple or plain way of religious understanding. Of his numerous works, *Kur'an'ın Temel Kavramları* is most relevant to the subject in hand. Here, he explains a good number of terms covered by the Qur'an with frequent reference to al-Raghib al-Isfahani's *al-Mufradat fi gharib al-Qur'an*.[9] Through style and substance, Öztürk's works are committed to reaching a perception of Islam through the themes and concepts of the Qur'an as distinct from traditional Islamic culture.[10] However, he is not interested in the interpretation of substantive practical themes in the Qur'an, such as legal issues, and for such matters would partly resort to Hüseyin Atay and Süleyman Ateş, recognising their authority in these.[11]

Ateş is a former head of the Religious Affairs Directorate and professor of Qur'anic studies. His fame developed around his controversial view that Heaven is a place not only for Muslims, but also for the *ahl al-kitab* who live up to the universal message of God. For Ateş, the Qur'an does not invalidate the previous Scriptures (mainly the Old and New Testaments), but in fact reinforces them. Ateş quotes a good number of Qur'anic verses throughout his work *Kur'an-ı Kerim'in Evrensel Mesajına Çağrı* to show that Heaven is not exclusive to Muslims. He received much popular attention for his argument that the *ahl al-kitab* are equal to Muslims, if they too abide by what God has asked of them.[12] Ateş's strength rests in his mode of defending Islam from the Qur'anic point of view, and proving that Islam is the true message of God and that God's message is inclusive for everyone. Ateş is also author of *Yüce Kur'an'ın Çağdaş Tefsiri*,[13] a twelve volume

Turkish commentary on the Qur'an which makes a useful reference book for students and scholars of Islamic studies.

If Öztürk is driven by the objective of presenting Qur'anic themes and terms coherently and in a manner that is simple and reconcilable with a modern understanding,[14] Ateş's main urge is to provide a broad-based and inclusive view of the Qur'an and Islam from within the Qur'anic content itself. Atay, the subject of this chapter, differs in his distinctive concerns and approach from both. He sees his contribution as one of producing practical solutions to substantive practical Islamic issues, based on his own views and interpretation of the legal content of the Qur'an. None of the scholars under discussion, Atay included, can be properly understood unless the prevailing socio-political context of modernity is taken into consideration. The underlying incentive which produces (or counter-produces) the attitudes of these scholars is inherent in the self-imposing nature of the sustained sense of modernism which has been prevailing in Turkey for almost two centuries.

The following overview of the life, career, works and thought of Atay is based as much on interviews conducted with him by the author as on his published works. Atay's views, developed over some forty years, are not always presented in a thematically focused manner in his publications. Consequently, interviews play an important role, providing an opportunity to bring different elements of his thought gleaned from his publications to his attention for further elaboration, substantiation or revision.

The life and works of Hüseyin Atay[15]

Born in 1930 in Güneyce (İkizdere, Rize) in North Eastern Anatolia on the edge of the Black Sea, Atay began recitation of the Qur'an and its memorisation in his early childhood. Later, while studying in Kadırga Primary School in Istanbul, he took private Arabic grammar lessons from Hacı Hasip Efendi. While attending Kumkapı Middle School, he continued these lessons under Mustafa Asım Hacı Bilaloğlu. Upon completing his middle school study in 1945, he took lessons in various Islamic disciplines from

244

Mustafa Gümülcineli for three years. In 1948, he moved to Baghdad to attend high school/lycee there. In 1954, he graduated from the Faculty of Shari'a in Baghdad. In 1956, he began his academic career at the Faculty of Divinity in Ankara University, as a Research Assistant in Islamic Philosophy. In 1960, he completed his Ph.D. thesis, entitled *Kur'an'a Göre İman Esaslarının Tesbiti ve Müdafaası.* In 1968, Atay assumed the post of Associate Professor, and in 1974 became a full Professor in the same Faculty. He spent two years in Israel, and just under two years in Chicago (during the early 1960s), and about one year in Harvard and again in Chicago during the mid 1970s. He taught for four years during the late 1980s at the King Fahd University of Petroleum and Mines in Dahran, Saudi Arabia, before resuming his post at Ankara University in 1991. Now retired from the university post, he maintains his scholarly activities within the Faculty of Divinity uninterrupted.

During his long academic career, Atay has produced a good number of works on various subjects. Some of his main works are: *Kur'an'a Göre İman Esasları,*[16] *Kur'an-ı Kerim ve Türkçe Anlamı,*[17] *Arapça-Türkçe Büyük Lügat,*[18] *Farabi ve İbn Sina'ya Göre Yaratma,*[19] *İbn Sina'da Varlık Nazariyesi,*[20] *Osmanlılarda Yüksek Din Eğitimi: Medrese Programları, İcazetnameler, İslahat Hareketleri,*[21] *Kur'an'a Göre Araştırmalar I-V,*[22] *Kur'an'daki İlkeler,*[23] *Kur'an'ın Reddettiği,*[24] *İslamın Siyasi Oluşumu,*[25] *İslam'ı Yeniden Anlama,*[26] *İrade ve Hürriyet.*[27] He has also edited Abu Hamid Muhammad al-Ghazali's *al-Iqtisad fi al-i'tiqad,*[28] Musa Ibn Maymun's *Dalalat al-ha'irin,*[29] Fakhr al-Din al-Razi's *al-Muhassal,*[30] and Abu al-Mu'in al-Nasafi's *Tabsirat al-adilla.*[31] In addition, he has published numerous articles in various fields of Islamic studies.

Atay and the Qur'an: a general outlook

Atay had memorised the entire text of the Qur'an before he was 15. His early contact with it did not remain confined to recitation and memorisation: as he continued to learn Arabic and Islamic sciences, he came to nurture an aspiration for understanding the Qur'an in a progressive manner. One of the first issues to grip his mind was the reference to the Mu'tazila in teaching sessions in Baghdad as 'al-Mu'tazila al-mukhalifa' (the 'opposing' Mu'tazila), in contrast with the references he had earlier heard in Istanbul teaching circles to 'al-Mu'tazila al-dalla' (the 'heretical' Mu'tazila). He began to grasp the notion that nothing escapes being interpreted, and that there was both a possibility and an indispensable need to engage in interpretation towards a progressive Islamic thinking. He was further stimulated in Baghdad during courses in the critique of traditional Islamic thought which he attended, taught by Abdallah Naqshbandi, a young professor from Arbil, Northern Iraq. During his Lycee years, Atay's mind was bewildered by his study of sociology text-books, but he always benefited from Abdallah Naqshbandi's guidance, in finding a clear direction. The key point that he grasped from Naqshbandi in the methodology of thought was 'to overwhelm the texts, rather than being overwhelmed by them'. This was the level of consciousness in relation to understanding texts from which Atay began his higher education in Islamic studies in Baghdad. As he advanced through the first and second years, as if defying the prevailing authority and bewildering complexity of the Islamic studies texts, he dared to understand the Qur'an directly, through his own analysis of its text, in a bid to free his mind from the convoluted textbook discourse.[32] Atay's continued interest in the relation of the text to reality surfaced during his Ph.D. study in Ankara. Encouraged by his professor Muhammad Tanji (of Moroccan origin), he directed his full attention to analysing the fundamentals of faith according to the Qur'an.

By demonstrating its absence from the Qur'an, Atay refutes belief in *qadar* (fate) as one of the traditionally accepted six principles of faith. The word *qadar* in the Qur'an, in Atay's view (based on references to various Qur'anic verses: 6: 91, 13: 26, 54: 12 and 49, 56: 60, 25: 2, 20: 40, and 42: 27), means limit, criterion, proportion or plan.[33] It never signifies a compulsory fate of the individual or society. Also, Qur'anic explanations such as 'no misfortune can happen ... but is recorded in a decree' (Q. 57: 22), signify that everything is within the knowledge of God.[34] Thus there is no written *qadar* that preempts the will and freedom of the person.

The reason that Sunni Islam included *qadar* in the body of principles of faith, Atay argues, lies in 'Abdallah Ibn 'Umar's defence of
it against some who claimed that there was no *qadar*, and that
things happened by chance.[35] Atay thus reduced the principles of
faith from six (belief in God, the angels, the holy books, the
prophets, the Hereafter, and *qadar*) to five, in 1960. In 1997, he
emphasised his view again, when he discovered during his editing
of the second volume of *Tabsirat al-adilla* of Abu al-Mu'in al-
Nasafi that the author there itemised the fundamentals of belief
as five, with no mention of *qadar* among them.[36] Driven by this
new sense of the legitimacy of his analysis, his concern to provide
remedies to practical problems in this case centred on the need to
liberate people from belief in a passive personality, that cannot
exercise its own will.

Discussing the authority of reason compared with that of the
general narrations of the hadith, Atay decides in favour of reason.
He stresses that the Mu'tazila in principle did not accept hadith as
a proper source for matters of belief/creed. Other scholars like
Abu Hanifa, al-Maturidi and al-Ash'ari did not easily accept the
hadith either, and for the same reason (unless a given hadith was
proven to be *mutawatir*, that is, narrated by a large generality of
people at each link).[37] Atay's hesitation in attaching serious
matters such as those of creed to the hadith emanates from his
concept of the significance of reason. Reason, in Atay's viewpoint,
in a sense has a supervisory role, against false attributions to the
Prophet. Atay's appreciation of reason is based on its nature as a
practical necessity. However it also stems from the fact that the use
of reason is sanctioned and given priority by the Qur'an.[38]

The legitimacy of a religious opinion, in Atay's view, is related
to a trio of interdependent sources: 'reason, the Qur'an and the
situation [context]'.[39] It is clear from this that his perception of
reason goes far beyond its instrumental role, in that he elevates it
to the status of a source of legitimacy at the same level of primacy
as the Qur'an itself. In his own words:

> The main sources of Islam are reason and the Qur'an. The words
> and acts of the Prophet Muhammad amount to examples in practice,
> methodology and interpretation and explanation or exegesis of

247

these two sources. These examples may change according to
different times, places, individuals or societies. Taking the Prophet
Muhammad as the model does not mean repeating literally what he
did or imitating him; it should mean rather producing examples, in
order to achieve goals in the interest of people.[40]

Naskh and understanding the Qur'an

A significant methodological area for understanding both the
Qur'an and Qur'an-based Islamic laws is the principle of abrogation. Atay does not recognise the theory of *naskh* (abrogation) in
his view of the Qur'anic text. His doubts concerning this concept
began during his years of study in Baghdad. Later, during his
academic career, he explicitly rejected the theory of *naskh*. Instead
of understanding the diverse or conflicting statements of the
Qur'an through this theory (which suspends abrogated verses),
Atay considers the entire text of the Qur'an to be valid for all times.
In his view, 'the abrogating and abrogated verses (e.g. those urging
war and those proposing co-existence in relation to non-
Muslims) continue to be part of life'. Hence there is nothing
redundant in the Qur'an. Corresponding to the societal realities of
life, Atay emphasises that the text of the Qur'an cannot be free of
diverse approaches. This avails the scholarly or political authority
the opportunity to resort to it at different times and places, and for
different solutions to different problems. By rejecting abrogation,
all Qur'anic verses, including those that differ from each other, are
seen to present a rich resource for solving a multitude of problems.
If the theory of abrogation is accepted, in Atay's view, the scope of
the Qur'anic text will be narrowed.[41]

In line with his rejection of *naskh*, Atay demonstrates a discli-
nation to understand the Qur'an through a historical contextualisation of the text. His reason is the same as for the theory of
abrogation: he argues that this would somehow diminish the
authority of the Qur'anic text for the present. If limited to the
time of revelation, a viable resource would at least in part be
literally incapacitated. Accordingly, Atay disagrees with Fazlur
Rahman's view that if, hypothetically speaking, the Qur'an is read

248

by a man in the North Pole who speaks Arabic but has no knowledge of Arabia/Arabic culture at the time of its revelation, this man would not be able to understand it properly. In Rahman's view, in order to understand the Qur'an, it is also necessary to understand the social and historical context of the Arab society of the time when it was revealed.[42] The Qur'an thus came into existence within a certain course of history and culture, and the reader must navigate this to arrive at a proper understanding of it. In contrast with Rahman, Atay believes in the need to liberate the reader's mind from historical and traditional culture, which in fact obscure a genuine understanding of the Qur'an. He insists rather that more attention should be devoted to developing a direct reading of the Qur'anic text.[43]

The Qur'an and legal methodology

In favour of a new understanding of Islam, Atay endeavours to explain the causes of stagnation in Islamic thought. He identifies the shift from the logic of induction to that of deduction in the Muslim world as the reason for the decline in Islamic thought.[44] He argues that the method of induction is proposed by the Qur'an itself (39: 18):

> Those who listen to the word and follow the best (meaning) in it. Those are the ones God has guided, and those are the ones endowed with understanding.[45]

In Atay's view, the Qur'anic injunction here is to apply the method of induction in making decisions.[46] While this claim is clearly an overstatement, his deliberation in Islamic legal thought may nevertheless be considered appropriate. Atay pursues his argument in this context by articulating the contrast between the Hanafi and Shafi'i schools of law in terms of the former being pro-induction, and the latter pro-deduction. He adds that the Hanafis first studied specific cases and then wrote about their methods. In contrast, the Shafi'is first established their methodological rules, and then dealt with specific cases (on the basis of these rules). Atay asserts further that these two methods were employed in contrast to each other until about the eleventh-century CE, when the Shafi'i-led method of deduction began to dominate. This, Atay believes, is the point of departure for the decline in Islamic thought.[47] Atay argues that the method of deduction leads to an authoritarian mentality as it is driven by the imposition of rules, rather than a pursuit of changing interests in changing cases.[48] Arguing in favour of the use of reason via the method of induction, Atay cites[49] three verses to demonstrate the significance the Qur'an attaches to reasoning:[50]

> ... They have hearts wherewith they understand not, eyes wherewith they see not, and ears wherewith they hear not. They are like cattle, – nay more misguided: for they are heedless (of warning). (7: 179)

> For the worst of beasts in the sight of God are the deaf and the dumb – Those who understand not. (8: 22)

> ... And he will place doubt (or obscurity) on those who will not understand. (10:100)

There is little doubt that Atay's strong insistence on the significance of reason betrays a profound anger with (and criticism of) the prevalence of traditionalism, contrasted with the authority of reason.[51]

The example of ablution and touching the Qur'an

In line with his critique of *taqlid* (contrasted with *ijtihad* and free use of reason), Atay holds the *fuqaha'* responsible for creating a formalism in religious thought and their interpretations, resulting ultimately in difficulty, instead of ease, in approaching and understanding the Qur'an. Motivated by an image of the Qur'an being hung in adorned cases high on the walls in people's houses (instead of being read and understood), Atay presents a critical outline of the roots of the formalistic attitude in the works of *fiqh*. He appears to have a twofold target here: demonstrating the vulnerability of certain traditional and formalistic juristic views when subjected to the plain authority of reason, and freeing peoples' minds from a perception of the Qur'an as something that is sacred and unapproachable. Atay discusses why it is that a state of ablution is regarded as a precondition for touching the Qur'an, tracing the origin of this requirement as far back as al-Shaybani (d. 805).[52] He believes the *fuqaha'* were generally enthusiastic about substantiating the established views of their schools of law, and tended to miss the main point while engaged in scholastic details.[53] In his criticism of 'Ala' al-Din Abu Bakr Ibn Mas'ud al-Kasani (d. 1191), a prominent Hanafi jurist who contributed to the classic era Hanafi School with his voluminous legal work *Bada'i' al-sana'i' fi tartib al-shara'i'*, Atay points out that he refers to Qur'an 56: 79 ('Which none shall touch but those who are clean') in order to prove that touching the Qur'an without holding ablution was not permissible.

In addition to this Qur'anic verse, Atay says, al-Kasani resorts to a Prophetic saying which reads: 'only the one who is clean can hold the Qur'an'. In Atay's analysis, al-Kasani understands these two texts as proofs for the requirement of ablution on the ground that respect for the Qur'an is necessary, and that it is not possible to respect it without ablution.[54] In his attempt to prove a progressive line of thought, Atay is in favour of Ibn Hazm (d. 1063), a leading Zahiri jurist, as he holds the view that, by 'those who are clean', the Qur'anic verse refers to angels.[55] Citing diverse opinions from different scholars of early Islam,[56] Atay argues that the view that the Qur'an could not be touched without ablution does not refer to the text of the Qur'an available to us. Rather it refers to the Qur'an in the *lawh mahfuz*,[57] which transcends the physical world in which we live.[58] He highlights Ibn Hazm's view in his own interpretation of Qur'an 56: 79, to deny the state of ablution as a precondition for touching the Qur'an.[59] The Qur'an is thus easy to touch, although it remains a sacred text. Once this has been established, Atay's priority is how to understand its contents with the objective of arriving at an appropriate practice of Islam. As undergraduate students of Islamic studies at Ankara University (1984), he would ask us to liberate our minds from what we carry in the way of history and culture, so that we might understand the Qur'an in a proper manner. The plainness of the Arabian desert, in Atay's thought, becomes a positive element for the Arabs in history, in viewing the Qur'an through a plain mind.[60] Atay's position here may be traced back to the thought of Ibn Hazm, in the sense that the Zahiri line of thought is keen to separate the Qur'an from the historical legacy of Islamic scholarship, in favour of stressing its sole authority. (Of course his thought remains distant from Ibn Hazm's denial of legitimacy to reason as a source of shari'a.)[61]

'Three perceptions of religion', and the issue of divorce[62]

Atay observes that there are 'three perceptions of religion' in the Muslim world. First is the religion of the people, comprising popular traditions and culture. Second is the religion of the scholars, made up from the literature of fourteen centuries, plus narrations from scholars, including the generation of the Companions. Third is the religion of the Qur'an, which is expressed by the Qur'an itself. Of these three, in Atay's view, the religion of the people differs from that of the scholars, and the religion of the scholars differs in part from that of the Qur'an. He explains through specific examples. Thus the practice of praying the noon-time *salat* in its complete form, including the obligatory (*fard*) and complimentary (*sunna*) parts just after the Friday prayer, exists in Turkey in the religion of the people, but it does not exist in that of the scholars, nor in that of the Qur'an. The validity of the sole expression of the *talaq* formula ('you are divorced') by husband to wife exists both in the religion of the people and the religion of the scholars, but it does not exist in that of the Qur'an.[63] Atay aims to refute both what he calls the religion of the people and the religion of the scholars, in order to prove that what he calls the religion of the Qur'an must be understood as clearly distinct from non-Qur'anic traditional perceptions. With regard to the issue of divorce, his main point is that the jurists neglected the procedure that culminates in divorce in the Qur'an. To Atay,[64] the valid procedure of divorce proposed by the Qur'an resides in the following two Qur'anic statements:

If ye fear a breach between them twain, appoint (two) arbiters, one from his family and the other from hers; if they wish for peace, God will cause their reconciliation: For God hath full knowledge, and is acquainted with all things. (4: 35)

Thus when they fulfill their term appointed, either take them back on equitable terms or part with them on equitable terms; and take for witness two persons from among you, endued with justice, and establish the evidence (as) before God ... . (65: 2)

Hence, when a married couple experiences a conflict that damages their relationship, their problem will first be put under the guidance of two arbiters (one from each side's family), in pursuit of a reconciliation, and in order to save the family. If and when this does not lead to the hoped-for results, then the case will be transferred to the care of the court or judge, where a divorce can be secured in the presence of two witnesses.[65] Atay's point here is that the *fuqaha'* principally entrusted the right to divorce to the husband, and neglected the Qur'an's proposed egalitarian procedure of divorce. Atay believes that the *fuqaha'* were overwhelmed by the patriarchal culture and the existing practice of divorce, and were not able properly to formulate the Qur'anic principle of equality between wife and husband, as regulated in the above two verses.[66]

The Qur'an and the issue of theft: Atay compared to al-Faruqi

In pursuit of a new methodology for understanding the Qur'an, Ismail R. al-Faruqi proposes what he calls 'the axiological systematization of the Holy Qur'an.'[67] Thus:

What is, therefore, paramountly imperative upon all Muslims at this stage of their history when pursuit of the Holy Qur'an as a constitution and the implementation of the message of Islam as an ideology are problems, is a systematic restatement of the Holy Qur'an's valuational system. Such statement must deduce from the instrumental goods the intrinsic; from the ought-to-do's the ought-to-be's; and from the elemental, preparatory or ethical values the final and most high. It must give us the values which God has expressed in a variety of ways in His Book, and then order them into a hierarchy showing the proper order of rank of each and the complexus of relations which relate it to other members of the realm. This is the axiological systematization of the Qur'an, and consequently, of Islam.[68]

Endeavouring to highlight the importance of escaping the literal barriers of the text in order to reach the spirit of the Qur'an, he continues:

Should the axiological systematization reveal, as it must, higher and lower values, it is un-Islamic to require unqualified literal obser-vance. Such an observance would put the higher values on a par with the lower, the moving supreme principle of the Holy Book with the detailed particularized ordinances ... .[69]

On the other hand, an axiologically systematized Qur'an will enable us to know and grasp its spirit ...[70]

He illustrates his 'axiological sytematization' through an example, as follows:

Consider, for instance, the Qur'anic verse, 'the man-thief and the woman-thief cut off their hands....' Literally the verse commands the realization of a real-existent state, *viz.*, having the hand cut off in the case of the proven thief. The values this verse seeks to realize are purification through penitence, education through example, and retribution. These are all values; but they do not stand on the same level. A cutting off the hand that realizes retribution but violates the other two cannot be deemed obligatory ... [71]

While Atay shares with al-Faruqi his sense of an urgent need for a new approach to the Qur'an in place of traditional Islamic views, he differs considerably from him in his *modus operandi*. Unlike al-Faruqi, Atay is not convinced of the utility of establishing hierar-chical principles for interpreting the Qur'an. He believes that a principle-based regulation bears the risk of an unrealistic and totalitarian approach, since it would inevitably impose similar solutions on differing problems, in line with the superior princi-ples established. Accordingly, Atay argues that it is necessary to develop solutions to each problem, on a case-by-case basis, in the light of the Qur'an.[72] As he does not give priority to the employ-ment of abstract principles in his interpretation, he cannot share the same level of concern as al-Faruqi to transcend the literal boundaries of Qur'anic statements. During the mid-1980s, Atay would tell his students that God mentions maximum level penalties in the Qur'an, which thus are not necessarily applicable. If ever they were applied, these penalties should be considered maximum penalties of last resort.[73] This position is akin to that of al-Faruqi, as Atay too seeks to avoid theft in society without resorting to the amputation of hands, thus giving priority to the ends, rather than the means.[74] The punitive letter of the Qur'an is thus proclaimed valid in the views of both scholars, while in practice it is given almost no chance of application.[75]

Conclusion

Atay's key point is to underline the significance of the diversity both in Qur'anic texts and in the societal problems addressed by the Qur'an. Thus the difference of one problem from another justifies the legitimacy of the difference in the solutions to these problems. Atay believes in the method of seeking solutions to problems on a case-by-case basis. It is presumably this tendency which impels him to explain his method of understanding the Qur'an in a sequence of three stages: '1. Reason; 2. the Qur'an; 3. the [actual] situation'.[76] He apparently projects the traditional dichotomy between reason and revelation in favour of reason, at least in principle. Reason is given the primary role, since it is essential for understanding the Qur'an and the problems to be addressed in society. Here, the inter-relationship of the three elements mentioned above functions as a mechanism for seeking solutions to changing problems in society. Atay's case-by-case approach leads him to reject the theory of abrogation concerning the Qur'an, since the idea of abrogation presupposes the replacement of some earlier rulings by some later ones within it. In fact, the idea of abrogation suggests a line of legislation that moves irreversibly forward, by always giving expression to the verses that were revealed later, of the two or more verses that differ with regard to one and the same issue. In contrast with the idea of abrogation, Atay emphasises the reversibility and repeatability of societal problems. For a utilitarian attitude such as that of Atay this is understandable, as the entire text of the Qur'an (without any abrogation) may provide a wider scope, to address more societal needs. Nevertheless, the concern to establish a systematic methodology of Qur'anic legislation is not prominent in Atay's thought. Instead, he tends to utilise the entire text of the Qur'an in finding solutions to practical problems in society.

Atay is careful to propose an Islamic viewpoint that is tolerant with respect to practice, and liberal with respect to theory. For example, he offers people the latitude of touching the Qur'an without ablution,[77] and of extending the duration of eating before fasting starts (*sahur*) from dawn time.[78] He upholds the permissibility for a woman to fast during menstruation.[79] At the same time, he exerts an effort to explain that the Qur'anic ruling for amputation of the hand in the case of theft is a penalty of last resort only. He holds that, if necessary, family planning is permissible on the basis of Qur'anic rulings,[80] and emphasises that there is 'no compulsion in religion'.[81] Hence, Atay's understanding of the Qur'an (and Islam) can potentially address people in a twofold manner: ordinary people for a simpler way of understanding religion and the daily practice of religious duties; and the elite, be it the ruling elite or intellectuals, primarily for a modern conception of religion.

The pro-modernist Turkish context provides a milieu in which a prominent academic such as Atay can publish his views for public consumption without observable resistance. It is also the religious-cultural reflex against the self-imposing nature of modernity which makes the audience in general both attentive to new ideas in religion, and at the same time reluctant to accept them, due to the 'foreignness' of the currently prevailing modernity (when compared with traditional Islam). As for Atay's influence in Turkish academic circles, it is not easy to find substantive analysis of his work, or works written about him. This is possibly due to three reasons. First, there are no legitimately surviving and officially recognised classical-style *madrasa*s in Turkey, which could have voiced views opposing certain of Atay's views. Second, academics in Faculties of Islamic Studies who might potentially disagree presumably feel a great deal of confidence in the established Islamic culture and literature and, thus, do not deem it necessary to write specifically to critique him. Finally, Atay's case-by-case approach makes his views appear sporadic; they do not appear as a cohesive theory, which might have generated substantive views or literature for or against him.

NOTES

1. For a survey of the late Ottoman and twentieth-century Republican eras, see Erik J. Zürcher, *Turkey: A Modern History* (London and New York, 1993).

2. For further analysis of the context of religion, religious education and the state, see Süleyman Hayri Bolay et al., *Türk Eğitim Sistemi: Alternatif Perspektif* (Ankara, 1996), pp. 45–47; Osman Taştan, 'Religion and [Religious] Minorities', in Debbie Lovatt, ed., *Turkey Since 1970: Politics, Economics and Society* (London and New York, 2001), pp. 147, 150–51.

3. See Yusuf Üevki Yavuz, 'Elmalı'lı Muhammed Hamdi', in *Türkiye Diyanet Vakfı İslam Ansiklopedisi* (Istanbul, 1995), Vol. 11, p. 58. It is noteworthy that Elmalı'lı Muhammed Hamdi Yazır was not only entrusted with the duty of writing a commentary on the Qur'an in Turkish language, but was also given seven point guidelines which he followed during its compilation. The fifth of these guidelines states the requirement that in belief-related issues, the *madhhab* of the Ahl al-Sunna should be followed, and in practice-related issues, the Hanafi *madhhab*. See Elmalı'lı Muhammed Hamdi Yazır, *Hak Dini Kur'an Dili: Yeni Mealli Türkçe Tefsir* (Istanbul, 1935), vol. 1, pp. 19–20.

4. For a full account of the introduction of Turkish language into Friday sermons, see Dücane Cündioğlu, *Bir Siyasi Proje Olarak Türkçe İbadet 1* (Istanbul, 1999), pp. 31–40.

5. For the debate for and against the call to prayer in Turkish, see Cündioğlu, *Bir Siyasi Proje Olarak Türkçe İbadet 1*, pp. 307–26.

6. See Halis Ayhan and Mustafa Uzun, 'Ezan'ın Türkçeleştirilmesi', in *Türkiye Diyanet Vakfı İslam Ansiklopedisi*, Vol. 12, pp. 38–42.

7. For a detailed survey of this issue, see Dücane Cündioğlu, *Bir Siyasi Proje Olarak Türkçe İbadet 1*, pp. 131–289.

8. Today, the number of the Faculties of Islamic studies in Turkey is in excess of 20.

9. Al-Raghib al-Isfahani, *al-Mufradat fi gharib al-Qur'an* (Cairo, 1324/1908). See Yaşar Nuri Öztürk, *Kur'an'ın Temel Kavramları* (Istanbul, 1991). For some examples of his references to al-Isfahani, see pp. 30, 36, 71, 124, 131 ff.

10. 'His aim', in the words of Neşe İhtiyar, 'is to present to the masses his main thesis, namely the return to the Qur'an and the elimination of superstitious beliefs'. See Neşe İhtiyar, 'Televangelism and the case of Yaşar Nuri Öztürk', *ISIM Newsletter* 9 (January, 2002), p. 22.

11. For some examples of Öztürk's references to Atay, see *Kur'an'daki İslam*, 6th edn (Istanbul, 1994), pp. 163, 271–72, 424–25, 453. For Öztürk's references to Ateş, see *Kur'an'ın Temel Kavramları* (Istanbul, 1991), pp. 344, 542, 643, 686, 722.

12. See Süleyman Ateş, *Kur'an-ı Kerim'in Evrensel Mesajına Çağrı* (Istanbul, 1990).

13. See Süleyman Ateş, *Yüce Kur'an'ın Çağdaş Tefsiri* (Istanbul, n.d.).

14. In addition to literature, Öztürk conveys his views to the masses through live television talks. Neşe İhtiyar may hardly be exaggerating in saying that 'since the mid 1990s almost every television viewer has become familiar with Öztürk's face and style'. İhtiyar, 'Televangelism', p. 22.

15. This section is mainly based on an interview with the author (16 April 2001).

16. Ankara, 1961; 1998.

17. With Yaşar Kutluay (Ankara, 1961). This is a Turkish translation of the Qur'an. Atay revised this translation in 1993 and again in 1998; a third revision is due for publication. For a critical analysis of how both translations of the Qur'an (including Atay's) and the interpretation of Qur'anic texts by Turkish scholars can be influenced by the impact of the prevailing context of modernism see Ömer Özsoy, 'Çağdaş Kur'an(lar) Üretimi Üzerine: "Karı Dövme' Olgusu Bağlamında 4. Nisa", 34 Örneği', *İslamiyat* V, 1 (2002), pp. 111–24. This considers the example of Qur'an 4: 34.

18. With İbrahim Atay and Mustafa Atay (Ankara, 1964). This Arabic-Turkish dictionary proceeds as far as the letter *ghayn* and thus is incomplete. A complete edition is currently in press.

19. Ankara, 1974.

20. Ankara, 1983; 2001.

21. Ankara, 1983.

22. Ankara, 1995–97.

23. Ankara, 1999.

24. Ankara, 1999.

25. Ankara, 1999.

26. Ankara, 2001.

27. Ankara, 2002.

28. With İbrahim Agah Çubukçu (Ankara, 1962).

29. Ankara, 1974.

30. Cairo, 1991.

31. (Ankara, 1993). The first volume only has been published: Atay and Şaban Ali Düzgün are currently working on the second volume.

32. This paragraph is based on an interview with the author (17 April 2001).

33. Hüseyin Atay, *Kur anda İman Esasları* (Ankara, 1998), pp. 133–136.

34. Ibid., p. 138.

35. Ibid., *Kur'anda İman Esasları*, p. 141.

36. Ibid., p. 146.

37. See Hüseyin Atay, *Kur'an'a Göre Araştırmalar V* (Ankara, 1995), p. 80.

38. The analysis is based on an interview with the author (18 September 2001).

39. See Hüseyin Atay, 'Niçin Kur'an'a Gidip Kur'an'dan Başlıyoruz', unpublished article.

40. Hüseyin Atay, 'Dinde Reform', *Ankara Üniversitesi İlahiyat Fakültesi Dergisi*, XLIII, 1 (2002), p. 6.

41. The above analysis is based on an interview with the author (1 August 2001). For further details on Atay's view on the issue of *naskh*, see Hüseyin Atay, *İslam'ı Yeniden Anlama* (Ankara, 2001), pp. 137–54.

42. For further details of his views, see Fazlur Rahman, 'Interpreting the Qur'an', *Inquiry*, (May 1986). pp. 45–49.

43. Interview with author (8 August 2001).

44. Hüseyin Atay, 'Dinde Reform', p. 9.

45. The English translation is by Abdullah Yusuf Ali, *The Holy Qur'an, Translation and Commentary* (UK, n.d.).

46. Hüseyin Atay, 'Dinde Reform', p. 8.

47. Ibid, p. 9.

48. Ibid.

49. Ibid.

50. The translation is from Abdullah Yusuf Ali, *The Holy Qur'an*.

51. See Hüseyin Atay, 'Dinde Reform', p. 9.

52. See Hüseyin Atay, *Kur'an'a Göre Araştırmalar V*, pp. 144, 151. Atay refers to al-Shaybani's *al-Jami' al-saghir* (Egypt, 1302 AH), p. 6.

53. For details of Atay's references, views and analysis see Hüseyin Atay, *Kur'an'a Göre Araştırmalar V*, pp. 139–46 ff.

54. Ibid., pp. 147–48. Atay refers to al-Kasani's *Bada'i' al-sana'i' fi tartib al-shara'i'* (Cairo, 1327/1911), vol. 1, pp. 23, 33.

55. For a detailed account of Ibn Hazm by Atay see ibid., pp. 157–59. Atay refers to Ibn Hazm's *al-Muhalla* (Egypt, 1357AH), vol. 1, pp. 83–84.

56. For details see ibid., pp. 159–67.

57. For the origin and translation of this term, see Abdullah Yusuf Ali, *The Holy Qur'an*, p. 1717.

58. See Hüseyin Atay, *Kur'an'a Göre Araştırmalar V*, p. 167.

59. Ibid., pp. 157–59.

60. Atay's views here were also reinforced during an interview with the author (8 August 2001).

61. For an analysis of the Zahiri line of thought as expressed in Ibn Hazm's work, see Osman Taştan, 'İslam Hukukunda Literalizm: Anahatlarıyla Mukayeseli bir Analiz', *İslami Araştırmalar*, IX, 1–4 (1996), pp. 146–51.

62. The expression 'three [perceptions of] religion[s]' is Atay's.

63. Hüseyin Atay, 'Niçin Kur'an'a Gidip Kur'an'dan Başlıyoruz'. For Atay's reference to the issue of the three perceptions of religion, see also Rainer Hermann, '"Den Koran lesen" – Ein türkischer Gelehrter will den Islam gegen die Last von Tradition und Dogmatik erneuern', *Frankfurter Allgemeine Zeitung*, 89 (17 April 2002), p. 14.

64. See Hüseyin Atay, *Kur'an'a Göre Araştırmalar I-III* (Ankara, 1997). pp. 20–25.

65. Ibid., loc. cit.

66. The analysis here is based on an interview with the author

Osman Taştan

(10 August 2001).

67. Ismail Ragi al-Faruqi, 'Towards A New Methodology for Qur'anic Exegesis', *Islamic Studies*, I, 1 (1962), pp. 45–46.

68. Ibid.

69. Ibid., p. 46.

70. Ibid.

71. Ibid., p. 48.

72. The analysis here is based on an interview with the author (2 August 2001). See also, Hüseyin Atay, 'Dinde Reform', p. 9.

73. Atay is now in the process of revising his view that the amputation of hands against theft is the maximum penalty. In this respect, he is now working on the etymology of the Arabic word *qati'* (cutting or amputating). As his revision of his view is not yet complete and established, it is not included in this discussion.

74. For al-Faruqi's views, see al-Faruqi, 'Towards A New Methodology', p. 48.

75. For a thorough study of the concept of fixed penalties in Islamic Law, see Mohamed S. el-Awa, *Punishment in Islamic Law: A Comparative Study* (Indianapolis, 1982).

76. See Hüseyin Atay, 'Nicin Kur'an'a Gidip Kur'an'dan Başlıyoruz', p. 3.

77. Hüseyin Atay, *Kur'an'a Göre Araştırmalar*, V, p. 139 ff.

78. Hüseyin Atay, 'Sahur Vaktinin Tayin ve Tesbiti', *İslam İlimleri Enstitüsü Dergisi*, V (1982), pp. 1–22.

79. Hüseyin Atay, *Kur'an'a Göre Araştırmalar I–III*, pp. 27–29.

80. Hüseyin Atay, 'Kur'an ve Hadiste Aile Planlaması', *Ankara Üniversitesi İlahiyat Fakültesi Dergisi*, XVIII (1970), pp. 1–22.

81. Hüseyin Atay, *Kur'an'a Göre Araştırmalar I–III*, pp. 37–48.

BIBLIOGRAPHY

Works by Hüseyin Atay

—— and Yaşar Kutluay. *Kur'an-ı Kerim ve Türkçe Anlamı (meal)*. Ankara, 1961.

—— and İbrahim Agah Çubukçu, eds. Abu Hamid Muhammad al-Ghazali, *al-Iqtisad fi al-i'tiqad*, Ankara, 1962.

—— and İbrahim Atay and Mustafa Atay. *Arapça-Türkçe Büyük Lügat*. Ankara, 1964.

——. 'Kur'an ve Hadiste Aile Planlaması', *Ankara Üniversitesi İlahiyat Fakültesi Dergisi*, XVIII (1970), pp. 1–22.

——. *Farabi ve Ibn Sina'ya Göre Yaratma*. Ankara, 1974.

——, ed. Musa Ibn Maymun, *Dalalat al-ha'irin*. Ankara, 1974.

——. 'Sahur Vaktinin Tayin ve Tesbiti', *İslam İlimleri Enstitüsü Dergisi*, V (1982), pp. 1–22.

——. *Osmanlılarda Yüksek Din Eğitimi: Medrese Programları, İcazetnameler, İslahat Hareketleri*. Ankara, 1983.

——, ed. Fakhr al-Din al-Razi, *al-Muhassal*. Cairo, 1991.

——, ed. Abu al-Mu'in al-Nasafi, *Tabsirat al-adillah*. Ankara, 1993.

Hüseyin Atay's approach to understanding the Qur'an

——. *Kur'an'a Göre Araştırmalar I–V.* Ankara, 1995–97.
——. *Kur'an'da İman Esasları.* Ankara, 1998.
——. *İslamın Siyasi Oluşumu.* Ankara, 1999.
——. *Kur'an'daki İlkeler.* Ankara, 1999.
——. *Kur'an'ın Reddettiği Dinler.* Ankara, 1999.
——. *İslam'ı Yeniden Anlama.* Ankara, 2001.
——. *İbn Sina'da Varlık Nazariyyesi.* Ankara, 2001.
——. 'Dinde Reform', *Ankara Üniversitesi İlahiyat Fakültesi Dergisi,* XLIII, 1 (2002), pp. 1–26.
——. *İrade ve Hürriyet.* Ankara, 2002.
——. 'Niçin Kur'an'a Gidip Kur'an'dan Başlıyoruz, unpublished article.

Interviews with Atay (Ankara, April–September 2001)

Atay's life, education and works
How to understand the Qur'an
Reason and Revelation
Divorce Procedure in the Qur'an
Naskh and the Qur'an
Methodology of Understanding the Qur'an

Other sources:

'Ali, Abdullah Yusuf. *The Holy Qur'an, Translation and Commentary.* UK, n.d.
Ateş, Süleyman. *Kur'an-i Kerim'in Evrensel Mesajına Çağrı.* Istanbul, 1990.
——. *Yüce Kur'an'ın Çağdaş Tefsiri.* Istanbul, n.d.
el-Awa, Mohamed S. *Punishment in Islamic Law: A Comparative Study.* Indianapolis, 1982.
Ayhan, Halis and Mustafa Uzun. 'Ezan'ın Türkçeleştirilmesi', in *Türkiye Diyanet Vakfı İslam Ansiklopedisi.* Istanbul, 1995, vol. 12, pp. 38–42.
Bolay, Süleyman Hayri, et al. *Türk Eğitim Sistemi: Alternatif Perspektif.* Ankara, 1996.
Cündioğlu, Dücane. *Bir Siyasi Proje Olarak Türkçe İbadet 1.* Istanbul, 1999.
Al-Faruqi, Ismail Ragi. 'Towards A New Methodology for Qur'anic Exegesis', *Islamic Studies,* I, 1 (1962), pp. 35–52.
Hermann, Rainer. '"Den Koran lesen" – Ein türkischer Gelehrter will den Islam gegen die Last von Tradition und Dogmatik erneuern', *Frankfurter Allgemeine Zeitung,* 89, 17 April 2002, p. 14.
İhtiyar, Neşe. 'Televangelism and the Case of Yaşar Nuri Öztürk', *ISIM Newsletter* 9, January 2002, p. 22.
Özsoy, Ömer. 'Çağdaş Kur'an(lar) Üretimi Üzerine: "Karı Dövme' Olgusu Bağlamında 4. Nisa", 34 Örneği', *İslamiyat* V, 1 (2002), pp. 111–24.
Öztürk, Yaşar Nuri. *Kur'an'ın Temel Kavramları.* Istanbul, 1991.
——. *Kur'an'daki İslam.* 6th edn, Istanbul, 1994.
——. *Kur'an'ın Temel Kavramları.* Istanbul, 1991.
Rahman, Fazlur. 'Interpreting the Qur'an', *Inquiry,* (1986). pp. 45–49.
Taştan, Osman. 'İslam Hukukunda Literalizm: Anahatlarıyla Mukayeseli bir Analiz', *İslami Araştırmalar,* IX, 1–4 (1996), pp. 144–56.
——. 'Religion and [Religious] Minorities', in Debbie Lovatt, ed., *Turkey Since 1970: Politics, Economics and Society.* London and New York, 2001, pp. 137–59.

Yavuz, Yusuf Üevki. 'Elmalı'lı Muhammed Hamdi', in *Türkiye Diyanet Vakfı İslam Ansiklopedisi*. Istanbul, 1995, pp. 57–62.

Yazır, Elmalı'lı Muhammed Hamdi. *Hak Dini Kur'an Dili: Yeni Mealli Türkçe Tefsir*. Istanbul, 1935.

Zürcher, Erik J. *Turkey: A Modern History*. London and New York, 1993.

10

'The form is permanent, but the content moves': the Qur'anic text and its interpretation(s) in Mohamad Shahrour's *al-Kitab wal-Qur'an*

ANDREAS CHRISTMANN

Introduction

THE appropriate term to describe the approach of the Damascene writer Mohamad Shahrour[1] to the study of the Qur'an is *de-familiarisation*: it describes the process in which language is used in such a way that its use suddenly attracts attention and is immediately perceived as uncommon, as deprived of 'automization, as deautomized'.[2] De-familiarisation is a subversive strategy to describe an object of art 'as if one were seeing it for the first time'; its aim is to counteract conventional 'habitualisation' in the way of reading art so that eventually very familiar objects become unexpectedly unfamiliar to the reader.[3]

What Mohamad Shahrour has in common with the Russian Formalists and the Prague School of Literary Theory, in which the terms 'de-familiarisation' and 'habitualisation' originated, is the explicit wish to undermine the well-established canon of interpretations and to suggest alternative ways of reading a text. He wants his readers to understand the Qur'an 'as if the Prophet has just died and informed us of this book' (*ka-anna al-nabi tuwuffiya hadithan wa ballaghana hadha al-kitab*),[4] that is, as if they were seeing it for the first time. This is meant to be a comprehensive programme of challenging traditional perspectives on the Qur'an, which he regards as being corrupted by the 'inherited dubious axioms' (*al-musallamat al-mawrutha al-mushkila*) of the Islamic discourse. Shahrour wants to demonstrate that the exact opposite of what 'habitualised', 'automised' interpretations say, is true.[5] It is no wonder, then, that his books have become a permanent object of fierce debate and criticism in the Arab–Muslim world.[6] They have also started to draw some attention in Western academic circles interested in Islamic reform and liberal thought in modern Islam.[7] However, although Shahrour has already been labelled as the 'Immanuel Kant in the Arab World'[8] or as 'a Martin Luther of Islam',[9] to introduce and explain his work to the Western reader is still a desideratum. For a better appreciation of his style and approach it is necessary first to introduce some biographical details of Mohamad Shahrour's life.

The most obvious thing in Shahrour's attempt to undermine the profession of the *mufassir* and *faqih* is that he himself does not belong to that profession. Born in 1938 in the Salihiyya quarter of Damascus, he was the fifth child of a dyer who decided to send his son not to the local *kuttab* and *madrasa*, but to the primary and secondary state school in al-Midan, the southern suburb of Damascus outside the walls of the old city.[10] His later career was quite typical of many post-independence intellectuals from former European colonies. In 1957 he was sent to Saratow, near Moscow, to study Civil Engineering (until 1964) and then, one decade later, in 1968, he was sent again to study abroad, this time to the University College in Dublin for his M.A. and Ph.D. degrees in soil mechanics and foundation engineering (until 1972). As a Professor of Civil Engineering at the University of Damascus (1972-99) and manager of a small private engineering company, Mohamad Shahrour went nowhere near scholarly Islamic institutions and he has never achieved a formal training or certificate in the Islamic sciences.

Consequently, the way Shahrour has gained knowledge in the diverse disciplines of the Islamic sciences is that of an autodidact. Here, we have to rely on what he reports in biographical notes about his route into the Islamic tradition.[11] As with many Arab intellectuals traumatised by the Arab defeat at the hands of Israel in 1967, Shahrour began to study the Islamic heritage (*turath*) hoping to find a way out of the political and intellectual crisis. But unlike others who chose to follow either political radicalism or a strict form of salafi Islam, he became disillusioned by what he calls the *madrasiyya* mentality, which he sees expressed in the regressive reiteration of ancient school traditions (including those of the Mu'tazila) that block the way to real innovative solutions to the dilemma of Arab-Muslims.[12] It is no wonder that we find in him an advocate of religious learning that is not school-based and even transgresses the boundaries of the Islamic religion itself. The list of scholars and thinkers he favours shows the typically eclectic, unorthodox and partially subversive character of an autodidact's choice: A.N. Whitehead, Ibn Rushd, C. Darwin, I. Newton, al-Farabi, al-Jurjani, F. Hegel, W. Fichte, F. Fukuyama, et al.[13]

Unsurprisingly, as someone who came from the outside into the field of Islamic teaching, the main, indeed almost exclusive, medium through which Shahrour can publicise and spread his ideas is that of published books. Lacking the opportunity to respond to his opponents via sermons, mosque-lectures, Islamic journals, or television programmes, Shahrour's opportunity to take part in public debates is basically restricted to the print media. Through his first and most innovative book *al-Kitab wal-Qur'an: qira'a mu'asira*, published for the first time in 1990 and now in its tenth edition, the then unknown Shahrour – at the age of 52 – was brought unexpectedly to the limelight of fame and public interest. His book has been subjected to the critical eye of the religious establishment with its scrupulous erudition. To date he has published (with the same publishing house al-Ahali)[14] four monographs edited as parts of a series called *Contemporary Islamic Studies* (*Dirasat Islamiyya mu'asira*).[15] In addition to this series, he has written a small booklet and a couple of newspaper articles.[16] Recently, as a result of a growing interest in his work outside Syria, he has started to use CD-Rom as a new means for the distribution of his ideas.[17]

As an unwelcome intruder into the field, Shahrour has had to

face the massed opposition of almost the entire body of professional specialists; at the same time, he lacks the institutional
support of either the academic or the *ma'had*-based networks.
These circles have accused him of being paid by foreign/Zionist
organisations to undermine the authority of the Qur'an and the
unity of the Islamic *umma*,[18] of being one of the lost sheep of
Marxism in the gardens of Islam,[19] of having created a completely
new religion,[20] of plagiarism,[21] or of having committed an unfor-
givable act of dilettantism in the field of Qur'anic exegesis.[22] In
Shahrour's eyes these accusations are all typical strategies to avoid
any serious, innovative discussion within the Islamic sciences.[23]
Even sympathetic scholars such as Nasr Hamid Abu Zayd, who
himself advocates change and reform, criticise Shahrour's
methodological naïveté.[24] Among the almost two dozen publications on his works, there is hardly any explicitly positive reaction,[25] not even from those who come from the same profession
as Shahrour himself (engineering),[26] which seems to indicate that
he is suffering the destiny of the prophet who is unheard by his
own people.[27] Based in his small office in the Muhajirun quarter
of Damascus and surrounded by only a small group of like-
minded engineers, editors, and journalists, Shahrour can only
rely on the support of a few individuals and the undeclared
backing of the Syrian government, which does not want a replica-
tion of the Abu Zayd affair.[28]

Given the very unorthodox and complex nature of Shahrour's
methods and theories, an introduction to the fundamental categories of his hermeneutical approach may pave the way to a more
equipped reading of his works as a whole. To that end, this discussion focuses on an exploration of Shahrour's concept of the
Qur'anic text and its interpretation. Related issues, such as his
theory concerning the process of revelation (*wahy*) or 'sending
down' (*tanzil/inzal*) of the Qur'an and the Qur'an's inimitability
(*i'jaz*), are also included. The aim is to show how much Mohamad
Shahrour has 'de-familiarised' basic concepts related to the
Qur'an, and to highlight the strategies he has applied in order to
estrange his contemporary readers from more conventional
explanations.

Shahrour's concept of the Qur'anic text

The best entry into Shahrour's ideas is still via his first book, *al-Kitab wal-Qur'an: qira'a mu'asira*. The subtitle of the book contains an early allusion to the position of the author in the process of (re-)reading the most authoritative text of the Islamic tradition: it is strictly *contemporary*. Shahrour uses this terminology in order to stress the necessity to keep an epistemological openness despite the overwhelming importance of the Arabic-Islamic heritage (*turath*). The main thrust of Shahrour's argument for a 'contemporary' reading is directed towards situating the interpretation of the Qur'an within the larger framework of human knowledge in general and, in particular, within the context of modern philosophy and linguistics and, with reference to his own qualifications as an engineer, of mathematics and the natural sciences. The theoretical basis for this is what Shahrour sees as the crucial distinction which must be made between two different forms of any religious discourse: at one level there is the divine reality, immutable, eternal, and absolute; while at the other level there is the human understanding of that divine reality, about which there is nothing divine, and which is changeable, partial, and relative. Since the latter is a product of interaction with the intellectual paradigms of specific human societies, it is in a constant process of evolving and perfecting. Moreover, the human capacity to grasp the complex realm of the divine will increases with the progress of scientific achievements; this notion has led Shahrour to conclude that contemporary attempts at interpreting the sacred realm are much better equipped and more advanced than previous Islamic scholarship throughout the centuries.

In a more specific way, Shahrour considers the distinction between the absolute divine and the relative human applicable to the Qur'anic text itself. He differentiates between the permanence of the textual form (*thabat sighat al-nass*), and the movement of its content (*harakat al-muhtawa*). Whereas the textual, linguistic form is the divine word of Allah, which is eternally valid and immutable, its actual content is materialised by its readers, whose context is changing from one generation to another, thus establishing a constantly moving content. This dialectical relationship between permanence and movement, stability and progress, objectivity and subjectivity is Shahrour's notion of the Qur'an's uniqueness, which will be discussed (further) below. What is already apparent is that Shahrour wants to be able to free himself in his contemporary reading of the Qur'an, on the basis of his premise to distinguish between the sacred and the human, from any restriction laid upon the exegetical process by previous *tafsir* and *fiqh* scholars. Since their exegetical work is a direct result of the intellectual paradigms of their societies, an adoption of their views would imply a regressing back to their horizons; this runs counter to Shahrour's appeal to interpret the text from a strictly contemporary point of view. As several of his critics have remarked, the problem with his overt break with the past is that Shahrour does not apply the same strict criteria to the other historical persons whom he quotes as a kind of alternative canon of authority (e.g. al-Jurjani, Abu Jinni, and al-Farisi). This is an epistemological problem which Shahrour was compelled to leave unresolved, unless he had wished to ground his work on no authority whatsoever.[29]

The key to the understanding of Shahrour's attempt to 'defamiliarise' the Qur'an in order to open it up for a new, contemporary understanding is the way in which Shahrour re-conceptualises familiar terminology related to the Qur'an. The entire first part of his book is dedicated to a radical reprogramming of Qur'anic terminology, while the other three parts can be seen as either an application or an illustration of that new scheme.[30] He first deconstructs common definitions of traditional terms and exposes them as naïve, illogical, or biased, then he discovers a new association with a not yet discovered textual evidence, before he finally introduces a redefinition of that terminology. Through his work nothing will stay as it used to be, Shahrour warns his readers. In the same manner that Newton, through his scientific findings, changed the religious doctrines of the Christian church, Shahrour's reading of the Qur'an will destroy the unquestioned paradigms of Islamic scholarship. No wonder that his new terms and concepts have made Shahrour's model so indigestable for the traditional scholar, and often incomprehensible for the common Muslim reader.

Let us first look at how the Qur'anic text is conventionally understood and how it has been conceptualised by Shahrour (the terms within these diagrams will be defined later on in the text):

Diagram 1a

The Conventional Understanding of the Qur'an

al-Kitab   =   al-Qur'an

Diagram 1b

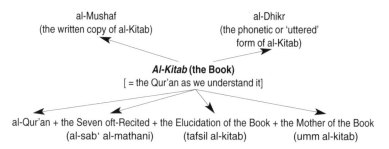

M. Shahrour's Understanding of the Qur'an

al-Mushaf
(the written copy of al-Kitab)

al-Dhikr
(the phonetic or 'uttered'
form of al-Kitab)

Al-Kitab (the Book)
[= the Qur'an as we understand it]

al-Qur'an + the Seven oft-Recited + the Elucidation of the Book + the Mother of the Book
(al-sab' al-mathani)   (tafsil al-kitab)   (umm al-kitab)

Diagram 2a

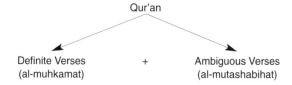

**Conventional Understanding of Definite and Ambiguous
Verses in the Qur'an**

Qur'an

Definite Verses   +   Ambiguous Verses
(al-muhkamat)   (al-mutashabihat)

Diagram 2b

M. Shahrour's Understanding of the Definite and Ambiguous Verses

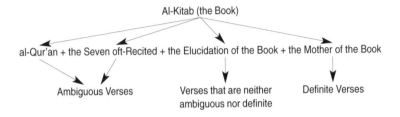

Diagram 3a

Conventional Understanding of Muhammad's Prophethood and Messengerhood

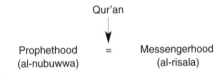

Diagram 3b

M. Shahrour's Understanding of Prophethood and Messengerhood

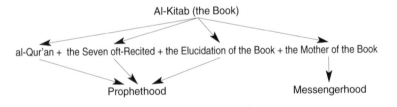

The diagrams 1b, 2b, and 3b are slightly revised and simplified versions of the chart which Shahrour presents at the beginning of his book. Shahrour immediately signals to his readers that they must drop their present understanding of the Qur'an and get involved in a new approach to the all too familiar Qur'anic vocabulary. What looks rather like a list of mathematical equations is, however, the outcome of basically three exegetical operations:

1. Shahrour applies al-Jurjani's principle of non-synonymy (*ghayr taraduf*) in poetical expressions to the Qur'anic text.[31] Terms which have achieved almost complete synonymy as *termini technici* in classical Islamic scholarship (e.g. *al-Qur'an* and *al-Kitab* as shown in Diagram 1a) are reorganised within their original Qur'anic context and explored as poly-synonymous expressions. Shahrour, convinced that not a single word can be replaced by another word without changing the meaning or corrupting the expressive power of the verses' linguistic construction, discovers fine distinct nuances of meanings between apparently synonymous terms. He differentiates the Qur'an – the book as we understand it – from *al-Kitab* and *al-Qur'an* on the one hand. On the other hand, he distinguishes between the latter two and *al-Dhikr* (the verbally acoustic form of *al-Kitab*). In this arrangement *al-Kitab* is the generic term (*ism 'amm*) which stands for the whole content of the written copy (*al-mushaf*), beginning with Surat al-Fatiha and ending with Surat al-Nas, while *al-Qur'an* is the more specific term (*ism khass*) that comprises only one part of *al-Kitab* (Diagram 1b). On the basis of these principles, Shahrour differentiates elsewhere between more than a dozen supposedly synonymous pairs or groups of terms, e.g. between *tanzil/inzal; furqan/Qur'an; imam mubin/kitab mubin; Umm al-Kitab/lawh mahfuz; qada'/qadr; zaman/waqt; mu'min/muslim; uluhiyya/rubu-biyya;* and *mann/salwa*, and he defines them separately.[32]

2. Shahrour rejects the idea of 'atomisation' (*ta'diya*), but interprets individual verses of the Qur'an on the assumption that they belong to organic single units within the overall larger unit of *al-Kitab*. According to him, the Book (*al-Kitab*) is neither uniform nor disjointed in its structure, but composed of many different sections. In the same manner in which Allah has revealed many different subject themes (*mawdu'at*), Shahrour groups these subjects as books (*kutub* – stated in the indefinite form)[33] within the entire *al-Kitab* (in its definite form):[34] e.g. 'the book of Creation', 'the book of the Last Day', 'the book of *al-'Ibadat'* and 'the book of *al-Mu'amalat'*. These books are again subdivided into other books: e.g. the book of *al-'Ibadat* is subdivided into the books of fasting, prayer, pilgrimage, etc., while the

book of prayer is similarly subdivided into the books of purification, *ruku'*, *sujud*, etc.[35] Based on the assumption of multiple
thematic subdivisions, Shahrour then goes one step further and
defines verses according to their metaphysical status as either
eternal, absolute, and objectively valid or as temporal, relative,
and subjectively conditioned. If Muhammad enjoyed the status of
the Prophet *and* the Messenger of Allah, Shahrour argues, the
Qur'an must reflect these two separate positions (conventionally
not perceived as separated, see Diagram 3a). While his prophethood represents the eternal and absolute side of Allah's revelation, his messengerhood represents its temporal and relative side
(Diagram 3b). This again is based on the distinction which
Shahrour makes between verses that are ambiguous
(*mutashabiha*), designating verses relating to prophethood; and
those that are definite (*muhkama*), the verses relating to messengerhood. These are supplemented by verses that are neither definite nor ambiguous (Diagram 2b).[36] Furthermore, by analogy
with his numerous subdivisions of thematic groups (*kutub*),
Shahrour assigns smaller units to the larger subgroups of *al-
Qur'an* and *Umm al-Kitab*, which can be best summarised in
another diagram (4)[37] (see p. 273).

3. Shahrour applies another principle of al-Jurjani's poetical
analysis, which is that of 'composition' (*al-nazm*). According to al-
Jurjani, 'not the smallest and superficially least significant element
of poetic composition can be ignored, for ignoring it may well
result in a total failure to comprehend and realise the structure of
meaning, or the levels of meaning, present in the composition.'[38]
Shahrour's concept of *al-Kitab*, with its complex structure and
substructures, is the result of his finicky search for the smallest vari-
ation in the syntactical position or grammatical expression of a
word. For each word there exists an etymological root which is for
Shahrour its essential, distinct meaning. The problem that lies in
such a literalistic and essentialist approach to meaning is – as many
critics have complained – that it prevents him from acknowledging
any symbolic or metaphorical meanings, inasmuch as it does not
allow any appreciation of the different usage of one term within the
Qur'an (e.g. *of al-Kitab*),[39] not to mention its diachronic

Diagram 4

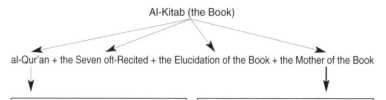

The Distinctive Nature of al-Qur'an and Umm al-Kitab

Al-Kitab (the Book)

al-Qur'an + the Seven oft-Recited + the Elucidation of the Book + the Mother of the Book

• **the Truth** (al-haqq) • **General laws that structure existence** (al-qawanin al-'amma al-nazima li al-wujud) • **the Laws of History** (qawanin al-ta'rikh) • **the Laws of Nature's Particles** (qawanin juz'iyyat al-tabi'a) • **the Conditioning of Nature's Phenomena** (tashrit ahdath al-tabi'a)	• **the 'Limits', including the Rites of Worship** (al-hudud bi ma fiha al-'ibadat) • **the General and Specific Guidance: the Commandments** (al-furqan al-'amm wal-khass: al-wasaya) • **Temporary Legal Prescriptions** (ahkam marhaliyya) • **Situational Legal Prescriptions** (ahkam zarfiyya: ayat mubayyanat) • **General Instructions, but not Legislation** (ta'limat 'amma, laysa tashri'at) • **Specific Instructions, but not Legislation** (ta'limat khassa, laysa tashri'at)

variations.[40] Because he also suspends any exegetical remarks by other interpreters (which are important only as part of the *turath*), and because he does not contextualise the meaning of the Qur'an through its historical origin (only the form is historical, the content is moving, i.e. contemporary), his resultant readings are quite unique and have a taste of arbitrariness. His exegesis of Qur'an 15: 87 ('And indeed, We have bestowed upon thee seven of the oft-repeated [verses], and [have, thus, laid open before thee] this sublime Qur'an ...'),[41] in which he establishes the meaning of the term *al-sab' al-mathani* ('the Seven Oft-Repeated', which Shahrour groups, together with *al-Qur'an*, the *Umm al-Kitab*, and the *Tafsil al-Kitab*, as one of the four fundamental parts of *al-Kitab*)[42] is one, possibly very extreme, example. Instinctively, he passes over all conventional understandings of the term 'the Seven Oft-Repeated', interpreted as referring either to the Qur'an's style in general, more particularly to the seven verses of Surat al-Fatiha, to seven long *suras* of the Qur'an, or to its seven punishment stories.[43] Instead, he looks at the etymological meaning of *al-mathani* – *tha'*, *nun, ya'* – and finds that several derivations point to the meaning 'the utmost part', the 'edge' or 'fringes' of a thing. He then concludes that the word *al-mathani* refers to the utmost part, the fringes of each chapter of the Qur'an, which he then confines only to their beginnings. Next, he checks all opening verses of each chapter and observes that there are seven combinations of eleven abbreviated letters (*al-muqatta'at*) which occur separately before the actual beginning of the chapter. *Al-muqatta'at* in other combinations are integral parts of a verse that contains more than these letters, which excludes them from being the 'utmost part' of the chapter. However, these remaining combinations contain three consonants which are not part of the other seven combinations – *qaf, ra', nun* – in which Shahrour sees the three roots of the word *al-Qur'an* (a term which Q. 15: 87 places in direct connection with *al-sab' al-mathani*), while *qara'a* expresses the same meaning as *qarana*, which is: to assemble or collect. Then he adds 3 to 11, which makes 14 (7x2), and explains that *al-sab' al-mathani* can be interpreted as the doubled or twofold seven! Clearly, Shahrour has managed to divert the attention from the significance of the number seven to the importance of the number eleven in the sense of 'collection/assembly of eleven'. But if *al-sab' al-mathani* alludes to 'collection/assembly of eleven', how does it come about that it is categorised together with *al-Qur'an* as part of *nubuwwa*, the *al-Kitab*'s prophetical part, which contains objective, absolute laws of the universe and of human life? Here, Shahrour fulfils his quest for strict contemporary exegesis and refers to new scientific results in modern linguistics which state that 11 consonants are the absolute minimal requirement of any human communication. *Al-Kitab*, thus, expresses an objective law of human life, and hence its place in Muhammad's prophetical message.[44]

Shahrour's concept of revelation

As in many modernist attempts to re-conceptualise the Qur'anic text, the issue of its revelation is central to Shahrour's new model of the Qur'an's nature, structure, and function. For his endeavour to introduce new boundaries within the text, the (re-)construction of the text's origins and first occurrence as Allah's revelation naturally plays a crucial role. The same three exegetical operations (discussed above) are again applied in challenging the traditional understanding of revelation. Firstly, Shahrour does not accept synonymy between the two terms *inzal* and *tanzil,* which are commonly used to describe the process of the Qur'an's 'coming down' as revelation to the Prophet Muhammad. Secondly, he asserts that the distinction between the two terms is based on the text's division into many variant sections, which differ in theme and status, with its main division between verses of prophethood and verses of messengerhood. Thirdly, he establishes this distinction by looking at linguistic composition, indexing all the references to both words in the Qur'an, and comparing the semantic nature of the difference between the second form of the verb *nazala* (*tanzil*) and the fourth form (*inzal*). By analogy with other verbs which imply processes of communication, e.g. *ballagha* (second form) / *ablagha* (fourth form),[45] Shahrour assigns to the fourth form *anzala* the delivery of a message by which its reception by all intended addressees is uncertain, while its reception is categorically implied with the usage of the second form *nazzala*. In order to justify this semantic operation he designs a plan of how mass media today are also technically operating in two different forms of communication:[46]

Phase 1: *al-ja'l* (transformation)

Football match in Mexico between Argentina and Brazil.

↓

The live action is filmed by cameras and then sent out into the world; sound and pictures are transformed into waves.

Phase 2: *al-tanzil*

Waves that transport sound and pictures from Mexico into the world.

It happens in the air and completely outside the human senses.

Phase 3: *al-inzal*

The process by which the TV/Aerial receives the waves and transforms them into sound and picture.

The result is a form of pictures and sounds that are perceivable by the human senses.

Phase 4: Perception

A viewer in Damascus can follow the football match in Mexico through his senses. The football match enters the viewer's knowledge.

The point Shahrour wants to stress is that it is possible to distinguish between ways of communication which either happen objectively and beyond human perception (the transfer of sound and pictures via waves from Mexico to Syria), or occur explicitly for the sensory perception of human beings (the re-conversion of the waves back into acoustic and optic signals for the reception of the TV-viewers). The term *al-tanzil* is assigned to the process of objective, other-human communication (reception by human beings is uncertain, impossible, or unintended), while the term *al-inzal* reflects the 'process of changing a matter outside the human mind from something unperceived to something perceived'.[47]

For Shahrour, the revelation of the Qur'an from Allah to the Prophet is based on the same technicalities of communication and can be explained in similar terms. According to him, *inzal* is the process of transforming (*ja'l*) the absolute laws of life and nature, which had been stored primordially in a 'preserved tablet'

(*lawh mahfuz*) and a 'clear guide' (*imam mubin*), or derive directly
from Allah's knowledge (*'ilm Allah*), into the linguistic form of the
Arabic language so that these laws, which were formerly outside
the human mind, can now be perceived, heard, and seen. On the
other hand, *tanzil* represents the objective transfer of *al-Kitab*'s
content into the Prophet's heart, from where he delivered it
afterwards to the people of Mecca and Medina. The whole point
of this distinction is that two different modalities of revelation
should be recognised. Shahrour suggests that revelation from
Allah took place either separately as *inzal / tanzil*, or simultaneously in both forms. If *inzal* and *tanzil* occurred separately, then
only *al-Qur'an* was revealed. If they happened simultaneously, the
other three remaining sections of *al-Kitab* (i.e. *Umm al-Kitab*, *tafsil
al-Kitab*, and *al-sab' al-mathani*) were uncovered. The difference
is that in the latter modus (the simultaneous occurrence of *inzal*
and *tanzil*) no pre-revelation takes place, since the revealed
messages are immediately available to Muhammad in their
perceivable (Arabic) version. Once again, tables might help to
illustrate this complicated notion of 'revelation'.[48]

(a) Revelation of al-Qur'an:

Lawh Mahfuz	Ja'l + Inzal		Tanzil		
General Laws of Existence	⇒ ⇒ ⇒ ⇒ al-Qur'an al-'Azim	- The Existence of an External Form of al-Qur'an in Arabic which is perceivable by humans. - occurred in the Laylat al-Qadr	⇒ ⇒ - an objective transfer of al-Qur'an outside Muhammad's consciousness via Jibril (Gabriel) - occurred throughout 23 years by Allah's command	- **Muhammad** records the Qur'an in his heart (and mind) - what he records is the Prophethood.	⇒ ⇒ ⇒ ⇒ - Prophethood is transferred to the **People** without any interpretation.
Imam Mubin The Initiation of Events in Nature The Recording of Events in History					

277

(b) Revelation of the Umm al-Kitab, the Tafsil al-Kitab, and al-Sabʿ al-Mathani:

Umm al-Kitab (al-Risala)	Issuing of Commands, Instructions, and Elucidations – revealed directly from Allah (Allah's Knowledge) ⇒ ⇒ ⇒ ⇒ It is a Transmission in Arabic without intermediate storage. – **Inzal and Tanzil** occur together within 23 years	Muhammad	Delivery of the Message to the **People** ⇒ ⇒ ⇒ ⇒
Tafsil al-Kitab (al-Nubuwwa)			
al-Sabʿ al-Mathani (al-Nubuwwa)			Transfer to 'those who are deeply rooted in knowledge' (Q. 3:7) ⇒ ⇒ ⇒ ⇒

In order to comprehend this model of 'revelation', some comments may help to clarify where exactly Shahrour's break with tradition begins. Clearly, his division of the revelatory process into two distinct categories with two different contents and separate chronological sequences runs counter to the mainstream opinion, which states that the *whole* Qur'an was sent down first from the 'preserved tablet' to the lowest heaven of this world (in the *laylat al-qadr* - traditionally the 27th night of Ramadan), and then revealed to the Prophet gradually over a period of 23 years until his death.[49] Even though Ashʿaris and Muʿtazilis differ over the question of whether the Qur'an was preserved in Heaven uncreated since eternity or created for the purpose of revelation, the unity of the Qur'an has never been questioned in either position. For Shahrour, however, a distinction is absolutely fundamental for the correct understanding of the Qur'anic text. According to him, the first category is the revelation of *al-Qur'an*, which contains the *mutashabihat* verses of Muhammad's prophethood. The second category is the revelation of the *Umm al-Kitab*, which contains the *muhkamat* verses of Muhammad's messengerhood, together with the *Tafsil al-Kitab* and *al-Sabʿ al-Mathani*. Whereas the first type is revealed from *lawh mahfuz/imam mubin*, transformed into Arabic and then transmitted via Jibril to the Prophet, the second type is given directly from Allah and stored in Muhammad's heart without any intermediary. The first represents what Shahrour calls *al-haqq*: the objective sources of existence, inasmuch as they are the general, absolute, and eternal laws of the universe, unaltered since the creation of the world, but for the first time revealed in a human (Arabic) language. The second type is designated by Shahrour *al-suluk*: guidance for human attitude and specific rules of social behaviour (see Diagram 4). They are not part of *al-haqq*, not absolute and general, but relative and particular, therefore not stored primordially in *lawh mahfuz/imam mubin*, but given directly to the prophets and messengers in correspondence with the historical, social, and intellectual context in which they lived.

There are at least three important implications of this division of the Qur'an's unity into two separate parts:

1. It shows that Shahrour does not want to identify himself wholly with either the Ash'ari or the Mu'tazili schools. In his model, only one section of the text (*al-Qur'an*) represents the *lawh mahfuz*, the 'uncreated, ever-existing and everlasting truth', which human beings are unable to fully understand in rational terms (the Ash'ari position).[50] The other sections of the text represent those verses whose exact verbal formulation and meaning are 'created' in the light of the historical context of revelation, and are thus subject to rational investigation (the position of the Mu'tazila).[51] Nevertheless, Shahrour does appear to support the position of the Mu'tazila through his insistence that the *muhkamat* verses do not form part of the eternally existing *al-haqq*, and through his claim that they are subject to alteration (*tabdil*), to the exercise of independent judgement (*ijtihad*) in the endeavour to understand them, and to rational investigation into their revelational circumstances (*asbab al-nuzul*).[52]

2. Through his distinction between *inzal* and *tanzil*, Shahrour avoids acknowledging any spatial dimension of revelation. In traditional exegesis the two recognised sources of revelation, the 'preserved tablet' or 'Allah's throne (*'arsh Allah*), were either interpreted in a literal sense or metaphorically, reflecting again the Ash'ari-Mu'tazili divide. But in both interpretations 'revelation' is conceptualised as a process of 'coming down' to earth from high above (the Heavens), the vertical connotation of this concept clearly imparts a spatial meaning to the term *nazala* in all its derivations. This traditional notion is unacceptable to

Shahrour, whose *horizontally* designed model of divine-human communication seems to indicate that he does not want to acknowledge any specific location of either *lawh mahfuz/imam mubin* or *'arsh Allah*, not to mention Allah himself. Were he to position the *lawh mahfuz/imam mubin* or *'arsh Allah* in the unseen world (*al-ghayb*) this would mean that they fall outside the reach of human reason, constituting a violation of his rationalist and 'scientific' claims, which he could not tolerate. Consequently, in an almost mystical fashion, Shahrour does not confer any spatial connotation on the sources of revelation, leaving it open – since he gives Muhammad only a passive role in the revelation process[53] – from where exactly the revelation occurred.[54]

3. Although Shahrour maintains the temporal dimension of revelation through his concept of *tanzil* (revelation in instalments over a period of 23 years), he challenges the traditional concept according to which the first and complete revelation of the Qur'an occurred during one night, the *laylat al-qadr*. First of all, he assigns only *al-Qur'an* (the universal, objective laws) to that revelation prior to the actual transfer (*tanzil*). Second, he describes that event not as (vertical) 'descent' (see point 2. above), but as *inzal*: the transformation of the imperceptible into the perceptible (Arabic) and as *ishhar*: the process of making *al-Qur'an* known. Third, since this process was *not* historically conditioned and since objective, absolute realities cannot be revealed within normal boundaries of time, Shahrour is at pains to deny the *laylat al-qadr* any specific temporality. Consequently, his exegesis of Q. 97: 1-5, to which he devotes a whole chapter, aims at voiding all relevant terms (*layla*; *shahr*; *matla' al-fajr*) of any temporal connotation.[55] Moreover, he denies the possibility that one can identify verses of *al-Qur'an* as either *nasikh* (abrogating) or *mansukh* (abrogated) [no objective law can ever be abrogated], inasmuch as it is impossible to establish their *asbab al-nuzul*, since they would have come as ontological necessities unconditioned, unrequested, and unasked.[56] The interesting effect of Shahrour's denial of any temporality/historicity to *al-Qur'an* is not only that he evokes again an almost mystical cloud around Muhammad's prophethood; he also creates a sharp dichotomy, through which

the temporality/historicity of the opposite part, the *Umm al-Kitab*, that is, the *muhkamat* verses, is even more accentuated. This dichotomy, one might argue, lies at the heart of the whole attempt to redefine revelation.

Shahrour's concept of *i'jaz* and the interpretation of the Qur'an

By looking specifically at Shahrour's concept of the 'wondrous nature/unparalleled uniqueness' (*i'jaz*) of the Qur'an and the principles of interpretation he upholds, the significance of the above distinction becomes even more apparent. Like many modern exegetes, Shahrour has some difficulty with the traditional explanation that the *i'jaz* of the Qur'an is based primarily on its linguistic and rhetorical style, its 'wonderful composition and high degree of eloquence, the perfection of which mankind is unable to imitate'.[57] However, he does not submit either to the modern equivalent of this explanation, that is to point primarily to its content, including all legal prescriptions, moral instructions, and spiritual guidelines, and assign to it the status of an 'intellectual-moral miracle which goes beyond the mere linguistic inimitability of the Qur'an'.[58] In Shahrour's view both explanations are too much concerned with an aesthetic admiration of the Qur'anic text, and neglect the fact that the Qur'an's *i'jaz* is much more connected with the problem of interpretation (*ta'wil*, see below), and is therefore to be found only in *al-Qur'an*, and not in the *Umm al-Kitab*. To explain that point, Shahrour develops an evolutionary philosophy of increasing participation in God's knowledge by human beings. According to his 'dialectics between the universal and human episteme', the only way to link the absolute, comprehensive knowledge, which is in Allah, and the relative, partial knowledge, which humans have, is to set up a total objective reality in linguistic form which corresponds with the understanding of each historical age. Once more, Shahrour presents the two elements: the stable, fixed, and eternal, which is *al-haqq* of *al-Qur'an* (not the *Umm al-Kitab*), and the movable,

changeable, and relative, which makes up the human understanding of *al-haqq*. The ambiguity of the verses of *al-Qur'an*
guarantees that human beings of whatever historical period or
intellectual background are constantly linked with and stimulated
by the objective truth. It is this ambiguity – a specific linguistic
shape of the text or perhaps a kind of unlocked semantic code –
which Shahrour regards as the fundamental aspect of *al-i'jaz*,
which he defines as the text's potential to allow a permanent
'assimilation' (*al-tashabuh*) between the temporal and eternal,
relative and total, partial and absolute.[59]

Shahrour's concept of interpretation (*ta'wil*) is embedded in
this view of *i'jaz*. Clearly, *ta'wil* in Shahrour's understanding does
not mean – as in the Sunni mainstream view – the metaphorical
interpretation which leaves the 'obvious' sense (*al-zahir*) and
dispenses with tradition, i.e. the opposite of *tafsir*.[60] For Shahrour,
ta'wil is rather the process of *tashabuh*: a permanent attempt to
harmonise the absolute nature of the Qur'anic verses with the
relative understanding (*nisbiyyat al-fahm*) of their human readers.
This harmony is achieved by moving the text's content
(meaning)[61] with the changing and progressing knowledge of the
interpreters, which they gain from the most advanced scientific
achievements of each period, and vice versa, by deducing scientific theories from the text of *al-Qur'an* itself. The ultimate aim of
each act of *ta'wil* is what Shahrour calls *ta'wil hissi*: perfect congru-
ence between humans' sensory perception of the world and the
content of *al-Qur'an*.

Among the examples of such a *ta'wil* which Shahrour cites are
Newton's theory of gravity, Darwin's theory of evolution, and
Einstein's theory of relativity, which are all taken from natural
scientists who were not Muslims. Shahrour's position here is that
since *ta'wil* is linked with *i'jaz*, and since *i'jaz* can only be found in
al-Qur'an, not in the *Umm al-Kitab* (i.e. the specific legal and
social law of *al-Kitab*), *ta'wil* can be carried out by everyone,
regardless of whether they are believers or unbelievers, Muslims or
non-Muslims, Arabic speakers or non-Arabic speakers. Shahrour
holds this view, which overturns everything that has previously
been prescribed as the prerequisites for *ta'wil*, on the basis of his

exegesis of Q. 3: 7, which has led him to the conclusion that 'those who are deeply rooted in knowledge' (*al-rasikhun fi al-'ilm*), are not, as conventionally assumed, the most learned and devout among the ulama and *fuqaha'*, but 'scholars and philosophers who occupy the most eminent place in society'.[62] The epistemological importance of this proposition derives from the underlying message that it is most important to invest in the authority of progressive science, rather than in regressive *tafsir* (which is based on the assumption that earlier commentaries are more authoritative than the later ones). The inclusion of modern science and philosophical theories will continuously expand *al-Qur'an*'s horizon, and – according to Shahrour's model of *i'jaz* – fuse it into the epistemological and social horizon of the modern age.

On the other hand, the ulama and *fuqaha'* are part of another interpretation process which Shahrour designates as the application of 'independent reasoning' (*ijtihad*) to achieve an understanding of the *Umm al-Kitab*. *Ijtihad* and *ta'wil* are described as two distinct forms of interpretation based on different assumptions and employing different methodologies. Since the *muhkamat* verses of the *Umm al-Kitab* are not revealed from the *lawh mahfuz* but directly from Allah in response to the historical situation in Mecca/Medina (*inzal* and *tanzil* together), their legal components (*ahkam*) are temporal, not eternal. They are definite, not ambiguous; hence for them there is no ground for *tashabuh*. Therefore the process of *ijtihad* is not, as many modern *ijtihad* theories argue, the attempt to harmonise the temporal needs of contemporary societies with the eternally valid *ahkam* of the Qur'an. On the contrary, it is the attempt to harmonise the temporal *ahkam* with the eternally valid laws of *al-Qur'an*. Shahrour holds that the *Umm al-Kitab* is in permanent need of active preservation (*hifz*), supervision (*raqaba*) and confirmation (*tasdiq*), while *al-Qur'an* is its *hafiz*, *raqib* and *musaddiq*.[63] This is the reason why the *mutashabihat* and the *muhkamat* verses are not separated in *al-Kitab*, but mixed together.[64] The significance of this aspect lies in the fact that it alludes explicitly to the debate about the implementation of the Islamic shari'a, which – in Shahrour's view – should never happen without recourse to the higher values and overarching principles of *al-Qur'an*. Moreover, since all humans, whether of Islamic faith or not, participate in interpreting *al-Qur'an*, a fusion between the state and a particular Islamic community would be detrimental to that process. Hence, Shahrour maintains, religion and politics should be separated.[65]

As for the methods of *ijtihad*, the exploration of the *asbab al-nuzul* and of possible abrogations (*naskh*) should be one of the main concerns of the *mujtahid*, if only applied to the *Umm al-Kitab*, not to *al-Qur'an*.[66] For both categories of text, however, Shahrour, in the manner of many other modernist thinkers, dispenses with exegetical reliance on the Sunna of the Prophet.[67] Quotations from hadith works are most sporadic and show neither competence nor real commitment. His overall method is one – as hinted above – of establishing direct hermeneutic contact with the Qur'anic text, and excluding any post-Qur'anic tradition. This issue has become one of the main targets of criticism by his opponents and has occupied much space on both sides of the fence.[68] Shahrour repeats again and again that the Prophet never himself interpreted *al-Qur'an*, but transferred it, uncommented upon, as a trust (*amana*) to the people. Even if he had done so, his interpretations of the absolute laws of the universe and nature would have been as temporal (*marhali*) as any other interpretation of the *tafsir* legacy after him, since absolute, perfect interpretation (*ta'wil mutlaq kamil*) is only possible for the one who represents that totality, Allah. As for the *Umm al-Kitab*, Muhammad's instructions about the *ahkam* were exclusively addressed to the people of his own time, which, as such, represent a perfect model of *ijtihad* (as a method), but not a binding example of conduct (as content). Had he done so, his instructions would have gained the status of the perfect, absolute, and immutable, which, in Islamic thought, cannot validly be claimed, since only Allah's revelation itself has such a status.[69]

The natural outcome of Shahrour's dispensing with tradition on the one hand, and demanding for constant inclusion of up-to-date sciences on the other, is that the thrust of authority in the interpretation of the Qur'anic text has been shifted onto the shoulders of the individual exegete. The possibility that each new exegesis of the Qur'an will institute its own tradition and authority is perhaps the underlying reason for the aggressive tone that colours the replies to Shahrour's work, but it only follows logically the pivotal point of his approach that 'only the text is permanent, but its content (meaning) moves'.

Conclusion

The genre of *tafsir*-commentaries functions like a contract. It serves as an agreement between exegetes, readers, and the general public enabling a circumscribed set of interpretations to be repeated in different religious sub-genres and other types of commentaries. This agreement may be based in the systems of meaning at work within a *tafsir* or schools of *tafsir* – that is, in familiar exegetical methods, narrative cues, and usage of *termini technici*. Or the agreement may be grounded in the engagement of readers' expectations and social attitudes by the persistent articulation of specific ideological values in *tafsir* commentaries. Alternatively, it may stem from a particular political climate that awards conformity with the conventional boundaries of the genre. Within a given school of Qur'an exegesis, the generic contract spells out the terms implicitly agreed upon by the *mufassirun* and their recipients so that the process of explaining and interpreting may continue, and so that a regulated set of cultural and ideological messages continues to be circulated in the process.

The uniqueness and originality of Shahrour's approach to the interpretation of the Qur'an lies in its conspicuous break with any agreement or contract – textually, linguistically, methodologically – pertaining to the *tafsir* genre. His proposal to virtually separate the Qur'an into two completely different texts (*nubuwwa/risala*) is certainly in itself a radical revocation of the dominant consensus – as some responses to similar approaches have shown.[70] Moreover, his assignment of the two parts of the text, firstly to two separate sources of origin (*lawh mahfuz/'ilm* Allah), secondly to two different modes of linguistic structure and code (*tashabuh/ghayr tashabuh*), and thirdly to two distinct forms of reception and interpretation (*ta'wil/ijtihad*), is against the generic contract, and by and large only to be found in marginal or minority positions within the history of *tafsir*. However, what makes his approach indeed original is his very bold 'crossing-over' among several other genres, disciplines, styles, and ideologies. Process theology, evolutionism, liberalism, Marxism, Sufism, mathematics, statistics, quantum physics, psychoanalysis, linguistics and communication theory: Shahrour synthesises many strands of thought without adhering to any one of them alone – to the puzzlement and chagrin of his critics. What is rarely mentioned in the many replies to his work is the fact that Shahrour has a *comprehensive* project of Islamic renewal in mind. It begins with a new philosophy of human and cosmological dialectics, and proceeds via the renewal of Qur'anic *tafsir* and Islamic *fiqh* to new foundations of Islamic economics, politics, ethics, and aesthetics, which finally will lead to the reform of the contemporary Arab-Muslim 'reality'. In order to appeal to as many readers as possible, who are indeed attracted by this comprehensive reform project, his work mixes at least four genres of Islamic religious literature (*tafsir, kalam, tasawwuf, fiqh*) with many disciplines of the modern human and social sciences. To judge his writings by the standards of only one of these genres and disciplines will not do his work any justice. This is because Shahrour's de-familiarisation strategies vigorously aim at challenging agreed standards and norms, and at exploring new boundaries between various genres and disciplines. To snatch away the Qur'anic text from the interpretive claims of exclusivist religious schools is his initial primary goal when he redefines the common terminology of Qur'anic Studies. What he writes about the Qur'an's texture, revelation, and interpretation may be recognised by many who are, like himself, outside these traditions as more plausible and logical than what has been said elsewhere. His guiding insight is that, within a world of changing social and ideological patterns, the authority to identify, mark, and measure the genre of Qur'an exegesis is diffused and subject to an ongoing and complex process of cultural negotiation.

NOTES

1. In spite of many different spellings, this article adopts the way Mohamad Shahrour himself transliterates his name in non-Arabic correspondence; other versions are kept if quoted in titles and citations.

2. Bohuslav Havránek, 'The Functional Differentiation of the Standard Language', in Paul Garvin, *A Prague School Reader on Esthetics, Literary Structure, and Style* (Washington, D.C., 1964), pp. 9–10.

3. Viktor Shklovsky, 'Art as Technique', 1965, p. 13, taken from Jeremy Hawthorn, ed., *A Concise Glossary of Contemporary Literary Theory* (New York, 1998), p. 40.

4. This is taken from his first book *al-Kitab wal-Qur'an: qira'a mu'asira* (cited hereafter as KQ), 1990, p. 44, also repeated in an interview with Mohamad Shahrour by the journalist Ali al-Atasi in *inamo*, no. 23/24, 6 (Autumn/Winter 2000), 'Ein Staat, wo kein Zwang in der Religion besteht', pp. 75–79.

5. KQ, p. 47.

6. See notes 17–25 below.

7. In particular in the work of Dale F. Eickelman, e.g. 'Islamic Liberalism Strikes Back', *Middle East Studies Association Bulletin*, 27, 2 (1993), pp. 163–68; 'Islam and the Languages of Modernity', *Daedalus*, 129, 1 (2000), pp. 119–35. (especially pp. 125 ff.); 'Muhammad Shahrur and the Printed Word', *ISIM Newsletter*, 7 (2001), p. 7; together with Jon W. Anderson, 'Print, Islam, and the Prospects for Civic Pluralism: New Religious Writings and their Audiences', *Journal of Islamic Studies*, 8:1 (1997), pp. 43–62 (especially p. 57). See also Peter Clarke, 'The Shahrur Phenomenon: a Liberal Islamic Voice from Syria', *Islam and Christian-Muslim Relations*, 7, 3 (1996), pp. 337–41; and Charles Kurzman, ed., *Liberal Islam: A Source book* (New York, 1998), M. Shahrour, 'Islam and the 1995 Beijing World Conference on Women' (trans. D.F. Eickelman), pp. 139–42.

8. D.F. Eickelman, 'Islamic Religious Commentary and Lesson Circles: Is there a Copernican Revolution?', in G.W. Most, ed., *Commentaries – Kommentare* (Göttingen, 1999), p. 140.

9. Rainer Nabielek, 'Muhammad Shahrur, ein "Martin Luther" des Islam', *inamo*, no. 23/24, 6 (Autumn/Winter 2000), pp. 73–74.

10. Details from an interview with M. Shahrour by the author, Damascus, May 2001.

11. KQ, pp. 46–48; interview, May 2001.

12. KQ, pp. 46–47.

13. Moreover, in his books he rarely acknowledges the sources of his inspiration. In his first book (KQ) there is no reference at all to any of the sources he has consulted. Only in his later publications does he sporadically include footnotes, in his latest monograph even endnotes, but bibliographies are still omitted.

14. In Syria regarded as one of the least prestigious, but quite unconventional ones, also famous for its left-wing, liberal publications, especially in the late eighties, when Shahrour began to write for them.

15. Interestingly, the first four editions of the first book did not yet bear

that series title, an indication perhaps that the idea of a series only developed after the success of the first title. The second book came out in 1994 as *Dirasat Islamiyya mu'asira fi al-dawla wal-mujtama'*, the third as *Islam wa iman* (1996); and finally *Nahw usul jadida li al-fiqh al-Islami* (2000). All of these books are elaborations of ideas which Shahrour had already developed in his first book. He applies in them also the same methodology of Qur'anic exegesis with only slight variations, so that, naturally, most observations in this article will be based on Shahrour's first book.

16. *Mashru' mithaq al-'amal al-Islami* (1999; trans. as 'Proposal for an Islamic Covenant' by Eickelman and Abu Shehadeh [2000]); 'al-Harakat al-libraliyya rafadat al-fiqh wa tashri'atiha wa lakinnaha lam tarfud al-Islam ka-tawhid wa risala samawiyya', *Akhbar al-'Arab al-Khalijiyya*, no. 20, 16 December 2000; 'al-Harakat al-Islamiyya lan tafuz bi al-shar'iyya illa idha tarahat nazariyya Islamiyya mu'asira fi al-dawla wal-mujtama'', *Akhbar al-'Arab al-Khalijiyya*, no. 21, 17.12.2000.

17. Shahrour distributes recordings of his TV appearance in January and February 2001 (satellite channel Orbit), when he explained in eight sessions to his host (the journalist 'Imad al-Din Adib) the content of his last monograph.

18. In particular Muhammad Sa'id Ramadan al-Buti, 'al-Khalfiyya al-Yahudiyya li-shi'ar qira'a mu'asira', *Nahj al-Islam*, 42 (December 1990), pp.17–21; Shawqi Abu Khalil, 'Taqattu'at khatira fi darib al-qira'at al-mu'asira', *Nahj al-Islam*, 43 (1991), pp.17–21. In fairness to his other opponents, not all the critics of his work share the view of conspiracy propounded by al-Buti and Abu Khalil. On the contrary, these latter were openly accused of 'scare-mongering' and 'ignorance' by other, not less critical writers (e.g. Mahir al-Munajjid, *al-Ishkaliyya al-manhajiyya fi 'al-Kitab wal-Qur'an': dirasa naqdiyya* (Damascus/Beirut, 1994), pp. 65, 79.

19. See Muhammad Sayah al-Ma'rawiyya, *al-Markslamiyya wal-Qur'an, aw: al-bahith 'an 'imama li Darwin wa Marks wa zawjat al-ni'man: 'qira'a fi da'wa al-mu'asira'* (n.p., 2000); Munir Muhammad Tahir al-Shawwaf, *Tahafut al-dirasat al-mu'asira fi al-dawla wal-mujtama'* (Beirut, 1993; Riyadh, 1995, previously published as: *Tahafut al-dirasat al-mu'asira* [Limassol, 1994]).

20. By Yusuf al-Qaradawi, during his television programme 'al-Shari'a wal-Hayat', 25 June 2001 (al-Jazira TV).

21. Like Mahir al-Munajjid, who doubts that M. Shahrour is the real author of the book; see *al-Ishkaliyya al-manhajiyya*, p. 12.

22. Among many: Yusuf al-Saidawi, who has counted 73 grave mistakes in KQ's 730 pages, 'every 10 pages one big error': *Baydat al-dik: naqd lughawi li kitab 'al-Kitab wal-Qur'an'* (Damascus, 1993), pp. 123–34; Salim al-Jabi, *al-Qira'a al-mu'asira li Duktur Muhammad Shahrur: mujarrad tanjim - kadhaba al-munajjimun wa law sadaqu* (Damascus, 1991); Tariq Ziyada, 'Tarafa fi al-taqsim wa gharaba fi al-ta'wil', *al-Naqid*, 45 (1992), pp. 57–60.

23. See *inamo* (2000), p. 79.

24. Nasr Hamid Abu Zayd, 'Limadha taghat al-talfiqiyya 'ala kathir min mashru'at tajdid al-Islam?', *al-Hilal* (October 1991), pp.17–27; and 'al-Manhaj al-naf'i fi fahm al-nusus al-diniyya', *al-Hilal*, March 1992.

Shahrour responded to Abu Zayd's first remarks, but left his second comments unanswered. M. Shahrour, 'al-Qira'a al mu'asira li al-Qur'an', *al-Hilal* (January 1992), pp. 128–34.

25. Perhaps with the exception of the very benevolent review by Na'im al-Yafi, 'al-Qur'an wal-Kitab [*sic*]: qira'a mu'asira', *al-Usbu' al-adabi*, 247 (1991), p. 3, and, perhaps as one might have expected, a review in the left-wing journal *Socialist Studies*: Bashir 'Ani, 'Muhammad Shahrur: manhaj fi al-qira'a al-mu'asira', *Dirasat Ishtirakiyya*, 164–65 (1996), pp. 46–54.

26. Ma'mun al-Jawijati, *al-Usus al-khasira li al-qira'a al-mu'asira*, 2nd ed. (Limassol, 1993); Jawad Musa Muhammad 'Affana, *al-Qur'an wa awham al-qira'a al-mu'asira – radd 'ilmi shamil 'ala kitab: 'al-Kitab wal-Qur'an: qira'a mu'asira'* (Amman, 1994).

27. Privately, Shahrour admits that his ideas are much more heard and accepted by Muslims who live outside the Arab-Muslim world, but he frequently quotes high-ranking officials in the Gulf states who revealed to him their (concealed) admiration for his work (interview, May 2001).

28. Shahrour acknowledges that Syria is the only place in the Arab-Muslim world where he can publish his work without fear of persecution, expulsion, or total ban of his books (interview, May 2001).

29. Ahmad 'Imran, *al-Qira'a al-mu'asira li al-Qur'an fi al-mizan* (Beirut, 1995), pp. 297 ff. The same criticism may be applied to Shahrour's frequent use of Ibn Faris's *Mu'jam maqayis al-lugha* (KQ, p. 44) for establishing the meaning of a word, since neither this dictionary nor his reading would be strictly contemporary, not to mention the tendency to make absolute the meaning of one age (that of the *Mu'jam*) over all others.

30. The four parts are called: (i) 'Remembrance' (*al-Dhikr*); (ii) The Dialectical Relationship between the Universe and the Human Being (*Jadal al-kawn wal-insan*); (iii) The Mother of the Book, the Sunna, and Jurisprudence (*Umm al-kitab wal-Sunna wal-fiqh*); (iv) About the Qur'an (*fi al-Qur'an*).

31. See K. Abu Dib, *Al-Jurjani's Theory of Poetic Imagery* (London, 1978), p. 7 ff. Like many other modern exegetes of the Qur'an (such as Amin al-Khuli, M. Khalafallah, Bint al-Shati', even Sayyid Qutb), Shahrour owes a good deal of his methodology to the work of Abu Bakr 'Abd al-Qahir al-Jurjani (d. 1078), whose philological and literary theories are extensively explained in two separate sections of KQ by the late Damascene Professor of Literary Studies, Ja'far Dakk al-Bab. In fact, al-Jurjani is the only source of inspiration Shahrour explicitly names. He seems to regard him as the only authority worth citing in support of his interpretation of the Qur'an. Al-Jurjani's teachings about the Qur'an have been analysed by Max Weisweiler, "Abdalqahir al-Curcani's Werk über die Unnachahmlichkeit des Korans und seine syntaktisch-stilistischen Lehren', *Oriens* 11 (1958), pp. 77–121. See also Helmut Ritter's introduction to his edition of *Asrar al-balagha* (Istanbul, 1954).

32. This is one of the most consistent methods in Shahrour's Qur'anic analysis and can be found in all of his major works, in particular in his third book *Islam wa iman* (1996).

33. E.g. in Q. 4: 103; 98: 2–3.

34. Based on Q. 2:1 and numerous other references.

35. KQ, p. 54.

36. Shahrour characterises these verses as a kind of commentary of other verses, which is provided by *al-Kitab* itself and which explains the text's typical self-referential character.

37. The diagram will be explained in greater detail below.

38. Abu Dib, *al-Jurjani's Theory*, p. 44.

39. Compare e.g. the subtle different nuances of *al-Kitab* as 'scripture' in the early Meccan period and as 'revealed scripture' in the late Meccan and early Medinan period, as noted by Tilman Nagel, 'Vom "Qur'an" zur "Schrift" – Bells Hypothese aus religionswissenschaftlicher Sicht', *Der Islam* 60 (1983), pp. 143–65; see also Arthur Jeffrey, *The Qur'an as Scripture* (New York, 1952), pp. 9 ff.; 69 ff.

40. See e.g. William A. Graham, *Beyond the Written Word: Oral Aspects of Scripture in the History of Religion* (Cambridge, 1987), pp. 79 ff.

41. Translation and parentheses by M. Asad, *The Message of the Qur'an* (n.p., 1980).

42. See Diagram 1b.

43. See for a summary of the diverse views, W.M. Watt, *Bell's Introduction to the Qur'an* (Edinburgh, 1970), pp. 134 ff.

44. KQ, pp. 98–99.

45. Based on Q. 5: 67 (*ballagha*), and 7: 93 (*ablagha*).

46. KQ, p. 174.

47. KQ, p. 149.

48. This is a simplified version from KQ, p. 175.

49. See for alternative views: Stefan Wild, '"We have sent down to thee the Book with the Truth": Spatial and Temporal Implications of the Qur'anic Concepts of *nuzul, tanzil,* and *inzal*', in S. Wild, ed., *The Qur'an as Text* (Leiden, 1996), pp. 138–153.

50. However, while in Shahrour's model *al-Qur'an* is transformed into Arabic through *inzal,* for the Ash'aris the Qur'an had always been stored in Arabic in the *lawh mahfuz.*

51. Again, Shahrour differs from the Mu'tazila in that he does not consider either Jibril or the Prophet as the agents of the exact wording in Arabic. The agent is rather Allah alone through simultaneous *inzal/tanzil.*

52. For the hermeneutical position of the Mu'tazila see the detailed study by Nasr Hamid Abu Zayd, *al-Ittijah al-'aqli fi al- tafsir*, 3rd edn (Beirut, 1993).

53. In this respect Shahrour seems to follow traditional patterns of explanation and, contrary to many modern concepts, does not assign to Muhammad an active/creative role in communicating the divine word. According to him, Muhammad received either 'abstract revelations' (*wahy mujarrad*) when he was unconscious, or 'sensory revelations' (*wahy fu'adi*) when he could hear or see the intermediary. In both situations Muhammad only recorded (*sajjala*) the messages 'directly into his innermost heart' (KQ, p. 383).

54. The irony in the fact that Shahrour vehemently attacks the positions of Sufism but nevertheless has frequent recourse to their metaphysical

ideas did not escape the attention of his critics. See Abu Zayd, 'Limadha taghat al-talfiqiyya', p. 26; and the remark by Wild, 'We have sent down to thee the Book', p. 152.

55. KQ, pp. 205–208. Interestingly, the possibility of a non-temporal reading of these terms (including the possibility of *layla* as a form of personification), or at least of reading them as an allusion to a complete dissolution of normal temporal boundaries, is also discussed by Michael Sells, 'Sound, Spirit, and Gender in *Surat al-Qadr*', *Journal of the American Oriental Society*, 111, 2 (1991), pp. 239–59.

56. KQ, p. 154.

57. See J.J.G. Jansen, *The Interpretation of the Koran in Modern Egypt* (Leiden, 1974), pp. 51–54.

58. As a good example see Muhammad Husain Tabataba'i, *Der Koran im Islam* (Bonn, 1986), p. 119 ff.

59. KQ, pp. 60 ff. and 185 ff.

60. For a summary of the difference between the two terms and some alternative explanations of *ta'wil*, see A. Rippin, 'Tafsir', in Mircea Eliade, ed., *Encyclopeadia of Religion*, pp. 236–44; I. Poonawala, 'Ta'wil', *EI²*, vol. 10, pp. 390–92.

61. Clearly, by 'content' Shahrour says 'meaning'. The fact that he does not use the Arabic terms for 'meaning' (*ma'na* or *dalala*) shows that he does not share the views of contemporary writers who approach the same subject from a more hermeneutical point of view. See e.g. N. Abu Zayd, *Mafhum al-nass* (Cairo, 1990), chs. 2–3; Tayyib Tizini, *al-Nass al-Qur'ani: amam ishkaliyyat al-binya wal-qira'at* (Damascus, 1997), in particular ch. 2. See also the collection of articles published in the Turkish *Journal of Islamic Research*, 1996, vol. 9, nos. 1–4 (the author owes this reference to Mr. Neçmettin Gokkir). That Shahrour is aware of their writings is obvious from sporadic quotations of their work, e.g. of Abu Zayd's *Ishkaliyyat al-qira'a wa aliyat al-ta'wil*, in: *al-Dawla wal-mujtama'*, p. 267.

62. Shahrour quotes alongside Newton, Darwin and Einstein al-Biruni, Ibn Rushd, al-Hasan Ibn al-Haytham, Kant, and Hegel (KQ, p. 193). Shahrour sparked a huge controversy among his opponents with this interpretation. His cross-reference to Q. 29: 49 – '*ayatun bayyanatun fi sudur alladhina utu al-'ilm*', 'signs of explanation in the hearts of those who are given knowledge', which Shahrour interpreted as 'signs clear to the most eminent who are given knowledge' (since the true meaning of *sudur* is to be taken from *sidara* = eminence/pre-eminence), was labelled as most obscure and arbitrary. Compare with more common interpretations as summarised in Mahmoud M. Ayoub, *The Qur'an and its Interpreters* (New York, 1992), vol. 2, pp. 20–46.

63. KQ, p. 160. On the basis of this distinction, Shahrour develops in the *fiqh* part of the book his theory of the dialectics between straightness (*istiqama*) and curvature (*hanafiyya*) in the evolution of human legislation; this is summarised by Wael B. Hallaq, *A History of Islamic Legal Theories* (Cambridge, 1997), pp. 245–53.

64. Paradoxically, although his views are so much concerned with the distinction between the two categories of verses, Shahrour nowhere gives

concrete hints as to how many of them there are in the book and how exactly they are differentiated. As for *al-ahkam,* for instance, their identification has always been one of the main concerns for the *fiqh al-Qur'an* scholarship. See M.H. Kamali, *Principles of Islamic Jurisprudence* (Cambridge, 1991), p. 19 ff.

65. KQ, p. 719; *al-Dawla wal-mujtama',* pp. 179–206.

66. Surprisingly, Shahrour, in his own *ijtihad,* did not consult at all the *asbab* or *naskh* sources, even when they could have improved his argument, e.g. in his exegesis of Q. 33: 53 and the issue of *al-hijab.* See KQ, p. 604 ff. and *Usul jadida,* p. 343 ff. Such consultation would have contradicted *his own* method of always seeking direct access to the Qur'anic text.

67. See for numerous similar positions in modern Islamic thought, Daniel Brown, *Rethinking Tradition in Modern Islamic Thought* (Cambridge, 1996), in particular pp. 60–80.

68. The most common expression used by his critics to denounce Shahrour's omission of tradition is *ta'wil shakhsi,* personal interpretation, which indicates their distaste for 'arbitrariness', 'eccentricity', 'uncontrolled personal passion' in the process of interpretation. In the *Usul al-tafsir* literature, this has been since al-Ghazali the standard response against *ta'wil* that is not guided and restricted by *tafsir.* See Muhammad Abul Quasem, *The Recitation and Interpretation of the Qur'an: Al-Ghazali's Theory* (Kuala Lumpur, 1979), Ch. 4, pp. 86–104.

69. These ideas reveal remarkable parallels to those expressed by the Ahl-i-Qur'an scholars in the Indian subcontinent. Note also that, perhaps similarly to Shahrour, they did not want to dispense with the authority of the Prophet altogether, but to protest against the manner in which the Prophetic authority is misrepresented by the traditional ulama. Brown, *Rethinking Tradition,* 1996, p. 71.

70. See e.g. the striking similarities in the distinction between these two textual types to the models developed by Mahmud Muhammad Taha (1909/11–1985) and his pupil Abdullahi Ahmed an-Na'im. See Mohamed Mahmoud, 'Mahmud Muhammad Taha's Second Message of Islam and his Modernist Project', in: J. Cooper, R. Nettler, and M. Mahmoud, eds, *Islam and Modernity* (London, 1998), pp. 105–128; also A.A. an-Na'im, *Toward an Islamic Reformation: Civil Liberties, Human Rights, and International Law* (Syracuse, NY, 1990), Chs. 2–3.

BIBLIOGRAPHY

Works by Mohamad Shahrour

——. 'al-Qira'a al-mu'asira li al-Qur'an'. *al-Hilal,* January 1992, pp. 128–34.
——. *al-Kitab wal-Qur'an: qira'a mu'asira.* Damascus, 1992.
——. *Dirasat Islamiyya mu'asira fi al-dawla wal-mujtama'.* Damascus, 1994.
——. 'Islam and the 1995 Beijing World Conference on Women' (trans. D.F. Eickelman), in Kurzman, Charles, ed. *Liberal Islam: A Sourcebook.* New York, 1998, pp. 139–142.

——. *Islam wa iman.* Damascus, 1996.

——. *Nahwa usul jadida li al-fiqh al-Islami.* Damascus, 2000.

——. *Mashru' mithaq al-'amal al-Islami.* (Trans. as 'Proposal for an Islamic Covenant' by Eickelman and Abu Shehadeh, n.p., 2000.) 1999.

——. 'al-Harakat al-libraliyya rafadat al-fiqh wa tashri'atihi wa lakinnaha lam tarfud al-Islam ka-tawhid wa risala samawiyya'. *Akhbar al-'Arab al-Khalijiyya*, no. 20, 16 December 2000.

——. 'al-Harakat al-Islamiyya lan tafuz bi al-shar'iyya illa idha tarahat nazariyya Islamiyya mu'asira fi al-dawla wal-mujtama''. *Akhbar al-'Arab al-Khalijiyya*, no. 21, 17 December 2000.

Other Sources

Abu Dib, K. *Al-Jurjani's Theory of Poetic Imagery.* London, 1978.

Abu Khalil, Shawqi. 'Taqattu'at khatira fi darib al-qira'at al-mu'asira'. *Nahj al-Islam*, 43 (March 1991), pp. 17–21.

Abu Zayd, Nasr Hamid. *Mafhum al-nass.* Cairo, 1990.

——. 'Limadha taghat al-talfiqiyya 'ala kathir min mashru'at tajdid al-Islam?' *al-Hilal*, October 1991, pp. 17–27.

——. 'al-Manhaj al-naf'i fi fahm al-nusus al-diniyya'. *al-Hilal*, March 1992.

——. *al-Ittijah al-'aqli fi al-tafsir.* 3rd edn, Beirut, 1993.

Abul Quasem, Muhammad. *The Recitation and Interpretation of the Qur'an: Al-Ghazali's Theory.* Kuala Lumpur, 1979.

'Affana, Jawad Musa Muhammad. *al-Qur'an wa awham al-qira'a al-mu'asira – radd 'ilmi shamil 'ala kitab: 'al-Kitab wal-Qur'an: qira'a mu'asira'.* Amman, 1994.

'Ani, Bashir. 'Muhammad Shahrur: manhaj fi al-qira'a al-mu'asira'. *Dirasat Ishtirakiyya*, 164–165 (1996), pp. 46–54.

Asad, M. *The Message of the Qur'an.* Gibraltar, 1980.

al-Atasi, Ali. 'Ein Staat, wo kein Zwang in der Religion besteht'. *inamo*, no. 23/24, 6, Autumn/Winter 2000.

Ayoub, Mahmoud M. *The Qur'an and its Interpreters.* New York, 1992.

Brown, Daniel. *Rethinking Tradition in Modern Islamic Thought.* Cambridge, 1996.

al-Buti, Muhammad Sa'id Ramadan. 'al-Khalfiyya al-Yahudiyya li shi'ar qira'a mu'asira'. *Nahj al-Islam*, 42 (December 1990), pp. 17–21.

Clarke, Peter. 'The Shahrur Phenomenon: a Liberal Islamic Voice from Syria'. *Islam and Christian-Muslim Relations*, vol. 7, 3 (1996), pp. 337–41.

Eickelman, Dale F. 'Islamic Liberalism Strikes Back'. *Middle East Studies Association Bulletin*, 27: 2 (December, 1993), pp. 163–68.

——. 'Inside the Islamic Reformation'. *Wilson Quarterly*, Winter 1998.

——. 'Islamic Religious Commentary and Lesson Circles: Is there a Copernican Revolution?', in G.W. Most, ed., *Commentaries - Kommentare*, Göttingen, 1999, pp. 121–46.

——. 'Islam and the Languages of Modernity'. *Daedalus*, 129: 1 (Winter 2000), pp. 119–35.

——. 'Muhammad Shahrur and the Printed Word'. *ISIM Newsletter*, 7 (2001).

—— and Jon W. Anderson, 'Print, Islam, and the Prospects for Civic Pluralism: New Religious Writings and their Audiences'. *Journal of Islamic Studies*, 8:1 (1997), pp. 43–62.

Graham, William A. *Beyond the Written Word: Oral Aspects of Scripture in the History of Religion*. Cambridge, 1987.

Hallaq, Wael B. *A History of Islamic Legal Theories*. Cambridge, 1997.

Havránek, Bohuslav. 'The Functional Differentiation of the Standard Language', in Paul Garvin, *A Prague School Reader on Esthetics, Literary Structure, and Style*. Washington, DC, 1964.

'Imran, Ahmad. *al-Qira'a al-mu'asira li al-Qur'an fi al-mizan*. Beirut, 1995.

al-Jabi, Salim. *al-Qira'a al-mu'asira li Duktur Muhammad Shahrur: Mujarrad tanjim - kadhaba al-munajjimun wa law sadaqu*. Damascus, 1991.

Jansen, J.J.G. *The Interpretation of the Koran in Modern Egypt*. Leiden, 1974.

al-Jawijati, Ma'mun. *al-Usus al-khasira li al-qira'a al-mu'asira*. 2nd edn, Limassol, 1993.

Jeffrey, Arthur. *The Qur'an as Scripture*. New York, 1952.

Kamali, M.H. *Principles of Islamic Jurisprudence*. Cambridge, 1991.

Mahmoud, Mohamed. 'Mahmud Muhammad Taha's Second Message of Islam and his Modernist Project', in J. Cooper, R. Nettler, and M. Mahmoud, eds, *Islam and Modernity*. London, 1998, pp. 105–28.

al-Ma'rawiyya, Muhammad Sayah. *al-Markslamiyya wal-Qur'an, aw: al-bahith 'an 'imama li Darwin wa Marks wa zawjat al-ni'man: 'qira'a fi da'wa al-mu'asira'*. n.p., 2000.

al-Munajjid, Mahir. *al-Ishkaliyya al-manhajiyya fi 'al-Kitab wal-Qur'an' - Dirasa naqdiyya*. Damascus/Beirut, 1994.

Nabielek, Rainer. 'Muhammad Shahrur, ein "Martin Luther" des Islam'. *inamo*, no. 23/24, 6, Autumn/Winter 2000.

Na'im, A.A. *Toward an Islamic Reformation: Civil Liberties, Human Rights, and International Law*. New York, 1990.

Nagel, Tilman. 'Vom "Qur'an" zur "Schrift" – Bells Hypothese aus religion-swissenschaftlicher Sicht'. *Der Islam* 60 (1983), pp. 143–65.

Poonawala, I. 'Ta'wil'. *EI²*, vol 10, pp. 390–92.

Rippin, A. 'Tafsir', in Mircea Eliade, ed., *Encyclopaedia of Religion*, pp. 236–244.

al-Saidawi, Yusuf. *Baydat al-dik: Naqd lughawi li kitab 'al-Kitab wal-Qur'an'*. Damascus, 1993.

Sells, Michael. 'Sound, Spirit, and Gender in *Surat al-Qadr*'. *Journal of the American Oriental Society*, 111, 2 (1991), pp. 239–59.

al-Shawwaf, Munir Muhammad Tahir. *Tahafut al-dirasat al-mu'asira fi al-dawla wal-mujtama'*. Beirut, 1993.

Tabataba'i, Muhammad Husayn. *Der Koran im Islam*. Bonn, 1986.

Tariq, Ziyada. 'Tarafa fi al-taqsim wa gharaba fi al-ta'wil', *al-Naqid*, 45 (March 1992), pp. 57–60.

Tizini, Tayyib. *al-Nass al-Qur'ani: amam ishkaliyyat al-binya wal-qira'at*. Damascus, 1997.

Watt, W.M. *Bell's Introduction to the Qur'an*. Edinburgh, 1970.

Weisweiler, Max. "'Abdalqahir al-Curcani's Werk uber die Unnachahmlichkeit des Korans und seine syntaktisch-stilistischen Lehren'. *Oriens* 11 (1958), pp. 77–121.

Wild, Stefan. '"We have sent down to thee the Book with the Truth": Spatial and Temporal Implications of the Qur'anic Concepts of *nuzul, tanzil,* and *inzal*', in S. Wild, ed., *The Qur'an as Text.* Leiden, 1996, pp. 138–53.

al-Yafi, Na'im. 'al-Qur'an wal-kitab [*sic*]: qira'a mu'asira'. *al-Usbu' al-Adabi,* 247, January 1991.

11

Modern intellectuals, Islam, and the Qur'an: the example of Sadiq Nayhum

SUHA TAJI-FAROUKI

THE FORCE of the Islamic resurgence of recent decades has been such that Muslim intellectuals who are products of a secular background and education, and are themselves essentially secular in orientation, have been drawn onto its discursive terrain. Moved to address the condition and future of Muslim societies and states, such intellectuals are faced with the unavoidable reality of a pervasive and powerfully influential Islamic discourse. To have an impact, their writings must appeal to the growing constituencies of those who have adopted a self-consciously Islamic identity and worldview. They must also be relevant to those who, while perhaps rejecting Islamist assumptions, remain uncomfortable with the exclusion of Islam as a source of guidance for modern life, and feel general concern for the Islamic heritage. Engagement with the Islamic textual tradition in general, and with the Qur'an in particular as its central text, provides 'Islamic' legitimisation for the arguments of such intellectuals in their aspiration to address these constituencies. Untrained in the methodologies and conventions of *tafsir* (as indeed in other Islamic disciplines), their approach to the Qur'an is direct and unfettered by its legacy. By advancing new readings themselves, such intellectuals implicitly suggest that multiple understandings are possible, calling into question a pronounced contemporary tendency, especially among Islamists, to insist that there is only one correct interpretation of Qur'anic meaning.

Given their secular orientation, the approach of such intellectuals might be dismissed as a merely 'ritualistic' acknowledgement
of Islam's primary text. While it is not easy to establish the
sincerity of their appeal to the Qur'an, it is equally difficult to
maintain that this is simply a strategem, recruited in the course of
a discursive struggle. Such intellectuals construe Islam, albeit re-
imagined from traditional understandings almost beyond recognition, as a source of inspiration and possible solutions in
confronting the problems of modern Muslim society. To that
extent, they must be distinguished from their counterparts who
deny religion any such role. The impulses and motives behind
their trajectory from a secular outlook towards an 'Islamic'
formula form an important dimension in the study of their
contributions, especially in the context of continuing debates of
wider application concerning the embrace of religion by modern
intellectuals, and their roles in modernisation.[1]

These themes are explored in this chapter through the example
of Sadiq Nayhum (1937–94), a literary personality from Benghazi.
While there is no intention to suggest the intrinsic merit or scholarly importance of Nayhum's ideas concerning Islam and the
Qur'an by presenting these here, justification for studying these
ideas derives from two factors. First, his writings have created
public controversy and he has himself become something of a
cultural phenomenon. More pertinently, these writings clearly
reflect the broader issues sketched above. In a similar vein, there is
no suggestion that his treatment of Qur'anic texts is intellectually
sophisticated or methodologically complex, or that it is highly
developed in the presentation of his arguments. Indeed, the
possibility that he might just as well have presented the same arguments *without* reference to Qur'anic texts informs the present
discussion, and shapes its central argument. Nonetheless, the
inclusion of an essay on Nayhum's writings in a volume on Muslim
intellectuals and the Qur'an is fitting as a rich case study in the
engagement of secular-oriented intellectuals with the sacred text,
encompassing their motives, methods, successes and failures in
this. Reflecting Nayhum's own treatment, and in contrast with

other essays in this volume, only a relatively small part of this chapter relates directly to issues of Qur'anic meaning. In the context of this volume, this contrast itself points to the widely divergent paths walked by contemporary Muslim intellectuals in appropriating and reading the sacred text, and their disparate points of departure and destinations in this. It thus serves the ultimate objective of this chapter: to probe such broader perspectives.

The chapter begins with a detailed survey of Nayhum's life-experience and career, which crystallises many of the competing forces and diverse impulses that shape the self-conscious intellectual of the Muslim twentieth century. It focuses thereafter on his later writings, exploring their ideological and literary aspects. The discussion sets out his thesis concerning the 'original' message of Islam, finally illustrating his recruitment of Qur'anic texts in its support through a translation of his 'commentary' on two Qur'anic *suras*. Concluding remarks investigate the bases of his projected authority as interpreter of these texts, and analyse his relation to the Islamic tradition, as reflected in the writings discussed, in his capacity as a Muslim intellectual of secular orientation who engages in a particular reading of Qur'anic texts.

Nayhum became well known in Libya from the mid-1960s for his contributions to the country's literary and cultural life, initially through the print media. His literary talents were soon recognised in wider Arab literary circles.[2] An awareness of his work in the larger Arab context mainly developed during the late 1980s and 1990s, however, with the appearance of three publications discussing Islam and Islamic history, and presenting a scathing critique of contemporary Arab culture, politics and society. First was *Sawt al-nas: mihnat thaqafa muzawwara* (1987), followed by *al-Islam fi al-asr: man saraqa al-jami' wa ayna dhahaba yawm al-jum'a* (1991). *Islam didda al-Islam: shari'a min waraq* (1994) became a best seller at the Arab Book Exhibition in Beirut the following year.[3] The latter two publications are collections of essays that had originally appeared in the Lebanese journal *al-Naqid* (launched in Beirut in 1988): its publisher notes that Nayhum's contributions provoked more response than any other.[4] All three publications were widely discussed among Arab intellectuals, and continued for some years to be debated in the Arab press.[5] In April 1995, they were impounded during a raid by the Lebanese general security forces on the offices of Riad El-Rayyes publishers in Beirut, prompted by a complaint concerning them by the state-appointed Mufti.[6] Interest in Nayhum's work grew due to the adverse publicity, leading to one or two references in Western media and academia.[7]

Arab perceptions of the man and his work are largely a product of Nayhum's controversial relationship with Libya's revolutionary authorities during the years immediately after the coup. His image in common Libyan perception suffers from several distortions and myths which are partly explicable in terms of his profound popularity with a generation of Benghazi youth, as well as his own individuality, bohemian lifestyle, and provocative views. This image also reflects a tendency to exaggerate both his abilities – reflecting the image of the intellectual as hero – and the opportunities that had been available to him to shape the developing thinking of Libya's new leaders, and to contribute to early policy formulation. Dashed expectations based on such assessments have led to accusations, common particularly within the Libyan opposition, that Nayhum failed Libyan society and abandoned all higher principles for personal gain. Such positions can be attributed at least in part to a projection of unresolved struggles, frustrations and disappointments concerning Libya's political development since the revolution. Nevertheless, perceptions concerning Nayhum's relationship with the Libyan authorities underpin a dismissive attitude towards his last publications which form the focus of interest here, among many Libyan and Arab intellectuals. Seen as an attempt to provide intellectual justification or support for Qaddafi's project of direct democracy and thus as essentially ideological, these are denied any intellectual worth. In contrast, they have been enthusiastically received by many general readers, one of whom recently described Nayhum's work as a 'beacon of liberated thought', for example.[8] A few intellectuals have also underlined Nayhum's contribution. A respected Moroccan writer thus recently referred to him as 'a great thinker, who represents enlightened, alive and democratic Islam'; he recommended that Nayhum's last publications be translated into English and French, to help portray to the West an authentic picture of Islam, free from distortion.[9] Nayhum's relationship with Libya's revolutionary authorities was more complex and ambivalent than its projection in many popular Libyan perceptions; this is overlooked in the simple reduction of his later publications to intellectual support for the foundations of the Qaddafi project.

Born in Benghazi in 1937, Nayhum grew up in a modest household.[10] His father served as a clerk at the city port, and was well known for his involvement in the Trade Union movement under the monarchy. Nayhum attended the local mosque Qur'an school, and Arabic primary and secondary schools in Benghazi. Graduating from school in 1957, he majored in Arabic at the Department of Arabic Language in the Faculty of Arts and Education at the Libyan University, the first branch of which had been opened in Benghazi just two years earlier. He was among one of the first few small classes to graduate from the university,[11] in 1961, and did so with honours, remaining attached to the Department as a teaching assistant. In 1965 he took up the scholarship he had been awarded and left for Cairo University, spending some time on higher studies but leaving without a degree. A widespread narrative maintains that the university refused to examine his doctoral work in comparative religion, supervised by 'A'isha 'Abd al-Rahman, because it was hostile to Islam, and possibly heretical. The same narrative has it that he then enrolled in the University of Munich, where he was eventually awarded a Ph.D. in comparative religion, proceeding on to further research in Arizona, a teaching post in comparative religion at the University of Helsinki, and finally at the University of Geneva. Attempts to verify this narrative, which has also been upheld by the publisher of Nayhum's later works,[12] expose the extent of the myths that colour perceptions of the man (and the bases of his authority to interpret Islam). For example, reliable sources point out that his premature departure from Cairo was partly due to his preference for literary over academic pursuits.

They observe that he never obtained a doctorate from any university,[13] and that claims of an impressive academic career (including proficiency in Hebrew and Aramaic) must be taken with more than a pinch of salt.

In 1967, Nayhum resigned from his position as teaching assistant in the Libyan University, and became occupied full-time as a writer for *al-Haqiqa*, an independent, Benghazi-based newspaper launched in 1964: he had been sending in articles (concerned with literary and socio-cultural criticism) from his temporary homes in Germany and Finland since 1965. He soon became something of a literary phenomenon: his fresh, spirited style has indeed been credited in some assessments with encouraging the Libyan public to read and develop cultural-literary interests (*al-Haqiqa* enjoyed the widest circulation of all independent newspapers in Libya until it was banned in 1972, and its success was closely associated with Nayhum as its most important writer[14]). During the two years leading up to the coup of 1969, his popularity in Libya grew steadily as he attended literary events hosted there and published his first literary works. He was fêted particularly among Benghazi's youth,[15] and became a symbol of intellectualism among Libyan students.[16] Nayhum's satirical critiques of Libyan culture and society, caught between old traditions and rapid modernisation, broached sensitive issues. There is a common perception that he singled out the '*figi*', the local mosque caretaker/Qur'an teacher, as contributing to Libyan backwardness by spreading incorrect Qur'anic understandings. His literary-critical essays (especially of modern Arabic poetry) were serialised in *al-Haqiqa*, and prompted lively debate. During the early 1970s, he published a first novel and a collection of short stories,[17] making central use of symbolism in both, as in later literary publications.[18]

At the time of the Free Officers coup in 1969, Nayhum had established a reputation in Libya, made largely from abroad, as a writer and intellectual. While remaining abroad for most of the next twenty-five years until his death, his relationship with Libya continued, mediated against the background of the unfolding revolutionary vision. In May 1970, he participated (along with other journalists, writers, teachers and students) in the televised

'Revolutionary Intellectual Seminar' (the forerunner of a series of public consultations in which the regime's elite councils discussed policy issues with experts, or the public).[19] His presence there reflected both a personal willingness, and popular good will towards the new leadership based on expectations aroused by their pledges on assuming power. This was Nayhum's first public encounter with Qaddafi. According to reliable Libyan narratives, he emerged something of a hero from the debate.[20] Qaddafi saw him as an important gain for the revolutionary regime. In line with his effort to connect with himself Libyans of outstanding ability or charisma, he took Nayhum into his inner coterie, paid attention to his ideas, and invited him to lecture to the Revolutionary Command Council (RCC) and broader political elites. This marked the start of his developing profile within certain official organs of the Arab Socialist Union party, to which he was appointed between 1971 and 1973,[21] and may have been behind his decision to take up residence in Tripoli in 1973, following frequent visits from his home in Helsinki. Indeed some have placed him among Qaddafi's 'regular ideas men' assembled during the early 1970s, to whom the leader would turn in testing out and developing the ideology of the new order.[22]

While intellectuals of Nasserist or al-Qawmiyyun al-'Arab orientation exerted most influence on the new leader during the early years, there is a widespread perception that Nayhum (who presumably had to accommodate his liberal principles to the specific ideological requirements of the new order) was also influential. He apparently entertained a belief at this time (perhaps reflecting an exaggerated perception of his own abilities) that he might make an impact, whether through his personal relationship with Qaddafi or his lectures to political elites, seeing Libya's new circumstances as an opportunity that could be turned to the benefit of the country and its people. On this basis he had persuaded others to support the new leadership and to refrain from unconstructive criticism. Announcement of the 'cultural revolution' in Zwara in April 1973 put an abrupt end to the 'honeymoon period', however. Claims to review the leaders' principles or actions were henceforth met with arrest or imprisonment, while ideological and political differences were crushed without exception. In such a climate it was inevitable that Nayhum's activities would meet with suspicion and censure from other Libyans. Disturbed by the popular conviction that he had made a significant contribution to the ideas behind the emerging Libyan order (with which he had come to be closely identified) and the impact of this on his reputation as an intellectual, Nayhum decided to publish the substance of his lectures to the RCC. *Niqash*, an attempt to explain what he had tried to convey to the regime's elites and thereby to set the record straight with the Libyan public, appeared in 1973. It was interdicted before it reached the market. In 1974, he resumed his voluntary exile, settling in Geneva after a short stay in Beirut. He established two publishing houses there, focusing on developing some of the first encyclopaedic projects in Arabic: this work continued along with the publication of literary works into the 1980s.

In Libyan circles and beyond, a strong popular perception has persisted that Nayhum was responsible for at least some of the RCC's ideas. Certain of his views may indeed have been appropriated (without acknowledgement) after May 1970. However, there is no basis for positing the persistence of his ideas as a possible source of influence on policy after the launch of the 'cultural revolution', in that domestic political developments were thereafter primarily, if not exclusively, dictated by the demands of power politics. Indeed, his departure from Tripoli in 1974 was apparently based on a realisation that he could not influence the authorities, and that it would be futile to continue trying. Unable to live in Libya under such circumstances and facing a life in exile, Nayhum appears to have struck a pragmatic compromise with the regime: by eschewing open criticism (and thereby avoiding its uncompromising attitude towards its critics and opponents), he could safeguard his personal freedom, and especially his freedom to visit whenever the need for home became pressing. Nayhum apparently retained a special relationship with the Libyan authorities (without the expectation that he write explicitly in support of their policies). There is thus a common perception that Qaddafi hosted him during his visits to Libya, and made sure that he was well provided for in Geneva (his publishing projects proceeded in collaboration with Libyan governmental agencies, albeit on a free-lance basis). There was also the personal friendship between the two men. The possibility of burning his bridges with Libya, which was the probable price of outright confrontation with the ideological establishment, was something he could not contemplate, given his inability to embrace exile wholeheartedly. Reliable narratives point out that Nayhum never engaged in apologetics on behalf of the Libyan establishment, whether during the early years or later. Neither did he promise a particular political contribution that he failed to deliver. Increasingly, however, he was judged against the uncompromising yardstick applied to all Libyan intellectuals, which deemed any relationship with the authorities deplorable.[23]

According to sources close to him, the experience of exile, both physical and existential, came to dominate Nayhum in later life, leading to a growing interest in his Islamic heritage, which furnished a remedy for his existential homesickness, a substitute homeland. In this interpretation, *Sawt al-nas* can be seen to reflect his intensifying existential crisis, revealing a yearning for 'Islam', a simple and clear source of inspiration, identity, and rootedness. As Nayhum's attention turned to expounding his views concerning the 'original' message of Islam and exposing its historical subversion, echoes of characteristic aspects of Libya's revolutionary system in his own exposition[24] have served to compound earlier speculation that he had been partly responsible (willingly or not) for aspects of the latter. A perception has taken root that Nayhum's last publications furnish *post-facto* justification for this system, accompanied at times by the accusation that their author produced them with the cynical aim of pleasing his paymaster. It is worth noting that, according to reliable sources, Nayhum in later times had no wish to be seen to have had a meeting of minds with Qaddafi. While the evident parallels in the ideas of the two men may prove to be no more than an interesting coincidence, what is underlined here is the persistence of debate concerning the ideological dimension, perceived or actual, of Nayhum's intellectual project, to the main thesis of which we now turn.[25]

Most of the essays republished from *al-Naqid* in *al-Islam fi al-asr* reiterate, clarify and develop more explicitly aspects of Nayhum's central thesis, presented in *Sawt al-nas*, applying or illustrating these with reference to the concrete contemporary Arab experience and at times relating them to current events, as was appropriate to the medium in which they first appeared. The longer essays of *Islam didda al-Islam* also relate to the thesis of *Sawt al-nas*, but a number of these also present a more detailed exploration of specific Islamic themes.[26] Reflecting his interest in comparative religion, the author at times cites Biblical texts in refuting traditional Islamic understandings. In *al-Islam fi al-asr*, Nayhum's concluding comment takes the form of a reply to the various reader responses that are published alongside his own essays. Recognising that some readers have misconstrued his project, he summarises the thrust of his thesis as presented in this volume in a few simple points, outlined here.[27] He argues that democracy can be guaranteed only if the people possess a constitutional voice, such that they oversee both the legislative and administrative apparatus. The Arabs are not in a position to acquire this within the capitalist version of democracy, because they do not possess its fundamental requirements.[28] The only way they can guarantee a genuine voice in administrative and judicial affairs is to discover a legitimate structure stemming from their own lived realities that can gather the majority beneath a single constitutional slogan. Nayhum posits the *jami'*[29] as the only such structure that can unite the Arabs in a single time and place, and under a unified political constitution, as it did historically. In their current situation, however, everything is confused. The *jami'* is thus lost behind the *masjid*; the voice of the majority has disappeared behind preachers' sermons, and Islam has been transformed from a constitution that guarantees the right of the living to justice, into a *fiqh* prescription for entering Paradise after death. Describing this as a civilisational catastrophe, he proceeds to defend direct democracy (*al-dimuqratiyya al-mubashira*) from readers' charges that it is chaotic or utopian, pointing to the Swiss Federation as one of several working examples.[30] He describes it as the 'firm foundation' on which parties can be established in a non-capitalist country, and from out of which a party coalition can emerge which is capable of representing all sectors of the community (*umma*), without its fragmentation. Accordingly, the real challenge the Arabs face is to liberate the 'Friday meeting' from the hegemony of clerics; to resurrect Islam from the grave-yard of *fiqh*; to extricate the *jami'* from the *masjid*, and to retrieve the citizen's voice, which has disappeared behind sermons. He observes that contemporary (Arab-Islamic) culture has failed to accept this challenge, while intellectuals have ensured that it is ignored by creating trivial disputes over peripheral issues. Returning to this challenge in the Introduction to *Islam didda al-Islam*, his comments wind up with a call for a practical step, to establish the vehicle (in the form of a popular party) that can develop the means to implement direct democracy in the Arab world.[31]

While all three publications address the diverse aspects of this thesis, our focus here is on the construction of 'original' Islam that stands at the heart of the seminal work, *Sawt al-nas*. Here the author develops his arguments more as abstract ideas and does not appear to identify his thesis explicitly in the terms introduced in his later comments, noted above. In contrast with the two later volumes, this presents a single, if loosely woven, narrative proceeding through a series of chapters in the form of short essays. Its elegant but accessible style is lively and compelling, showcasing the author's literary talents. There is widespread use of literary devices, metaphors and symbolism. Important points are often developed through a listing of contrasting pairs, rather than elaborate argumentation. Chapters open and conclude with striking effect, drawing the reader into the narrative. Scenes from the past are brought to life through the painting of imaginary scenarios, using the present tense to engage the reader as dramatic witness, developing a sense of urgency to the message conveyed. Nayhum's construction of the 'original' Islamic message is elaborated against a broad historical canvas, drawing on political, social, ideological, religious and intellectual aspects of the ancient world, of pre-modern and modern Europe, and of early, classical and modern Islamic civilisation. Perhaps inevitably, sweeping generalisations and over-simplifications are common-place. There is some lack of conceptual clarity, as precise or systematic definitions are typically absent. While endnotes provide some definitions (and an array of relevant data), there is virtually no source documentation.[32] *Sawt al-nas* is a popular work (which may pretend to a semblance of scholarship). Its rhetorical, polemical and provocative style aims to alert Arab-Muslim readers to the crisis that engulfs them, and to show what must be done to resolve it. Historical accuracy, detail, and nuanced evaluation are thus sacrificed to the author's tendentious project.

Nayhum argues that the *raison d'être* of religion – *per se*, but his concern is with Islam specifically – is to uphold the rights of the oppressed. This is what distinguishes it from politics, and makes it capable of changing the law of the jungle and its underlying maxim, 'survival of the fittest'. Unlike politics, religion addresses the people themselves, rather than (state) institutions. In prac-tical terms, it translates into a system in which the people them-selves are responsible for directing the administration, and hold all associated powers. As laws are drafted in the 'language' of the community (*jama'a*), this system is characterised by a collective law (*al-shar' al-jama'i*). This distinguishing characteristic is used as a shorthand in *Sawt al-nas* for the system of collective adminis-tration (*idara jama'iyya*) upheld by religion:[33] it alone can guar-antee the adoption of specific legislation to safeguard the rights of the most vulnerable in society.[34]

According to Nayhum, Islam upholds a definition of the oppressed that encompasses the entire human family. The advent of Islam saw the institution of an administrative system founded on a challenge to the logic of force: it aimed to 'liberate the people's paradise from the law of the jungle'.[35] The duty of jihad (defined in this context as the fight to defend the oppressed) was therefore made applicable to humanity as a whole, obligating every individual to defend the collective law. Islam thus came to challenge and supplant the 'feudal system', for it is 'the collective law itself … It is an administrative system which aims to achieve real justice, by subjugating the administration to the authority of the majority (*sultat al-aghlabiyya*)'.[36] Islam demonstrated that humanity could unite under a single law, and meet under a single, world administration: for 'seven thousand years of civilisation' prior to that, people had known themselves by many names, but had not discovered 'their authentic, common, name' (as the people: *al-nas*).[37]

Nayhum construes world history as a struggle between the forces of 'feudalism' (which have assumed diverse forms) and 'the people'. The former (both as an abstract idea and a concrete system) is ultimately doomed, while the notion of the collective law cannot be extinguished, as it is a natural law, which humanity will inevitably establish. Even where Islam did not penetrate Nayhum holds that history has demonstrated the inevitability of feudalism's demise in the face of the people. The English revolution furnished evidence of these facts (after the world had forgotten their first expression, in the language of Islam): it witnessed the rise of an alternative form of the collective law (as 'large landowners and traders assembled under a single roof, inaugurating the age of modern capitalism').[38] The Islamic system of collective law is unique, however, because its source (the Qur'an) is protected against change: its preservation in its correct form is thus guaranteed.[39]

Islam brought a distinctive paradigm for collective administration. Its system reflects two fundamental Islamic principles: the illegitimacy of mediation (*wisata*), and the notion that Islam embraces, and undertakes to co-exist positively with, other faiths. The first principle translates into a rejection of deputised representation (as the duty of jihad applies to every individual, 'every citizen is personally responsible for the actions of the administrative apparati').[40] The second necessitates the institution of an apparatus that can bring together different confessions (and ethnicities), under a single collective administration. According to Nayhum, this apparatus is the *jami'*.[41] This is not a mosque (*masjid*), but a framework for convening an inclusive administrative conference that has a higher authority than that of the state, and is constitutionally charged with drafting laws. Islam has specified a time for its meetings; the *jami'* has given its name to the day

309

on which this arises (*yawm al-jum'a*). It must meet at the set time, without postponement or cancellation. The obligatory status of this conference derives from the fact that certain obligatory matters can only be properly executed within its framework (the duty of jihad and the Qur'anic injunction to enjoin good and forbid evil, for example). The duty to prohibit interest (*riba*) illustrates the line of argument: its implementation necessitates that the community as a whole has administrative control over the movement of capital.

Nayhum argues that the *jami'* system brought together diverse groups under a single administration, liberated from the whims of sectarian and military institutions, for the first time ever.[42] They met with the aim of understanding each other in the name of the people. This 'world administration' recorded glorious deeds 'on the first page of the book of collective rule'. Although it lasted a brief twenty-four years out of Islam's fourteen centuries, Nayhum posits this fleeting period as the source of everything that Muslims deem legitimate in their administrative culture.[43] Hence this was the time of the only 'rightly-guided' caliphs, whose legitimacy derived from the *bay'a* of the community, which alone possesses legitimate authority.

As it is incumbent upon every individual to protect the collective law (in accordance with the duty of jihad), Nayhum maintains that Islam deems the professional army (which supports feudalism) illegitimate, and considers the fight against it a war in God's path. Dubbing the professional soldier 'a sword up for rent' in accordance with a Roman contract from the first century BCE,[44] he contrasts the latter with the Islamic contract summed up in 'the constitution of jihad'. In the Roman contract, the army is a weapon in the hands of the administration; it acts only on the Emperor's command (to defend him), and the decision to go to war does not involve the people. In the jihad constitution, the people decide whether to go to war; war is fought to protect their right to a single administration, and is engaged only for the sake of God and the oppressed.[45] Islam upholds 'the legislation of collective defence', witnessed by mankind for the first time in the Islamic duty of jihad. This introduced a criterion for determining whether a war was fought for legitimate reasons (that is, in defence of the people's right, engaged under a collective administration, and under the people's immediate direction). Under Islam a new fighter arose, defending not the interests of feudalism, but his own: 'the first world liberation army witnessed in history was mustered. In it Muslims, Copts, Jews, Blacks, Berbers and Persians fought to free their necks from the grasp of feudal administrations and their paid armies in the Arabian Peninsula, Persia and Byzantium.'[46]

The arch-villain in Nayhum's reading of Islamic history is Mu'awiya. As governor of Syria, he flagrantly violated the principle of jihad by establishing a professional army along Byzantine lines (this was done with the permission of the Caliph 'Umar, who thereby committed a grave error). While this development met with popular suspicion, 'Uthman refused to deal with the situation on assuming power. According to Nayhum, 'the apparati of collective administration' pressed openly for 'Uthman's removal, in 'the first clash in Islam between the collective authority and the authority of the state'.[47] Mu'awiya then adopted 'Uthman's assassination as a pretext for denying the legitimacy of the system of collective administration. His agreement to engage with 'Ali at Siffin was a ruse, aimed at implementing a premeditated political plan that would strike this system with a fatal blow. By raising the Qur'an, his intention was to establish a recognition that 'the rules of the *fiqh*, and not those of the community, are the source of legitimacy in Islam.' Thus for 'Ali the search for a decision from the Qur'an signified appealing to the opinion of the majority; for Mu'awiya, it meant appealing to 'the knowledgeable among the *fuqaha''*.[48] Now that majority authority had been terminated, Nayhum argues:

> Islam suddenly disappeared from the people's reality. There emerged a pressing need to compensate them with an 'Islam' that does not touch their reality. This necessitated that the *fuqaha'* become the source of legitimacy in place of the majority, and that they assume responsibility for issuing fatwas concerning affairs of administration, in place of the people as a whole.[49]

The outcome of the arbitration was the disappearance of the collective law behind the fatwas of the *fuqaha'*, in a political manipulation of Islam directed against the Muslims themselves. Mu'awiya's machinations had brought Islam's journey to an end before it had begun. He proceeded to eradicate the administrative conference in the *jami'*, concealing this behind the congregational prayer in the *masjid*.[50] While Mu'awiya had acquired a state for his family, the Muslims had lost everything. Henceforth, paid employees ran the state, a professional army protected it, and a paid accountant administered its coffers:

> The Muslims' world was turned upside down from Mu'awiya's time. It remains inverted today, although Muslims remain unaware of this. Hence the *jami'* is absent, and the age of the Rightly-Guided Caliphs has ended. The administration has been taken out of the community's hands, and the majority has lost the right to decision-making. The principle of personal responsibility has been suspended. The state has taken control of *bayt mal al-Muslimin*, the *mujahid* has lost his weapons, and the citizen no longer has a right to justice.[51]

Mu'awiya had transformed Islam into an Islamic *fiqh* without an administrative apparatus: the institutionalisation of the professional army and the installation of a caliph as deputised representative of all Muslims marked its final demise. The Muslims became divided into political factions disguised as *fiqh* schools, destroying the integrity of the community and its collective authority. Losing the quality that sets religion apart from politics, Islam was stripped of its capacity to preserve the rights of the oppressed. From the time of Mu'awiya until the twentieth century, Nayhum maintains, the *fuqaha'* have written about human rights, while administrations the Muslim world over remained ignorant of them, and neglected in particular the rights of the vulnerable.[52]

Having repudiated the Islamic system of collective rule, Nayhum maintains that the Umayyad rulers had transferred their administrative systems from Byzantium. They faced a profound problem, unknown to feudal rulers before them. Their state was thus compelled to coexist with the state constitution encapsulated in the Qur'an, which contradicted it comprehensively. While they had created an Islamic state modelled on Byzantium, the Qur'an called for Byzantium's overthrow. It openly instigated the people against 'the authority of Pharoah',[53] calling them to armed revolt. Having decided that it was too dangerous to impound the Qur'an, the Umayyad Caliph set about the discovery of an alternative '*qur'an*' which, unlike the original, would not be a declared enemy. The hadith served this purpose: as a source of legislation, it provided him with 'a *fiqhi* way out'.[54] Nayhum rejects the hadith as a source of legislation. He argues that it was used to confer the status of successor to God's Messenger, and hence legitimate rights in administrative and judicial affairs on 'an Umayyad caliph who has not been elected by the majority'.[55] The real purpose of the science of hadith was indeed to grant the *fuqaha'* authority to legislate on behalf of the majority. Nayhum faults al-Shafi'i for excluding the authority of the people from the sources of legislation, arguing that Muslims only uncovered this 'fateful error' after the rise of democracies in the West. Its result was that the Islamic *fiqh* turned its back on the only legitimate authority, and sought its solutions in the Companions' sayings. This issued in the rise of countless schools of *fiqh* as the voice of the majority disappeared behind that of the *fuqaha'* and Islam became thoroughly fragmented.[56]

As the *fiqh* was introduced to speak in the language of Islam in the absence of Islam itself,[57] 'through the words of a *faqih* well-versed in *fiqh*' the Umayyads were able to construe their radical, comprehensive revolution against the Islamic doctrine as a particular (legitimate) interpretation of this doctrine. Implementing its 'deadly deception' in the language of Islam, the *fiqh* transformed the significance and function of pivotal Islamic principles and institutions. Thus while the Prophet had brought a collective law that embraces all religions, based on the *fiqh* interpretation of the rules of the Sunna Islam was now upheld merely as an additional religion.[58] The *jami'* was stripped of its administrative function, being retained as a House of God and a school for teaching *fiqh*. Friday lost its function as the appointed time for a meeting between all religions, becoming refashioned as a day for prayer during which Muslims would meet to hear a sermon on *fiqh* delivered by a *faqih* (a state employee). The original purpose of jihad (the defence of the oppressed) was supplanted by the *fiqh* notion of spreading Islam (minus its administrative system). Although the principle of personal responsibility was not expunged from the law, it came to signify responsibility for ritual observance to the exclusion of the administration. This led to production of more detailed studies in *fiqh*, while no one noticed that Islamic principles were comprehensively violated in the systems of government. With the termination of the collective law, the affairs of state thus centred on one man. Although this amounted to a blatant deviation from every Islamic principle, Nayhum argues that the *fuqaha'* permanently bound this arrangement to Islam by insisting on descent from Quraysh as the primary stipulation concerning the head of state.[59] The *fuqaha'* inverted the interpretation of fundamental concepts. For example, while the *fiqh* schools deem it permissible to shed the blood of someone who opposes the (tyrannical) ruler (on the pretext that he has seceded from the community), they do not deem the ruler's blood legally permissible (although he has usurped the rights of the entire community).[60]

In sum, the *fiqh* deliberately transformed Islam from a doctrine with an integral administrative system to a doctrine employed to serve an alternative (feudal) administration. It thereby terminated the collective state and subjugated the majority to rule by the few. The *fuqaha'* adopted 'the language of magicians' in place of the people's language, and presented an interpretation of religion based on absent realities. For example, according to a hadith (of which Nayhum cites eleven different variations), Friday encompasses the hour in which God grants whatever is requested of Him. There is no mention of its original status as the appointed day for a collective administrative conference.[61] Since the Umayyad period, the *fiqh* has spoken on behalf of Muslims – who have lost the ability to speak for themselves. Nayhum posits the ensuing catastrophes of Islamic history as an inevitable consequence.[62] Referring to the demise of the Abbasids at the hands of the Mongols:

> Hulagu was met by an unarmed, bare-headed caliph surrounded by
> a retinue of unarmed *fuqaha'*... The upshot of the collective law's
> disappearance behind the fatwas of the *fuqaha'* was the surrender of
> the Islamic administration to a bloody butcher.[63]

Islam failed to direct world civilisation and to achieve its (true)
global identity while capitalism rose 'like an alternative world religion': it was held back in the Old World, its peoples struck with
poverty and ignorance, 'under the guard of *fuqaha'* absent from
history'.[64] The civilisation of the East was doomed in the absence
of the collective law, but the triumph of capitalism, which upholds
the interest of institutions (rather than the people) and aims to
serve capital at the expense of everything else, was a tragedy for all
people, East and West.

His account of its early outward demise notwithstanding, Nayhum
nevertheless points to the continued (hidden) survival of the
Islamic paradigm of collective law and majority rule, in contemporary Arab-Muslim countries. Organically connected to its concepts
and categories, the Arabic language is thus itself a repository,
guardian and indelible reminder of this paradigm, and hence
cannot be employed in any other system of administration.
Consequently, the substitution of alien administrative terms for
original Arabic-Islamic ones has spawned a contemporary situation
where two languages 'live side by side in an artificial peace ... in an
eternal tug-of-war, between an administration that does not recognise the people, and a people who do not recognise the administration.'[65] While one denotes concepts of alien provenance, the other
carries within it the worldview that underpins the Islamic system of
collective administration. Contemporary Arab governments are
thus forced to coexist with the Islamic paradigm of collective
administration, surviving in 'the language of the people'.[66]

Nayhum finds further evidence of the survival of this paradigm
in *al-adhan* (the call to prayer formula), and the celebration of
the Islamic festivals (*al-a'yad*). He construes the call to prayer as a
symbolic expression of loyalty to 'a hidden state' (that of the
collective administration), and thus a repudiation of the modern
Arab nation states. As an affirmation of the exclusive legitimacy of

collective rule, this formula represents a withholding of allegiance
from existing governments and a call to change their underlying
systems.[67] Applying a similar approach to the Islamic festivals (Eid
al-Fitr and Eid al-Adha, for example, which he notes are celebrated more enthusiastically than national ones[68]), Nayhum
construes these as commemorations of the invisible state of
Islam's collective law, which rejects the legitimacy of all other
states. Elucidating their symbolic significances,[69] he argues:

> The Muslim is a citizen in an invisible state that has lived secretly
> among the people since the cancellation of the system of collective
> administration in Mu'awiya's time. When he terminated the *jami'*
> system, Mu'awiya did not kill the system of collective rule; he merely
> tied its hands ... it became a call in the people's hearts, which they
> pass among the generations. They celebrate its festivals and carry
> out its rites, anticipating the hour of salvation ...[70]
>
> Mu'awiya believed he had taken possession of Islam's state by
> putting an end to its collective law. However Islam's state is still the
> state of the collective law. It raises its slogans five times a day from
> the minarets. Each year millions celebrate its birth in the *hijra*, feel
> sad at its loss at Karbala', celebrate its leader's birthday, and
> slaughter a sheep, announcing their willingness to sacrifice them-
> selves for its sake ... The situation says quite simply that although
> Mu'awiya died, the thing he killed did not.[71]

In the sphere of popular culture, Nayhum finds in Juha (a
pseudo-historical literary character and the most popular
protagonist of humorous tales in the Arab world) 'the voice of the
people' responding to the illegitimate rule suffered by Muslims
since the restoration of the feudal age. Juha, who always lives at
the mercy of a tyrant, expresses what most people say in secret. He
transmits this openly in political communiqués disguised through
humour; his tales are thus a vehicle for the critique of power by
the powerless. Nayhum suggests that Juha's message is articulated
'in the language of the Qur'an', which has taught him the treas-
ures of the collective law and its associated wisdom, and an awareness of his legitimate right to a life free from fear and poverty.
Juha thus knows that his civilisation rests on a collective administration, that the ruler has stripped him of this, and that it is his
duty to oppose him. His cause is hence 'to withhold recognition of

the legitimacy of Timerlane's rule, and to mock his judges, *fuqaha'* and paid soldiers unceasingly'.[72]

Nayhum's fascination with the literary uses of symbolism has been evident throughout his career as a writer. His interest in the symbolic dimensions of the Qur'anic text specifically first appeared some twenty years before the publication of *Sawt al-nas* in a controversial essay serialised in *al-Haqiqa*. In *Dirasat al-ramz fi al-Qur'an* (1967), Nayhum attempted to show that a symbolic discourse can be excavated from the literal expressions of the Qur'anic text. To this end, he argued that the text deliberately employs expressions that are expansive in their compass, and are susceptible of multiple interpretations. Thereby, it is able perpetually to accommodate the knowledge of all historical eras, however this might change. He illustrated his thesis through an analysis, among others, of the tale of 'the Men of the Cave' (Q. 18: 9 ff). Departing from the opinions of classical exegesis, he argued that the Qur'anic tale does not incorporate anything at its surface that is of a miraculous nature. Beneath its literal surface, however, the Qur'anic text yields a parallel and precise *symbolic* narrative that is both more comprehensive in its compass than the specific tale, and goes beyond the possible scope of historical knowledge in the Prophet's time. It is here that the text's miraculous nature comes to light, located in the expansive extent of its expression (which is not merely rhetorical in nature, nor a phenomenon prevalent in linguistic usage of seventh-century Arabia). As far as the tale of the 'Men of the Cave' is concerned, Nayhum suggested that the underlying symbolic discourse of the text narrates the entire history of Christianity, beginning 'in the caves of monks', and ending 'in the Stock Exchanges of cities' (in the modern period).[73] Such discussion of the Qur'an was unprecedented, using an implicitly literary discourse and focusing on its symbolic dimensions in the medium of a newspaper accessible to the general reading public. Reflecting the deep-rooted traditionalism of Libyan society, there was a public outcry against it. This culminated in a popular campaign (orchestrated by various religious scholars and individuals with 'Islamist' leanings) denouncing Nayhum's views as tantamount to apostasy, with the aim of intimidating *al-Haqiqa* into discontinuing publication of the series: it finally bowed to public pressure.[74]

In *Sawt al-nas*, Nayhum effectively unveils within the Qur'an his thesis concerning the authentic Islamic message and its formula for the good society, and his arguments concerning its historical subversion, outlined above. Throughout this work, he cites specific Qur'anic phrases or concepts. As illustrated above, he also attributes various intentions and meanings to the Qur'anic message as a whole, without specific illustration or elaboration. A verse by verse 'commentary' is presented on two specific *suras*, however: al-Fatiha (Q. 1) and al-Jum'a (Q. 62). Nayhum posits al-Fatiha (recited several times a day during the obligatory prayers) as the encapsulation of a hidden expression of the identity of the authentic Islamic citizen, who upholds Islam's collective law. It survives in this 'protected fortress' like 'the soul in the breast of a bird in a cage on a remote island', where it is safe from falsifications dictated by the whims of politicians.[75] The constituent elements of this identity are elucidated through his commentary,[76] translated below, with the Qur'anic text reproduced as it appears in his elaboration:[77]

PRAISE BELONGS TO GOD, THE LORD OF ALL BEING
There is nothing here about the Shi'a, the Sunna [i.e., the Sunnis], the Christians, the Jews, or the Communists. This is because the Arab citizen who has been educated by Islam is a world citizen, whose exclusive affiliation is to this universal, human doctrine. Such a citizen does not permit himself to be put to the service of partisan or disputatious doctrines. Neither is he legally prepared to serve such doctrines.

THE ALL-MERCIFUL, THE ALL-COMPASSIONATE
The world citizen's doctrine is compassion (*rahma*), because this is the only doctrine that is directed at the people, and not their institutions. Every slogan – apart from the slogan of compassion – can be put, philosophically speaking, to the service of the interests of institutions, at the expense of the people themselves.

THE MASTER OF THE DAY OF RECKONING
Religion is not politics, and it does not address the state, but the people.

THEE ONLY WE SERVE; TO THEE ALONE WE PRAY FOR SUCCOUR
This is a community (*jama'a*) that openly speaks with the conscience of the community. It is not just a solitary Muslim citizen.

GUIDE US IN THE STRAIGHT PATH
Someone who asks for guidance knows that the decision, first and last, rests with him. He knows that whatever befalls him in his life (and in the lives of his children after him) is not the responsibility of some administrative or ideological agency. Rather, he is himself personally responsible for this: specifically, he is responsible for every atom's weight of it.

THE PATH OF THOSE WHOM THOU HAST BLESSED,
The distinguishing feature of this path is that it leads to goodness and happiness, in a society that guarantees the right of the community, encompasses its outward differences, and brings it together in an efficient administrative system, erected on compassion and mutual human understanding, love and respect.

NOT OF THOSE AGAINST WHOM THOU ART WRATHFUL,
There are many other laws, apart from the collective law, which are also capable of bringing the people together. However, these do not show compassion towards the people, because they are not able to protect them from the tyranny of the powerful.

NOR OF THOSE WHO ARE ASTRAY.
The mark of someone who is astray is that they are a solitary person, far away from their world. For without the collective law, the people are captives in cities, at the mercy of feudalism. Without any administration, they are tribes wandering aimlessly in the desert.

If al-Fatiha encapsulates the identity of the authentic Muslim citizen, according to Nayhum, Surat al-Jum'a preserves a record of the original purpose of Friday as a meeting between all religions. As noted earlier, Nayhum maintains that once the collective law was cancelled, Friday became a day dedicated exclusively to prayer, based on 'extraneous political interpretations that intentionally distorted the original model',[78] but were compelled to coexist with the Qur'anic reminder of it. His commentary on this *sura* elucidates this original function, and provides support for his broader construction of the original Islamic message. Portions of this are translated below (bold text replicates that in his own elaboration):[79]

In the beginning of Surat al-Jum'a, the noble Qur'an announces the rise of a new *umma* out of the illiterate Arabs, whom Islam had brought together under a single law. They thereby became a wise, blessed *umma*, possessed of a Book. This introduction sings the praises not of the Arabs, but of the collective law:

IT IS HE WHO HAS RAISED UP FROM AMONG THE COMMON PEOPLE A MESSENGER FROM AMONG THEM, TO RECITE HIS SIGNS TO THEM AND TO PURIFY THEM, AND TO TEACH THEM THE BOOK AND THE WISDOM, THOUGH BEFORE THAT THEY WERE IN MANIFEST ERROR ...
The Arabs did not become **ulama**; they became **liberated** from the authority of ignorance and feudalism. This is a truly eternal blessing, because it constitutes a victory for all people, of all generations:

... AND OTHERS OF THEM WHO HAVE NOT YET JOINED THEM. AND HE IS THE ALL-MIGHTY, THE ALL-WISE.
The collective law – and not **learning** (*al-'ilm*) – is the people's treasure, their only refuge from oppression and poverty, and their only route to general prosperity and happiness:

THAT IS THE BOUNTY OF GOD; HE GIVES IT TO WHOM HE
WILL, AND GOD IS OF BOUNTY ABOUNDING.
The first four verses in Surat al-Jum'a do not speak about **salat**,
but about the administration. They do not say that the Muslims'
salat is the people's route to **Paradise**. Rather they say that **their
collective law** is the route; that this is wisdom and learning, and
that it is the only law, outside of which there is no other.

In addressing the Qur'anic debate with the Jews encapsulated
in the next verses, Nayhum suggests that it had first to settle the
matter of the Jews and their 'segregationist claim' (unique in its
being based on a heavenly book), before turning to the Friday
meeting. As it constituted 'the only obstacle to a world meeting
encompassing all religions', the Qur'an was intent on exposing
the falsity of this claim. Turning to the next verse, he continues:

O BELIEVERS, WHEN PROCLAMATION IS MADE FOR PRAYER ON
THE DAY OF CONGREGATION, HASTEN TO GOD'S REMEM-
BRANCE ...
'**Believers**', in the Qur'anic language, is a term encompassing
Muslims, Jews, Christians, Whites, Blacks, Persians and Arabs.
The call for them to remember God on Friday does not mean
that they should carry out (together) the rituals of **one salat**, but
that **they should come together in one meeting**, which starts
with the *salat*, because the congregational *salat* prevents vile
deeds and evil[80] collectively:

... AND LEAVE TRAFFICKING ASIDE; THAT IS BETTER FOR YOU,
DID YOU BUT KNOW.
Non-attendance of the meeting thus constitutes a sure loss,
even if this absence was for the purpose of some gain. This is
because the citizen who loses his place in overseeing the
administration becomes liable to other losses, which he does
not know of: his shop might be closed down without his
knowing, and his children might be sold in the market:

THEN, WHEN THE PRAYER IS FINISHED, SCATTER IN THE LAND
AND SEEK GOD'S BOUNTY, AND REMEMBER GOD FREQUENTLY;
HAPLY YOU WILL PROSPER.

The collective law alone can thus ensure the right to strive for
everyone, just outlays, and a clear and ongoing distinction
between seeking God's favour, and seeking the favour of other
than Him.

Thereafter, the conclusion of the *sura* furnishes God's words:

BUT WHEN THEY SEE MERCHANDISE OR DIVERSION THEY
SCATTER OFF TO IT, AND THEY LEAVE THEE STANDING. SAY:
'WHAT IS WITH GOD IS BETTER THAN DIVERSION AND
MERCHANDISE. GOD IS THE BEST OF PROVIDERS.'

The prevalent exegesis of these verses is that a trading caravan
entered Medina while the people were performing the *salat*.
They went out to do trade, leaving the Prophet standing alone in
prayer. This exegesis disregards the fact that the Qur'anic text
mentions not only trade, but entertainment and fun too.[81] In
fact it is not speaking about people leaving the *salat* – which is an
unthinkable notion anyway – but their leaving an administrative
conference, from which it is forbidden for them to be absent.

Concluding remarks

Sawt al-nas has resonated with the interests, concerns, and preferences of a particular segment among contemporary Arab-
Muslim readerships whose world has partly been shaped by the
Islamic resurgence and the rise to prominence of the Islamist
vision. They may seek an 'Islamic' alternative to this vision, or
agitate for a reform of political institutions in Muslim societies
based on culturally 'authentic' paradigms. By using an Islamic
idiom and engaging with the Qur'an, Nayhum appeals to such
readers. By these means, he also implicitly challenges the claims
and assumptions of the Islamist worldview, and suggests an alternative application of 'Islamic' cultural resources. For modern-

educated readers who increasingly see the traditional discourses of the specialised Islamic elite as impenetrable and irrelevant, his lack of traditional ('ulamatic') credentials as an interpreter of Islam is of little consequence. Presented in a popular, quasi-literary work, the appeal of his thesis lies in its accessibility, and the simple yet persuasive eloquence of its exposition. Its direct relevance is exemplified in its plea to 'the people' to shake off the yoke of contemporary 'feudalists' in the Arab-Muslim world, against a backdrop of unjust regimes and oppressive states. As with many others, the general bases of Nayhum's authority as one of Islam's 'new interpreters' can be excavated from the structural changes that have transformed Muslim societies in the course of modernisation.[82] Specifically, mention must be made of his image and status as a talented intellectual, and the impact of this on public perceptions and expectations, the tarnishing of his reputation due to his encounter with power[83] and the modesty of his scholarly training notwithstanding.[84]

For his part, Nayhum had no interest in established Islamic communities of meaning. His projection of the 'original' message of Islam and his critical reading of Islamic history indeed entail a wholesale dismissal of all post-Qur'anic Islamic authorities, including the hadith, *fiqh* and *tafsir*. His views concerning the hadith and the *fiqh* in its 'satanic alliance' with feudal power aimed at silencing the voice of the people were elaborated above. As far as *tafsir* is concerned, he attacks what he describes as its claim to constitute 'a sacred knowledge that is beyond criticism'. Arguing that the Qur'an is not a 'coded book', and does not require a 'science' for its interpretation, he insists that it is simply a call to establish the collective law, with the mission of destroying the feudal system.[85] In his treatment in *Sawt al-nas*, it becomes a canvas emptied of all received meanings, on which the broad outlines of a vision of the good society is sketched, reflecting a profound suspicion of the modern state with its intrusive and oppressive tendencies.[86] Although his recourse to the Qur'anic text is selective, he effectively presents al-Fatiha and al-Jum'a as a show-case for how the Qur'an as a whole should be read, leaving the reader in no doubt as to the thrust of its 'meaning'.

Critics may legitimately question the originality of the ideas presented in Nayhum's writings discussed here,[87] and the rigour and extent of their elaboration. These writings are methodologically weak, whether judged from the perspective of the Islamic tradition, or that of systematic scholarship. His lack of commitment to the latter is evident, for example, in the absence of references to relevant authors, debates and texts, while he appears effectively to indulge in a monologue, conducted from within a virtual philosophical and textual void. This has contributed to the dismissive attitude towards these writings among many scholarly audiences, and the difficulty in characterising their genre and context, and, indeed, in working with them.

The attempt to characterise the impulses behind Nayhum's later publications must balance the possibility of a 'ritualistic' recruitment of the Qur'anic text for purposes of legitimisation, with perceptions among those close to him of the sincerity of his later engagement with 'Islam', alluded to above. In his early writings, Nayhum's concern appears to have been with exposing whatever he considered obstructive to the modernisation and progress of Libyan society, like the role of the '*fiqi*'. Intensified by exile, his own experience of modernity as overwhelmingly fragmenting had reportedly brought him to what has been described by a close friend as a 'quest for wholeness'. The alienating exilic condition perhaps contributed to the framing of this quest in terms of an appeal to a nativist legacy, 'Islam', essentialised as a single, integrating principle, its history and foundational text rewritten accordingly.

This principle, which perhaps reflects Nayhum's encounter with power and his resulting marginalisation and exile as much as his own liberal orientation, is political emancipation. Nayhum argued that Islam came with the aim of liberating people from state oppression, and effectively projected the Qur'anic text as a manifesto for universal liberty and freedom. He thereby underscored the relevance of the Qur'anic message for post-colonial Muslim society, and signalled his commitment to a culturally 'authentic' prescription for its political organisation. However, as suggested earlier, he might well have presented his arguments for political emancipation and direct democracy without reading these into Qur'anic texts, and without a pretence of 'Islamic' scholarship.[88] The path he chose in *Sawt al-nas* bears witness to the powerful forces and impulses that propelled him, and perhaps continue to propel intellectuals like him, towards a 'Qur'anic' formula. Firstly, this path speaks to the influence of a pervasive Islamic discourse, and its implications for those who enter discursive struggles within and concerning the future of Muslim societies. Secondly, it bears witness to the appeal of the Islamic tradition as a refuge from the fragmentation, disjunctures and alienation that form an integral part of the experience of modernity for some such intellectuals. Finally, it illustrates the reconstruction to which this tradition is subject, and its implications for the projection of Qur'anic meaning. An important mode in this, exemplified here in the case of an exilic intellectual, upholds an idealised, reconstructed tradition as a bridge between an original culture (of a Muslim Libya 'lost' through exile), and universal ideals associated with modernity. It is articulated through an essentialised Qur'anic meaning which, at the same time, furnishes the possibility of an integrating, 'totalising' foil to the fragmenting impacts of modernity and exile.

NOTES

1. Compare with Juan R.I. Cole, ed., *Comparing Muslim Societies: Knowledge and the State in a World Civilization* (Ann Arbor, 1992), Introduction, pp. 20–1; Charles D. Smith, 'The Intellectual, Islam, and Modernization: Haykal and Shari'ati', in ibid., pp. 163 ff.

2. The Iraqi revolutionary poet 'Abd al-Wahhab al-Bayati reportedly described him in 1973 as among what he deemed 'the five most important Arab writers', for example. Ahmad al-Maqinni, 'al-Tajriba al-fikriyya al-multabisa li al-katib al-Libi al-rahil al-Sadiq al-Nayhum', *al-Hayat*, 15 December, 1995.

3. All three works were published in Beirut and/or London by Riad El-Rayyes.

4. Riad El-Rayyes, 'Qabl al-rahil: azmat thaqafa muzawwara, ba'd al-rahil: azmat thaqafa musadara, *al-Naqid*, 83 (1995), p. 7. *Al-Islam fi al-asr* is a collection of 24 articles that first appeared in *al-Naqid* (1988–91), together with readers' reactions and the author's response to these. *Islam didda al-Islam* brings together six essays from *al-Naqid* (1993–4), with readers' reactions and the author's responses to these.

5. For a recent example, see *al-Ahdath al-Maghribiyya*, 21 July and 13 September 1999.

6. The head of the general security forces impounded the books without recourse to a court, as required by Lebanese law. Some argued that the Mufti had come under pressure from Saudi Arabia to make the complaint, and that while then Prime Minister Hariri could have inter-vened, he feared possible offence to his Saudi friends. El-Rayyes publishers launched a lawsuit against the Lebanese state, arguing that the impounded books neither contained any abasement of any faiths, nor anything that might arouse sectarian chauvinism, nor did they threaten the state. See David Hirst, 'How Riyadh stifled a free Arab voice', *The Guardian*, 21 April 1995; Riad El-Rayyes, 'Qabl al-rahil', p. 7 ff.

7. For example, Dale F. Eickelman and James Piscatori, *Muslim Politics* (Princeton, NJ, 1996), p. 156.

8. Letters to the editor, *al-Naqid*, 83. Letters from various Arab coun-tries published in this issue of the journal, dedicated posthumously to Nayhum, illustrate the popular esteem in which he is held.

9. Comments by Abdou Filali-Ansari, cited in *al-Naqid*, 83, p. 9.

10. The biographical sketch presented here has been constructed largely on the basis of oral sources, including independent academics, independent critics of the Libyan system, and those close to it. Certain of those consulted make credible claims to present factual and accurate accounts (by virtue of their independence, their closeness to Nayhum for a significant part of his life, and the absence of any agenda that might colour the narratives they uphold). The account sketched here draws mainly on such sources which in this context are described as reliable. Reflecting their explicit wish or general preference, none of the sources consulted are identified. For a discussion of the difficulties surrounding the attempt to reconstruct Nayhum's biography (and for further detail on aspects of this sketch and sources used) see Suha Taji-Farouki, 'Sadiq Nayhum: An Introduction to the Life and Works of a Contemporary Libyan Intellectual', *The Maghreb Review* 25, 3–4 (2000), pp. 242 ff.

11. During the first academic year, the university had only thirty-one students and eleven teachers. Henri Labib, *Libya: Past and Present* (Malta and Tripoli, 1979), p. 231.

12. It is recorded thus on the inside covers of his last three publications, presumably with the author's approval.

13. Indeed, he did not make use of such a title, nor was it used in refer-ring to him.

14. The main readership for the small official and independent press under Idris was in Tripoli and Benghazi: literacy rates elsewhere remained low. Copies of *al-Haqiqa* were reportedly snapped up and Nayhum's articles were discussed by regular readers. This was so unusual that other newspa-pers reportedly spoke of the 'Nayhum phenomenon': see Ahmad Ibrahim al-Faqih, 'Sahib al-nufudh', *al-Naqid*, 83, p. 46.

15. A report in the *Sunday Times* described him as the 'enigmatic hippy' responsible for many of the ideas of Benghazi's youth; ibid.

16. Salim al-Hindawi, 'al-'A'id ila Benghazi', *al-Naqid*, 83, pp. 38–40.

17. *Min Makka ila huna* (Benghazi, 1970); *Min qisas al-atfal* (Benghazi, 1972).

18. Nayhum's literary achievements have received high praise. According to al-Faqih, for example, his originality 'secured him a lofty place in the history of Arabic literature as a pioneering writer, an important renewer, and the architect of a school of literary treatment and style unique to itself'; al-Faqih, 'Sahib al-nufudh', p. 47. Al-Maqinni points out that Nayhum adopted the linguistic techniques of free verse (especially its symbolic and mythical usages) and the artistic devices of the foreign novel (its weaving of realism with symbolism). He maintains that the writer was influenced by Steinbeck, Caldwell and Hemingway; see Ahmad al-Maqinni, 'al-Tajriba al-fikriyya'. According to reliable sources, Nayhum himself reportedly identified Taha Husayn as a major literary influence, in addition to the American novelists who had been translated into Arabic. Apart from his literary talents, such sources also point to Nayhum's admiration for Husayn's modernism and critical outlook.

19. While there are conflicting views of the seminar [for details, see Taji-Farouki, 'Sadiq Nayhum', pp. 260–2], the following comment by Davis is notable: 'men of action gain more assent from "average Libyans" if men of learning support or justify them, if the evanescent deed is attached to eternal values by the approbation of qualified persons'; John Davis, *Libyan Politics: Tribe and Revolution* (London, 1987), p. 79. Compare with Ruth First, *Libya: The Elusive Revolution* (Harmondsworth, 1974), p. 124 ff.

20. For conflicting views concerning Nayhum's role in the seminar, see Taji-Farouki, 'Sadiq Nayhum', pp. 260–2.

21. Viz., the Founding Committee, the Section on Thought and Instruction, and the Special Committee for Education, Science, Culture and Information.

22. David Blundy and Andrew Lycett, *Qaddafi and the Libyan Revolution* (London, 1987), p. 92.

23. Early perceptions that he had sold out to the system followed Nayhum to the end. While his body was flown back to Benghazi following his death, and was accompanied by the acclaimed Libyan novelist Ibrahim al-Kuni (among others), the funeral was a very modest affair by Benghazi standards, attended by perhaps twenty-five people.

24. *Sawt al-nas*, according to one Libyan opinion, was thus interpreted as a translation of Qaddafi's ideas set out in the first part of the *Green Book* ('The Solution to the Problem of Democracy: the Authority of the People' [al-Dimuqratiyya: sultat al-sha'b], first published during late 1975), and practically implemented in full following the Sebha declaration of March 1977; see al-Maqinni, 'al-Tajriba al-fikriyya'. There are notable parallels, for example, in the two men's suspicions of the state and its institutions, which are seen as a threat to the people (Nayhum's views point towards a notion that Islam came to free the citizen from the yoke of the state). There are also parallels in their rejection of representation and parties, in their insistence on the people's self-supervision, and in their concept of an instrument of governing that comprises the people as a whole: Nayhum's projection of Friday as the day for popular meetings thus resonates with

Qaddafi's popular congresses and peoples' committees. There are signifi-cant differences in specific concepts and in terminology, in the frameworks within which their arguments are constructed, and in their motivations and contexts. What ultimately unites them is a vision of democracy in which the people supplant the government administration.

25.   This debate points to the broader question of the relation to power of writings that recruit Qur'anic justifications, such as those discussed here.

26.   For example, essays address the Prophet's illiteracy and the signifi-cance of the *muqatta'at*; see *Islam didda al-Islam*, 2nd edn (1994), pp. 21 ff; 107 ff. References throughout are to this edition.

27.   *al-Islam fi al-asr*, 3rd edn (1995), p. 363. References throughout are to this edition.

28.   This emerged in specific European circumstances, based on a unique balance between the power of the workforce and capital. Here, capital was the means to liberate the administration from feudalism, whereas in the Arab context Islam had provided the means to achieve such liberation; compare with *Sawt al-nas* (London, 1987) p. 191.

29.   Literally the congregational mosque; in Nayhum's project it repre-sents a particular administrative system.

30.   *al-Islam fi al-asr*, p. 364.

31.   *Islam didda al-Islam*, p. 17.

32.   The author refers in the text to a handful of authors of Muslim provenance, including al-Shafi'i, Ibn Kathir and Taha Husayn, and a few 'Western' ones (Spinoza, Marx and Rousseau, for example).

33.   *Sawt al-nas*, p. 75.
34.   Ibid., p. 76.
35.   Ibid.
36.   Ibid., p. 61.
37.   Ibid., p. 42.
38.   Ibid., p. 139.
39.   Ibid., p. 108.
40.   Ibid., p. 42.
41.   Ibid.
42.   Ibid.
43.   Ibid., p. 46.
44.   Ibid., p. 58.
45.   Ibid., p. 58–9.
46.   Ibid., p. 59.
47.   Ibid., p. 60.
48.   Ibid., p. 61.
49.   Ibid.
50.   Ibid., p. 27.
51.   Ibid., p. 78.
52.   Ibid., p. 77.
53.   Ibid., p. 108.
54.   Ibid., p. 109.
55.   Ibid., p. 110.
56.   Ibid., p. 111.

57. Ibid., p. 78.
58. Ibid., p. 112.
59. Ibid., p. 78.
60. Ibid.
61. Ibid., p. 79.
62. Ibid., p. 81.
63. Ibid., p. 124.
64. Ibid., p. 138.
65. Ibid., p. 27.
66. Ibid., p. 26.
67. Ibid., pp. 25–6.
68. Ibid., p. 239.
69. Ibid., pp. 240–4.
70. Ibid., pp. 243–4.
71. Ibid., p. 243.
72. Ibid., pp. 153–63. On Juha, see U. Marzolph, 'Juha' in Julie Scott-Meisami and Paul Starky, eds, *The Cambridge Encyclopedia of Arabic Literature* (London and New York, 1998), pp. 417–8.
73. 'Dirasat al-ramz fi al-Qur'an', reprinted in *al-Qahira* (July, 1996), pp. 52–62. It is tempting to speculate that this reflects Nayhum's study under 'A'isha 'Abd al-Rahman in Cairo from 1965.
74. It might also be noted that Nayhum's essay pointed implicitly to the use of symbolism as a time-honoured Islamic literary tradition. This had political significance, at a time when symbolism was used as a means to articulate oppositional ideas indirectly under the monarchy.
75. Ibid., p. 23.
76. Ibid., pp. 22–3.
77. The translation of Qur'anic text is from Arthur J. Arberry, *The Koran Interpreted* (Oxford, 1964), with one or two modifications.
78. Ibid., p. 43.
79. Ibid., pp. 43–5.
80. An allusion to Q. 29: 45.
81. While recording varying accounts, the classical *tafasir* generally converge on the notion that verse 11 was revealed at a time when the Prophet used to lead the Friday prayer first, and then deliver the *khutba*. In the course of the latter, the goods' caravan of a merchant who had not yet embraced Islam arrived, and was greeted by his family with drums and entertainment. Most of those listening to the *khutba* rushed out, leaving the Prophet standing at the pulpit: only twelve men remained. This happened on three occasions, and the Prophet was moved to reverse the order of the Friday prayer and the *khutba*. See, for example, al-Tabari, *Jami' al-bayan 'an ta'wil ayat al-Qur'an*, 2nd edn (n.p., 1954), vol. 26, pp. 103–5; *Tafsir al-Jalalayn* (Beirut, n.d.), pp. 742, 769. The 'fun' referred to in the verse is described in the classical *tafasir* as a reference either to the entertainment greeting the trading caravan, or to the fact that, when girls married, they would proceed to the sound of drums and pipes, which also caused those gathered during the *khutba* to go out and watch. Nayhum's research on this point was evidently superficial.

82. These include the influence of modern mass education, the rise of professions, and the power and pervasive influence of modern information technology and modes of communication, for example. Such changes have resulted in ever-widening claims to interpret Islam's foundational texts, and the opening up of the interpretive act itself to new techniques and approaches. See Dale F. Eickelman, 'Mass Higher Education and the Religious Imagination in Contemporary Arab Societies', in George N. Atiyeh, ed., *The Book in the Islamic World: The Written Word and Communication in the Middle East* (New York, 1995), pp. 255–72; Frances Robinson, 'Technology and Religious Change: Islam and the Impact of Print', *Modern Asian Studies* 27, 1 (1993), pp. 229–51; Dale F. Eickelman and Jon W. Anderson, eds, *New Media in the Muslim World: The Emerging Public Sphere* (Bloomington, 2000).

83. In one possible (sympathetic) interpretation of this encounter, his failed attempt to 'speak the truth to power'. Cf. Hans J. Morgenthau, *Truth and Power: Essays of a Decade, 1960–70* (London, 1970), p. 15. Such an interpretation is of particular interest in light of Nayhum's own critique of contemporary Arab intellectuals as 'new magicians', who support the feudalists and justify their policies. *Sawt al-nas*, p. 192.

84. Entrenched perceptions that he received formal training in comparative religions at various Western universities are likely to be baseless.

85. For these views on *tafsir*, see *al-Islam fi al-asr*, p. 164 ff.

86. His 'commentaries' on Qur'anic texts can hence be described as an 'over-interpretation', to borrow Eco's term. See Umberto Eco, with Rorty, Culler and Brooke-Rose, ed. Stefan Collini, *Interpretation and Overinterpretation* (Cambridge, 1992).

87. Many have highlighted the nature of the Friday congregation as a potentially political association. The Tunisian writer al-Safi Sa'id refers to parallels between Nayhum's projection of the *jami'* and the Tanzanian President Julius Nyerere's 'call for socialism based on the notion of the *jama'a* and *jami'*. See 'Burtray min al-khajal wal-bayad', *al-Naqid*, 83, p. 24.

88. It is notable in this respect that he did not raise or address directly the relationship between Islam, modernity, freedom, and political power in any of his writings.

BIBLIOGRAPHY

Works by Sadiq Nayhum

——. *Sawt al-nas: mihnat thaqafa muzawwara.* London, 1987.

——. *al-Islam fi al-asr: man saraqa al-jami' wa ayna dhahaba yawm al-jum'a?* 3rd edn, Beirut and London, 1995.

——. *Islam didda al-Islam: shari'a min waraq.* 2nd edn, Beirut and London, 1994.

——. *Dirasat al-ramz fi al-Qur'an*, reprinted in *al-Qahira* (July, 1996), pp. 52–62.

Other Sources

Arberry, Arthur J. *The Koran Interpreted.* Oxford, 1964.

Blundy, David and Andrew Lycett. *Qaddafi and the Libyan Revolution.* London, 1987.

Cole, Juan R. I. 'Introduction', in idem., ed., *Comparing Muslim Societies: Knowledge and the State in a World Civilization.* Ann Arbor, 1992, pp. 1–28.

Davis, John. *Libyan Politics: Tribe and Revolution.* London, 1987.

Eco, Umberto, with Richard Rorty, Jonathon Culler and Christine Brooke-Rose, ed. Stefan Collini. *Interpretation and Overinterpretation.* Cambridge, 1992.

Eickelman, Dale F. 'The Art of Memory: Islamic Education and its Social Reproduction', in Juan R.I. Cole, ed., *Comparing Muslim Societies: Knowledge and the State in a World Civilisation.* Ann Arbor, 1992, pp. 97–132.

——. 'Mass Higher Education and the Religious Imagination in Contemporary Arab Societies', in George N. Atiyeh, ed., *The Book in the Islamic World: The Written Word and Communication in the Middle East.* New York, 1995, pp. 255–272.

Eickelman, Dale F. and Jon W. Anderson, eds. *New Media in the Muslim World: The Emerging Public Sphere.* Bloomington, IN, 2000.

——. 'Print, Islam and the Prospects for Civic Pluralism: New Religious Writings and their Audiences', *Journal of Islamic Studies*, 8, 1 (1997), pp. 43–62.

Eickelman, Dale F. and James Piscatori. *Muslim Politics.* Princeton, NJ, 1996.

First, Ruth. *Libya: The Elusive Revolution.* Harmondsworth, 1974.

Hirst, David. 'How Riyadh stifled a free Arab voice', *The Guardian*, 21 April 1995.

Labib, Henri. *Libya: Past and Present.* Malta and Tripoli, 1979.

al-Maqinni, Ahmad. 'al-Tajriba al-fikriyya al-multabisa li al-katib al-Libi al-rahil al-Sadiq al-Nayhum', *al-Hayat*, 15 December 1995.

Marzolph, U. 'Juha', in Julie Scott-Meisami and Paul Starky, eds, *The Cambridge Encyclopedia of Arabic Literature.* London and New York, 1998, pp. 417–8.

Morgenthau, Hans J. *Truth and Power: Essays of a Decade, 1960-70.* London, 1970.

al-Naqid, 83 (1995).

al-Qathafi, Muammar [sic]. *The Green Book.* n.p., n.d.

al-Qadhdhafi, Mu'ammar. *Al-Kitab al-akhdar.* n.p., n.d.

Robinson, Frances. 'Technology and Religious Change: Islam and the Impact of Print', *Modern Asian Studies* 27, 1 (1993), pp. 229–51.

Sa'id, al-Safi. 'Burtray min al-khajal wal-bayad', *al-Naqid*, 83 (1995).

Smith, Charles D. 'The Intellectual, Islam, and Modernization', in Juan R. Cole, ed., *Comparing Muslim Societies: Knowledge and the State in a World Civilization.* Ann Arbor, 1992, pp. 163–90.

al-Tabari, Abu Ja'far Muhammad Ibn Jarir. *Jami' al-bayan 'an ta'wil ayat al-Qur'an.* 2nd edn, n.p., 1954.

Tafsir al-Jalalayn. Beirut, n.d.

Taji-Farouki, Suha. 'Sadiq Nayhum: An Introduction to the Life and Works of a Contemporary Libyan Intellectual', *The Maghreb Review*, 25, 3–4 (2000), pp. 242-74.

Index

Index

Index

thinkable, the, 147
thinkers
   as agents of Westernisation, 12
   critiques of Muslim regimes, 4–5
   individuality of, 5
   major themes illustrated by, 3
   modernisation, 4
   new readings of the Qur'an, 297–8
   polarisation of, 2
   reformists, 9
   Western interest in, 7
Throne, the, 279–80
Tillich, 153
tradition
   democratisation of, 14
   as substance of change, 1–2
traditional Islam, 40–2
transformationists, 78
truth
   Absolute (*Haqq*), 86
   infinite and finite, 204
Turkey
   influence of Rahman's ideas, 39
   modernisation policy, 241–2

ulama, 12, 44
'Umar ibn al-Khattab
   adherence to the spirit of the
      Qur'an, 109–10
   professional army, 311
   reactualisation, 82
Umayyad rule, 41, 139, 312–13
universality, 195–6. *See also* subjec-
      tivity
unthought
   concept introduced, 125
   premises of, 147
   rethinking Islam, 130
'urfi, 217
usul al-fiqh, 48
usury, 310
'Uthman ibn 'Affan, 311

veil, the, 102–3
velayat-e-faqih, 217–18
vicegerent, man as, 197
Vincennes, University of, 129
volition, 208
Wadud, Amina
   background, 97–8
   career and works, 100–6
   critique of traditional *tafsir*, 101–6
   gender relationships, 101, 111–12
   on the headcovering, 102–3
   hermeneutics of equality, 106–12
   introduction to, 22
   as a Muslim woman, 98–100
   ostracising of, 100
   Qur'an from a woman's perspec-
      tive, 113–17
Wahid, Abdurrahman, 78
war, legitimate, 311
Waugh, Earl H., 39
Western society
   Arab internalisation of, 11–12
   interest in Islamic thinkers, 7
   See also modernity
White Fathers, 128
Whitehead, A. N., 265
women
   rights of, 38, 216
   status of, 227–8, 233
   See also family law
world administration, 310
World War One, 11

yawm al-jum'a, 310
Yazır, Elmalı'ı Hamdi, 242
Yogyakarta, 74
Yusuf Ali, Abdullah, 91

Zahiri legal school, 251–2
zawj, 114
al-Zarkashi, 174
zuhd, 41

DATE DUE
